OXFORD STUDIES IN ANALYTIC THEOLOGY

Series Editors
Michael C. Rea   Oliver D. Crisp

D0999227

OXFORD STUDIES IN ANALYTIC THEOLOGY

Analytic Theology utilizes the tools and methods of contemporary analytic philosophy for the purposes of constructive Christian theology, paying attention to the Christian tradition and development of doctrine. This innovative series of studies showcases high-quality, cutting-edge research in this area, in monographs and symposia.

Metaphysics and the Tri-Personal God

WILLIAM HASKER

OXFORD

UNIVERSITY PRESS

OXFORD
UNIVERSITY PRESS

Great Clarendon Street, Oxford, OX2 6DP,
United Kingdom

Oxford University Press is a department of the University of Oxford.
It furthers the University's objective of excellence in research, scholarship,
and education by publishing worldwide. Oxford is a registered trade mark of
Oxford University Press in the UK and in certain other countries

© William Hasker 2013

The moral rights of the author have been asserted

First published 2013
First published in paperback 2017

Published in the United States of America by Oxford University Press
198 Madison Avenue, New York, NY 10016, United States of America

British Library Cataloguing in Publication Data
Data available

Library of Congress Cataloging in Publication Data
Data available

ISBN 978-0-19-968151-8 (Hbk.)
ISBN 978-0-19-880314-0 (Pbk.)

Honoring the Memory of Professor John McIntyre, 1916–2005

Contents

PART III: TRINITARIAN CONSTRUCTION

Introduction

It is no secret that the past sixty years—roughly, since the mid-twentieth century—has seen a remarkable outpouring of trinitarian theology. Initially spurred on by Karl Barth, but with many other theologians from various confessions joining in, the volume and variety of work on this doctrine may have exceeded any previous period since the fourth century. It is perhaps less widely known, however, that important work on the Trinity has occurred in fields other than systematic or dogmatic theology. Over the last three or four decades there have been extremely important developments in scholarly understanding concerning the formative stages of trinitarian doctrine, with the result that assumptions that had been accepted for centuries have had to be abandoned. Still more recently, there have been important investigations of the Trinity coming from a somewhat unexpected source—namely, analytic philosophers of religion. The focus of this philosophical work has been narrower than for the systematic or historical studies; it has been primarily concerned with what may be termed the "three-in-oneness problem," the problem of what it means to say that there are three trinitarian Persons but only one God. Is this something we can understand? Is it something we can express without contradiction? Is it really possible that the doctrine is true? Such questions, to be sure, are but a small part of everything that needs to be said about the Trinity, but they are crucial; if those questions do not have good answers, then everything else about the doctrine is called into question.

Ideally speaking, the results produced by these three movements in trinitarian theology should converge, with the best results of the historical and philosophical studies incorporated into an enriched theological synthesis. In practice, however, this seems not (or not yet) to have happened, at least not to any substantial degree. So far as one can tell, the results of the new understanding of the formative period of trinitarian doctrine are only just beginning to be taken account of by systematic theologians. And there is even less inclination, in many theological circles, to make use of the recent philosophical investigations of the doctrine (though there are exceptions to this generalization). No doubt there are reasons for this failure of integration, reasons of historical inertia and also, perhaps, a certain amount of protection of disciplinary turf. But however that may be, the need for integration and synthesis remains. The present volume represents an attempt to contribute to such integration; an attempt which inevitably, given the author, is most heavily focused on the philosophical contribution. I have endeavored, however, to place that contribution within a broad theological context and also to take account, insofar as this is possible for a non-specialist, of the new consensus which is gradually emerging concerning the origins of trinitarian doctrine.

The first part of the book, "Trinitarian Foundations," finds those foundations primarily in the work of the "pro-Nicene" theologians, especially Gregory of Nyssa late in the fourth century, and Augustine of Hippo early in the fifth. My contention is that it is their grasp of the doctrine of the Trinity that needs to be the starting point for our own reflections; if we were to conclude that they got things fundamentally wrong, the prospects for our arriving at a doctrine of the Trinity that would succeed where they had failed would be vanishingly small. At the same time, I argue that we need to examine their formulations in the light of the questions as they present themselves to us in the present time, and we must be prepared to challenge some of the philosophical assumptions that are involved in their versions of the doctrine. This sets up what may be the most important methodological tension for the book as a whole. Some will consider that the philosophical doctrines I am prepared to jettison (in particular, the strong doctrine of divine simplicity) are integral to the doctrine of the Trinity, and removing them leaves us with but a pale simulacrum of the real thing. There will be others who think that, by barring the way to a more drastic revision of the tradition, I have prevented any real theological progress and have condemned trinitarian theology to stagnation. In the nature of the case there can be no single, conclusive answer to such criticisms; I can only ask that the perspective I put forward be given fair consideration and a chance to show its strengths.

The second part of the book, "Trinitarian Options," reviews and assesses some of the main proposals that have been advanced concerning the divine three-in-oneness. We begin with four theologians, then go on to consider six different philosophical proposals on the topic. None of the proposals is found to be completely satisfactory, but taken together they provide important resources for a more adequate solution. The final part, "Trinitarian Construction," builds up step by step my own constructive proposal for the doctrine of the Trinity. Here we engage what is perhaps the most important, and most difficult, philosophical problem confronting my proposal (as well as many other versions of the doctrine): Is it possible to affirm consistently that the trinitarian Three are *persons*, in a sense that is strongly analogous with our ordinary concept of a person, and yet that they share a single concrete divine nature—a single "trope of deity"? The part concludes with a concise summary of the metaphysical account of the Trinity that is being proposed.

It may be helpful to say a little here about the book's organization. The three parts, as sketched in the two previous paragraphs, define the main structure of the book as a whole. There are many subdivisions of these parts, they vary considerably in length, and some of them are too short to qualify as chapters as normally understood. It might have been possible to combine them into chapters of more uniform length, but I believe that doing so would tend to obscure rather than clarify the development of thought throughout the book. If things go well, it will be perceived that each chapter marks a distinct step which advances, in a larger or smaller degree, the process through which the overall thesis is set out and defended. (And just what is that thesis, you may ask? For that, see the last chapter of the third part—preferably, however, having read the rest of the book first as preparation.)

No book written on this topic can be a solo performance. My indebtedness to those who have written before me will be evident from the references in the footnotes throughout the book. I am also greatly in the debt of all those who have engaged in discussion or provided clarification of various points, mostly by email. These include Jeff Brower, Bill Craig, Steve Davis, Jonathan Evans, Brian Leftow, Alan Padgett, Mike Rea, Richard Swinburne, Peter van Inwagen, and almost certainly some I have forgotten. Dale Tuggy and Joseph Jedwab read the manuscript and provided many valuable comments. Thomas McCall was the reader for Oxford University Press; his suggestions were extremely beneficial. My appreciation goes also to the series editors, Oliver Crisp and Michael Rea, and to Tom Perrin at Oxford, for their encouragement and support.

Finally, I come to the man to whom this book is dedicated. John McIntyre (1916–2005) was Professor of Divinity at New College, Edinburgh, from 1956 until his retirement in 1986. In addition to his numerous books and articles, his many distinctions included serving as Principal of New College, Chaplain to the Queen in Scotland, and Moderator of the General Assembly of the Church of Scotland. Far down on the list of his contributions is the fact that during 1959–61 he was the advisor for my Ph.D. dissertation, "The Social Analogy in Modern Trinitarian Thought." (Only a few of the words from that dissertation survive here, but the work done then became the foundation for what is contained in the present book.) At first McIntyre was dubious about the topic, fearing that not enough material would be available. (Those were as yet early days in the trinitarian revival.) But once he was convinced, I could not have asked for a more helpful and accommodating advisor. I recall not only his academic guidance but his personal consideration as well, shown especially in arranging for me a month-long "preaching vacation" in a Highland pulpit at a time when my wife and I were greatly in need of such a respite.

I conclude these comments with a small episode that should not be lost to posterity. It occurred during a term when I was sitting in on McIntyre's course in divinity (for American readers, philosophical theology). One of the Scottish students posed a provocative question: "Would it be an unforgivable heresy," he asked, "to say that it was a terrible shame that the Old Testament and the New Testament were ever bound together as a single book?" Without missing a beat, McIntyre replied: "You're right about the heresy; it's not for me to say whether it is forgivable." It is my hope that, were he to read the present volume, he would find it free of heresy, and that the mistakes which undoubtedly remain would be judged to be forgivable.

Part I

Trinitarian Foundations

1

Prelude: Where are the Foundations?

Establishing the foundations for the doctrine of the Trinity is a monumental task. Central to this task is the revelation, or what is taken to be the revelation, of God in Jesus of Nazareth. I have inserted the qualification because it is not uncontroversial that the events concerning Jesus constitute such a revelation. Having said that once, however, I will from now on largely ignore the need for the qualification, for a simple reason: Anyone who does not believe that such a revelation occurred has no need to concern herself with the doctrine of the Trinity, unless for the purpose of refutation, or perhaps with a purely historical interest. My primary audience consists of persons who accept that there was indeed a revelation in and through Jesus, and who wish to consider whether the doctrine of the Trinity represents a reasonable and defensible construal of that revelation, and, if so, what form of the doctrine best accomplishes that task.

So we begin by postulating a revelation in Jesus. But doing this merely brings us to the point of departure for a long and demanding journey. Supposing that the events concerning Jesus do constitute some sort of divine revelation, that revelation is available to us only if we have some reasonably reliable information as to what those events actually were. The events, however, are accessible to us only through the writings of the New Testament. Because of this, establishing that we can have reliable knowledge concerning the events in question plunges us into the entire maze of critical and historical studies of the biblical literature. Furthermore, we need to be convinced not only that the New Testament documents convey some modicum of historical information concerning Jesus, but that the interpretations of Jesus' life, ministry, and person they offer us are on the whole reliable and trustworthy. Establishing that this is so, and the sense in which it is so, is in itself a monumental theological task. I do not say here that some particular view concerning the inspiration of the biblical writings is essential; what view should be taken of those matters is itself a topic requiring extensive theological investigation. But if we are not able to reach some sort of positive conclusion about these topics, the path leading to the doctrine of the Trinity will be effectively blocked.

All this is merely the beginning. If we suppose that the writings of the New Testament do give us some access to Jesus as he actually lived, died, and rose again, as well as interpretations of the revelation in and through Jesus that are worthy of our belief, there lies before us the enormous task of understanding and interpreting those writings. And of course, this cannot well be accomplished without similar attention to the writings of the Hebrew Bible, called by Christians the Old Testament; those writings are in every respect the presupposition and foundation for the distinctively Christian writings of the New Testament.

By this point we have well and truly begun, but only begun. It is by this time generally conceded that the Church's doctrine of the Trinity is not as such to be found in the New Testament; rather, it was the product of a historical development that took place over several hundred years. Indeed, that development arguably is not complete even in the present time, inasmuch as new proposals and interpretations of trinitarian doctrine continue to be put forward today. Tracing these historical developments is an additional, and monumental, task, over and above those already mentioned. But especially with regard to the earlier centuries, the task is an essential one; we cannot well understand the product of this developmental process without understanding the process itself. Furthermore, the nature of the process raises a further, and vitally important, theological question: To what extent does the divine guidance believed to have been present in the formation of the New Testament writings continue in the life and thought of the Church in subsequent centuries?

Much more could be added to all this by way of elaboration, but one thing should by now be abundantly clear: one can hardly think to address the foundations of the doctrine of the Trinity armed with anything less than the contents of an entire theological library. Every single topic mentioned has been the subject of dozens, hundreds, perhaps even thousands of books, and new contributions are constantly appearing.

What sense, then, can be made of the idea of a book of moderate length that begins with a chapter on "Trinitarian Foundations"? Should the reader be prepared for a lightning summary of the historical and literary criticism of the biblical literature? Followed by an abbreviated but hopefully compelling argument for some particular construal of the inspiration of the biblical writings? Next in order would be a concise argument for particular theological interpretations of those biblical writings most directly pertinent to the doctrine of the Trinity. All this to be capped off by a rapid review of the historical development of doctrine, combined with a theological argument supporting the claim that this development was an appropriate one that has led in the direction of authentic theological knowledge. Given all this, we would at last be ready for the task of doctrinal construction!

Readers who expected our account of trinitarian foundations to take this course will be disappointed—or more likely, relieved—to learn that nothing of the sort is in prospect. To be sure, all of this may really be required to set out the trinitarian foundations in full. In order to take the doctrine of the

Trinity seriously we have to assume—at the very least, to hope—that positive results can be obtained in each of the areas mentioned. But over and above the impossibility of attempting all this in a single volume, there are good reasons why a somewhat different approach may be justified and appropriate. It was mentioned at the beginning that we would assume without argument that a revelation from God has indeed occurred, centered around the person and ministry of Jesus. The justification for assuming this was simply that anyone unwilling to make this assumption can scarcely have any positive interest in the doctrine of the Trinity. But if this procedure is defensible, similar moves can take us a good deal farther along the road. Persons who think that little or no information is available concerning Jesus, or that the New Testament teachings concerning him belong properly to mythology, will likewise be unlikely prospects for a serious and constructive interest in the Trinity. The same will be true of those who think the relevant New Testament writings have been radically misinterpreted,[1] or who consider that the turn to trinitarian speculation in the Church was part and parcel of the Fall into Philosophy in the early centuries—a Fall that obscured the original message and led eventually to its virtual disappearance.[2]

If we consider the actual formation of the doctrine of the Trinity, we note that the doctrine in its received form was formulated in the late fourth century, most notably in our "Nicene Creed," which is actually the creed of the council held at Constantinople in 381. This resolution was reached after an intense controversy in which most if not all of the plausible alternative views were considered. The Nicene Creed has arguably the best claim of any Christian confession to have defined a central Christian doctrine in a way that has met with acceptance by the Church as a whole.[3] If we credit the assertion that divine providence has been at work in guiding the Church in its understanding, and in preventing it from falling into destructive errors, this particular development stands out as an especially plausible example of such guidance.[4] If we are reluctant to rely on the assumption that this sort of guidance has occurred, we are still confronted with the question: Is it at all possible for human beings to arrive at a credible and defensible understanding of the matters treated in that Creed? If this is not possible, then no doctrine of the Trinity is deserving of our acceptance and we had best turn our energies and attention to other

---

[1] For instance, those unitarians who consider their faith to be biblically based.

[2] Harnack, and the Ritschlian school of theology generally.

[3] The Creed expresses a consensus of Roman Catholic, Eastern Orthodox, Nestorians and Monophysites, Protestants, and Pentecostals, among others.

[4] "The assumption that Jesus Christ did not quite abandon His Church at this time, and that therefore in spite of all that might perhaps rightly be said against her, it would be in place to listen to her, as we listen to the *Church*—this assumption might in any case have a very definite advantage over the opposite one." Karl Barth, *Church Dogmatics, i/1. The Doctrine of the Word of God*, tr. G. T. Thomson (Edinburgh: T. & T. Clark, 1936), 433. (Here as elsewhere, I have replaced the s p a c i n g for emphasis, retained from the German by the translator of this volume, with italics.)

matters. But if we are not willing to be trinitarian skeptics, I submit that we will do well to take seriously the consensus of the universal Church, rather than going off in a fundamentally different direction on our own.

In the light of these reflections, I propose that the best place to begin in our investigation of the doctrine of the Trinity is with the Church Fathers of the late fourth century. They are the giants on whose shoulders we need to stand, if we are to arrive at an understanding of these matters.[5] And this suggests a different approach to the issue of trinitarian foundations than the one that was discussed above and rejected as impracticable. It suggests that we need to begin by ascertaining, as clearly as we can, what the fourth-century consensus amounted to. This requires, crucially, an understanding on our part of their way of understanding both the threeness of the divine Persons,[6] and the oneness of the divine nature that is common to the three. We will need also to consider their understanding of the biblical witness on which, in their own estimation, their doctrine of the Trinity was founded. Putting it this way assumes, to be sure, that there actually was a consensus on these matters; that is one of the assumptions that will need to be tested. If we can arrive at defensible conclusions about the doctrine as it emerged in the late fourth century, we will be in a position to consider how the doctrine can best be articulated for the Church of the third millennium.

Here is another way of understanding my proposal: this is not a Cartesian project, in which the objective is to demolish our existing edifice of belief, scour the building site down to bedrock, and build all over again with imperishable materials. What I am proposing is rather in the spirit of Reidian epistemology, in which certain deliverances of "common sense" are taken as given, indeed as indispensable, though not infallible, and we seek to improve and extend the edifice of knowledge even as we continue to dwell therein. (Also pertinent is Neurath's image of the ship that must be repaired at sea, even as we continue to rely on it to stay afloat and carry us towards our desired destination.) To be sure, the Nicene doctrine of the Trinity can hardly be characterized as "common sense." For Christians, it is rather uncommon sense, the sense of the marvelously uncommon Gospel whose message it encapsulates.

To begin our quest, however, we need to come to terms with the fourth century, as it was and as it has recently become.

---

[5] Here for once I find myself in agreement with Brian Leftow, who wrote, "Historic Christian orthodoxy represents the best effort of nearly 2000 years of Christian minds to plumb God's nature. It is possible that they have all been wrong, even fundamentally wrong. But it would be hubris for a twentieth-century trinitarian to conclude this so long as any orthodox approach is not utterly exhausted." "Anti Social Trinitarianism," in Thomas McCall and Michael C. Rea (eds), *Philosophical and Theological Essays on the Trinity* (Oxford: OUP, 2009), 87.

[6] Here and throughout I use "Persons" as a designator for the trinitarian Three, without commitment as to the nature of the Persons. The lower-case "person" is used, on the other hand, to express a concept at least closely analogous with our ordinary conception of a person.

2

The "New" Fourth Century

The fourth century is not what it used to be—in fact, it never was. That perhaps cryptic remark is meant to signal the fact that our understanding of this crucial period in the history of Christian doctrine has undergone a remarkable revision in the past three decades or so. What has been known, or rather assumed, to be true of this period has turned out to be, in certain respects, an egregious case of "history written by the winners." A truer history has begun to emerge—one that does not, to be sure, differ in all respects from that previously accepted, but with some rather large shifts of emphasis and interpretation. This "new" fourth century has barely begun to be taken account of by systematic theologians, and most philosophers, even those who have concerned themselves with trinitarian doctrine, seem hardly to be aware of its existence.

In order to give the reader some sense of these developments, I will provide here a brief summary of the previously entrenched understanding of the fourth-century trinitarian controversy, followed by an explanation of some of the ways in which the received understanding has been revised. What is said here cannot, of course, reproduce or replace what is available in the detailed scholarly treatments of the subject.[1] Nor can we assume that consensus has been reached on all points, but I believe what is presented here is a fair reflection of the still-developing mainstream understanding of the fourth century.

Here, then, is a brief statement of the way in which the fourth century has been understood until very recently: The Church of the second and third centuries held generally to a basically orthodox (as judged by later definitions) conception of the Trinity, though with some inaccuracies of statement and inadequate means of expression. In the early fourth century, however, this

---

[1] The reader will quickly become aware of my indebtedness to Lewis Ayres, *Nicaea and its Legacy: An Approach to Fourth-Century Trinitarian Theology* (Oxford: OUP, 2004). Also helpful are Frances M. Young, *From Nicaea to Chalcedon: A Guide to the Literature and its Background*, 2nd edn (Grand Rapids, MI: Baker Academic, 2010); Khaled Anatolios, *Retrieving Nicaea: The Development and Meaning of Trinitarian Doctrine* (Grand Rapids, MI: Baker Academic, 2011); and R. P. C. Hanson, *The Search for the Christian Doctrine of God: The Arian Controversy, 318–381* (London: T. & T. Clark, 1988; paperback edn, Grand Rapids, MI: Baker Books, 2005).

broad consensus was disrupted by Arius, a presbyter of Alexandria, with his teaching that the Son was merely a creature. Motivated by philosophical considerations, Arius created a separation between the "true God" and the divine Word or Logos, and his rhetorical and argumentative skills persuaded many to become his followers. In order to rectify the resulting confusion the first ecumenical council was called at Nicaea in 325. In principle, this council settled the question and re-established the orthodox doctrine by defining that the Son is *homoousios* with the Father. However continued agitation by Arius and his followers, with support from some Arian-leaning emperors, meant that in practical terms the controversy remained alive, especially in the Eastern Church. (The West, meanwhile, remained largely faithful to the orthodox Nicene doctrine.) Had it not been for the lifelong, heroic, and to a large extent single-handed, advocacy of Athanasius, Arianism might even have triumphed. Towards the end of the century, however, the Nicene cause was taken up by the Cappadocian Fathers, Basil of Caesarea, Gregory of Nazianzen, and Gregory of Nyssa. They emphasized the full Godhood of the Holy Spirit, which had been left somewhat obscure by earlier theologians, and coined the crucial formula for the trinity in unity: God is one *ousia* in three *hypostases*. With their encouragement the emperor Theodosius convened the second ecumenical council at Constantinople in 381, which effectively settled the controversy and gave us what has come to be known as the Nicene Creed.

Not everything in this brief summary is wrong, of course. Arius did indeed play a crucial role in instigating the controversy, but it is a mistake to see him as an innovator motivated almost exclusively by philosophical considerations. (Then, as now, the charge that someone's theological views were unduly influenced by philosophy could be an effective way to discredit those views.[2]) In fact, Arius has come to be seen as a somewhat extreme representative of a type of theological thinking that was widely disseminated in the Church of that age.[3] Other representatives in the early fourth century included the bishops Eusebius of Caesarea (the church historian), and Eusebius of Nicomedia. If Arius had been purely an innovator, it would be hard to understand the widespread and sustained influence of his ideas. And on the other hand, later "Arianism" turns out to have been less dependent upon Arius than has been generally assumed.[4] Since Arius had been condemned at Nicaea, it was possible to secure a polemical advantage by labeling all who held similar views as

    [2] Note, however, that the claim of Gregg and Groh (Robert C. Gregg and Denis E. Groh, *Early Arianism: A View of Salvation* (Philadelphia: Fortress Press, 1981)) that Arius was primarily concerned with soteriology rather than cosmology has not been widely accepted. See Ayres, *Nicaea*, 55–6.

    [3] "Older narratives tended to assume that 'heresies' were novel creations divergent from a pre-existing orthodoxy.... [W]hat later counts as heretical at times preceded what came to be counted as orthodoxy, and was itself seen as orthodox at that earlier stage." Ayres, *Nicaea*, 78.

    [4] A helpful assessment of the later "Arians," and of their similarities and differences from Arius' own views, is given by Anatolios, *Retrieving Nicaea*, 53–79.

"Arians"; it was Athanasius who exploited this opportunity, and in so doing has misled historians ever since. (Ayres characterizes the 340s as the decade of "the creation of 'Arianism'."[5])

More pertinent to the work of contemporary trinitarian theorizing is the fact that, at the time of the council of Nicaea, there was no single, well-developed "Nicene" theology. Rather, there were several theological trajectories, varying somewhat among themselves, that were able to join together in repudiating Arius and his doctrines. Most likely the term *homoousion* was chosen precisely because it was known that Arius could not accept it; terminology derived from scripture, on the other hand, was accepted by him and interpreted in accordance with his own theological views. But the term played no part in the controversies of the period immediately following the council; it was not until some twenty years later that Athanasius came to see the strategic importance of *homoousion* and the related phrase *ek tēs ousias tou patros* ("from the being of the Father"), and to emphasize them in his polemical writings.

An interesting consequence of these developments in historiography is that they tend to call into question the idea of Nicaea and Constantinople I as "ecumenical" councils which as such possessed definitive theological authority. In the early fourth century, the notion of a council as promulgating a creed that would be universally binding, and would function as a "rule of faith" for the entire Church, simply did not exist. It was only gradually, during the latter part of the century, that a number of thinkers came to perceive Nicaea and its definitions—notably, the *homoousion*—as an important rallying-point for those opposed to the diminished status for the Son that was affirmed by those they termed "Arians."[6] It was of course the council of Constantinople that gave us our "Nicene" Creed, the one trinitarian document that has the best claim to having been received as definitive by the entire Church. But here also the pre-eminent status of the council's deliverance is more a product of a later evaluation than a reflection of the perception at the time when it was produced. One indication of this is that the first record we find of the text of that Creed occurs in the acts of the council of Chalcedon a half century later![7] None of this indicates, of course, that these two councils are not deserving of the importance that has historically been accorded to them. But it suggests that, rather than being bestowed by the "ecumenical" character of the councils themselves, their authority is best seen as arising from their subsequent

---

[5] In view of the apparently limited influence of Arius on later opponents of Nicaea, Ayres employs the adjective "Arian" only in contexts where Arius's direct influence is evident. This is commendable in its insistence on historical accuracy, but I have permitted myself the broader use of "Arian" which is familiar in standard histories of doctrine.

[6] For an illuminating summary of the way in which the conception of orthodoxy, and the appeals by which orthodoxy was established, developed during the 4th cent., see Ayres, *Nicaea*, 78–84.

[7] See Ayres, *Nicaea*, 253.

reception and appreciation by the Church at large, as it found their deliverances to be clear and trustworthy renditions of its faith.[8]

Much more could be said to illustrate the complex development of
fourth-century trinitarian orthodoxy. The notion that there was a clear-cut
separation between the Western, or Latin-speaking, and the Eastern, or
Greek-speaking, churches with respect to trinitarian belief is now regarded
as untenable; there were a variety of positions that had adherents in both
East and West. An interesting feature of the controversy is the alliance, for a
number of years, between Athanasius and Marcellus of Ancyra. Marcellus is
a somewhat shadowy figure whose views are difficult to spell out with precision, as is the case with many who came to be deemed heretical. He emphasized the unity between the Father and the Son, or Word, in a way that led to
his being accused of Sabellianism, though this was not strictly accurate. He
seems to have held that the Logos became more of a distinct existence at the
time of creation, and that this process would be reversed at the end of time,
when the Son would surrender his kingdom back to the Father. (The phrase,
"and his kingdom shall have no end," incorporated into the Nicene Creed
and many other creeds of the period, is explicitly anti-Marcellan.) There is
no indication that Athanasius ever shared these views, yet he allied himself
with Marcellus, worked closely with him even after his deposition in 335,
and apparently never completely repudiated him. For Athanasius, Marcellus'
lack of clear affirmation of the eternally distinct existence of the Logos was
apparently overshadowed by his welcome insistence on the community of
nature between Father and Logos. Not surprisingly, suspicion of Marcellus
fed into a more general suspicion of and resistance to the Nicene formulas he
had supported.

These developments in historiography point to certain conclusions
about how we should go about understanding the theological content of
fourth-century trinitarianism. They suggest that it is a mistake to focus nar-
rowly on the council of Nicaea, in an attempt to determine what was "really
meant" by *homoousion*. Most likely there is no answer to that question beyond
the bare minimum: the Son is divine like the Father, and so cannot be a created being, as Arius had said. Beyond this, the council simply did not reflect a
unified, clearly defined theological perspective.[9] We need to respect the developmental process that went on throughout the fourth century, leading up to

---

[8] I believe that something along these lines is what Michel René Barnes means by "the process
of orthodoxy."

[9] "Nicaea's terminology is...a window onto the confusion and complexity of the early
fourth-century theological debate, not a revelation that a definitive turning-point had been
reached." Ayres, *Nicaea*, 92. Hansen's comment is even sharper: "However we regard it, the Creed
produced by the Council of Nicaea was a mine of potential confusion and consequently most
unlikely to be a means of ending the Arian Controversy." *The Search for the Christian Doctrine of
God*, 168.

but not concluding with the council of Constantinople. Nor, for that matter, should we focus solely on that council's creed, as if it were a "stand-alone" document waiting for our favored interpretation. I believe, in fact, that we need to give pride of place to the late fourth-century theologians who have collectively been termed "pro-Nicene." These men believed that the way forward theologically lay in a reaffirmation of the central thrust of Nicaea, and developed some common strategies by which to establish what should count as sound trinitarian doctrine. The boundaries of the group are not precise, but Ayres suggests three criteria that are marks of pro-Nicene theology:

1. a clear version of the person and nature distinction, entailing the principle that whatever is predicated of the divine nature is predicated of the three persons equally and understood to be one (this distinction may or may not be articulated via a consistent technical terminology);

2. clear expression that the eternal generation of the Son occurs within the unitary and incomprehensible divine being;

3. clear expression of the doctrine that the persons work inseparably.[10]

But is not such an approach in danger of giving excessive weight to a comparatively small group of thinkers who represent, after all, only a fraction of all that has been written on the doctrine of the Trinity? In response to this question, I point to the fact that the thinking of these men, represented in but not exhausted by the Nicene Creed, presents what the Christian Church as a whole has come to accept as the definitive statement of the doctrine of the Trinity. The chain of inferences leading to this doctrine is by no means incontestable, as is shown by the plausible appeals to scripture and to reason made by the different varieties of heretics. Nevertheless, the Church has judged that this doctrine gives a good and faithful account, one that best synthesizes the rich variety of scriptural data and provides a basis for a fruitful understanding of both revelation and redemption. I submit that if the Church got this fundamentally wrong—if Nicene trinitarianism is not in fact a substantially correct reading of what has come to us as divine revelation—then it is doubtful that we will be more successful in crafting substitutes of our own. Putting such substitutes forward as "the doctrine of the Trinity" may create the impression that we are using a traditional formula as a fig leaf to cover our own radical departure from that tradition.

It is important to see what is and is not being claimed here. I do not suggest that all of the arguments urged in support of Nicene trinitarianism, much less all of the scriptural exegesis that was deployed, should be accepted as sound. Nor do I imply that we must, or that we should, accept without question the philosophical views that influenced the expression of the doctrine. To be sure, there never was a single, well-developed, consistent philosophical system that

---

[10] Ayres, *Nicaea*, 236.

was generally accepted as normative. Rather, particular philosophical ideas tended to be used on an *ad hoc* basis insofar as they were perceived to be useful in a particular theological context. In all of these respects—soundness of argument, biblical exegesis, and philosophical construction—I believe that *we can and should do better* than the pro-Nicenes of the fourth century were able to do—just as they themselves did better than the earlier theologians on whose shoulders they stood. But for all that, we should, I claim, respect their right to show us, through their writings, what the doctrine of the Trinity is and must be.

To be sure, approaching matters in this way sets up an inevitable tension: if we deviate from the pro-Nicenes in a certain respect, are we explaining in a clearer and more cogent manner the doctrine that we and they hold in common, or are we departing from the tradition in a way that threatens to undermine the doctrine?[11] Such questions cannot be decided in advance; we must consider particular questions as they arise, and act on our best (fallible) judgment. This parallels the familiar idea that we acknowledge the pre-eminence of the divine revelation in scripture even while we recognize that our present-day knowledge of both science and history is superior in many respects to that which is reflected in the biblical writings. To say this is not to place the pro-Nicene Fathers of the Church on the same level as scripture. But I believe it will be difficult to maintain anything approximating an orthodox trinitarianism if we refuse to acknowledge a role for the Holy Spirit in guiding the Church in its understanding of the trinitarian nature of God. In either case, negotiating the issues promises to be a sensitive and difficult process. Did someone say that all this was supposed to be easy?

A further question that arises is on whom among the pro-Nicenes should we concentrate our attention? The group has a fair number of members, and the task of comparing and correlating all their views is one for the historical scholar, not for a philosopher or theologian attempting to arrive at a constructive proposal. Fortunately, the question is not too difficult to answer. There is no doubt that Augustine's theology of the Trinity represents the culmination of trinitarian reflection in the Latin-speaking Church of the fourth century. No single Eastern figure stands out to the same degree, but there is widespread agreement on the pre-eminence of the Cappadocian Fathers, Basil of Caesarea, Gregory of Nyssa, and Gregory Nazianzen. Among these three it is widely, though not universally, thought that the writings of Gregory of Nyssa reflect the most sophisticated and well-developed understanding of

---

[11] A recent work that sees any significant deviation from the tradition as undermining the doctrine in its entirety is Stephen R. Holmes, *The Holy Trinity: Understanding God's Life* (Milton Keynes: Paternoster Press, 2012). Holmes dismisses virtually all recent restatements of trinitarian doctrine on the basis that they deviate from the summary that he presents as "The Harvest of Patristic Trinitarianism" (see pp. 144–46; also p. 206). At the same time, he sees no need to defend the coherence and possibility of the beliefs included in the summary.

trinitarian doctrine available in the Eastern Church of the era.[12] Accordingly, our primary question at this point will be, what can we reasonably conclude about the doctrine of the Trinity as understood by Augustine and Gregory of Nyssa? (This will not preclude our introducing and commenting on the views of other theologians as this becomes appropriate.)

This decision in turn sets the stage for the approach to be taken in the next few chapters. Two main questions that need to be answered are: How do Gregory and Augustine understand what is meant by saying that the trinitarian Three are *hypostases* or *personae*? What, in other words, is meant by "person" as applied to the Persons of the Trinity? And, how do these theologians understand the oneness of *ousia* or *essentia* that they ascribe to the trinitarian Persons? In other words, what is the nature of the unity and the diversity in the Trinity? It will hardly surprise anyone that these questions should be asked. However, the way in which they are asked may raise some eyebrows. I shall begin each chapter by asking how we should understand the pro-Nicene Fathers *in terms of the questions as they arise for contemporary trinitarian discussion.* Historians may consider that this is inappropriate—that if we are to interrogate these historical figures we ought to do so in terms of the questions and the alternatives as they appeared to them in their own time. Such an approach is only right and proper—for a historian. But there is, all the same, a further question to be asked and answered: How does their understanding of the Trinity appear *in the light of assumptions and questions that are viable for us today?* If that question remains unanswered, then we are at a loss what to make of their doctrines—unless, that is, we suppose that we can somehow transport ourselves back into the thought-world of the fourth century, and take up residence there. Those who find that to be a serious possibility may be uninterested in the questions I am asking. For the benefit of the rest of us, I press on. I begin each of these topics by posing the issues as they present themselves to our contemporary understanding. Then I consider how, in the light of their actual statements, we should understand the views of Gregory and Augustine in relation to these issues. The suspicion may arise, of course, that I am distorting their thought by viewing it in the light of our own understanding of the questions; whether this happens or not will have to be seen in the light of the actual development of my argument. I will try to develop and defend my interpretations on the basis of the actual texts, though I hope I will not be found to have overlooked well-informed scholarly interpretations of their writings. And from

---

[12] For a differing estimate, see Christopher A. Beeley, *Gregory of Nazianzus on the Trinity and the Knowledge of God* (Oxford: OUP, 2008). According to Beeley, Gregory of Nazianzus's trinitarian doctrine is superior to that of Gregory of Nyssa, and indeed is "the most powerful and comprehensive Trinitarian doctrine of his generation" (p. 319; see also pp. 303–9). I have chosen to go with the majority view, but there is no reason to think the conclusions would have been substantively different had Gregory of Nazianzus been chosen.

time to time I will discuss some of the philosophical assumptions made, and positions endorsed, by these men, offering explanations as to why we can or cannot undertake to think along the same lines ourselves. Readers are asked to postpone a judgment about the soundness of this way of proceeding until they have seen the result.

3

The Divine Three: What is a "Person"?

"When the question is asked, 'What Three?'...the answer is given 'Three persons', not that it might be spoken, but that it might not be left unspoken."[1] These famous words of Augustine seem to suggest that, for him, "person" (*persona*) in the doctrine of the Trinity serves as a mere logical token; it fills a needed grammatical role without conveying any positive information about the divine Three. As we shall see, consideration of his actual use of the term conveys a somewhat different impression. But the puzzlement is real, and it persists. For us today, an answer to this question is a crucial requirement for a viable and intelligible account of the Trinity. And if we are to arrive at a workable understanding of the pro-Nicene doctrine, we need to understand the answer(s) that are either explicit or implicit in its account of the Trinity.

As it happens, there is a contemporary movement in trinitarian theology that offers a relatively clear answer to Augustine's question, and I believe this answer can serve as a useful tool in sorting out the views of fourth-century pro-Nicene trinitarians. I am referring here to Social trinitarianism, a movement that claims historical precedents but appears in definitive form in the twentieth century.[2] In part, the movement can be seen as a reaction against the widespread claims that the ancient terms *hypostasis* and *persona* are not properly seen as equivalent to "person" as we understand the notion today. Leonard Hodgson, the theologian whose writings first brought Social trinitarianism into prominence,[3] insisted on the contrary that the trinitarian Persons are persons "in the full, modern sense." This being the case, the unity between the Persons must be genuinely a social unity, one characterized by mutuality and reciprocity. Drawing on insights from philosophy, psychology, and sociology,[4]

[1] Augustine, *On the Trinity*, tr. A. W. Hadden (Edinburgh: T. & T. Clark, 1873), bk. 5, ch. 9. Here I have preferred the Hadden translation, but otherwise references will be to St Augustine, *The Trinity*, with introduction, translation, and notes by Edmund Hill, OP (Hyde Park: New City Press, 1991).

[2] A useful capsule history may be found in Carl Mosser, "Fully Social Trinitarianism," in McCall and Rea, *Philosophical and Theological Essays*, 131–50.

[3] Leonard Hodgson, *The Doctrine of the Trinity* (New York: Charles Scribner's Sons, 1944).

[4] Sources mentioned by Mosser include John Laird, *Problems of the Self* (London: Macmillan, 1917), and John MacMurray, *The Self as Agent* (London: Faber, 1957).

Social trinitarians point out that genuine personhood not only permits but actually requires social interaction with other persons: a human being who severs all relationships with others has in the process abrogated important aspects of his or her own personhood. (Thus, the unitarian picture of God as a solitary person becomes extremely unattractive, unless we view the created universe as a necessary complement which provides God with an "other" to relate to.[5]) Carl Mosser helpfully provides a set of four propositions that summarize these core contentions:

1. Inter-personal unity is irreducibly social in nature.
2. The members of the Trinity are persons in the full, modern sense.
3. Therefore, the unity of the Trinity is genuinely social in nature.
4. The divine persons interpenetrate, co-inhere, and mutually indwell one another in *perichoresis*.[6]

This final proposition is added in order to reinforce the divine unity and to counteract the suspicion of tritheism which might otherwise attach itself to the Social conception of the Trinity.

Social trinitarians reject the charge that their conception is a modern innovation; they claim historical precedent for their view, often appealing especially to the Cappadocians and to the trinitarian tradition of the Eastern Church. The constructive view of Social trinitarianism need not depend for its validity on the precise accuracy of a particular historical reconstruction.[7] It is fair to say, however, that the lack of any substantial historical precedent for their view would strike a heavy blow against its viability as a proposal for contemporary theology.

Hodgson was the pioneer, but Social trinitarians have become a numerous brood, including (among many others) theologians such as Jürgen Moltmann, David Brown, and Cornelius Plantinga, Jr., and philosophers such as Richard Swinburne, William Lane Craig, and Keith Yandell.[8] Although they are

[5] For a counter-argument to this claim, see Dale Tuggy, "On the Possibility of a Single Perfect Person," in C. P. Ruloff (ed.), *Christian Philosophy of Religion* (Notre Dame, IN: University of Notre Dame Press, forthcoming 2013).

[6] Mosser, "Fully Social Trinitarianism," 133–4.

[7] Mosser lays heavy emphasis on the fact that the narrative typically endorsed by Social trinitarians (including a fairly strong contrast between the "social" Cappadocians and the more "modalist" Augustine, and in general between the Eastern and Western conceptions of the Trinity) is one that has increasingly been rejected by recent scholarship. In response, I make two points. (1) This narrative, whatever its weaknesses, is by no means the sole possession of Social trinitarians; something very much like it has been the received wisdom until very recently. (2) If constructive presentations of trinitarian doctrine are to be disqualified because they embrace a defective historical narrative, we shall probably have very few contenders left. Almost certainly Athanasius will be one of the first to go, on account of his broad-brush labeling of his opponents as "Arians."

[8] See Jürgen Moltmann, *The Trinity and the Kingdom*, tr. Margaret Kohl (Minneapolis: Fortress Press, 1993); David Brown, *The Divine Trinity* (La Salle, IL: Open Court, 1985); Cornelius Plantinga, "Social Trinity and Tritheism," in R. J. Feenstra and C. Plantinga, Jr. (eds), *Trinity, Incarnation, and*

generally united in support of the themes suggested above, there are also important differences among them. They all maintain that "person" in the doctrine of the Trinity is significantly similar to our modern conception of personhood, but there are disagreements as to how close the similarity should be said to be. Is the use of "person" in the doctrine strictly univocal with its use in common speech, or should an element of analogy be recognized? According to Mosser, "The general tendency in all varieties of ST is to employ [*person* and *social*] as univocal terms but some Social Trinitarians ultimately back away from this."[9] Mosser himself, in his critique of Social trinitarianism, provides reasons why analogy needs to be kept in play here. He writes,

> Human beings simultaneously experience interconnected political relation-ships, economic relationships, workplace relationships, sexual relationships, and extended family relationships. We also experience many social relationships that require inequality of position, e.g. parent–child, teacher–student, doctor–patient, commander–soldier, patron–client. Can we really say that the Trinity is a society or even like a society if it contains nothing even remotely correspond-ing to these various elements of human society? Proponents of ST may assert that God is a society, but the narrow range of social relationships they ascribe to the Trinity makes the Trinity *like* a society in only a few modest respects. Hence, the social constitution understanding of personhood requires us to say that the trinitarian members are *like* modern persons in only a few modest respects.[10]

Surely there is an element of exaggeration here: no sensible person would deny that a small, primitive village, or perhaps even a single family living alone, constitutes a "society" in a very meaningful sense of that term, even though many of the sorts of relationships evident in a complex modern society are missing. Still, Mosser's words serve to caution us against an over-simple equa-tion of trinitarian persons and trinitarian sociality with these notions as they occur in everyday contexts.[11]

It is important to recognize that the notion of Social trinitarianism is one that is understood differently by various authors. Mosser, in the conclusion of his article, complains that "Social Trinitarians who are ostensibly committed to creedal orthodoxy have not done enough to clarify the commitments and

---

Atonement: Philosophical and Theological Essays (Notre Dame, IN: University of Notre Dame Press, 1989), 21–47; Richard Swinburne, *The Christian God* (Oxford: Clarendon Press, 1994); J. P. Moreland and William Craig, *Philosophical Foundations for a Christian Worldview* (Downers Grove, IL: InterVarsity, 2003), ch. 29 "The Trinity" (Craig is primarily responsible for the section on the Trinity); and Keith Yandell, "How Many Times does Three Go into One?" in McCall and Rea, *Philosophical and Theological Essays*, 151–68.

[9] Mosser, "Fully Social Trinitarianism," 136.
[10] Mosser, "Fully Social Trinitarianism," 146.
[11] Mosser's critique of Social trinitarianism depends on his leaning heavily on the univocal end of the spectrum; his essay concludes with the suggestion that perhaps we ought to recognize Mormons as the "fully social trinitarians" (see pp. 149–50). One would like to think this is an attempt at humor, but it seems that the actual intent is to establish guilt by association.

boundaries of their model."[12] McCall and Rea, in the introduction to their edited volume, state the first "core tenet" of Social trinitarianism as follows: "The Father, the Son, and the Holy Spirit are 'of one essence', but are not numerically the same substance. Rather, the divine persons are consubstantial only in the sense that they share the divine nature in common.... Furthermore, this sharing of a common nature can be understood in a fairly straightforward sense via the 'social analogy' in which Peter, James and John share human nature."[13] This may indeed be held by some Social trinitarians, but not by all. For instance, it would be rejected both by William Craig and by myself; both of us are present in the McCall–Rea anthology as representatives of Social trinitarianism!

For purposes of the present study it will be useful to have available a fairly minimal definition of Social trinitarianism, one that will capture the core commitments of the position while leaving open the various points on which Social trinitarians disagree with one another. The formula I shall offer comes from Cornelius Plantinga, Jr., author of an article that provided an important impulse for recent work in Social trinitarianism. Plantinga states,

> By a strong or social trinitarianism, I mean a theory that meets at least the following three conditions: (1) The theory must have Father, Son, and Spirit as distinct centers of knowledge, will, love, and action. Since each of these capacities requires consciousness, it follows that, on this sort of theory, Father, Son, and Spirit would be viewed as distinct centers of consciousness or, in short, as *persons* in some full sense of the term. (2) Any accompanying sub-theory of divine simplicity must be modest enough to be consistent with condition (1), that is, with the real distinctness of trinitarian persons.... (3) Father, Son, and Spirit must be regarded as tightly enough related to each other so as to render plausible the judgment that they constitute a particular social unit. In such social monotheism, it will be appropriate to use the designator *God* to refer to the whole Trinity, where the Trinity is understood to be one thing, even if it is a complex thing consisting of persons, essences, and relations.[14]

Of the three conditions stated, the first is clearly the most important, and this is the one to which I shall mainly refer in the subsequent discussion.[15] Condition (2) is a requirement for logical consistency, specifically a requirement that Social trinitarian view should not include other commitments that contradict

---

[12] Mosser, "Fully Social Trinitarianism," 150.

[13] McCall and Rea, *Philosophical and Theological Essays*, 3. Michael Rea repeats this in his characterization of social trinitarianism in his own essay on the Trinity; see "The Trinity," in Thomas P. Flint and Michael C. Rea (eds), *The Oxford Handbook of Philosophical Theology* (Oxford: OUP, 2009), 413.

[14] "Social Trinity and Tritheism," 22.

[15] The term, "center of consciousness" may be found insufficiently precise by some; those who find it so are invited to substitute "subject of consciousness."

condition (1). (As Plantinga notes, and as we shall see, there are special reasons for stressing this requirement in relation to the doctrine of divine simplicity.) Condition (3) is one that all Social trinitarians will claim to have satisfied in their own theories, although some critics will dispute whether the Trinity so conceived can indeed be said to be (only) one God.

Two additional points may be made briefly concerning Plantinga's formula. First, note that the insistence that Father, Son, and Spirit are persons "in some full sense of the term" leaves it open that the term can legitimately have a variety of senses, and thus allows (though it does not require) the recognition of an analogical element in the use of "person." But second, it should be noted that the formula as stated does not require that the three Persons should share merely an abstract essence, as opposed to a numerically identical concrete nature. It is true that some Social trinitarians (including Plantinga himself) have thought of the divine oneness in terms of generic unity among the Persons. I believe, however, that this is because they found themselves unable to understand how distinct persons could share a numerically identical concrete nature, rather than because they found the notion of a merely generic unity of the Persons inherently compelling. As has already been noted, there are thinkers who are generally recognized as Social trinitarians, and who so regard themselves, who have insisted on the numerical identity of the divine essence,[16] so it is undesirable to include "merely generic unity" as a defining characteristic of Social trinitarianism.[17]

Having said this, I want to acknowledge that those who wish to use "Social trinitarianism" in a more restricted sense are within their rights to do so. In that case, "Social trinitarians" on their definition will be a subclass of the Social trinitarians discussed in this book. It may then turn out that there are criticisms that are applicable to the narrower group which need not apply to Social trinitarianism as I understand it. On the other hand, there is at least one major advantage that might accrue if the sort of definition I am proposing should become widely accepted. It is my observation that there are a good many theologians and philosophers who are in sympathy with Social trinitarianism to some degree; however they are reluctant to accept the label because there are other aspects of the views of well-known "Social trinitarians" (e.g. Moltmann) that give them pause. The acceptance of a clear-cut definition such as the one proposed here could clarify the situation, and enable scholars generally to identify themselves clearly as Social trinitarians or as opposed to Social trinitarianism—or perhaps as straddling the fence between the two camps.

---

[16] See Moreland and Craig, *Philosophical Foundations for a Christian Worldview*; also William Hasker, "Tri-Unity," *Journal of Religion*, 56/1 (Jan. 1970), 1–32.

[17] Consider also the following: "The central commitment of social trinitarianism is that in God there are three distinct centers of self-consciousness, each with its proper intellect and will." Moreland and Craig, *Philosophical Foundations*, 583.

Given this way of understanding Social trinitarianism, how are we to use this notion in order to clarify the ancient pro-Nicene conception of the Trinity? To begin with, I believe it would be infelicitous to describe any ancient or medieval thinker as a Social trinitarian. As we have seen, the movement in its present form is inescapably indebted to insights drawn from recent philosophy, psychology, and sociology. To refer to Gregory of Nyssa (e.g.) as a Social trinitarian would be (at best) to ignore this indebtedness and in effect to delete from Social trinitarianism much of what makes it a distinctive and interesting movement. Still worse, such a move might tempt us to attribute to Gregory, and other ancient Fathers, ideas and views which we have no reason to suppose they ever entertained. This is a real danger, as is shown by the example of an important work on Gregory by Lucian Turcescu. Turcescu writes, "The question arising now is 'What causes the Father, Son, and Holy Spirit to be divine persons and not mere "collections of properties"?'"[18] He then answers his own question as follows: "Gregory makes communion among the three persons the important factor that transforms them from mere collections of properties into persons."[19] This seems misguided for at least two reasons. First of all, the idea that persons become persons by interacting with other persons is a distinctive insight of modern psychology and sociology; the texts cited by Turcescu fail to provide any evidence that a similar notion was entertained by Gregory in the fourth century. Secondly, Turcescu himself provides evidence that shows that the very question Gregory is supposed to be answering—the question, "What causes the Father, Son, and Holy Spirit to be divine persons and not mere 'collections of properties'?"—is a question that *would not arise* for Gregory himself. For us today, to be sure, it seems extremely plausible that a person has to be "something more" than a mere collection of properties. For the philosophy of that time, however, this was not the case. In Neoplatonism, an individual was *defined as* a collection of properties; Gregory echoes this when he states, "a *hypostasis* is also the concourse of the peculiar characteristics."[20] Later on, Turcescu explains that "If one adds to each divine person (*hypostasis*) other properties besides the ones that uniquely characterize each of them, one describes each divine person as a unique collection of properties."[21] I find it strange that Turcescu fails to recognize that, in citing this notion of a "divine person as a unique collection of properties," he has undercut his own reason for supposing that, in Gregory's view, Father, Son, and Spirit are caused to be persons by their mutual intercommunion. The only explanation I can find for this is that he was so captivated by the ideas connected with the modern

---

[18] Lucian Turcescu, *Gregory of Nyssa and the Concept of Divine Persons* (Oxford: OUP, 2005), 58.

[19] Turcescu, *Gregory of Nyssa*, 59.

[20] Turcescu, *Gregory of Nyssa*, 54. (I have transliterated the Greek letters in Turcescu's text, a practice followed throughout this book.)

[21] Turcescu, *Gregory of Nyssa*, 57.

conception of a person that he could not resist the temptation to attribute those same ideas to Gregory, however defective his evidence for doing so.[22]

I shall not, then, describe the pro-Nicenes, or any other ancient theologians, as Social trinitarians. I propose, however, to identify as *pro-Social* those trinitarians who are committed, either explicitly or implicitly, to the view that the Persons are distinct from one another in the way indicated by the first of Plantinga's three criteria: they are "distinct centers of knowledge, will, love, and action...distinct centers of consciousness." And on the other hand, *anti-Social trinitarians* are those who, while recognizing a real, objectively existing divine Trinity, reject the idea that they are distinct persons in the way specified.[23] Clearly, it may sometimes be open to dispute whether a particular thinker qualifies as pro-Social, especially when we must rely on inferences rather than on explicit statements. And it may well be that some cases are indeterminate, in that the evidence does not support a clear answer. Nevertheless, I believe that the concepts as so defined can prove a valuable tool in coming to terms with the trinitarian views of the ancient Fathers. Equipped with these tools, we now turn to examine the views of Gregory of Nyssa and of Augustine concerning the divine Persons.

---

[22] Interestingly, Turcescu himself criticizes John Zizioulas for attributing to the Cappadocians notions that are actually derived from modern sources; see his "'Person' versus 'Individual', and Other Modern Misreadings of Gregory of Nyssa," in S. Coakley (ed.), *Re-Thinking Gregory of Nyssa* (Oxford: Blackwell, 2003), 97–109. In spite of this, it does seem that he has fallen into the same error himself.

[23] Proponents of anti-Social trinitarianism are not, of course, antisocial persons; nothing of the sort is intended or implied.

4

Gregory of Nyssa and the Divine Persons

Recent discussions of Gregory of Nyssa's trinitarian views have largely revolved around his short treatise, On "Not Three Gods," to Ablabius,[1] often referred to by its Latin title, Ad Ablabium. Scholars have protested, with good reason, at the neglect of Gregory's other writings on the Trinity in favor of this one piece. But the interest in Ad Ablabium is natural and perhaps inevitable. (Lewis Ayres, one of the leading protesters, nevertheless organizes his own exposition of Gregory's trinitarian views around a close examination of Ad Ablabium.) This is the locus for the deployment of the "three men" analogy for the Trinity, which has played a major role in the debate over the interpretation of Gregory's trinitarianism as Social or pro-Social. And since that is our interest as well, we need to see what this treatise has to say on the topic.[2]

The "three men" analogy needs, however, to be approached in the light of the treatise as a whole. Gregory begins by stating that he has been asked by Ablabius, a younger cleric, to respond to a particularly challenging question posed by the opponents of trinitarian doctrine. The question takes the form of a dilemma: "either to say 'there are three Gods',... or not to acknowledge the Godhead of the Son and the Holy Spirit."[3] Obviously neither of these alternatives is at all acceptable, so the question urgently demands an answer.

The answer proposed by Gregory takes the form of another dilemma (this time a constructive dilemma), though this does not become apparent right away. The dilemma hinges on the interpretation of the word theotēs ("Godhead" or "deity"). Does the word designate the divine nature, or some activity taken to be characteristically divine? In addressing the first alternative, Gregory admits that "Peter, James, and John, being in one human nature, are called three men."[4] Why then are not Father, Son, and Holy Spirit, who by hypothesis share the one divine nature, three Gods? Gregory's response here is rather surprising: it

---

[1] Nicene and Post-Nicene Fathers, 2nd ser. 5/331–6.

[2] For discussions of the source of the "three Gods" objection, and the polemical context of Ad Ablabium, see Ayres, Nicaea, 345–7; also Michel René Barnes, The Power of God: Dynamis in Gregory of Nyssa's Trinitarian Theology (Washington, DC: Catholic University of America Press, 2000), 297–305.

[3] Ad Ablabium, 331.   [4] Ad Ablabium, 331.

is actually a mistake, a "customary misuse of language," to call Peter, James, and John "three men." When referring to the plurality of individuals we ought to do so by some designation peculiar to them (for instance, by their names), rather than by the name of their common nature. To refer to them as "men," in the plural, suggests that there are "many human natures," which we know to be false. (This parallels the error of those subordinationists who think that there is a distinct nature for each of Father, Son, and Holy Spirit.)

Gregory admits, however, that it would be impracticable to attempt to reform common usage in such a way as to eliminate plural references to "men" and other kinds of entities in terms of their common nature. And since no actual harm results from this usage, we must simply tolerate, in this case, the logical infelicity involved. Not so, however, in the case of the deity: "in the case of the statement concerning the Divine nature the various use of terms is no longer so free from danger: for that which is of small account is in these subjects no longer a small matter."[5] Here, then, we must insist on strict logical propriety, and must refuse to "pluralize" the divine nature, speaking always of Father, Son, and Spirit as *one* God and not as three Gods.

So far, we are assuming that *theotēs* designates the divine nature as such. There is, however, an alternative: we may assume that this word designates, not the divine nature, but some characteristically divine activity. Gregory himself accepts this interpretation, holding that "every term either invented by the custom of men, or handed down to us by the scriptures, is indeed explanatory of our conceptions of the Divine Nature, but does not include the signification of that nature itself."[6] What activity, then, is signified by *theotēs*? Gregory proposes that "Godhead, or *theotēs*, is so called from *thea*, or beholding, and that He who is our *theotēs* or beholder, by customary use, and by the instruction of the scriptures, is called *theos*, or God."[7] He argues at some length that the activity of "surveying and inspecting" thus expressed is common to the three divine Persons. He does not, however, insist on this interpretation of *theotēs*; rather, it functions in his argument as the second horn of the dilemma, parallel to the previous discussion in which *theotēs* is taken to signify the divine nature.

The interpretation of *theotēs* as signifying an activity does not, however, suffice to silence the objection. Gregory acknowledges that

> we find in the custom of mankind that not only those who are partakers in the same nature, but even any who may be of the same business, are not, when they are many, spoken of in the singular; as we speak of "many orators," or "surveyors," or "farmers," or "shoemakers," and so in all other cases.... [S]ince it has been established by what has been said, that the term "Godhead" is significant of operation, and not of nature, ... we ought all the more to call those "three Gods" who are contemplated in the same operation.[8]

---

[5] *Ad Ablabium*, 332.   [6] *Ad Ablabium*, 332.
[7] *Ad Ablabium*, 333.   [8] *Ad Ablabium*, 333.

In response, Gregory argues that our plural references to farmers, orators, and the like are explained by "the fact that men, even if several are engaged in the same form of action, work separately each by himself at the task he has undertaken...For instance, supposing the case of several rhetoricians, their pursuit, being one, has the same name in the numerous cases: but each of those who follow it works by himself, this one pleading on his own account, and that on his own account."[9] But not so with regard to God; rather,

> every operation which extends from God to the Creation...has its origin from the Father, and proceeds through the Son, and is perfected in the Holy Spirit. For this reason the name derived from the operation is not divided, because the action of each concerning anything is not separate and peculiar, but whatever comes to pass, in reference either to the acts of His providence for us, or to the government and constitution of the universe, comes to pass by the action of the Three, yet what does come to pass is not three things.[10]

Since, then, the divine activity of "beholding" is one and not three, we must also confess one "beholder" (*theos*) and not three. Gregory here appeals to the doctrine of the "inseparable operation" of the trinitarian Persons, a doctrine deeply entrenched in pro-Nicene trinitarianism, and one that plays a crucial role in the defense of the divine unity. It follows, then, that whichever interpretation of *theotēs* is accepted, we are correct to say that there is one God, and the argument for "three Gods" misses its mark.

What shall we say about these arguments? With regard to the first argument, where *theotēs* is taken to refer to the divine nature, I think we must admit that Gregory is simply wrong. When we speak of many men, or many cows, or many birds, we are in no way indicating a multiplicity of human natures, or bovine natures, or avian natures. Rather, we are speaking about a plurality of individuals, all of which share in one and the same nature.[11] The claim that we misspeak when we say these things is not merely incredible as an account of linguistic usage; it misunderstands and misstates the claims that are actually being made. And Gregory's failure at this point is by no means trivial; it places all the weight of his argument on the case for the second horn of his dilemma, and on the interpretation given to it.

The other case, where *theotēs* is taken as indicating an operation, is more complex. Gregory appropriately points out the contrast between the ordinary human situation, where (e.g.) various lawyers (his "rhetoricians") are each pursuing their individual cases, with the situation in the Trinity where the Persons always act inseparably. He neglects, however, to ask how we ought to speak in situations where human agents are working closely together. Think of three attorneys working together on a particular case—or an even simpler

---

[9] *Ad Ablabium*, 334.   [10] *Ad Ablabium*, 334.

[11] Christopher Stead remarks, "Gregory needs to convince us that Moses, Eunomius, and Cleopatra are 'all one man'!" *Philosophy in Christian Antiquity* (Cambridge: CUP, 1994), 184.

example, three singers maintaining a perfect unison throughout a lengthy piece of music. In these sorts of situations, it is beyond doubt that we will still speak in the plural, of "attorneys," or "singers." And the reason for this is that, in spite of the close cooperation involved, we can still discern in each case a plurality of *personal agencies*. This in turn suggests that in order for Gregory's argument to succeed the trinitarian Persons must work, not only inseparably, but *indistinguishably*, so that in each and every instance there is only a single agency involved. This interpretation of "inseparable operation" is tempting if one is seeking to maintain a strong doctrine of divine unity. According to Lewis Ayres, Gregory "uses a model of causality to present the three not as possessing distinct actions, but as together constituting *just one distinct action* (because they are one power)."[12]

This understanding of trinitarian activity is not, however, without its problems. One difficulty that immediately comes to mind concerns the incarnation, where the "action" of becoming incarnate, and indeed the subsequent actions of the incarnate Word, seem to be quite definitely actions of the Son and not of the Father or the Spirit. Even more pertinent in the present context is the fact that this interpretation does not correspond to the extended example given by Gregory himself:

> For as when we learn concerning the God of the universe, from the words of Scripture, that He judges all the earth, we say that He is the Judge of all things through the Son: and again, when we hear that the Father judgeth no man, we do not think that the Scripture is at variance with itself,—(for He Who judges all the earth does this by His Son to Whom He has committed all judgment; and everything which is done by the Only-begotten has its reference to the Father, so that He Himself is at once the Judge of all things and judges no man, by reason of His having, as we said, committed all judgment to the Son . . .)[13]

Here we see that the Father "judges all the earth" precisely by *delegating* the office and authority of judgment to the Son. One thinks of monarchical systems in which judgment is pronounced in the name of the monarch, but where the king or queen does not personally participate in the activity of reaching and announcing the verdict. Here there can be no doubt that the Son is said to perform an action, judging, that is *not* in the same way an action of the Father or the Spirit, though it is done in a way that accords with their will and intention. Given this example, Ayres's claim that the trinitarian Three have together "just one distinct action" apparently cannot be maintained.[14]

---

[12] Ayres, *Nicaea*, 357–8.   [13] *Ad Ablabium*, 334.

[14] Khaled Anatolios states, "I would qualify Ayres's assertion that Gregory 'present[s] the three not as possessing distinct actions, but as together constituting *just one distinct action* (because they are one power)' (*Nicaea*, 358). Such a judgment leaves out of account statements in which Gregory distributes the one divine action distinctly among the *hypostaseis* by using different verbs, as in the passage discussed above wherein the one divine *energeia* 'originates in the Father, proceeds through the Son, and is complete in the Holy Spirit' (*Ad Ablabium*: GNO 3.1.47)." *Retrieving Nicaea*, 220n.

But lacking this, Gregory's defense of his "not three Gods" claim fails for this horn of the dilemma as well.

That Gregory's argument is unsuccessful does not of course entail that the "three Gods" objection cannot be answered, much less that his doctrine of the Trinity is fundamentally flawed. One suspects that it may have been a mistake for him to argue on the basis of common linguistic usage, instead of appealing directly to the unique features of the trinitarian situation. Some of his remarks made in passing in *Ad Ablabium* may actually be more promising than the arguments he deploys at length, and which we have examined here. For instance, he imagines an objector conceding that "If, indeed, Godhead were an appellation of nature, it would be more proper . . . to include the Three Persons in the singular number, and to speak of 'One God', by reason of the inseparability and indivisibility of the nature."[15] If the divine nature is understood to be one numerically and not, like the nature of humanity, merely generically, such an argument might show genuine promise. However, our main concern here is with the implications of the "three men" analogy, and to this we now turn.

Those who oppose a Social interpretation of Gregory's trinitarianism point out that the "three men" analogy is introduced in *Ad Ablabium* in the name of an objector, as part of an argument against Gregory's own view.[16] That much is certainly correct, but it does little to diminish the force of this analogy as evidence for Gregory's view. First of all, Gregory endorses the analogy in another context, where he explicitly cites the relation between person and nature in the human case as a basis for understanding the Trinity:

> If now of two or more who are [man] in the same way, like Paul and Silas and Timothy an account of the *ousia* of men is sought, one will not give one account of the *ousia* of Paul, another one of Silas and again another one of Timothy; but by whatever terms the *ousia* of Silas is shown, these same will fit the others as well. And those are *homoousios* to each other, who are described by the same formula of being. . . . If now you transfer to the doctrine of God the principle of differentiation between *ousia* and *hypostasis* that you acknowledge on the human level, you will not go astray.[17]

But even if we limit ourselves to *Ad Ablabium* the objection is weak. The question that must be considered is this: *Why does Gregory consent to conduct the*

[15] Ayres, *Nicaea*, 333.

[16] See Sarah Coakley, "'Persons' in the 'Social' Doctrine of the Trinity: A Critique of the Current Analytic Discussion," in S. T. Davis, D. Kendall SJ, and G. O'Collins SJ (eds), *The Trinity: An Interdisciplinary Symposium on the Trinity* (Oxford: OUP, 1999), 132.

[17] The quotation is from Basil of Caesarea, Epistle 38; tr. Johannes Zachhuber, *Human Nature in Gregory of Nyssa: Philosophical Background and Theological Significance* (Leiden: Brill, 2000), 70. This epistle is now generally believed to have been written by Gregory rather than Basil. Coakley references Epistle 38 and attributes it to Gregory, but she fails to note that in it he introduces the "three men" analogy while speaking in his own voice.

entire discussion in terms of this analogy?[18] It is clear that the "three Gods" of the objection are thought of as analogous to the many gods of contemporary paganism—gods that are without question conceived as personal agents, indeed as quite distinctive personalities. If he had pointed out right at the beginning that this analogy was defective and unsuitable, he could have scuttled the objection with much less fanfare. Recent anti-Social trinitarians such as Barth and Rahner[19] take precisely this course. Neither pays much attention to the charge of tritheism as a problem for his own view; such a charge evidently is not applicable to views such as theirs, according to which "person" as used in the doctrine of the Trinity is at most very remotely analogous to the usage of "person" as referring to human beings.

To be sure, Gregory's failure to take this line might be understandable if he had available to him some other clear, conclusive, and relatively simple way of refuting the objection. This, however, is not the case. I say this not merely because of his own protestations concerning the difficulty of the problem; that might be merely a rhetorical ploy, designed to secure the close attention of readers to his argument. But when we examine the actual argument, we see that it is complex, requiring considerable dialectical ingenuity—and in the end, of dubious success. So it begins to appear that *he accepted the analogy precisely because the analogy is appropriate in the light of his own understanding of the doctrine of the Trinity.* Note that the passage about the Father's having delegated the task of judgment to the Son meshes seamlessly with the "three men" analogy: only a person can pass judgment, and only a person can delegate the task of judging to another person. This passage, furthermore, is not the result of an anti-trinitarian objection; rather, it was deliberately introduced into the discussion by Gregory himself, in order to illustrate his doctrine of inseparable operation. This impression is confirmed by a move made by him in the less polemical context of his *Great Catechism.* After a general survey of trinitarian doctrine, he remarks:

> The Jewish dogma is destroyed by the acceptance of the Word, and the belief in the Spirit; while the polytheistic error of the Greek school is made to vanish by the unity of the Nature abrogating this imagination of plurality. While yet again, of the Jewish conception, let the unity of the Nature stand; and of the Hellenistic, only the distinction as to persons; the remedy against a profane view being thus applied, as required, on either side.[20]

---

[18] Anatolios states, "It should be noted that nowhere in the course of this ingenious response does Gregory simply repudiate altogether the example the three human individuals sharing a common nature as supplying a logical analogy for the formal relation of common-particular in *ousia-hypostasis* and kindred analogies. Rather, Gregory assumes the validity of the comparison and indeed validates trinitarian language by reference to it." *Retrieving Nicaea,* 228.

[19] For the trinitarian views of Karl Barth and Karl Rahner, see the discussion of their doctrines in Part II of this book.

[20] *The Great Catechism, NPNF* 2nd ser. 5/477.

Gregory actually commends as sound the Greek view of "the distinction as to persons"; it is hard to see how he could have spoken in this way if, in his view, the Persons of the Trinity were not in some fairly strong way analogous with the multiple personages of the pagan pantheon.[21]

At this point it may be helpful to introduce briefly some themes from Gregory's *Contra Eunomium*. It is beyond question that for Eunomius the Son/Logos was a person distinct from the Father—distinct, and also distinctly inferior. In principle, there were two ways in which Gregory could have attacked that position. He might have argued that the Son was *not* a distinct person from the Father in the way Eunomius was assuming. Or, he could argue that the Son, while he was indeed a distinct person, *was not inferior* to the Father, but was indeed fully divine in the same way that the Father is divine.

Significantly, Gregory consistently pursues the second of these strategies rather than the first. Indeed, the main theme throughout the lengthy work is the equivalence of the Son's nature to that of the Father; that this is so is too obvious to require lengthy argument. It is interesting that there were resources, in the traditional trinitarian discourse, that could have been exploited in favor of the former strategy. The often-repeated examples of a spring from which flows a stream, or the sun which sends out rays of illumination, could lend themselves to the view that it is the Father who is the "real substance" of the Godhead, and the Son merely an aspect or function of the Father. For that very reason, however, Gregory feels the need to correct these implications of the familiar images:

> For once having taken our stand on the comprehension of the Ungenerate Light, we perceive that moment from that vantage ground the Light that streams from Him, like the ray co-existent with the sun,...not being a later addition, but appearing at the first sight of the sun itself...or rather...*it will not be a ray of the sun that we shall perceive, but another sun blazing forth*, as an offspring, out of the Ungenerate sun, and simultaneously with our conception of the First, and in every way like him, in beauty in power, in lustre, in size, in brilliance, in all things at once that we observe in the sun.[22]

By substituting a "second sun" for the emitted ray Gregory in one way spoils the example, for we do not in fact perceive a sun producing as an offspring a second sun. But he powerfully underscores the full equivalence of the being of the Son with that of the Father. And since the Father, for Gregory, is unequivocally a person, the same must be true of the Son as well. Indeed, Gregory freely

---

[21] Once again, I quote from Anatolios: "With regard to [the social analogy], it must be conceded that we do not find an extended and focused discussion of the likeness between the unity-in-distinction in the human realm and that in the divine realm as a central theme in Gregory's theology, certainly not to the extent that we find in modern proponents of this approach or even in Richard of St. Victor. However, the tendency to dismiss scattered allusions to such a likeness takes the matter too far in the other direction." *Retrieving Nicaea*, 232.

[22] *Against Eunomius* 1.36 (*NPNF* 2nd ser. 5/84–5); emphasis added.

and without hesitation or embarrassment attributes to the Son all manner of personal functions and activities: he has marked out the heavens, he upholds the earth and encompasses the waters, and directs all that is in motion, but he also was born among us, healed sufferings by his touch, saves the lost, and judges the sinner—and so on and on.[23] Anyone who, in the face of this, refuses to admit that Gregory affirmed the full personhood of the Son has a steep mountain to climb.

I believe that the discussion so far constitutes significant evidence for the overall character of Gregory's trinitarian doctrine. At this point, however, it will be helpful for us to move on to another aspect of the pro-Nicene doctrinal development.

AN APOLLINARIAN INTERLUDE

Apollinarius of Laodicea is known to history as the architect of one of the heresies that was laid to rest on the way to the eventual settlement of the christological issue at Chalcedon. But Apollinarian, and Apollinarian-like, views played a role also in the evolution of trinitarian doctrine, and I believe an understanding of this role can play a part in our own grasp of the character of pro-Nicene trinitarianism. This part of the story really begins with Athanasius. There has been a debate about his views concerning the presence or absence of a human soul in Christ: according to Frances M. Young, "Athanasius never seems to have faced the question whether Christ had a human soul or mind."[24] The reason this issue never became salient for him stems from the character of his theology of the incarnation. Young summarizes some key ideas as follows:

> To Platonists, human existence was the soul's experience of being trapped in the flesh and succumbing to its temptations. If Athanasius understood human life in this way, then in general terms his view of the incarnation was perfectly legitimate. The Logos had the experience of being human because he, like us, was trapped in flesh and, like us, was tempted by it, but the subject of the experience being the Logos, he did not in the process succumb to sin, because of his very nature. This was no docetic charade, but a real experience of the conditions of human life, the only difference being that he could have no guilt or sinfulness.[25]

---

[23] All these from *Against Eunomius* 5.4 (p. 186).

[24] *From Nicaea to Chalcedon*, 248. Earlier, however, she states, "the weight of the evidence supports those who argue that Athanasius did not think that Christ had a human soul; his was a Word-flesh Christology, and he was Apollinarian before Apollinarius" (p. 63). If we are to reconcile these assertions, it will have to be on the assumption that Athanasius' "Apollinarianism" was latent in his thought rather than explicit.

[25] *From Nicaea to Chalcedon*, 63.

In view of this a human soul, even if present, could not play a significant role of its own in the incarnate life; as Young says, "The question of the human soul of Christ does not appear within Athanasius' horizon."[26]

Now, there can be no doubt that such a view of the incarnation has serious shortcomings, and the threat of some kind of docetism lies close at hand. It is not sufficient to assert that the "flesh" of Christ suffered. Flesh does *not* suffer, unless appropriately linked to a conscious mind, and the mind in question, the divine Logos, is immune to suffering and weakness. (The approach of modern kenotic christology, in which the Son literally laid aside his divine attributes, would not have been countenanced by any ancient theologian.) So a dilemma looms: either affirm the real suffering of Christ, and thereby compromise the immutability and perfection of the divine Logos, or deny that suffering and with it the reality of Christ's human experiences. It was with good reason that later theologians insisted on the presence in Christ of a human soul.

Our present concern, however, is not with these christological issues as such, but rather with the implications of Athanasius' christology for his view of the Trinity. The important point, which must not be lost sight of, is this: *For Athanasius, the psychological subject of the human experiences of Jesus is the divine Logos.* According to J. N. D. Kelly,

> the Word for Athanasius was the governing principle, or *hēgemōn*, in Jesus Christ, the subject of all the sayings, experiences and actions attributed to the Gospel figure. It was, for example, one and the same Word Who performed the miracles and Who wept and was hungry, prayed in Gethsemane and uttered the cry from the cross, and admitted ignorance of the date of the last day.... If Scripture says that Jesus advanced in wisdom and grace, its real meaning is that there was a parallel and progressive development of His body and disclosure of His deity. When He is reported to have professed ignorance, it was a case of feigned, not genuine, ignorance.... [Athanasius] represented the Word as the unique subject of all Christ's experiences, human as well as divine.[27]

In view of this, the character of Athanasius' trinitarian doctrine as pro-Social seems beyond question.[28]

The friendship between Athanasius and Apollinarius is well attested. When Athanasius was returning from exile in 346, Apollinarius offered him communion after he had been refused by the bishop of Laodicea; the bishop retaliated by excommunicating Apollinarius. The two men maintained an extensive correspondence, and Athanasius consulted with Apollinarius on theological

---

[26] *From Nicaea to Chalcedon*, 64.

[27] J. N. D. Kelly, *Early Christian Doctrines* (London: Adam & Charles Black, 1958), 285–6, 287.

[28] It should perhaps be stated that the presence or absence of a human soul in Christ, according to Athanasius, remains a matter of controversy. For present purposes, however, that is not the most important point. The important point is that, as Kelly says, "the Word for Athanasius was...the unique subject of all Christ's experiences, human as well as divine." About this there seems to be no doubt.

matters. "As far as Athanasius was concerned, Apollinarius was a staunch supporter of Nicene orthodoxy."[29] Apollinarius, unlike Athanasius, made explicit the doctrine that Christ was without a human mind: the incarnation consisted in the assumption by the Logos of "flesh," which is to say, a human body. It follows, of course, that for Apollinarius also the psychological subject of the human experiences of Jesus is the Logos. Once again, the Persons of the Trinity must be "distinct centers of knowledge, will, love, and action." Apollinarius also must be recognized as a pro-Social trinitarian.[30]

The story does not end there. Early in his career Basil of Caesarea engaged in a correspondence with Apollinarius, with an emphasis on trinitarian doctrine. Indeed, it was under Apollinarius' influence that Basil came to accept the *homoousion*; previously, Basil was inclined to reject this term in favor of "unalterably like" (*aparallaktōs homoiou*).[31] Later on, after Apollinarius had come under suspicion of heresy, Basil tried to dissociate himself, but there is no evidence for any substantial difference in their trinitarian views. Indeed, Young concludes that Apollinarius' view of the Trinity was "not far from the position reached by the Cappadocians."[32] Perhaps it is conceivable that Basil differed fundamentally from Apollinarius with regard to the nature of the trinitarian Persons, with no evidence of this divergence having been preserved. In the absence of such evidence, however, the more reasonable supposition seems to be that there was a basic agreement between Apollinarius and Basil—and, by a reasonable extension, the two Gregories as well.[33] If so, this agreement adds to the other evidence that justifies classifying the Cappadocians also as pro-Social trinitarians.

Interestingly, Apollinarius seems to have preached his particular view on the person of Christ for many years without causing much consternation thereby. Young's plausible explanation is that, so long as Arian views remained a serious threat, the question of a human soul in Christ remained largely in the background. Only after 381, when the accession of Theodosius and the council of Constantinople had secured the victory of the Nicene cause, did the two Gregories undertake the task of refuting Apollinarius' christology.

This connection between Athanasius, Apollinarius, and the Cappadocians seems to me to offer an important window into the character of Greek pro-Nicene trinitarianism, and it is surprising that more has not been made of

---

[29] Kelly, *Early Christian Doctrines*, 245.

[30] According to Anatolios, Apollinarius "combines an emphasis on the three distinct subsistences—or *prosopa*, in his preferred terminology—with a strongly unitive Christology that denies ascribing duality to Christ...In this schema, the humanity of Christ can be integrated into the Son's relation to the Father but, it seems, only by being harmonized with the divinity to a degree that compromises its own integrity." *Retrieving Nicaea*, p. 93.

[31] See Hanson, *Search*, 695–7.   [32] Hanson, *Search*, 253.

[33] According to Young, "Gregory Nazianzen's Trinitarianism also seems indebted to him [viz., Apollinarius]" (*From Nicaea to Chalcedon*, 161). Christopher A. Beeley goes further, pointing out extensive similarities between the two, not only in trinitarian doctrine but especially in christology, in spite of their disagreement about Christ's human mind. See Beeley, *Gregory of Nazianzus on the Trinity*, 285–92.

it in the literature. Conceivably this might be due to a reluctance to draw attention to the problematic character of Athanasius' christological views.[34] But if this is the reason, it is surely a bad reason. In the first place, good history has to be done "warts and all"; we need not fear that Athanasius will lose his place in history by our pointing out flaws in his theology.[35] In the second place, while Apollinarian christology clearly requires a Social or pro-Social trinitarianism, the converse is not true: the Cappadocians, and many others since then, have maintained such a doctrine of the Trinity together with a full commitment to the completeness of Jesus' humanity, body and soul. But before I rest my case, we need to listen to an important dissenting voice.

THE PERSONS AND DIVINE SIMPLICITY

One scholar who objects to classifying Gregory of Nyssa as a Social or pro-Social trinitarian is Richard Cross.[36] His argument to this effect applies also to Augustine, Aquinas, and a host of later figures, but our present concern is especially with Gregory. We need to examine the reasons for this objection, reasons which stem directly from the endorsement by these thinkers of the doctrine of divine simplicity. According to Cross, all of them held "that the essence is the only real constituent of each divine person, and that the essence is numerically identical in each divine person."[37] Furthermore, the only distinction between the divine essence and the divine persons, and between the divine persons themselves, is relational. But "relations are not real entities or things in the world, and to this extent we might think of the distinction between the essence and a divine person as mind-imposed."[38] (I take it that by "mind-imposed" Cross means that the distinction exists only insofar as it is perceived or thought about in the mind of some person.) Given this much (though I am greatly abbreviating

---

[34] Concerning Athanasius, Anatolios states, "Eternally in possession of the fullness of divinity, the Word manifests the self-humbling divine love in the self-emptying of his humanity. The scriptural identity of Jesus Christ is the single subject of this twofold drama.... To read the scriptural christological narrative correctly involves distinguishing between the two accounts while attributing both to the single subject of the Word incarnate." *Retrieving Nicaea*, 124. He also states, summarizing Athanasius' views, "Ultimately, the church can speak about God most truly by *sharing in the mutual conversation within God* of Father, Son, and Holy Spirit" (p. 133; emphasis added; see also p. 153). He does not, however, connect this pro-Social reading of Athanasius to the latter's silence concerning the human soul of Christ.

[35] One scholar who has no such hesitation is R. P. C. Hanson. He is highly appreciative of Athanasius' contribution to the trinitarian debate, but states that "The result of this refusal to accept the existence of a human soul or mind in Jesus was that when Athanasius has to deal with Jesus as a human person with human limitations he is immediately in difficulties." *Search*, 453. Hansen gives a useful history of recent scholarly opinion on the subject; see *Search*, 446–58.

[36] Richard Cross, "Latin Trinitarianism: Some Conceptual and Historical Considerations," in McCall and Rea, *Philosophical and Theological Essays*, 201–13.

[37] Cross, "Latin Trinitarianism," 204.   [38] Cross, "Latin Trinitarianism," 205.

Cross's subtle and complex discussion), he has available a quick argument against a Social, or pro-Social, interpretation of the trinitarian doctrine held by these thinkers. "The views of the theologians I have been discussing here—Gregory of Nyssa, Augustine, and Aquinas—to the extent that they entail that the only features that distinguish the persons are relations, are on the face of it incompatible with the claim that there are three mental subjects in God, since distinction of mental subject seems to be more than just a relational matter, and it certainly seems to be more than a question of relations *between* the persons, such as the Trinitarian relations are supposed to be."[39]

In my opinion, Cross is on the track of an important argument. But he does not formulate the argument rigorously, and as a result draws a weaker conclusion than is warranted by the argument itself. So we need to try for a more precise formulation:

According to Cross, Gregory, Augustine, and Aquinas held the following:

(1) The only real constituent of each divine Person is the divine essence.

(2) The divine Persons are distinguished from each other only by the relations between them.

(3) Relations are not real items in the world but are rather mind-dependent.

To these premises, I now add a fourth, which I claim to be a necessary truth:

(4) For any items x and y, if x and y differ only in some respect that is mind-dependent, then x is identical with y.

This last proposition is implicitly accepted by Cross, when he says, "relations are not real entities or things in the world, and to this extent we might think of the distinction between the essence and a divine person as mind-imposed."[40] And it is readily confirmed by reflection: if the only difference between x and y consists in the way they are considered in someone's mind, then between x and y in themselves there is no difference at all—which is to say, they are identical. (In the philosopher's legend of the Morning Star and the Evening Star, Phosphorus was initially identified as being "the bright star which, at certain seasons, appears low in the eastern sky before sunrise," whereas Hesperus was identified as being "the bright star which, at certain seasons, appears low in the western sky after sunset." Once it was recognized that this is the *only* difference between Hesperus and Phosphorus, it was acknowledged that they are in fact identical, being in reality the planet Venus.)

---

[39] Cross, "Latin Trinitarianism," 213.

[40] Cross states that, in this traditional view, "There are two controversial claims here: first, that relations are not real things in the world, and secondly that two things could be distinct *merely* by such relations." Cross, "Latin Trinitarianism," 205. He refrains (perhaps unfortunately) from pursuing these controversial questions.

But from (1)–(4), it follows that this traditional trinitarian view entails

(5) The Father is identical with the Son, and each of them is identical with the Holy Spirit.

At this point we are confronted with a difficult choice. Three options are available, none of them especially attractive. The options are as follows:

    I. Gregory, Augustine, and Aquinas accepted (5).

    II. Cross is mistaken in his interpretation of the traditional view.

    III. The traditional view is incoherent.

Of the three, I reject I out of hand. (I trust there will be no controversy over this.) It might seem appealing to accept II, since this would allow us to avoid concluding that this traditional view is incoherent. The obstacle to this, over and above Cross's not inconsiderable scholarly authority, is that it is difficult to come up with a plausible revision of the views attributed to the three theologians that would do the job. A contemporary philosopher might be inclined to reject (3); it is an important insight of modern logic and metaphysics that relations can be real items in the world, just as much so as monadic properties. If attributing this view to these men seems overly anachronistic, we might consider attributing to them a rejection of (2). That is to say, it could be that the relations, while in themselves mind-dependent, are grounded in real, objectively existing properties of the Persons. But rejecting either (2) or (3) in this way would also require the rejection of (1); it would mean that there is in each Person another real constituent, over and above the divine essence. This, however, would compromise the doctrine of divine simplicity, and very likely would not have been accepted by Gregory,[41] Augustine, or Aquinas.[42]

It seems, therefore, that we have no viable alternative to accepting III, which states that this traditional view (also held, let us not forget, by a host of others) was logically incoherent. This need not entail any gross negligence; these thinkers may simply have been unaware of the necessary truth of (4). Nor does

---

[41] Actually it is not quite clear that this is true in the case of Gregory. Andrew Radde-Gallwitz has argued convincingly that Gregory held a modified doctrine of simplicity and may not in fact have endorsed (1) in the argument given above. He writes, "[I]t is hard to see how, on [Gregory's] account, the persons can be simple.... Divine simplicity, I conclude, was useful as a blunt instrument to bludgeon Eunomius with (and for Eunomius to bludgeon in return), but was not fully and coherently integrated into Gregory's own trinitarian theology." *Basil of Caesarea, Gregory of Nyssa, and the Transformation of Divine Simplicity* (Oxford: OUP, 2009), 217. If Radde-Gallwitz is right about this, Cross's argument concerning Gregory still fails, but for a different reason than the one given in the main text.

[42] Aquinas recognized the problem, but it is doubtful that he arrived at a successful solution. Christopher Hughes argues that "there is a fundamental incoherence in Aquinas' theory of the Trinity, arising from his desire to eat his cake and have it too—*viz.*, to have a God who is at once triune and free from composition of any kind": *On a Complex Theory of a Simple God: An*

it rule out the possibility of a revision of their views that would salvage coherence and at the same time retain the most central features of their trinitarian theology. (My rejection of option I is based on the conviction that for these men the real distinction between the Persons is more important than inferences that could be drawn from the doctrine of simplicity.)

For our purposes, however, the immediately relevant point is that this shows why Cross's objection to a pro-Social reading of Gregory is misguided. He deploys the argument based on divine simplicity in a one-sided fashion, using it to rule out a Social trinitarian interpretation while leaving unscathed Gregory's commitment to a real, objectively existing divine Trinity. Once we realize that a strong doctrine of simplicity of the sort explained by Cross is incompatible with *any* objectively existing Trinity, it becomes apparent that a fundamental revision of the simplicity doctrine is the only way to restore coherence. And with this, the illusion that Cross's argument poses some special threat for a Social interpretation of Gregory is dispelled.

Investigation in Aquinas' Philosophical Theology (Ithaca, NY: Cornell University Press, 1989), 188. Writing in another context, Richard Cross observes that "if the distinction between the divine essence and the Son is merely a rational matter, with no corresponding extra-mental distinction, it is hard to see how we can plausibly deny the application of the indiscernibility of identicals, and thus deny that, if the divine person suffers, the divine nature suffers too": Richard Cross, *The Metaphysics of the Incarnation: Thomas Aquinas to Duns Scotus* (Oxford: OUP, 2002), 149. If we apply this same reasoning to the Trinity, we get the result spelled out in the text.

5

Augustine and the Divine Persons

Just as the Cappadocians represent the culmination of Greek pro-Nicene trinitarianism, Augustine occupies that position for the Western Church. The relationship between the two is, however, a matter of contention. Augustine was well aware of the Greek discussion, and considered himself to be in agreement with its conclusions. But he clearly was baffled by the distinction being drawn between *ousia* and *hypostasis*; he translated the trinitarian formula, one *ousia* and three *hypostases,* into Latin as one *essentia,* three *substantiae.* He concludes that the Greeks adopted *hypostasis* as the general designation for the trinitarian Three for the same reason the Latins spoke of *persona*—in order to have something to say when no really appropriate term was available.

Certainly there is an initial impression that Augustine emphasized the divine unity more strongly than the Cappadocians, and was more cautious than they were concerning any explicit statement about the distinctions between the Persons. He expresses his dislike for views that find the image of the Trinity in a group of human individuals. (One would be hard pressed to imagine Augustine commending as sound the pagan view of "the distinction as to persons," as did Gregory of Nyssa.) He very often uses "God" to refer to the Trinity as a whole, rather than to the first Person.[1] He uses singular pronouns in speaking of "God" in contexts where the reference is clearly to the entire Trinity. Above all, there is his well-known insistence on "psychological analogies" for the Trinity, as deployed at length in *De Trinitate.* In spite of this, Lewis Ayres argues that all of the key moves made by Augustine are already present in the Cappadocians, and that it is a mistake to drive a wedge between East and West on this issue. In view of this, there is need for us to examine carefully Augustine's thought on the subject.

Augustine's writings on the Trinity are voluminous, and cannot all be reviewed here. Since our initial concern is with his conception of the Persons, an appropriate place to begin is with the famous "psychological analogies"

[1] e.g.: "From this we can go on to infer that the apostle Paul's words, *who alone has immortality* (I Tim 6:16), do not refer to the Father alone but to the one and only God which the trinity is." Augustine, *The Trinity,* tr. Edmund Hill OP (Hyde Park, NY: New City Press, 1991), bk 1, p. 73. Subsequent citations in this chapter are given with book and page number in the text.

which occupy most of books 9 through 14 of *De Trinitate*. The plural, "analogies," is significant here. Augustine is convinced from scripture that it is in the human soul that the image of God—that is, of the Trinity—is to be found. His response to that is not, however, to seize at once on a single image. Rather, he treats the soul and its various functions as, in Lewis Ayres's term, an "analogical site" that can be exploited in a variety of different ways to yield images that may help us in our effort to grasp the Trinity which is God. In the end he does point us to one of those ways as the true and proper image of God, but a lot of ground needs to be covered before we arrive at that destination.

The first of these analogies actually makes its appearance at the end of book 8, where Augustine speaks of "the lover, what is being loved, and love" (bk 8, p. 257). As an analogy for the Trinity, this suggests the now-familiar idea of the Holy Spirit as the bond of love between the Father and the Son. It is a bit ironic that this has been one of the most influential of all Augustine's analogies, yet it is abandoned by him (at least in *De Trinitate*) almost immediately. At the beginning of book 9, he reflects on the fact that the mind may love itself, and thus we have only a duality: the lover, and the love with which it loves itself. But, he reasons, "the mind cannot love itself unless it also knows itself" (bk 9, p. 273), and taking this into account we have a second trinity: the mind, its knowledge of itself, and its love of itself. It will occur to us at this point that the members of this trinity (as well as of the first) are not equal: on the one hand we have the mind, which is a substance, and on the other hand knowledge and love, not substances but rather activities of the mind. Augustine, however, disagrees: "lover or knower is substance, knowledge is substance and love is substance" (bk 9, p. 273). He gives various arguments for this, arguments that are likely to strike us as unconvincing. The important point is stated by Hill: "as a Christian neoplatonist, with John for his authority, he is quite sure that God is love substantively."[2] We will return to this point later; for now, Augustine must be allowed his own way of thinking about the matter.

The next trinity discovered in the mind appears at the end of book 10; this is the trinity of memory, understanding, and will, which in various forms remains with us until the end. In book 11, however, Augustine turns to a trinity based on the "outer man," with his sensory experience, in particular the experience of vision. (He supposes that this will be more readily grasped by some readers.) This trinity consists of "the thing we see, a stone or flame or anything else the eyes can see," the "actual sight or vision" (as we might say, the visual sensation), and the "conscious intention," which "holds the sense of the eyes on the thing being seen" (bk 11, p. 304). He remarks that these three "are not only manifestly distinct, but also of different natures" (bk 11, p. 304);

---

[2] Augustine, *The Trinity*, tr. Hill, bk 9, p. 273n. Later on, Hill comments "there is no doubt…that Augustine took *Deus caritas est* [1 John 4: 8 and 16] to mean 'love is God' just as much as 'God is love'" (bk 15, p. 402n.).

this of course renders them less appropriate as an analogy for the Trinity. He then derives from this still another trinity, taken from the situation when we are not actually perceiving some object but recall it in imagination from an earlier experience of perception. In this case we have "another trinity, out of the memory and internal sight [viz., the memory-image which we recall] and the will which couples them together" (bk 11, p. 309).

Book 12 does not present to us any new trinitarian image, but it contains some important reflections on the general nature of Augustine's enterprise. He states,

> It will be clear that I do not find the opinion very convincing which supposes that the trinity of the image of God, as far as human nature is concerned, can be discovered in three persons; that is, that it may be composed of the union of male and female in their offspring, in which the man suggests the person of the Father, what proceeds from him by way of birth that of the Son, and thus the third person of the Holy Spirit, they say, is represented by the woman. (bk 12, p. 324)

It is not clear who was propounding this view of the image, or where Augustine encountered it. He does, however, state explicitly why he finds the proposal unacceptable: this is because in scripture

> God said, *Let us make man to our image and likeness* (Gn 1:26), and a little later on it adds, *And God made man to the image of God.* "Our," being plural in number, could not be right in this place if man were made to the image of one person, whether of the Father or the Son or the Holy Spirit; but because in fact he was made in the image of the trinity, it said *to our image.* (bk 12, p. 326)

The interpretation of the plural in Genesis 1: 26 as referring to the Trinity may not commend itself to modern exegetes, but for Augustine this was a sure and established interpretation, one that governs all his work on the topic.

In book 12 Augustine has included some comments on the sad state of fallen humanity; in turn, a great deal of books 13 and 14 consists of reflections on the soul's redemption and return to God, leading to the perfected heavenly state. It might occur to us to wonder just why these particular ideas occupy an important place in a discourse on the Trinity. To be sure, Augustine would never have considered time wasted that was spent meditating on the mysteries of our redemption. But there is a structural reason for the inclusion of this material at this point in the text. If it is in the human mind that the image of God is to be found, then that image must be the greatest and most excellent thing about the mind; surely, then, it cannot be something that will be lost or left behind as the soul progresses towards its ultimate perfection. Furthermore, it is Augustine's conviction that the image, while never entirely destroyed, has been effaced, rendered faint and nearly invisible, in fallen humanity. Because of this, it is especially in our final, perfected state that the image may be most clearly seen. He also holds that "not everything in creation which is like God in some way or other is also to be called his image, but only that which he alone is higher than. That alone receives his direct imprint which has no other nature interposed between him and itself" (bk 11, p. 312). So the image is to be found in the soul, which is the highest part of a human being, and in the highest and best activities of the soul, which are naturally to be found especially in the soul's restored and perfected state. In order to reach this state, to be sure, faith must play an important role, and this in turn yields a kind of trinity: "whatever notions this faith and life [viz., the life of faith that works through love] produce in the consciousness of the believing man, when they are contained in the memory, and looked at in recollection, and please the will, they yield a trinity of its own kind. But the image of God...is not yet to be found in this trinity" (bk 13, p. 369). This is so, because in our final state faith will have disappeared, having been replaced by sight, whereas the image of God must be something that we will never lose.

The search for the image reaches its culmination in book 14. Augustine insists that the true image must be found, not in sense experience (which we share with the beasts), or in the "knowledge" of external things, but in the "wisdom" which consists in the contemplation of eternal truths. Consider, then, the mind's contemplation of its own nature: "Here we are then with the mind remembering itself, understanding itself, loving itself. If we see this we see a trinity, not yet God of course, but already the image of God" (bk 14, p. 379). ("Remembering" here does not mean, as it did for Plato, recalling what was learned in a previous existence. It is more a matter of calling to mind "innate ideas.") To be sure, this trinity of memory, understanding, and love appeared much earlier. But only now, after extensive reflection on the purification of the soul and on the differences between sense experience, knowledge, faith, and wisdom, can it be properly appreciated. Augustine also says, "This trinity of the mind is not really the image of God because the mind remembers and understands and loves itself, but because it is also able to remember and understand and love him by whom it was made. And when it does this it becomes wise" (bk 14, p. 384). Later on, he cites 1 John 3: 2: *We know that when he appears we shall be like him, because we shall see him as he is,* and adds, "From this it is clear that the image of God will achieve its full likeness of him when it attains the full vision of him" (bk 14, p. 392). And with this, Augustine's search for the trinitarian image reaches its climax.

With this material in hand (albeit brutally compressed), what shall we make of Augustine's trinitarian analogies? A first point to keep in mind is that he is *not* developing the analogies in order to enable us to arrive at the correct doctrine of the Trinity. On the contrary: that doctrine is assumed throughout to be already fixed by scripture and the faith of the Church; the endeavor here is to enable us better to understand, and in some way to grasp imaginatively, this already established doctrine. The entire project is very much a matter of "faith seeking understanding."[3] A second point to notice is that the question that for us looms in the forefront of such a study is by no means equally central for Augustine. Given the recent trinitarian debate, the inescapable question for us is: One person or three? Is the Trinity most properly seen in terms of a single person, in our ordinary sense of "person," or as a triad of such persons? Augustine was not unaware of this question, but it was by no means as important for him as it is for us, and if we assume the contrary we are likely to be misled. That is to say, we are likely to see his insistence on "psychological" analogies as an answer to *our* question—but as I shall now argue, it is no such thing.[4]

It will now be argued, that is to say, that it is a mistake to interpret Augustine as an "anti-Social" trinitarian, on the basis of his preference for psychological analogies. To begin with, notice his reason for rejecting the trinity of father, mother, and child. The reason is *not* that the comparison of the trinitarian Persons to individual human persons is inherently inappropriate. Even the notion of the Holy Spirit as wife of the Father and mother of the Son need not, in itself, cause us to shun such an image (see bk 12, p. 325). The objection he gives is, as we have seen, simply and solely that scripture indicates that the image of God—that is, of the Trinity—is to be found in the *single* human being, and not in a plurality. It is true, to be sure, that he has reservations about the word "person"—but here also, we need to attend to what he actually says. The objection he states is that "person is a generic name; so much so that even a man can be called person, even though there is such a great difference between man and God" (bk 12, p. 328). That is to say, there ought to be a specific (not merely generic) term by which to refer to the divine Persons, but no suitable term is available. What he does *not* say is that there is an equivocation when "person" is used both of human persons and of the trinitarian Three—but that is just what modern anti-Social trinitarians would say; they would not by any means admit that "person" can serve as an appropriate generic term covering both human beings and the Persons of the Trinity.[5] (Rahner, for instance, makes it quite clear that he would be happy to abandon the word "person" entirely, were he not constrained by the Church to retain it.)

Augustine's treatment of specific analogies also fails to support the notion that he is promoting an anti-Social conception of the Trinity. Take the analogy of the mind, its knowledge of itself, and its love of itself. An anti-Social theorist would surely take advantage of this to point out that there is here, in reality,

[3] According to Lewis Ayres, "Trinitarian faith guides as much as it is explored by Augustine's dialectical reasoning": *Augustine and the Trinity* (Cambridge: CUP, 2010), 317.

[4] Ayres once again: "his use of these mental analogies in *De trinitate* should not be taken as providing any warrant for the view that Augustine's Trinitarian theology treats the Trinity as most like a unitary self-thinking mind": *Augustine and the Trinity*, 175–6.

[5] Later on he says that in God "there are three persons of one being, not, like any single man, just one person" (bk 15, p. 404). Here especially an anti-Social trinitarian would have been bound to point out the supposed equivocation on "person."

a single being or substance, the soul; knowledge and love may be activities or functions of the soul, but there is really only one person involved. But as we have seen, Augustine spoils that "lesson" from the analogy by insisting that each of the three—mind, knowledge, and love—is substance. He just is not saying what an anti-Social trinitarian would want him to say.

What benefit, then, is Augustine deriving from his analogies, if they are not to be understood as indicating a preference for an anti-Social trinitarianism? The answer, I think, is quite clear in the text, though it is something a modern reader might easily pass by without noticing. A primary interest in his use of the analogies concerns the *metaphysical relationships* between the terms in the analogies—relationships which, as he develops them, parallel and thereby illuminate the metaphysical relationships that obtain within the Trinity. One passage to this effect will have to suffice, out of many that could be cited:

> These three then, memory, understanding, and will, are not three lives but one life, nor three minds but one mind. So it follows of course that they are not three substances but one substance. When memory is called life, and mind, and substance, it is called so with reference to itself; but when it is called memory it is called so with reference to another. I can say the same about understanding and will; both understanding and will are so called with reference to another. But each of them is life and mind and being with reference to itself. For this reason these three are one in that they are one life, one mind, one being; and whatever else they are called together with reference to self, they are called it in the singular, not in the plural. But they are three in that they have reference to each other. And if they were not equal, not only each to the other but also each to them all together, they would not of course contain each other. In fact though they are not only each contained by each, they are all contained by each as well. (bk 10, p. 301)

A very little reflection will show how in this passage Augustine is illustrating key aspects of his trinitarian doctrine through the relationships between memory, understanding, and will. (To see this, substitute "Father," "Son," and "Spirit" for "memory," "understanding," and "will" in the passage; the result is completely acceptable as a statement of Augustine's doctrine of the Trinity.[6])

I have argued that, on the basis of what he has written, Augustine should not be understood as an anti-Social trinitarian. Still, doubts may linger. It is after all still true that he insisted on psychological analogies for the Trinity, and rejected the one version of a social analogy that he mentions. And some of what he says about the unity of the Trinity—for instance, the remarks in the preceding quotation—may give us pause if we seek to classify him as a Social, or pro-Social, trinitarian. Have I perhaps been engaging in special pleading,

---

[6] In *Augustine and the Trinity*, chs 11 and 12, Ayres provides a much more detailed and complex explanation of the benefits Augustine derives from his trinitarian analogies. I have not incorporated his results into the present discussion, but I believe his conclusions are consistent with what is stated here.

giving reasons for one interpretation while ignoring equally strong reasons on the other side? Such doubts may seem appropriate, in the light of what has been shown so far. But before we come down on the side of the doubts, we need to look at the fifteenth and last book of *De Trinitate*—the book that is titled (ominously) by the translator as "The Absolute Inadequacy of the Perfected Image" (bk 15, p. 395).

The book begins with a point-by-point review of the conclusions that have been established in the earlier books. But when he contemplates the trinities in the mind that have been identified as the image of the Trinity which is God, he finds himself in difficulty. Earlier I claimed that for Augustine, unlike for us, the entire enquiry does not center around the question, One person or three? He had other things on his mind—in particular, the metaphysical relations between memory, understanding, and will to which I have briefly referred. But that other question did not escape his attention entirely—and now in the fifteenth book he does attend to it, with a result that threatens to undermine all his previous hard work:

> [W]hether we talk about mind in man and its knowledge and love, or whether about memory, understanding, will, we remember nothing of the mind except through memory, and understand nothing except through understanding, and love nothing except through will. But who would presume to say that in that trinity the Father does not understand either himself or the Son or the Holy Spirit except through the Son, or love except through the Holy Spirit, but only remembers either himself or the Son or the Holy Spirit through himself? Or, in the same way, that the Son does not remember either himself or the Father except through the Father, and only loves through the Holy Spirit, while through himself he only understands both the Father and himself and the Holy Spirit? And likewise that the Holy Spirit remembers the Father and the Son and Himself through the Father, and understands the Father and the Son and himself through the Son, while through himself he only loves both himself and the Father and the Son? All this, as though the Father were his own memory and the Son's and the Holy Spirit's, while the Son would be his own understanding and the Father's and the Holy Spirit's, and the Holy Spirit his own and the Father's and the Son's charity. Who would presume to imagine or affirm such a view about that trinity? (bk 15, p. 404)

Having spelled out at such length (and quite indignantly, we might add) the rejected option, he indicates how we must rather think of the matter:

> So here we are then with these three, that is memory, understanding, love or will in that supreme and unchangeable being which God is, and they are not the Father and the Son and the Holy Spirit but the Father alone. And because the Son too is wisdom, begotten of wisdom, it means the Father does not do his remembering for him or the Holy Spirit his loving any more than the Father or the Holy Spirit do his understanding, but he does it all for himself; he is his own memory, his own understanding, his own love, but his being all this comes to him from

the Father of whom he is born. The Holy Spirit too does not have the Father for memory and the Son for understanding and himself for love, because he is wisdom proceeding from wisdom, and he would not be wisdom if another did his remembering and another his understanding for him, and he himself only did his own loving. No, he himself has these three, and he has them in such a way that he is them. But its being so with him comes to him from where he proceeds from. (bk 15, p. 405)

Frankly, it is difficult to see what more would have to be said, or that could be said, to make it clear that for Augustine each of the trinitarian Persons is, in Plantinga's words, a "distinct center of knowledge, will, love, and action." If this does not qualify Augustine as a pro-Social trinitarian, what more would it take?

In the subsequent pages of book 15 Augustine pursues the idea that, although the images he has presented have been shown to be inadequate, they may nevertheless enable us to *see through a mirror in an enigma* (1 Cor. 13: 12). (Augustine explains that an enigma is "an obscure allegory.") This endeavor is carried on at considerable length, and he clearly believes we can make some progress thereby in understanding the Trinity. Nevertheless, he never retracts the conclusion that was reached about the inadequacy of the images he has developed. Towards the end he says,

So great has this difficulty been, that every time I wanted to bring out some comparative illustration of this point in that created reality which we are, having promised in the second book of this work that I would talk about the matter later on, I found that no adequate expression followed whatever understanding I came to; and I was only too well aware that my attempt even to understand involved more effort than result. In the one person which a man is, I did indeed find an image of that supreme trinity...And yet the three things of one person were quite unable to match those three persons in the way our human plan requires, as we have been demonstrating in this fifteenth book. (bk 15, p. 435)

It is my claim that the passages quoted here, and the longer development which they epitomize, decisively confirm the classification of Augustine as a pro-Social trinitarian. Interpretations of Augustine that ignore these developments in the concluding book of *De Trinitate* are missing the point in a profound way and are difficult to take seriously.[7]

One scholar who does not ignore book 15 (at least, not completely) is Lewis Ayres. Ayres acknowledges Augustine's insistence that each Person possesses, and indeed is identical with, his own memory, understanding, and love. I do

---

[7] According to Michel René Barnes, "Augustine has been read in bits and pieces. Indeed, in bits and pieces sometimes seems to be the only way that Augustine has been read." "Rereading Augustine's Theology of the Trinity," in Davis *et al., The Trinity,* 147. This material from bk 15 seems to be one of the bits that has often been left out!

not see, however, that he registers the disappointment which seems evident in the remarks of Augustine cited above.[8] (Whose is the "human plan" that would seek to match the three Persons with the functions of memory, understanding, and will, if not Augustine's own? And why the heavy emphasis here on "seeing through a mirror in an enigma"?) In any case, after emphasizing that for Augustine Father and Son are each his own wisdom Ayres goes on to say, "If the Son is wisdom itself, and the Father is wisdom itself, then we can go a step further and say that the Son's essence must be identical with the Father's essence. There cannot, obviously enough, be two instances of wisdom itself."[9] Is this in effect taking back what was previously granted, in such a way that the real distinction between the Persons comes into question?

This prompts us to ask what, in Ayres's view, is the nature of the Persons according to Gregory and Augustine? This is not a particularly easy question to answer. His general overview of pro-Nicene trinitarianism could be not unfairly summarized by saying that the three Persons are distinct in a way we are incapable of understanding, but are also united in a way we are incapable of understanding.[10] To get beyond these rather unhelpful results we need to pay close attention to various things said in different contexts. There is some reason to suspect that Ayres would object to our classifying these thinkers as Social or pro-Social trinitarians. He is quite critical of Social trinitarian Cornelius Plantinga.[11] And in discussing Gregory's views he is highly resistant to attributing "dense psychological content" to the trinitarian Persons.[12] Just what is involved in this psychological content is, however, left unexplained.

Nevertheless, there is more to be said. Ayres describes Augustine's trinitarian language as "analogically personalist," explaining that "This language considers foundational Scripture's primary dramatic language concerning the interaction of Father, Son, and Spirit."[13] To say that this "dramatic language" is foundational amounts to saying that the most fundamental way to think about Father, Son, and Spirit is to think of them *as persons*—which is

---

[8] According to Hill, "XV is a ruthless exposé of the inadequacy even of the genuine trinitarian image in man at its highest peak of intensity for representing the divine Trinity itself, and thus a confession that the author has failed—but how splendidly!—in his quest." *The Trinity*, 27.

[9] Ayres, *Nicaea*, 379.

[10] Ayres, *Nicaea*, 295–301. A similar point is made vividly by Andrew Radde-Gallwitz, who follows Ayres's view closely. Commenting on Basil of Caesarea's doctrine, he writes, "Basil's claim is rather that the *ousia* is the common term, which is individuated by bundles of *idiomata* into God knows what, but we'll call it a *hypostasis*." *Basil of Caesarea, Gregory of Nyssa, and the Transformation of Divine Simplicity*, 136.

[11] Ayres, *Nicaea*, 365n.   [12] Ayres, *Nicaea*, 338n.

[13] *Augustine and the Trinity*, 320–1. Later on, he writes, "Scripture offers the language of Father and Son and does so in ways that invite us to imagine those terms as if they referred to two individual agents of the kind that we are familiar with as human beings. At the same time, Scripture itself troubles that implicit analogy when it speaks of the Son as Word and Wisdom and Image." *Augustine and the Trinity*, 325.

exactly what Social trinitarians maintain. Also telling is Ayres's assertion that Augustine "consistently founds the unity of God in the Father's eternal act of giving rise to a communion in which the mutual love of the three constitutes their unity of substance."[14] The notion that the unity of substance is *constituted by* the mutual love of the three is very much a theme of Social trinitarianism, but perhaps this point should not be pressed.[15] However, the very idea of *mutual love* has inescapable Social implications. Mutual love can only occur *between persons*; moreover, it entails the recognition by the Father, for example, that "I the Father love *the Son*," and "I the Father *am loved by* the Son." The Son, however, would recognize that "I the Son love *the Father*," and "I the Son *am loved by* the Father." If this does not constitute distinctive "psychological content" for the Persons, it is unclear what would constitute this. In any case, the idea of mutual love between the Persons is the central core of Social trinitarianism, and it is precisely this idea that Ayres attributes to Augustine. (Recall in contrast that it is this mutual love which is specifically rejected by the anti-Social Rahner.) I conclude that, whatever precisely Ayres finds objectionable in recent Social trinitarianism, his conclusions on balance reinforce our assessment of Augustine as a pro-Social trinitarian.[16]

---

[14] *Nicaea*, 319.

[15] See the earlier comment from Ayres: "we can say that we never find [in the pro-Nicenes] descriptions of the divine unity that take as their point of departure the psychological inter-communion of three distinct people." *Nicaea*, 292. Careful exegesis would seem to be required, if this is to be rendered consistent with the remark quoted from *Nicaea*, 319.

[16] Stephen Holmes asserts, "The practice of speaking of three 'persons' in this [modern] sense in the divine life, of asserting a 'social doctrine of the Trinity', a 'divine community' or an 'ontology of persons in relationship' can only ever be, so far as I can see, a simple departure from (what I have attempted to show is) the unified witness of the entire theological tradition." *The Holy Trinity*, 195. This rather dogmatic claim is not, however, backed up with very much in the way of argument. Holmes never addresses the sorts of evidence to the contrary cited in this and the previous chapter of this book. His eleven-page discussion of Augustine on the Trinity never even mentions bk 15 of *De Trinitate*. He mentions Richard of St Victor's claim that "the highest moment of love is when a lover wishes that another should love, and be loved by, the beloved as fervently as the first lover does" (p. 153), but apparently sees no relevance of this to the issue dividing Social and anti-Social trinitarianism.

6

The Divine Oneness: What is a "Nature"?

Augustine, who posed the question about the divine Three, did not raise the corresponding question about the divine oneness. Yet the question, "One what?" also needs to be answered, if we are to have a satisfying answer to the metaphysical problem of the divine three-in-oneness. To be sure, the question can easily be answered, "One God," and all trinitarians will agree to that. But to say that much merely presents the problem over again; it does little to resolve it. Nor is the problem to be resolved by simply referring to the ancient terms *ousia* and *physis*, or *substantia* and *essentia*; all these terms had multiple uses and senses, and their meanings in trinitarian contexts have to be puzzled out by close attention to those contexts.[1] Still less can an answer be found by searching out the original meaning of *homoousion* as it was incorporated into the creed of the council of Nicaea; as already noted, there probably was no well-defined original meaning, except that the term was meant definitely to exclude Arius and his theology.

The best approach to take here, I believe, is the one already followed with respect to the divine Persons: first, formulate as clearly as possible *in our own terms* the issue at stake here, and then try to find the answer the pro-Nicenes gave, or would have given, to that question. To the complaint that doing this distorts their views by placing them in a modern, and alien, philosophical context, my answer must be the same as before: try to withhold judgment on that question until the result of the inquiry has been presented. My contention will be that the philosophical gulf between us and them, though real, is not so vast as to preclude success in the enterprise as outlined.

There is agreement among trinitarians on at least this much: the three divine Persons share a single, common nature or essence, a single *ousia* or *physis* or *essentia*. An initial way of putting the question that must be answered is this: Is the divine nature thus specified merely generically one in the three Persons, or

---

[1] G. Christopher Stead, in *Divine Substance* (Oxford: Clarendon Press, 1977), and in *Philosophy in Christian Antiquity* (Cambridge: CUP, 1994), sets out in detail the large number of uses in ancient literature of the key words in the trinitarian and christological debates. This is important because it counteracts the tendency to think there are just two or three relevant senses among which interpreters must choose in a particular passage.

do they share the numerically identical nature? I do not think this way of putting the matter is wrong, but I believe another way of approaching the question may prove more illuminating. I propose to put the question by asking whether the "one divine nature" shared by the three Persons is *abstract* or *concrete*. Admittedly, the distinction between abstract and concrete entities is controversial, in that there is no single, generally recognized criterion for distinguishing between them. (One suggested criterion is that concrete entities can enter into causal relations, whereas abstract entities cannot. But this is not universally accepted, and may have exceptions.[2]) I believe, however, that we can make the distinction between abstract and concrete as applied to natures and essences even without arriving at such a general criterion. Once we have done this we can ask, in which of these categories does the "one divine nature" belong?

We can approach this question by thinking about the essences of "natural kinds," such as gold or water. An essence in this sense is a *set of properties*, properties which are individually necessary and jointly sufficient for a thing's belonging to the kind in question. These essences are undoubtedly abstract: shareable properties are paradigmatic examples of abstract entities. The essence of gold, as we now understand the matter, is that it is a chemical element with atomic number 79, with further physical and chemical properties that follow (given the laws of nature) from that fact. The essence of water is that it is a compound with the formula H_2O, again with further properties that follow from its molecular composition. The essence of gold does not, as such, cause anything, and it seems reasonable to hold that, should all the actual gold in the universe be annihilated or transmuted into some other element, the essence of gold would not thereby be extinguished. (If some stuff with atomic number 79 were subsequently produced, that stuff would be gold.) However, there being an object with the properties specified in the essence does have causal consequences. The essence is abstract; the gold bar, or chain, or whatever, is concrete. To say that a number of objects share a common essence, in this sense, is to say that each of the objects exemplifies all of the properties specified in the essence, and is thereby an instance of the natural kind that corresponds to the essence. The implications of this as applied to trinitarian doctrine seem initially clear: the three Persons share the common essence of *Godhood* or *deity*, in that each of them has all those properties or attributes, the conjunction of which is both necessary and sufficient for *being God*. There will, however, be doubts in some quarters as to whether having the same essence in this sense is sufficient for the three Persons to constitute a *single* God. (Compare the "three Gods" challenge addressed by Gregory.)

But what of the other alternative? How are we to understand the notion of natures, or essences, as concrete? Here I think we will do well to avail ourselves

[2] See Joshua Hoffman and Gary S. Rosenkrantz, "Platonistic Theories of Universals," in M. J. Loux and D. W. Zimmerman (eds), *The Oxford Handbook of Metaphysics* (Oxford: OUP, 2003), 46–74.

of a concept that has become prominent in contemporary metaphysics, the concept of a *trope*.[3] A trope is an *instance* of a property, and as such is not shareable, at least not in the way in which ordinary universals are shareable. Furthermore, tropes as property-instances arguably have causal consequences. The universal property of brightness does not cause anything, but the brightness of a particular light may cause me to blink or to shield my eyes. A trope of the divine essence would, then, be a *particular instance* of the divine essence, the divine essence *as instantiated in* a divine being. Understanding the divine essence in this way once again brings causality into play: power as a universal causes nothing, but the power *of God* is responsible for the existence of all things whatsoever. Presumably this is what Robert Merrihew Adams had in mind in saying that the divine essence "is no mere logicians' plaything but a supremely powerful cause."[4]

This proposal, however, may give rise to an objection: If we view the divine essence as concrete, as a trope, then it is not shareable as between the divine Persons; each would need to have his own trope, and we would not after all have a single divine essence, as all the pro-Nicenes insisted that we must. Brian Leftow, indeed, makes precisely this point as part of his argument against Social trinitarianism. First, he presents a quotation from Aquinas:

> among creatures, the nature the one generated receives is not numerically identical with the nature the one generating has ... But God begotten receives numerically the same nature God begetting has.[5]

He then introduces the notion of a trope as an "individualized case of an attribute," and proceeds:

> With this term in hand, I now restate Thomas' claim: while both the Father and Son instance the divine nature (deity) they have but one trope of deity between them, which is God's. While Cain's humanity ≠ Abel's humanity, the Father's deity = the Son's deity = God's deity. But bearers individuate tropes. If the Father's deity is God's this is because the Father *just is* God: which last is what Thomas wants to say.[6]

At a later stage a good deal will need to be said about this objection. But I need to respond at least briefly in the present context, lest the objection be taken to preclude an option that it is important to keep alive for the ensuing

---

[3] I am indebted to Brian Leftow for this suggestion.

[4] Robert M. Adams, "Divine Necessity," *Journal of Philosophy*, 80 (1983); repr. in Robert M. Adams, *The Virtue of Faith and Other Essays in Philosophical Theology* (New York: OUP, 1987), 215. In view of this interpretation, I withdraw my previous suggestion that Adams's assertion represents a "combination of excitement and obscurity"! See William Hasker, "Analytic Philosophy of Religion," in W. J. Wainwright (ed.), *The Oxford Handbook of Philosophy of Religion* (Oxford: OUP, 2005), 439.

[5] The reference is to the *Summa Theologiae* Ia.39.5 *ad* 2.245a; Leftow's tr., in Brian Leftow, "A Latin Trinity," *Faith and Philosophy*, 21/3 (July 2004), 305.

[6] Leftow, "A Latin Trinity," 305.

discussion—the option, namely, that the doctrine of a single concrete divine essence may be compatible with a Social or pro-Social doctrine of the Trinity.

A first observation is that, if Leftow is right about Aquinas, this has unfortunate consequences for Aquinas's doctrine of the Trinity. If, as Leftow interprets Aquinas, "the Father *just is* God"—that is, is identical with God—it will also be the case that "the Son *just is* God." But then it will follow (by the transitivity of identity) that "the Father *just is* the Son," that is, that Father and Son are identical. Since this conclusion is formally heretical, and was certainly disavowed by Aquinas, we must hope that it is possible to keep from accepting Leftow's reading of Aquinas at this point.

How then shall we go about rescuing Aquinas from the predicament in which Leftow has placed him? Aquinas is clearly committed to the view that "Father and Son...have but one trope of deity between them." ("God begotten receives numerically the same nature God begetting has.") It is not so clear, on the other hand, that he is committed to Leftow's claim that "bearers individuate tropes," a claim which Leftow understands as entailing that there is a one-to-one correlation between bearers and the tropes of a property that is common to them. Still, it must be admitted that this claim is initially plausible. It does seem to follow, from the fact that Cain and Abel are different individuals, that Cain's trope of humanity must be a different trope than Abel's. And if Cicero's trope of humanity is identical with Tully's trope of humanity, this can only be because Cicero = Tully. But, we may ask, must this one-to-one correlation between bearers and tropes hold universally? I will now suggest that it need not always hold, and in support of this I will appeal to another significant idea in recent metaphysics, the notion of *constitution*.

Consider a case proposed by Michael Rea: A builder has crafted an object which is at once a supporting pillar for a building, and a statue of a person.[7] What is the relation between the pillar and the statue? An apparently plausible, common-sense view is that the two are identical: the pillar *just is* the statue. Philosophers, however, will recognize that this cannot be correct. If pillar and statue are identical, then all the properties of the pillar must be properties of the statue, and vice versa. But their properties are not identical; in particular, they differ in their *persistence conditions*. If a very small amount of marble is removed, obliterating the features that create the resemblance to a human being, the statue will be no more, but the pillar will still persist. Or, the pillar might be destroyed, by hollowing out the block of marble so that it is incapable of bearing a load, while the statue remains essentially intact. So the statue is distinct from the pillar, but there both of them are, standing in the exact same spot on the porch of the town hall. There are various possible ways of dealing with this situation conceptually, but one promising approach makes use of the technical notion of constitution: the same piece of marble is said to *constitute*

---

[7] Michael C. Rea, "The Trinity," in Flint and Rea, *Oxford Handbook of Philosophical Theology*, 418.

both the pillar and the statue, even though pillar and statue are not identical (and the piece of marble is not identical with either of them).[8]

Now, ask yourself this question: How many tropes of "marbleness" are there in the pillar-statue? The most natural answer, I suggest, is one. If you doubt this, go back in thought to an earlier stage in the process, when the block of marble has been given the appropriate general shape for a pillar, but where there is no particular resemblance to a human being. Then the sculptor goes to work, and by removing a comparatively small amount of marble (say, 5 percent or less of the whole), creates a shape that bears a credible likeness to the person being honored. Is it plausible to say that by doing this the sculptor has created an additional instance of the property, "being made of marble"? I for one doubt that it is. Someone might possibly think that, by removing some of the original stone, the sculptor has brought about that a new trope of marbleness exists, replacing the one that was there before. But even if (unlike me) you find this plausible, there would still be only one trope of marbleness in the resulting pillar-statue. In order for the answer to be two, it looks as though the sculptor would need to make a trip to the quarry to obtain additional marble—but this he has not done. So it does seem that, in this case, we have two distinct entities, the pillar and the statue, that have between them just one trope of the property, *being made of marble*. And if this is possible, then it may be possible that, in the Trinity, Father, Son, and Spirit have between them one and only one trope of deity.

All this, let me emphasize, is merely provisional and exploratory. If these ideas are to be incorporated into a formal proposal for trinitarian doctrine, much more will be needed by way of both explanation and defense. For the present, it is sufficient if enough has been done to keep the ideas in play—to convince the reader that they are worth considering, as we explore the views of the pro-Nicene Fathers on the divine unity.

---

[8] There are other ways available of describing the situation, so a bit more discussion will be needed later on. All I need at present, however, is that the description here proposed is a coherent one that enables us to gain an initial grasp of the way in which the constitution relation might be applied to the doctrine of the Trinity.

7

Interlude: Simplicity and Identity

Before we proceed to assess the view(s) of the pro-Nicenes on divine unity, we need to consider a philosophical concept that plays an important role in their development of that theme. The concept in question is that of divine simplicity. Though devoid of biblical warrant (unlike most of the other classical divine attributes), this notion was axiomatic for Christian thinkers of the fourth century, and for many since then. We have already seen that the doctrine of simplicity creates problems for both Gregory of Nyssa and Augustine, but at this point we need to probe a little deeper into the reasons for their attachment to the doctrine. To be sure, divine simplicity in some sense is unavoidable for theists. All will agree that God is not assembled out of parts and cannot be decomposed into parts. But the doctrine of simplicity held by the pro-Nicenes—by Augustine in particular[1]—went far beyond this, and that is what we must now investigate.

While I was expounding Augustine's "psychological analogies" I remarked at the oddity of considering what seems to be a divine action or activity as a "person," in whatever sense that term bears in Augustine's trinitarian discourse. How, for instance, is an inner word or thought (God's Word or *Logos*) a distinct person, coordinate with the person who is the thinker of that thought? How is the "bond of love" between two persons itself a third person? At the time, we passed by this difficulty and went on, but now we need to consider the philosophical doctrines that made that move seem feasible for Augustine. One such doctrine is found in the claim that "everything that is said about God is said substance-wise."[2] This is a claim that was made by the Arians (e.g. by Eunomius), who argued as follows: Everything that is said about God refers to the divine substance. Therefore, "unbegotten" said of the Father, and "begotten," said of the Son, refer to the substance of the Father and the Son

---

[1] As has been noted, Andrew Radde-Gallwitz has shown (in *Basil of Caesarea, Gregory of Nyssa, and the Transformation of Divine Simplicity*) that Basil and Gregory developed a conception of simplicity significantly different than the one which was held by Augustine and which went on to predominate in the Western Church. The theological implications of this "transformed" concept of simplicity have yet to be thoroughly explored, so the remarks in this chapter apply primarily to Augustine.

[2] Augustine, *The Trinity*, bk 5, p. 191.

respectively. But unbegotten and begotten are contraries, and cannot both be true of the same substance. It follows that the substance of the Father is different from the substance of the Son. Augustine must contest this reasoning, but he agrees with the main premise, with one qualification which we will come to in a moment. First, though, his reasons for accepting the premise (apart from that qualification).

When something is said of God, it seems that the alternatives are two: either it denotes the divine substance, or it denotes an accident (Hill, "modification") attaching to that substance. Augustine observes,

> We usually give the name 'modification' to something that can be lost by some change of the thing it modifies. Even though some modifications are called inseparable, *achorista* in Greek, like the color black in a crow's feather, it does lose it, not indeed as long as it is a feather, but because it is not always a feather.... *So there is no modification in God because there is nothing in him that can be changed or lost.*[3]

In view of this, it is not surprising that "Word" and "love" are understood as substance-terms. Hill states, "as a Christian neoplatonist, with John for his authority, he is quite sure that God is love substantially."[4] Augustine insists, however, that not everything said about God designates the divine substance. For some things said of God express *relations*: "begetting," said of the Father, and "begotten," said of the Son, are prime examples. These terms do not, therefore, signify the divine substance, and so the conclusion drawn by the Arians fails.

So far, it seems, Augustine is in the clear. But a further question looms: *What is it that is related* by the relation-terms "begetting" and "begotten"—or, for that matter, "Father" and "Son"? The answer, no doubt, is that these terms relate the divine persons—but this means that we need, in turn, a further explanation of the ontological status of the persons. We shall return to this shortly. Another point that should be noted is the following: In this doctrine that (with the exception of the relations) everything said of God denotes the divine substance, we have a powerful impetus in the direction of a strong doctrine of divine simplicity. "God is good"—"God is just"—"God is powerful"—"God is wise": each of these predicates is said to denote the divine substance. But there is, of course, only one divine substance, so it follows that God's goodness, God's justice, God's power, and God's wisdom are each identical with that one substance, and with each other, and with God himself. Indeed, even God's actions must be identical with God, for otherwise they would be accidents, modifications. It follows from this that the inner activity of conceiving the Word is substantial, as is the eternal activity of love between Father and Son, which explains why those analogies seemed more cogent to Augustine than they do to us.

---

[3] Augustine, *The Trinity*, bk 5, pp. 191–2; emphasis added.
[4] Augustine, *The Trinity*, bk 9, p. 273n.

This, then, is one of the impulses behind the doctrine of divine simplicity, but it is far from being the only one. It is evident that the philosophical atmosphere of the fourth century was suffused with Platonism; one did not have to be a serious philosopher in order to be influenced by it, any more than a person today needs to be a philosopher to be influenced by scientific naturalism. Consider, then, the Platonic idea of participation. The notion is difficult to explain precisely, as Plato himself learned, but the intuitive idea is fairly clear. The Good is the ultimate Good Reality; it is both the source and the standard of goodness for everything that is good. All good things derive their goodness from the Good itself; it is as though the Good were a spring or fountain from which goodness flows to each thing in accordance with its ability to receive, without ever in any way diminishing the store of goodness possessed by the Good. Similarly, Wisdom itself is the source from which all wisdom flows; a horse is a horse in virtue of its participation in the True Horse, and so on.

Now, consider the attributes of God. God is good, wise, powerful, and all the other things that are rightly said of him. But if we think of God's goodness along the lines of participation, as described above, we run into difficulties. If God is good through participation in the Good, then God's goodness is dependent on something other than God, which is unacceptable even if God has the absolute maximal degree of goodness.[5] So the Good in virtue of which God is good must somehow be brought within the being of God himself; all theistic Platonists have realized this.

But how are we to think about this? Is the Good only one of the various "elements" in God's being, alongside of Wisdom, Power, and whatever else may be needed? This would suggest that God is, as it were, assembled from various parts, which is clearly unacceptable. It also suggests that the "part" of God that is the Good is dependent for wisdom on the "part" that is Wisdom, and so on, somewhat as the various organs in our bodies are dependent on each other to perform their different functions—on the lungs to oxygenate the blood, on the heart to pump it, on the stomach to digest food, and so on. But this, again, seems clearly inappropriate in the case of God. So we are led to say that God's goodness is simply identical with God himself, or with his essence or his substance, and so also with God's wisdom, God's power, and all the other attributes. But if each of these is identical with God, or with God's essence, then they must each be identical as well with each other. So we get the doctrines that God is identical with God's goodness, and that in God goodness is identical with wisdom, which is identical with power, and so on.

Already we have arrived at a strong doctrine of divine simplicity. But it is necessary to consider also God's actions. Particular divine actions are not,

---

[5] In bk 11 of *The City of God*, Augustine emphasizes that God does not have his attributes by way of participation.

it would seem, identical with the divine substance. But nor, according to Augustine, can they be accidents or modifications. He says, "So it is clear that anything that can begin to be said about God in time which was not said about him before is said by way of relationship, and yet not by way of a modification of God, as though something has modified him.... So too when he is said to be angry with the wicked and pleased with the good, they change, not he; just as light is harsh to weak eyes, pleasant to strong; but it is the eyes, not the light, that change."[6] Here the actions are said of God by way of relationship. But we recall, from our discussion of Richard Cross on Gregory, that relations are merely mental items, not ingredients in reality. The basis for our attribution of relations, however, must be a real property in one or both of the relata. In the comment just quoted, Augustine anticipates the medieval doctrine that God is not "really related" to creatures—that is, that *there does not exist* any real property in God, in virtue of which God is related to creatures in one way or another, though there is a real property in the creature in virtue of which it is related to God. (If there were such a real property in God, it would constitute an accident or modification in God himself, which by hypothesis cannot exist.) So God's being either angry or pleased with creatures does not signify two different states of God, but only two different states of the creatures themselves. All this is nicely summed up by a remark of Rowan Williams: "God's action has been held, in orthodox Christian thought, to be identical with God's being—that is, what God does is nothing other than God's being actively real."[7] Pressing this a little farther (as was done by some Muslim philosophers, such as Avicenna), it becomes problematic to think of God even as having any awareness of particular, contingent reality. If he were so aware, it would seem that this would entail God's being contingently (because the creatures themselves are contingent) in one state rather than another, which would constitute an accident in God. Augustine, of course, did not carry things this far, though it is hard to see how he can consistently avoid such a conclusion. In any case, what we have said shows clearly that, for a theistic Platonist, a strong doctrine of simplicity is unavoidable.

But now we return to the question: Given that "Father" and "Son" denote relationships, what are the relata? This question is the occasion for a fascinating exposition by Lewis Ayres of the theological benefits Augustine derives from divine simplicity. He notes that, for Augustine, "every essence which is spoken of relatively is something apart from that relative predication."[8] Thus, "The Father is something in himself and only *because* the Father is such an essence can the Father be spoken of in relation.... The individual reality of the

    [6] Augustine, *The Trinity*, bk 5, p. 204.
    [7] Rowan Williams, "Redeeming Sorrows," in D. Z. Phillips (ed), *Religion and Morality* (Basingstoke: Macmillan, 1996), 143.
    [8] *Trin.* 7.1.2; quoted in Ayres, *Nicaea*, 378. (It follows from this that Augustine did *not* have the later idea that a Person simply *is* a "subsistent relation.")

Father is thus affirmed."[9] But the Father generates the Son, who is also God. Furthermore, "The grammar of simplicity means that we must say that if God the Father is to generate another, a Son, both the generator and the generated must be wisdom and God in themselves: the grammar of simplicity allows us to say truly that 'the Father has given the Son to have life in himself' (John 5: 26)."[10] So now we have the individual reality of both Father and Son (and, by implication, of the Spirit as well). "However, the language of divine simplicity enables and demands a further step. If the Son is wisdom itself, and the Father is wisdom itself, then we can go a step farther and say that the Son's essence is identical with the Father's essence. There cannot, obviously enough, be two instances of wisdom itself."[11] Ayres sums up this process of thought as follows:

> The Father generates the Son who is light from light, wisdom from wisdom, and essence from essence. The Son is an essence in Himself, not just a relationship: to talk of the person of the Son is to talk of the Son's essence. And yet, because the Father's and the Son's essences are truly simple, they are of one essence.... Thus, in using the grammar of simplicity to articulate a concept of Father, Son, and Spirit as each God, and as the one God, we find that the more we grasp the full reality of each person, the full depth of the being that they have from the Father, the more we are also forced to recognize the unity of their being.[12]

Without doubt, we have here before us an elegant intellectual structure. Yet a problem remains, which Ayres seems not to have noticed—a problem which arises from the very concept of identity. Identity, as this notion is understood by logicians, is a relation that is symmetrical and transitive: if A is identical with B, and B with C, then A is identical with C. So if the Father is an essence in himself, and the Son also is an essence in himself, and yet their essences are identical, it follows inexorably that the Father is identical with the Son, a heretical conclusion that cannot possibly be accepted—and of course, Augustine does not accept it. It does not help to point out at this juncture that Father and Son cannot be identical, because they are related by the "begetting" relation, a binary relation that a thing cannot have to itself. That is true enough, but it in no way cancels out the entailment noted from the concept of identity; it just brings out explicitly the contradictory character of the theological system so understood.

At this point, I submit that we have a problem in interpreting Augustine. What should we assume his attitude to have been towards the problem thus stated? Abstractly considered, there are three possibilities. It could be that Augustine understood very well, in general, that identity is a transitive relation, but that he simply failed to notice the implications of this in the case of the Trinity. Frankly, I am unwilling to attribute to Augustine (and with him,

⁹ Ayres, *Nicaea*, 378.   ¹⁰ Ayres, *Nicaea*, 378–9.
¹¹ Ayres, *Nicaea*, 379.   ¹² Ayres, *Nicaea*, 379–80.

the entire subsequent tradition) such a gross logical blunder, in a matter that was obviously of deep concern to him. Another possibility is that Augustine recognized that his doctrine was contradictory, but insisted that it was true nevertheless. Again, I am unwilling to attribute to Augustine (and with him, again, the subsequent tradition) this outright defiance of the requirement of logical consistency.

What then is left? Only this, I think: Augustine *did not affirm* an identity between each of the Persons and the divine substance, *in the sense of identity that is recognized by modern logicians.* That is to say: He *did not have such a conception of identity.*[13] Some may find this incredible, but I think they underestimate the logical sophistication involved in that conception. If Augustine was not working with the conception of identity thus understood, then the heretical conclusion, "The Father is identical with the Son and with the Holy Spirit," need not follow from his view. Since the other two interpretations of his intention seem clearly unacceptable, I think this is the one we must adopt.

This, however, leaves us with yet another question; one to which, so far as I know, no answer is available in ancient philosophy and theology. Here is the question: What *is* the concept of identity with which Augustine is working here? What sort of notion is this, of an "identity" (or sameness) that is not both symmetrical and transitive? If there is an answer to this, I do not know where to find it. If what has been said is correct, this is a question to which an answer is urgently needed, but for which no answer is available. (Later on, we will be discussing some candidates for such a relation that have been proposed by modern philosophers.)

My provisional conclusion is that the philosophical doctrines we have been discussing in this chapter amount to a tangle of confusion which cannot be resolved by any amount of tinkering, but only by outright rejection. The distinction between substance and property, we must insist, is not the same as between that which can and cannot be changed. The names of God's essential attributes—those that absolutely cannot change—are still the names of properties, and not of substances, or of the divine substance. Many of God's actions are indeed accidental to him, in the sense that they need not have occurred. (God need not have created Augustine, or me, or the reader.) If God is in time, then these are indeed "modifications" in God, though they do not involve changes in God's essential nature. The Platonic doctrine of participation should be jettisoned. A horse is not a horse by participating in the True Horse; it is a horse in virtue of having the genetic structure, morphology, etc. that qualifies it as a member of that species. That God's goodness is not identical with God does not mean that God is "dependent upon" something other

---

[13] If you find this too paradoxical, feel free to assume instead that Augustine did have this conception, but failed to clearly distinguish it from other "sameness" concepts in the neighborhood. The practical implications will be the same either way.

than God in order to be good. The strong doctrine of divine simplicity, which threatens to become a cognitive black hole that swallows up everything positive we might want to say about God, needs to be excised.[14] (To be sure, it will still be true that God is "simple" in that God is not assembled out of parts and cannot be decomposed into parts. But saying this falls far short of the doctrine of simplicity as it was embraced by Augustine and the medievals.) The divine Persons are not identical with the divine nature; what the relationship in question is, is a matter for further investigation.

All this, however, looks forward to the constructive part of our project. In interpreting the Fathers—who for all that I have said are eminently worthy of our respect and admiration—we must grant them the logical and metaphysical doctrines they espoused and make the best sense we are able to of the result. To that task, we now return.

---

[14] One reader of the manuscript objected that "it is hard to see how [the rejection of the strong doctrine of simplicity] could be justified *on the basis of the pro-Nicene theology of Gregory and Augustine.*" My answer is straightforward: our examination of their theology justifies the rejection of simplicity, because that examination (in this chapter and in Chs 4 and 5 above) has shown that, if consistently maintained, this doctrine of simplicity would force these theologians to abandon the real, objective distinction between the divine Persons. I take it for granted that their commitment to such a distinction was bedrock and non-negotiable.

8

The Pro-Nicenes and the Divine Nature

The task we have set ourselves is that of determining whether, for the pro-Nicenes Gregory of Nyssa and Augustine, the one divine nature (*ousia*, *essentia*) is best understood as abstract or concrete. This task differs in a significant way from the corresponding task with respect to the divine Persons. The idea of a person is fundamentally a natural and intuitive one, however much the nuances may have changed over the centuries. We can presuppose, but can also readily verify, that the theologians of the ancient world possessed the concept of a personal agent, and we can then look and see how that concept comports with what they say, and refrain from saying, about the Persons of the Trinity. We cannot make the corresponding assumption with respect to abstract versus concrete "natures" of things. These notions are not provided ready-made by common sense; they are philosophical conceptions that reflect a considerable degree of sophistication. Nevertheless, I believe it is possible to interrogate the pro-Nicenes with respect to their (partially implicit) stance in regard to these matters, and to come up with a definitive answer. This is so, even though (as we saw in the last chapter) some of the specific philosophical idioms they employ (such as the strong doctrine of divine simplicity) are ones we cannot ourselves adopt.

With regard to Augustine, the point should hardly need much argument. Augustine's many critics have never claimed that his trinitarian doctrine was burdened with too weak a conception of divine unity, as it would be if the Persons were united only by sharing the same abstract nature or essence. The complaint has been, rather, that he failed to grasp adequately the distinctness of the Persons.[1] Nevertheless, it is worth our while to detail some of the specific features of his teaching that support the conclusion that he conceived of the divine substance (or *ousia*[2]) as concrete. Consider then his objection, in book 6 of *De Trinitate*, to the idea that the Trinity is "triple, or three by

---

[1] See Ayres, *Augustine and the Trinity*, 319ff.

[2] For the equivalence of substance and *ousia*, see *The Trinity*, bk 5, p. 197. It is true that Augustine accepted *substantia* as a translation for *hypostasis* in the Greek doctrine, but he makes no use of this equivalence in his own presentation.

multiplication."[3] Here we may contrast the Trinity with a group of three men—say, Abraham, Isaac, and Jacob. In such a group we have three individuals sharing a common (abstract) nature, but given the three of them there is "three times as much manhood" as in Abraham alone—in our terminology, three tropes of human nature. But no such multiplication can exist in the case of the trinitarian Persons; unlike the "three men" case, those Persons have only one trope of divinity between them, which is why "the Father alone or the Son alone or the Holy Spirit alone is as great as Father and Son and Holy Spirit together."[4] Another telling passage occurs in book 7:

> If however being (*essentia*) is a species word like man, and those three which we call substances or persons have the same species in common, as Abraham, Isaac, and Jacob have in common the species which is called man; and if while man can be subdivided into Abraham, Isaac, and Jacob, it does not mean that one man can be subdivided into several single men—obviously he cannot, because one man is already a single man; then how can one being be subdivided into three substances or persons? For if being, like man, is a species, then one being is like one man.[5]

This requires some unpacking; both the syntax and the thought are complex. What I think Augustine means is this: While "man" is a species-word, and the species man can be subdivided (i.e. multiply exemplified), it does not follow that *an individual man* can be so divided. But then, neither can *an individual being* (in the divine case) be subdivided into three "substances[6] or persons." The argument has force precisely because Augustine assumes that the divine being (*essentia*) is individual and concrete, like a man, and not an abstract universal like "manhood." (Otherwise, just as "man can be subdivided into Abraham, Isaac, and Jacob," it would follow that "God can be subdivided into Father, Son, and Holy Spirit.") The divine *ousia*, in other words, consists of a single trope of Godhood or divinity.

A similar conclusion follows from Augustine's reading of the biblical saying that "God is love." We have already noted Hill's comment that "Augustine took *Deus caritas est* [1 John 4: 8 and 16] to mean 'love is God' just as much as 'God is love'." The love which is God cannot be for Augustine (as it is for some liberals today) the abstract property of love; it is rather the *concrete instance* of love which is identical with God; that it is so identical is an implication of divine simplicity. (I am not withdrawing my earlier assertion that we cannot accept the strong doctrine of simplicity. Nevertheless, we are bound to take it into account in interpreting Augustine.) But if God is concrete rather than

---

[3] *The Trinity*, bk 6, pp. 212–13.   [4] *The Trinity*, bk 6, p. 212.

[5] *The Trinity*, bk 7, pp. 232–3.

[6] This disjunct is included because Augustine is going along, at this point, with the Greek use of *hypostasis* for the trinitarian Persons, and he accepts the linguistic equivalence of *hypostasis* and *substantia*. However, he goes on to argue against the propriety of saying there are "three substances" in God (bk 7, p. 231).

abstract (and surely he is that; the biblical God is a mighty causal agent), then so must the love that is God be concrete. And since God's love is identical with the divine essence as a whole (again, an implication of simplicity), we must conclude that the essence is itself concrete—a single trope of Godhood.

Arguments to this effect could easily be multiplied, but I take it there is little to be gained by doing so. That the divine *essentia* is a concrete, individual instance of Godhood or deity is fundamental to Augustine's thinking; there is no good reason for disputing this.

In contrast to Augustine, it may seem initially plausible to suppose that Gregory of Nyssa understood the divine essence or nature to be abstract. Unlike Augustine, he views the divine nature as a shareable universal; also telling is the fact that he specifically invites us to apply to the Trinity the relationship between *hypostasis* and *ousia* as we understand it in the case of human beings. ("If now you transfer to the doctrine of God the principle of differentiation between *ousia* and *hypostasis* that you acknowledge on the human level, you will not go astray."[7]) Since the essence of humanness is most readily conceived as an abstract universal, it would seem that the same should be said of the divine *ousia*.

However, there are good reasons to question this conclusion. Here I would invite us to compare Gregory's reflections on the nature of human beings, as contained in *Ad Ablabium*, with Augustine's comments on the same topic, as cited earlier in this chapter. Augustine, we will recall, argued that

> if while man can be subdivided into Abraham, Isaac, and Jacob, it does not mean that one man can be subdivided into several single men...then how can one being be subdivided into three substances or persons? For if being, like man, is a species, then one being is like one man.

Here Augustine recognizes that the species "man" can be "subdivided" into several individuals; however this is not true of the divine essence, which is not an abstract universal but rather a concrete property-instance or trope. Gregory, however, confronts the problem in a different way: his surprising claim, as we saw above, is that it is a "customary abuse of language" to refer to those who share the identical human nature as "men" in the plural. No doubt he fails to convince us that this really is a mistake, but what we need to attend to is his reason for insisting on this. He seems to think of the common essence of humanness as a *real unity* that somehow exists *as a whole* in each individual human being.[8] But what sort of unity is this? Or to put the question differently,

---

[7] From Basil of Caesarea (= Gregory of Nyssa?), epistle 38. As previously noted, most scholars attribute the letter to Gregory.

[8] "[Y]et their nature is one, at union in itself, and an absolutely indivisible unity, not capable of increase by addition or of diminution by subtraction, but in its essence being and continually remaining one, inseparable even though it appear in plurality, continuous, complete, and not divided with the individuals who participate in it." *Ad Ablabium*, 332.

why is he unwilling to allow that the *ousia* of humanness can be divided among various human beings? If this *ousia* were merely an abstract common nature, the problem of "subdividing" it would have little bite. To "divide" an abstract nature would presumably mean to separate the various properties contained in the nature—for instance, animality from reason, in the famous definition of man as a rational animal. But it goes without saying that natures cannot be divided in this way; to separate the properties comprised in an essence is simply to destroy that essence and replace it with others. And on the other hand, to "divide" an abstract nature in the sense that it is multiply exemplified does not pose any problem. If, however, we think of the *ousia* as a concrete property-instance—in our terminology, as a trope—then it seems perfectly plausible to suppose that there is a distinct trope for each individual human being. Gregory, however, needs to resist this precisely because *he intends to transfer to the Trinity the relation between ousia and hypostasis that obtains for human beings.* Having stated (perhaps unwisely) that the distinction between *hypostasis* and *ousia* can be transposed directly from the human case to that of the Trinity, Gregory now has to interpret (we might rather say, to distort) the human situation in order to render it parallel with the conclusion he wants to draw concerning the Trinity. To make sense of all this, we have to recognize that for him the divine *ousia* is not merely an abstract set of properties, but rather something concrete and individual.[9]

The objection to "dividing the nature" surfaces once again in a passage in *The Great Catechism* (477), where Gregory writes,

> For, in personality, the Spirit is one thing and the Word another, and yet again that from which the Word and Spirit is, another. But when you have gained the conception of what the distinction is in these, the oneness, again, of the nature admits not division, so that the supremacy of the one First Cause is not split and cut up into differing Godships.[10]

Here the indivisibility of the nature is directly related to its causal power and activity. But as we have seen, causality is found in concrete property-instances and not in abstract universals. If *per impossibile* there were several distinct beings, each possessing its own trope of the divine nature independent of the others, that might indeed look like "differing Godships."

There is yet another line of thought concerning the divine unity in Gregory, and perhaps this is the one that lies closest to the center of his thought. This argument appears in *Ad Ablabium*, but a little background is needed for it to be properly appreciated. Michel René Barnes has pointed out that Gregory

---

[9] At least, I say that we need to recognize this. But suppose someone were to reply that the abstract/concrete distinction is not within Gregory's purview and that we should not attribute to him any view on the question? I respond by saying that the question, once it has been formulated, is a good and indeed an inescapable one, and we can certainly ask which answer fits better with everything Gregory says about the divine essence.

[10] *NPNF* 2nd ser. 5/477.

employs a particular technical understanding of the relation between natures, powers, and activities (*physis* or *ousia, dynamis, energeia*). Barnes traces a long history for these ideas in earlier Greek thought, but the immediate background figure is most likely Plotinus. A key point here is the necessary relationship between natures and powers, which is illustrated (among many other examples) by the relationship between fire and heat. Fire necessarily produces heat, and (in ancient physics) wherever there is heat, there must of necessity be fire as well.[11] The "power" of heat is displayed, in turn, by its effects in various circumstances—it softens bronze, hardens mud, melts wax, and destroys flesh. The relation here is both ontological and epistemological. Fire necessarily has the power of heat, which is active in producing the effects just noted; but heat is recognized by its effects and is in turn the key to our recognition of the nature involved, namely that of fire.

All of this, when properly considered, transfers nicely to the divine case. Here, however, Gregory wants to emphasize that the divine nature as such is unknown to us; what we can know is the power of that nature as seen in its activities—activities, that is, such as creation and redemption. And now we are in a position to see the full import for Gregory of the characteristic pro-Nicene doctrine that the Persons of the Trinity work inseparably. He writes,

> But in the case of the Divine nature we do not similarly learn that the Father does anything by Himself in which the Son does not work conjointly, or again that the Son has any special operation apart from the Holy Spirit; but every operation which extends from God to the Creation…has its origin from the Father, and proceeds through the Son, and is perfected in the Holy Spirit. For this reason the name derived from the operation is not divided, because the action of each concerning anything is not separate and peculiar, but whatever comes to pass, in reference either to the acts of His providence for us, or to the government and constitution of the universe, comes to pass by the action of the Three, yet what does come to pass is not three things.[12]

These works, then, are the activity of the three Persons working as one, inseparably. As such they manifest the one, indivisible, divine power, which points us in turn to the one, unknowable but surely indivisible, divine nature or *theotēs*. Quite appropriately, Ayres concludes, "The activity of divine persons shows God's power (and hence the divine nature) not to be individuated as is human nature."[13] What we see in operation is a *single*, unitary divine power—not, as in the human case, multiple (though perhaps qualitatively indistinguishable)

---

[11] Barnes, *Power of God*, 278–88. Barnes states, "Gregory understands power as the capacity to act that is distinctive to a specific existent and that manifests the nature of that existent." *Power of God*, p. 305.

[12] *Ad Ablabium*, 334.

[13] Ayres, *Nicaea*, 358. This confirms what was earlier suggested—that it was unwise for Gregory to assert that the relation between *hypostasis* and *ousia* for human beings could be simply transferred to the Trinity.

"powers" residing in multiple human beings. There is, for Gregory, but a single trope of the divine nature.[14]

At this point I need to acknowledge a certain awkwardness in these arguments, inasmuch as I am interpreting Augustine's and Gregory's doctrines in terms of concepts that are not explicitly present in their respective conceptual vocabularies. By way of extenuation, I have to say that, even if doing this proves difficult, making the attempt is preferable to the alternatives. Those alternatives, so far as I can see, are two. With much liberal theology, we can simply dismiss the whole way of thinking of the Fathers with a wave of the hand, as tied to outmoded forms of philosophical thought: we then excuse ourselves from taking anything they say seriously, unless we happen to come across some gem that can be fitted into a scheme that is more acceptable to our modern (and therefore superior) sensibility. Or we can follow the lead of some patristic scholars, and try to convince ourselves that we can remain within the conceptualities of the ancient writers, making our permanent intellectual home in the ancient world. (This often seems to go along with the assumption that the philosophical conceptions employed by the Fathers were a mere *façon de parler* and need not be seriously examined for their conceptual coherence.) The journey between this Scylla and that Charybdis may be a hazardous one, but surely the effort is worth making.

[14] Nathan Jacobs argues at length that the relation between *hypostasis* and *ousia* in the Cappadocian Fathers is to be understood in terms of the Aristotelian distinction between primary and secondary substance: "On 'Not Three Gods'—Again: Can a Primary–Secondary Substance Reading of *Ousia* and *Hypostasis* Avoid Tritheism?" *Modern Theology*, 24/3 (2008) (corrected version available at www.nathanajacobs.com.) This in turn entails that the unity of the divine *ousia* is that of an abstract, repeatable universal, contrary to what has been argued here. Jacobs goes on to argue that such a reading is compatible with the *homoousion* and with monotheism. Jacobs does well in marshaling the passages which support his interpretation. I believe, however, that he pays insufficient attention to the themes and passages in the Cappadocians which indicate that they were not satisfied with the interpretation of the divine essence as merely an abstract universal.

9

The Fathers, the Trinity, and Scripture

To this point in our study, comparatively little has been said about the Fathers' use of scripture. And this, it has to be said, is typical of much of the scholarly treatment of the subject; tracing the various possible philosophical influences on their doctrines has often seemed a more attractive project than wading through page after page of patristic exegesis. However, the emphasis in their own writings is quite different. Much of Athanasius' *Three Orations* is taken up with text-by-text refutations of Arian appeals to scripture. The first four books of Augustine's *De Trinitate* are occupied primarily with biblical topics; all this before, in book 5, he gets down to "serious" matters of logic and ontology. Similar emphasis on exegetical matters can be found in other pro-Nicene theologians, as well as in the anti-Nicene authors they are opposing.

One might wonder, then, why this material has received comparatively little emphasis in the scholarly literature on the subject. One explanation might be that scholarship tends to look for distinctive ideas and emphases in various writers, whereas the appeals to scripture among the pro-Nicenes tend to be more uniform. There is also the undeniable fact that some of their exegesis strikes us as patently unsound. We have noted Augustine's assumption that the plural in Genesis 1: 26 ("Let us make man to our image and likeness") refers to the Trinity—not an interpretation that commends itself to modern exegetes. Also worth noticing is Augustine's insistence that New Testament references to "the one God" must be referring to the Trinity—a claim that is reasonable only on the assumption that the New Testament writers had clearly in mind (though they failed to mention the fact) something like the pro-Nicene doctrine of the Trinity.[1] Similar problems can be found in other Fathers as well. Ayres seems at times to suggest that, in defiance of contem-

---

[1] Joseph Jedwab asks, "Why can't Augustine say that even if the human authors didn't have the pro-Nicene view of the Trinity in mind, God, who inspired the human authors, did have this in mind?" (Private communication.) Supposing Augustine were to say this, the reply must be that it simply is not responsible, for us today, to interpret scripture in a way that by-passes the human authors and what they thought they were saying.

porary biblical scholarship, we ought to accept pro-Nicene interpretations of scripture as correct.[2] This suggests the following argument:

(1) We ought to accept the pro-Nicene doctrine of the Trinity as being true.

(2) If we accept the pro-Nicene doctrine of the Trinity as true, we ought also to accept as correct the exegesis of scripture on which the doctrine is based. Therefore,

(3) We ought to accept the pro-Nicene exegesis of scripture as correct.

One problem with this argument is that, for many scholars, it will seem more plausible to read it as a *modus tollens* than as a *modus ponens*. That is to say, rather than the doctrine leading us to accept the exegesis, the flaws in the exegesis may tend to discredit the doctrine. Surely, however, there must be a middle ground here. It could be that, while some of the texts the Fathers take as referring to the Trinity have no such reference, there are other texts for which their interpretations can be endorsed and affirmed by good contemporary biblical scholarship.[3]

Some relevant biblical questions will be discussed in the final, constructive chapter of this book. Our present concern, however, is with the Fathers, and we need to ask: What do their interpretations of scripture tell us about the content of their doctrine(s) of the Trinity? In particular, how do these interpretations bear on their views concerning the two main questions posed in this part of the book: the nature of the divine Persons, and the right way to understand the one divine nature?

With regard to the unity of the divine nature, I doubt that there is a great deal to be learned in this way. The scriptures do not contain, nor did the Fathers believe they contained, a philosophical analysis of the divine unity. God is one; of that there can be no doubt. But the explication of just how it is that God is one is not something to be found in the biblical text.

On the other hand, I believe that very interesting and important results can be obtained if we ask: What does the Fathers' reading of scripture tell us about their conception of the divine Persons? Let me begin with a concession made by Richard Cross in the midst of his argument against a Social interpretation of the trinitarian tradition. As we saw above, he argues that the view of divine simplicity accepted by the Fathers precludes our attributing to them anything like a Social doctrine of the Trinity. However, he acknowledges in a footnote that

---

[2] I say this by way of a general summary of various remarks made by Ayres in *Nicaea*. However, I am by no means certain that he would endorse without qualification the argument given below in the text.

[3] As an example (among others that could be given) of such a mediating approach I cite the book by Gerald O'Collins, *The Tripersonal God: Understanding and Interpreting the Trinity* (New York: Paulist Press, 1999). O'Collins interacts extensively with contemporary critical scholarship, yet finds in the biblical texts ample warrant for an orthodox doctrine of the Trinity.

It seems to me that there is one powerful argument in favour of a social theory of the Trinity. Clearly, on any account of the divine persons, such persons are subjects of mental properties and states. If they are in some sense just one subject—as is entailed by the denial of the social view as I am characterizing it here—then Patripassianism is true. At the very least, the Son must be able to become a separate subject of (human) mental states in virtue of his assumption of human nature. The claim that there would be two divine psychological subjects during the Incarnation (one the Father and Spirit, and the other the Son) seems remarkably implausible, though not I suppose unorthodox.[4]

In order to explore this point further, I turn to Paul Gavrilyuk's study, *The Suffering of the Impassible God*.[5] Gavrilyuk finds a clear statement of the view that God the Father suffered in Noetus, who wrote: "I am under necessity, since one is acknowledged, to make this One the subject of suffering (*hypo pathos pherein*). For Christ was God, and suffered on account of us, being Himself the Father, that He might be able also to save us."[6] Hippolytus, replying to Noetus, objected to his "confusion between the Father and the Son, which resulted in identifying the subject of suffering with the Father, rather than with God the Word. In response, Hippolytus appealed to selected scriptural passages that made it clear that Christ was not talking to himself when he addressed his Father, that the one addressed was distinct from the one addressing."[7] Gavrilyuk cites with approval Thomas Weinandy, who states that "while patripassianism (early third century) was condemned, the real issue was not that the Modalists attributed suffering to the Father, but rather that they failed to distinguish adequately between the Father and the Son. Patripassianism was primarily a trinitarian and not a christological heresy."[8]

Later on, in the fourth century, Gregory of Nyssa was confronted by Eunomius with the claim that the Son's suffering on the Cross showed him to be different in nature from the impassible Father. He responds,

> We hold that the God who was manifested by the cross should be honored in the same way in which the Father is honored. For them [the Eunomians] the passion is a hindrance to glorifying the only-begotten God equally with the Father who begot him.... For it is clear that the reason why he [Eunomius] sets the Father above the Son, and exalts him with supreme honor is that in the Father is not seen the shame of the Cross.[9]

---

[4] Richard Cross, "Two Models of the Trinity?" *Heythrop Journal*, 43 (2002), 275–94; repr. in M. Rea (ed.), *Oxford Readings in Philosophical Theology*, i. *Trinity, Incarnation, Atonement* (Oxford: OUP, 2009), p. 124n.

[5] Paul Gavrilyuk, *The Suffering of the Impassible God: The Dialectics of Patristic Thought* (Oxford: OUP, 2004).

[6] Quoted from Hippolytus, *Contra Noetum* 2.7, in Gavrilyuk, *Suffering*, 93–4.

[7] Gavrilyuk, *Suffering*, 94–5.

[8] Thomas Weinandy, *Does God Suffer?* (Notre Dame, IN: University of Notre Dame Press, 2000), 176; in Gavrilyuk, *Suffering*, 92.

[9] Gregory of Nyssa, *Eun.* 3.3; quoted by Gavrilyuk, *Suffering*, 131.

What Gregory does *not* say here is that Eunomius was wrong to attribute the suffering on the Cross just to the Son and not to the Father as well. Where Eunomius has gone wrong, rather, is to suppose that such suffering, along with other human experiences, disqualifies the Son from being fully and equally God along with the Father. Gregory asks: "Who is then ashamed of the Cross? He who, even after the passion, worships the Son equally with the Father, or he who even before the passion insults the Son...?"[10]

The implications of this should perhaps already be clear, but I will spell them out anyway. The core of the objection to patripassianism is that *the sufferings of Jesus on the Cross are the sufferings of God the Son and not in the same way of God the Father.* But if it is possible for one Person and not the other to suffer, it must be that, in Cross's words, they are distinct "subjects of mental properties and states."[11] Or, to revert to the words we have borrowed from Cornelius Plantinga, the Persons must be "distinct centers of knowledge, will, love, and action." This is as clear as anything can be, and it has enormous implications for our understanding of the trinitarian Persons. Cross, as we have seen, acknowledges this, yet he allows these implications to be outweighed and overridden by the consideration that, for Gregory, the Persons are distinguished only by the intra-trinitarian relations. I submit that this represents a case of skewed priorities. The opposition to patripassianism, to Sabellianism, and to monarchianism generally, was deeply entrenched in fourth-century trinitarian discourse. These were the "recognized heresies" that had to be avoided by any position that had any claim to be taken seriously in the fourth-century debate. It is simply out of the question to suppose that Gregory, and the other pro-Nicenes, would be neglectful of these entrenched, consensus positions. Yet Cross in effect supposes that these considerations were brushed aside by the pro-Nicenes in the interest of honoring a speculative conclusion (a conclusion drawn by him, not by the Fathers themselves) from a particular metaphysical analysis of the nature of the Persons. I do not think this is at all credible—no more than it is credible that, under pressure from that same metaphysical analysis, Gregory would have abandoned the doctrine that there is a real, objective difference between Father, Son, and Spirit.

In the debate with Arianism an important role was played by the words of Jesus, "The Father is greater than I" (John 14: 28). This and similar sayings were naturally interpreted by the Arians as indicative of the difference in nature and status between Father and Son. The standard reply, at least since the time of Athanasius, was that "subordinationist" texts such as this pertain to Christ's status viewed in terms of his self-humbling in the incarnation,

---

[10] Gregory of Nyssa, *Eun.* 3.3; quoted by Gavrilyuk, *Suffering*, 131.

[11] I do not think we can take seriously Cross's tentative suggestion that, during the incarnation, there were for the first time "two divine psychological subjects." This would postulate a *change in the nature of God the Son*—a postulation which (*pace* Cross) would surely be unorthodox by 4th-cent. pro-Nicene standards.

whereas "unity" texts such as "I and the Father are one" (John 10: 30) reveal his eternal divine status as co-equal and co-essential with the Father. For our present purposes, however, a different question becomes important, namely this: *Why did this text (John 14: 28) present a problem for trinitarian theology in the first place?* Once asked, the question is easily answered: *The text presented a problem because the words and actions of Jesus were understood to be words and actions of God the Son, the second Person of the Trinity.* If it were merely a human being who said, "The Father is greater than I," there would be no problem for theology, unless the fact that a mere human being—*any* mere human being—found it necessary to state such an overwhelmingly self-evident fact were taken as suggesting overweening pride.

Those words, however, were *not* attributed to any merely human person, but instead to the Word, the divine Logos, the second of the three trinitarian hypostases. But of course, not only those words were so attributed; rather *all* the words, and works, of Jesus were ascribed to the eternal, divine, Son of God. This fact constitutes the biblical core of the Fathers' argument for the distinctness of the Persons—and it also provides decisive evidence in support of a pro-Social interpretation of their views. Here, then, is a more or less random selection of texts illustrating this point.

For Augustine, I cite a lovely paragraph in which he explains the reason why Christ, after his resurrection, needed to ascend to the Father:

> So it was necessary for the form of a servant to be removed from their sight, since as long as they could observe it they would think that Christ was this only which they had before their eyes. This explains his words, *If you loved me you should rejoice at my going to the Father, for the Father is greater than I* (Jn 14: 28), that is, "This is why I must go to the Father, because while you see me like this you assume from what you see that I am inferior to the Father, and thus with all your attention on the creature and on the adopted condition, you fail to understand the equality I enjoy with the Father." It also explains the other text, *Do not touch me, for I have not yet ascended to the Father* (Jn 20: 17)....He did not want this heart, so eagerly reaching out to him, to stop at thinking that he was only what could be seen and touched. His ascension to the Father signified his being seen in his equality with the Father, that being the ultimate vision which suffices us.[12]

Gregory of Nyssa, in support of his claim that the trinitarian Persons share inseparably the operation of "seeing," argues as follows:

> For Scripture attributes the act of seeing equally to Father, Son, and Holy Spirit. David says, "See, O God our defender" [Ps. 84: 9]: and from this we learn that sight is a proper operation of the idea of God, so far as God is conceived, since he says, "See, O God." But Jesus also sees the thoughts of those who condemn Him, and questions [*sic*] why by His own power He pardons the sins of men? for it says, "Jesus, seeing their thoughts" [Matt. 9: 4]. And of the Holy Spirit also, Peter says

---

[12] *The Trinity*, bk 1, p. 82.

to Ananias, "Why hath Satan filled thine heart, to lie to the Holy Ghost?" [Acts 5: 3] showing that the Holy Spirit was a true witness, aware of what Ananias had dared to do in secret, and by Whom the manifestation of the secret was made to Peter.[13]

Here the "seeing" done by Jesus is an act of God the Son, parallel to the actions of the Father and the Holy Spirit.

Christopher A. Beeley offers the following comments on Gregory Nazianzen's practice of interpreting christological passages:

> Grander titles like "God," "Word" (Jn 1. 1) and "Christ the power of God and the wisdom of God" (I Cor 1. 24) indicate Christ's identity as the divine Son of God in his eternal relationship with the Father...Alternatively, lowlier expressions like "slave," "he hungered," and "he wept" (Phil 2. 7; Mt 4. 2; Jn 11. 35)—and above all Christ's cross and death—refer to the Son of God as he has assumed human existence in the person of Jesus and is now "composite," a single mixture of God and human existence....By referring the lesser sayings to the Son in his incarnate form, Gregory is able to counter the claim that such texts prove that the Son is merely a creature and therefore not fully divine. Yet at the same time, when he distinguishes between unqualified and qualified reference to Christ, Gregory is saying that both kinds of statements refer to *the same Son of God*.[14]

It is, then, the eternal, divine Son who hungers, weeps, suffers, and dies—all *personal actions,* actions of that *person* who is in fact the Second Person of the holy Trinity.

In Athanasius' *On the Incarnation,*[15] he unhesitatingly attributes all the words and deeds of Jesus to the divine Logos. It was "the most holy Son of the Father" who "came to our region to renew man once made in his likeness, and find him, as one lost, by the remission of sins; as he says himself in the Gospels: 'I came to find and to save the lost'."[16] And "from the works he did in the body he made himself known to be Son of God. Whence also he cried to the unbelieving Jews: 'If I do not the works of my Father, believe me not. But if I do them, though ye believe not me, believe my works; that ye may know and understand that the Father is in me, and I in the Father'."[17] Here "my works"—Jesus' works—are the works of the Father's Son, the eternal divine Logos.

Tertullian's *Against Praxeas*[18] was written against the monarchians of his time, those who denied the personal distinction of Father from Son. (One could say that he was writing against an early version of "anti-Social" theology!) According to Tertullian, when Christ approved of Peter's faith in saying of him, "Thou art the son of God" (Matt. 16: 16), he

---

[13] *Ad Ablabium,* 333.
[14] Beeley, *Gregory of Nazianzus on the Trinity,* 133 (emphasis in original).
[15] *St. Athanasius on the Incarnation,* tr. Archibald Robertson (London: D. Nutt, 1891).
[16] *St. Athanasius on the Incarnation,* 24–5 (Luke 19: 10).
[17] *St. Athanasius on the Incarnation,* 31 (John 10: 37–8).
[18] *Tertullian's Treatise Against Praxeas,* tr. Ernest Evans (London: SPCK, 1948).

approved the distinction of both persons, the Son on earth whom Peter had recognised as God's Son, and the Father in heaven who had revealed to Peter what Peter had recognized, that Christ is God's Son.[19]

Indeed the very text which the monarchian heretics loved to cite, "I and the Father are one," could itself be turned against them:

> For if he had said, "are one [person]" he would have been able to assist their cause: for "one [person]" is apparently an indication of the singular number. Yet when he says that two, of the masculine gender, are one [thing], in the neuter, which is not concerned with singularity but with unity, with similitude, with conjunction, with the love of the Father who loveth the Son, and with the obedience of the Son who obeys the Father's will—when he says, "One [thing] are I and the Father," he shows that those whom he equates and conjoins are two.[20]

It is, then, precisely the distinction of genders—masculine versus neutral—that turns the "unity" text into an affirmation of the distinction of Persons.

Many, many more texts could be cited, but I trust the point is by now sufficiently clear. For the Fathers, the words and actions of Jesus are the words and actions of the trinitarian Son, the divine Logos. We may or may not decide to embrace this way of interpreting the Gospel narratives for ourselves. But in seeking to understand the doctrine of the Trinity held by the pro-Nicenes, we ignore this point at our peril. It shows them to be pro-Social trinitarians.

---

[19] *Tertullian's Treatise Against Praxeas*, 160.   [20] *Tertullian's Treatise Against Praxeas*, 164.

10

Postlude: Are the Foundations Stable?

We have now completed our search for the foundations of trinitarian theology, as laid out in Chapter 1. As was there proposed, our main concern has been to get as clear as possible about the nature of the doctrine of the Trinity that was embraced by the pro-Nicene theologians of the late fourth century. At this point, it may be helpful to set out the main points that emerge from our study—points that, it is hoped, will provide helpful guidance as we seek a formulation of trinitarian doctrine that is viable for us today. Four points stand out:

1. It has been argued that, for the pro-Nicene Fathers, the trinitarian Persons are indeed "distinct centers of knowledge, will, love, and action." The pro-Nicenes, I have claimed, are also pro-Social trinitarians.

2. The unity of the divine Persons is to be found, not merely in a common abstract essence, the shared possession of the essential divine attributes, but in their having in common a single concrete divine nature—a single trope of deity.

3. The Persons are related to one another by the "relations of origin": the Son is eternally begotten of the Father, and the Spirit proceeds from the Father. This has not been stressed heretofore, because it is uncontroversial that the Fathers held this doctrine, but it will be important to keep in mind as we go forward.

4. I have indicated briefly part of the biblical basis for the doctrine of the Trinity as the Fathers understood such matters. A key role is played by their understanding of the relationship between Jesus and his heavenly Father, as depicted in the New Testament, as a relationship between trinitarian Father and Son.

This of course leaves an enormous amount still to be done, if one intends really to secure the foundations of trinitarian thought. There is the important question as to whether the Fathers' interpretations of scripture are, if not beyond challenge, at least sufficiently sound to provide support for the main doctrinal conclusions they drew from the biblical text. Pressing still further back in the chain of argument, there remain all of the historical and critical questions with which students of the biblical literature are inundated. Later on, a bit more will be said about issues of interpretation. Excavations which delve into those deeper levels of the foundations, and the support for the foundations, and the support for the support, will be left to others.

But leaving all that to one side for the moment, or (what amounts to the same thing) taking it all for granted, there remains one major problem, the problem it is the task of this book to address. *Are the foundations stable?* Does the pro-Nicene doctrine of the Trinity provide a stable, secure basis for the edifice of theology that has been erected upon it? Now, in one sense the stability of the trinitarian doctrine is hardly open to question. Nicene trinitarianism has in fact endured as a critical element in the faith of millions upon millions of Christians for over a millennium and a half—for the Roman Catholic and Orthodox churches, for evangelical and conservative Protestants, and for others besides. Not too many doctrines or theories can claim a similar record of success and stability.

This, however, is a work of philosophical theology and not of church history, and the claim to historical continuity of belief is not sufficient to show that the foundations are stable in the sense at issue here. From the present standpoint, the crucial issue is one of logical and philosophical coherence. Is the doctrine of the Trinity developed by the fourth-century pro-Nicenes something that can be built upon without collapsing into incoherence or unintelligibility? I claim to have shown that these theologians held to a pro-Social doctrine of the Trinity—that they affirmed, both implicitly and to some extent explicitly, that the trinitarian Persons are "distinct centers of knowledge, will, love, and action." I have also argued that these theologians should be viewed as holding that the three Persons have between them but a single trope of deity—a single instance of the property, *being God*. But is this combination of views logically consistent? Is it something we can even understand, in such a way as to assess its possibility and plausibility? Appeals to mystery are all very well, but eventually the doubt is likely to surface whether such appeals may be a smokescreen to cover up an ultimate incoherence.

At this point, it seems to me that further appeals to the Fathers are of questionable value. It is not clear whether any of the fourth-century pro-Nicenes had solutions to this problem that are viable for us today. I have argued that the strong doctrine of simplicity, held by many if not all of them, is something we cannot maintain. Such a doctrine may secure the divine unity, but it threatens to erase the distinctness of the Persons. The claim that each Person is identical with the divine essence leads directly to the conclusion that each Person is identical with each other Person, a conclusion that is fatal for the doctrine. It may be that there is some sense in which each Person "is" the one divine substance, according to which the "is" represents something other than strict Leibnizian identity. And perhaps charity should lead us to attribute something along these lines to the theologians of the orthodox trinitarian tradition—indeed, I am inclined to think we should do just that. But if there is such a sense, it has not to my knowledge been elucidated by any ancient theologian. If we are to have a viable and coherent trinitarianism for our own time, *we need to do better* in this respect than they were able to do. They are the giants on whose shoulders we must stand—but, standing on those shoulders, we may indeed be able to see a little farther than they did. That at least is what we must hope for; to see whether the hope can be fulfilled is the project of the remaining two parts of this book.

Part II

Trinitarian Options

11

Surveying the Options

The first part of this book has measured the foundations of the doctrine of the Trinity, insofar as those foundations can be found in the pro-Nicene theologians of the late fourth century. Our next task is to consider some of the options for trinitarian theorizing that are presented by theologians and philosophers in recent times. The views selected for examination here have two main characteristics in common. First, each of them intends to be loyal to the main trinitarian tradition—to be orthodox, in the sense of the Nicene Creed as this has been understood by the Church. It is hoped that by now this will occasion no surprise. Our endeavor in these pages is to clarify and, if possible, to defend *the doctrine of the Trinity*. And the doctrine of the Trinity precisely *is* what has come down to us from those theologians and from the Church that has enshrined their teachings. If we were to conclude that such a venture is hopeless and that we need to strike out in fundamentally new directions in our attempts to understand the nature of God, it would be misleading and perhaps disingenuous to label the results of such an endeavor as "the doctrine of the Trinity."

The other characteristic of the views discussed here is that each of them tries to go beyond simply repeating the formulas by which ancient and medieval theologians have articulated the doctrine. To be sure, it may not be obvious to everyone that going beyond those formulas is something that needs to be done. If we intend, as we surely do, to respect their thought-processes as well as the conclusions they reached, then there is a presumption that we will take seriously the particular detailed formulations at which they arrived. On the other hand, however, it cannot be denied that those formulations were influenced in important ways by the general intellectual climate, and in particular by the philosophical environment, of the times in which they were crafted. It cannot be simply taken for granted that everything that was then found satisfactory will still pass muster in the light of all that has been learned and thought in the intervening centuries. We, at least, will not take that for granted! And most likely readers who have persevered to this point will be willing at least to consider the possibility of the need for fresh formulations that will preserve the core commitments and affirmations of Nicene trinitarianism.

The trinitarian views to be considered here fall into two main groups. First, the theologians: we begin with two theologians who played a crucial role in instigating and stimulating the revival of trinitarian theology: the Protestant Karl Barth and the Roman Catholic Karl Rahner, both of them, in our terms, "anti-Social" trinitarians. We then go on to consider two theologians whose work emerged later in that revival: Jürgen Moltmann, another Protestant, and the Orthodox theologian John Zizioulas, both of whom are Social trinitarians. Following this, we consider a series of six different accounts of the doctrine by analytic philosophers of religion. As with the theologians, we will begin with views that are distinctly hostile to Social doctrines of the Trinity, and progress to those that are explicitly Social in their understanding of the doctrine. Or more generally, we progress from views that emphasize most strongly the divine unity and affirm the distinction of Persons only with stringent qualifications, towards views with somewhat weaker characterizations of the unity of God and with stronger affirmations concerning the three distinct Persons in the Godhead. (There is one exception to this general progression, for reasons which will become apparent when we reach that point.)

It is evident that the selection of just these philosophers and theologians for discussion can be questioned. Readers may ask, why is this or that person included? And why was so-and-so's important contribution neglected? I can only reply that selection was essential, if the book was to be kept to a reasonable length, but I have no guarantee that other and better choices could not have been made. Those who find other presentations of the Trinity more appealing are invited to bring them forward and advocate them. But it may occur to some readers to ask, why the emphasis on work done by philosophers on what is, after all, a quintessentially theological topic? A key to this is found in a statement by theologian Thomas McCall: "Systematic theology of recent vintage has done surprisingly little to address this dilemma [of divine threeness in oneness]. Given that many of these theologians criticized the traditional (especially Latin) formulations, it is both surprising and disappointing that they have not set themselves to the task of addressing the problem."[1] Upon further reflection, however, this may not be so surprising after all. There can be no doubt whatsoever that the divine three-in-oneness is, at bottom, a metaphysical problem. But there are excellent reasons why comparatively few

---

[1] Thomas H. McCall, *Which Trinity? Whose Monotheism? Philosophical and Systematic Theologians on the Metaphysics of Trinitarian Theology* (Grand Rapids, MI: William B. Eerdmans, 2010), 11–12.

of our recent systematic theologians are well equipped to deal with such a problem.[2] Insofar as these theologians have been trained in contemporary philosophy, most of them will have concentrated their efforts on varieties of philosophy which offer few resources in the realm of metaphysics; indeed, many are openly contemptuous of it.[3] Certainly neither hermeneutics nor postmodernism in their many varieties, however much they may contribute to theology in other respects, have much to offer that might assist the project of trinitarian metaphysics. Many theologians are still mightily impressed by the Kantian and post-Kantian critique of metaphysics, and are quite unaware of the vigorous response to this critique that has been mounted over the last several decades.[4] For many, their main exposure to analytical types of philosophy came in the form of an encounter (often remembered with strongly negative affect) with logical positivism and its successors. (Once when attending a theological gathering I heard a distinguished European theologian refer dismissively to "the heyday of analytic philosophy," as something that lay in the distant, and unlamented, past. I felt constrained to point out to her that *"This is* the heyday of analytic philosophy!") But in the years since about 1970 there has been a vigorous resurgence of metaphysics among analytic philosophers—not least, among Christians who are analytic philosophers—and it is this domain of philosophy that, at present, offers the most promising resources for a reexamination of the metaphysics of the Trinity.[5] Thomas McCall, immediately following the remark quoted above, goes on to say, "Fortunately, however, philosophers of religion working in the so-called analytic tradition do address this issue."[6] I believe this is indeed fortunate, and it is

[2] Kevin Giles provides a brief discussion of the trinitarian theologies of Robert Jensen, Wolfhart Pannenberg, Thomas Weinandy, and David Coffey, pointing out that in each case they involve fairly radical departures from the historic tradition of trinitarian orthodoxy. (See Kevin Giles, *The Eternal Generation of the Son: Maintaining Orthodoxy in Trinitarian Theology* (Downers Grove, IL: IVP Academic, 2012), 245–55.) Like Giles, I believe we ought to trust the trinitarian tradition of the Church, and to uphold it unless it is conclusively shown to have failed.

[3] A major exception to this generalization will be found in the process theologians who are influenced by the philosophies of Alfred North Whitehead and Charles Hartshorne. However, there are characteristics of these philosophies that tend to distance their adherents from the sort of Christian orthodoxy that might lead them to take seriously the traditional doctrine of the Trinity.

[4] Nicholas Wolterstorff trenchantly remarks: "It's possible to recover from Kant." "Between the Pincers of Increased Diversity and Supposed Irrationality," in W. J. Wainwright (ed.), *God, Philosophy, and Academic Culture: A Discussion between Scholars in the AAR and the APA* (Atlanta, GA: Scholars Press, 1996), 13–20; quotation from p. 20.

[5] A selection of essays by both theologians and philosophers, exploring the possibilities for theology opened up by analytic philosophy, will be found in O. D. Crisp and M. C. Rea (eds), *Analytic Theology: New Essays in the Philosophy of Theology* (Oxford: OUP, 2009).

[6] *Which Trinity?*, 12.

precisely this body of work that forms the main contents of my Part II.[7]
Let me also state that the inauguration of the Oxford Series in Analytic
Theology shows great promise for alleviating the condition of estrange-
ment that has existed between Christian theologians and their analytic
philosophical colleagues.

---

[7] An ironic commentary on the present state of affairs is provided (unintentionally) by Fergus
Kerr's essay, "Trinitarian Theology in the Light of Analytic Philosophy," in G. Emery OP and
M. Levering (eds), *The Oxford Handbook of the Trinity* (Oxford: OUP, 2011), 339–45. Kerr
devotes a cursory half-page to Swinburne, but seems completely unaware of the contributions of
any of the other philosophers discussed in this part, or of the work contained in T. McCall and
M. C. Rea, *Philosophical and Theological Essays on the Trinity* (Oxford: OUP, 2009). He concludes,
"As regards the impact of analytic philosophy in any substantial way on the doctrine of the Trinity,
however, we must await the development of analytic theology" ("Trinitarian Theology," 345). No
doubt we should also await the appearance of a commentator who has read the available material.

12

Barth and Rahner: Persons as Modes of Being

Without any doubt, Karl Barth is one of the principal instigators of the renewed interest in the Trinity in the twentieth century. In the face of the rejection or reduction of this doctrine in liberal theology, he affirmed what he intended as a restatement of the orthodox doctrine enshrined in the writings of the Fathers and the confessions of the Church. Interestingly for our present purposes, his version is clearly a kind of anti-Social trinitarianism—though not quite unambiguously so, as we shall see.

Unlike most (though not quite all) earlier theologians,[1] Barth places the doctrine of the Trinity at the very beginning of his dogmatics, prior even to the consideration of the divine attributes. This unusual placement of the doctrine is for him inevitable. Since he rejects natural theology, his own theology must begin with divine revelation, and this immediately raises the question: What God is it whose revelation we are dealing with? The answer to this question must be that it is the Christian God of whom we speak—and the Christian God is none other than the Trinity. More than this, however, according to Barth the trinitarian nature of God is an immediate implication of the very fact of revelation. When confronted with such revelation, we are compelled to ask: *Who* is the self-revealing God? But then we must also ask: How does it *happen* that God reveals himself? And further: What is the *effect* of this revelation upon the person to whom it happens? When we ask these things, "the answer to each special question, is essentially identical with the answers to the other two questions. *God* reveals Himself. He reveals himself *through Himself.* He reveals *Himself*" (p. 340). These answers are summed up in a single sentence, which Barth designates as the "root of the doctrine of the Trinity": "*God reveals Himself as the Lord*" (p. 351). God, the Revealer, is himself immediately present in his revelation, and the effect of revelation on the hearer is revealed

---

[1] Barth mentions Peter Lombard and Bonaventure as medieval theologians who likewise began with the Trinity. Karl Barth, *Church Dogmatics*, i/1. *The Doctrine of the Word of God*, tr. G. T. Thomson (Edinburgh: T. & T. Clark, 1936), 345. In this chapter, further references to this work will be given by page numbers in the text.)

in the Lordship which God exercises and which must be recognized and accepted by the recipient of revelation. In every instance of revelation there is the revealing God, there is the concrete person, object, or event through which revelation occurs, and there is the resulting relationship of Lordship which obtains between God the revealer and the recipient of God's revelation.

There is, however, a certain ambiguity about the status of this statement, "God reveals himself as the Lord," which is the root of the doctrine of the Trinity. Barth states explicitly that this is an "analytical judgment" (p. 351). The context seems to indicate that we should understand this claim in a roughly Kantian sense—that the concepts of God, revelation, and lordship are mutually implied in each other in such a way that, if we know the meanings of the terms, we see at once that the proposition must be true. However, Barth says other things that cast doubt on this interpretation of the "root." He tells us that, on the basis of things said in "the first edition of this book" (i.e. *Christlichen Dogmatik*, i, published in 1927), he was accused of "practising the very thing I otherwise oppose, namely deriving the mysteries of revelation from that data of a generally comprehensible truth" (p. 340)—the truth, namely, of the sentence "God speaks," *Deus dixit*. Barth, of course, is eager to repudiate such an interpretation; he notes that

> Attentive readers of goodwill had already at the time noted the sense in which [those words] were used; namely that these words naturally did not themselves aim at being a proof but merely at reducing in a preliminary way a proof already achieved.... Naturally I never dreamt then, nor do I now, of deriving the truth of the dogma of the Trinity from the general truth of such a formula; but from the truth of the dogma of the Trinity the truth of such a formula is perhaps derivable for this definite purpose, to wit, for the dogma of the Trinity. (p. 340)

These remarks serve to exonerate Barth from the charge that he was practicing (horror of horrors!) a "natural theology of the Trinity." But they seem seriously inconsistent with his designation of the "root" as an "analytical judgment." Surely an analytical judgment does not require a "proof," other perhaps than the proof involved in pointing out that the formula is in fact analytic and therefore necessarily true. Furthermore, one looks in vain for this "already completed proof" of the doctrine—at least, Barth never tells us where the proof is to be found, or of what it consists. If there were such a proof, one would think that this proof would constitute the real "root" of the doctrine, rather than the formula that supposedly has been *derived from the doctrine itself*, a doctrine already proved in some other way.[2]

---

[2] It should be said here that Barth's assertions about the "root" of the doctrine of the Trinity have been subject to diverse interpretations; on this see George Hunsinger, "Karl Barth's Doctrine of the Trinity, and Some Protestant Doctrines After Barth," in Emery and Levering, *Oxford Handbook of the Trinity*, 296–7.

For the time being, however, we must pass by this ambiguity about the root of the doctrine, and see what it is that Barth derives from the root. An important point to notice is that the conception of revelation here is quite general, encompassing all of the revelatory episodes reported in the Bible. The revelation in and through Jesus is of course mentioned, but it is not at this juncture given any special status; it functions here merely as one instance of the revelation referred to in the statement which is the root of the doctrine of the Trinity. What counts is the three-fold structure present in all genuine revelation, the structure of Revealer, Revelation, and Revealedness.

This in turn leads to two additional questions. First, what is the connection between this three-fold structure of revelation and the three-foldness in the very *being* of God? That is, what is the relation between the "economic" Trinity of revelation, and the "immanent" Trinity in God's own being? And secondly, what is the nature of the immanent Trinity—of the three-fold distinction within the being of God? (This, of course, is the problem we have been wrestling with all along, the question: What is a divine Person?) With regard to the first question, Barth's answer is perhaps surprising. We are forced by scripture, Barth tells us, to conceive of God in this three-fold way—"as Revealer, Revelation, and Revealedness, or as Creator, Reconciler, and Redeemer, or as Holiness, Mercy, and Loving-Kindness" (p. 427). We cannot "do away with these distinctions without exegetical violence" (p. 427). However, "The limit of our conception lies in the fact that in *conceiving* these distinctions we *do not conceive* the distinctions in the divine modes of existence. These *do not consist* of such distinctions in the acts or attributes of God. If that were our assumption, we should be assuming three gods or a tripartite essence of God" (p. 427). That is to say, the immanent Trinity, the Trinity in God's own being, *is not directly present* in God's revelation to us. Barth here appeals to the classic doctrine, *opera trinitatis ad extra sunt indivisa*. (The external works of the Trinity are undivided.) When we take one element in one of the triads of revelation and assign it especially to one divine Person—for instance, creation to the Father, as in the Apostles' Creed—we are engaging in *appropriation*; we are "appropriating" to one Person in particular what really belongs equally to all three Persons of the Trinity. So the triadic structure of revelation *calls our attention* to the trinitarian nature of God in Godself; the revelational structure is *analogous* to the structure of God's own being. But that is all that can be said; the Trinity that is God is nowhere directly present in his revelation to us.[3]

---

[3] One thing Barth says in this connection is especially striking: "[T]he appropriation must not be exclusive.... What is appropriated belongs in fact to all the modes of existence, and the real distinction between the modes of existence cannot really be achieved by any appropriation, *in the last resort not even by the designations Father, Son, and Spirit*" (p. 429, the final emphasis has been added).

But if this is so, the question becomes inescapable: *How do we learn about the distinctions within the being of God?* If the distinctions that are present in revelation do not, in fact, exhibit to us the distinctions within God himself, is there any necessary reason for positing such distinctions at all? Certainly, God really is in himself as he reveals himself to be. But as Cyril Richardson has observed, "The consequence of finding a different person in the Godhead to account for each distinct way in which God comes to us is to have a Trinity with an infinite number of terms."[4] And so we are bound to ask: Is the immanent Trinity as expounded by Barth merely an *arbitrary postulation*?

Barth, however, does affirm an immanent Trinity, and certainly does not regard it as an arbitrary postulation. But what is the nature of the internal distinctions within God? In his answer to this question Barth clearly identifies himself as (in our terminology) an anti-Social trinitarian. In his customary emphatic style, he states,

> [I]t is to the one single essence of God, which is not to be tripled by the doctrine of the Trinity, but emphatically to be recognised in its unity, that there also belongs what we call to-day the *"personality"* of God.... "Person," in the sense of the Church doctrine of the Trinity has nothing directly to do with "personality." Thus the meaning of the doctrine of the Trinity is not that there are three personalities in God. That would be the worst and most pointed expression of tritheism, against which we must here guard. (p. 403)

In a lengthy review of the usage in trinitarian doctrine of the concept of "person," Barth emphasizes that the meaning of the concept was never fully clarified. However, a decisive turn was taken in the nineteenth century when the attribute of *self-consciousness* became part of this concept. At this point, theology was faced with the choice, "either of attempting to complete the doctrine of the Trinity by assuming the concept of Person with this new accentuation, or of holding to the old concept of Person which, since this accentuation of linguistic usage, has become completely obsolete and incomprehensible outside monastic and a few other studies" (p. 410). The first option is (in Barth's opinion) tritheistic, while the second has nothing in its favor except the authority of tradition. In view of this, Barth states,

> We prefer ... to say not "Person" but *"mode of being"*, with the intention of expressing by this concept the same thing as should be expressed by "Person", not absolutely but *relatively* better, more simply and more clearly.... The statement "God is one in three modes of being, Father, Son, and Holy Spirit" thus means that God is what He is not in one mode only, but—we appeal in support simply to the result of our analysis of the Biblical concept of revelation—in the mode of the Father, in the mode of the Son, in the mode of the Holy Spirit. (pp. 412–13)

---

[4] Cyril Richardson, *The Doctrine of the Trinity* (New York: Abingdon Press, 1958), 110–11.

The expression "modes of being" (*Seinsweisen*) is a translation of *tropoi hyparxeos*, used by the Cappadocian Fathers; Barth includes an extensive discussion of the justification of this terminology in relation to various things that have been said in the trinitarian traditions of the Church. The central point, however, can be stated succinctly: "modes of being" indicates that there is a real, ontological distinction between Father, Son, and Holy Spirit, while it avoids the tritheistic connotations that now seem inescapable if we were to say that there are three *persons* in God.

We may still wonder, however, what the *positive content* is of Barth's expression, "modes of being." What difference does it make, we ask ourselves, that the one divine person, God, exists (or subsists) in three distinct modes of being? In order to answer this question, we shall need to look further at the use he makes of this concept, and of the doctrine of the Trinity, throughout his dogmatics. Before doing this, however, it will be helpful to consult the thought of another important twentieth-century trinitarian, Karl Rahner.

KARL RAHNER

Although they were essentially contemporaries, the intellectual contexts for the trinitarian theologies of Karl Barth and Karl Rahner were substantially different. For Barth, his reinvigoration of the doctrine of the Trinity was part and parcel of his lifelong battle against the theological ravages wrought by Protestant liberalism. For Rahner, writing in the aftermath of the Second Vatican Council, the main struggle was against the rigid, formalized version of Catholic theology known as "neo-scholasticism," which in his opinion had in effect removed the doctrine of the Trinity from real religious life. He protested that "Christians are, in their practical life, almost mere 'monotheists.'... [S]hould the doctrine of the Trinity have to be dropped as false, the major part of religious literature could well remain virtually unchanged."[5] In spite of this difference of context, there is a considerable amount of similarity in Barth's and Rahner's respective treatments of the doctrine, a similarity which has prompted their being paired together in this chapter.

One point of similarity between the two theologians is their common opposition to the arrangement of theology that considers "the one God" separately and in advance of the doctrine of the Trinity. Another element of this similarity is the insistence of both theologians on grounding the doctrine of the

---

[5] Karl Rahner, *The Trinity*, tr. Joseph Donceel, with introduction, index, and glossary by Catherine Mowry Lacugna (New York: Crossroad, 1997), 10–11; see also Lacugna's Introduction. For this work also, page numbers will be given in the text; as it happens there is no overlap with the pages from Barth's Church Dogmatics, and thus no danger of confusion.

Trinity in the history of salvation. Rahner, in fact, goes considerably farther than Barth in this regard. Barth, as we have seen, insists that whereas the three-fold structure of Revealer, Revelation, and Revealedness is the root from which the doctrine of the Trinity has sprung, it is nevertheless the case that the "immanent Trinity," the trinity in God's own being, *is not directly present* in the three-fold structure of revelation. Barth, therefore, makes heavy use of the doctrine of appropriations, by which elements which in reality are common to Father, Son, and Holy Spirit are nevertheless especially associated with one or another of the divine modes of being. In Barth's theology (no doubt contrary to his own intention), the connection between the "immanent" Trinity and the "economic" Trinity is hard to discern.

For Rahner, things are much different. The central, and much-discussed, axiom of his trinitarian doctrine is, "*The 'economic' Trinity is the 'immanent' Trinity and the 'immanent' Trinity is the 'economic' Trinity*" (p. 22).[6] He points out that at least one instance of this thesis is dogmatically beyond question: the Son, and *only* the Son, became incarnate in Jesus of Nazareth. But he wishes to go beyond this single instance and insist that there are also genuine, "not-appropriated relations of the divine persons to the justified" (p. 34).[7] This does not mean that Rahner rejects the doctrine of appropriations, but he will not allow the distinctiveness of the Persons to be obscured by that doctrine in such a way that there is nothing that can be properly attributed to one Person as opposed to the other two. Alongside of the doctrine of appropriations, there is the doctrine of the *missions* of the divine Persons into the world, which deserves at least equal emphasis.

All this, however, is preliminary to Rahner's main exposition. In developing his doctrine, he first wishes to set out "a 'systematic' conception of the 'economic' Trinity" (p. 82). He does this in terms of a two-fold "self-communication" of God, which he develops by means of four pairs of aspects: "(a) Origin-Future; (b) History-Transcendence; (c) Invitation-Acceptance; (d) Knowledge-Love" (p. 88). His discussion of these aspects will not be reproduced here; the important point is that he groups the first member of each pair (Origin, History, Invitation, Knowledge) as one of the "basic modalities" of God's self-communication (and thus, of the "mission of the Son"); and the second member of each pair (Future, Transcendence, Acceptance, Love) as the other basic modality (thus, the "mission of the Spirit"). In this way we arrive at the

---

[6] One important criticism is that Rahner does not clearly acknowledge the difference between the necessity of the intra-trinitarian relations, and the contingency of creation and the economic Trinity. See John Thompson, *Modern Trinitarian Perspectives* (Oxford: OUP, 1994), 26–30. For a review of the diverse responses to "Rahner's Rule," see Fred Sanders, "Entangled in the Trinity: Economic and Immanent Trinity in Recent Theology," *dialog*, 40/3 (Fall 2001), 175–82.

[7] In an interesting footnote (p. 34), Rahner mentions that, in the traditional theology of the beatific vision, it is asserted that the blessed will enjoy an immediate intuition of the Trinity. In order for this to be possible, he points out, there must be here also a direct, not-appropriated relation of each of the divine Persons to the created person.

conclusion that "the divine self-communication possesses two basic modalities: self-communication as truth and as love" (p. 98).[8] This enables Rahner to assert that "we may have succeeded in some way in conceptualizing the 'economic' Trinity." He goes on to say, "The question now arises whether, with our concept of the 'economic' Trinity, we have also practically been speaking of what in the Church's statement about the Trinity is meant by Father, Son, and Spirit, hence of the 'immanent' Trinity" (p. 99). It is this key transition—a transition which we saw to be somewhat lacking in the case of Barth—that we need to examine.

There are two questions we now must pose. First, why must we suppose that there is an immanent Trinity at all? And second, what is the nature of this Trinity—which is to say, what is the meaning of the assertion that there are in God three Persons, or three hypostases? Here is Rahner's answer to the first of these questions:

> [T]he differentiation of the self-communication of God in history (of truth) and spirit (of love) must belong to God "in himself," or otherwise this difference, which undoubtedly exists, would do away with God's *self*-communication. For these modalities and their differentiation either are in God himself (although we first experience them from our point of view), or they exist only in us, they belong only to the realm of creatures as effects of the divine creative activity.... Then they can only be that communication of God which occurs precisely in creation, in which what is created contains a transcendental reference to the God who remains forever beyond this difference, thus at the same time "giving" him and withdrawing him. Hence there occurs no self-communication.... God would be the "giver," not the *gift itself*, he would "give himself" only to the extent that he communicates a gift distinct from himself. (pp. 99–101)

The dialectic is subtle, but the argument fails to convince. A human person can give herself to others in different ways both in knowledge[9] and in love (say, a university professor who is an outstanding teacher, but who also devotes much of her time to assisting newly arrived refugees), without this requiring any special internal division within the person herself, above and beyond the sorts of complications normally present in any other person. In the same way, God could give himself to humans in all of the ways indicated by Rahner's "modalities" without this requiring any internal differentiation within God

---

[8] It is noteworthy that in this way Rahner arrives at a two-fold schematization of God's self-communication, corresponding to the missions of Son and Spirit, whereas Barth's schematization is three-fold, in which one aspect is appropriated to each of the three Persons. Comparing the two, it is hard to avoid the conclusion that the schematization in each case is determined by the desired dogmatic result rather than by anything apparent in the divine revelatory activity as such.

[9] It should perhaps be noted that what Rahner means by "knowledge" is rather different from the ordinary uses of that term (see *The Trinity*, 95–6); however this does not affect the point made in the text.

that a unitarian would need to object to. It begins to look as though Rahner, as well as Barth, fails to establish a convincing connection between the economic Trinity and the immanent Trinity, in spite of Rahner's heavy emphasis on the "axiom" connecting the two. He goes on to state that the differentiation of the immanent Trinity "is constituted by a double self-communication of the Father, by which the Father communicates *himself*" (p. 102)—that is, by the "relations of origin," the generation of the Son and the procession of the Spirit. But this is not an answer to the question we are now asking. That question concerns, not the ontological grounding of the immanent Trinity, but rather our epistemic access to these distinctions. That access can only be by way of the economic Trinity—that is, by God's revelatory activity in the world—and both Barth and Rahner fail to show how this is possible.

Again as with Barth, however, we must acknowledge that Rahner does intend to speak of an immanent Trinity, and must go on to see what this amounts to. The key to this is found in his section on "The Problem of the Concept of 'Person'" (pp. 103–15). The discussion in this section becomes quite complex, as Rahner interacts both with ordinary uses of the term "person" and with what has been said about this concept in the theological tradition. Yet his basic perspective becomes clear when he says,

> [W]hen *today we* speak of person in the plural, we think almost necessarily, because of the modern meaning of the word, of several spiritual centers of activity, of several subjectivities and liberties. But there are not three of these in God—not only because in God there is only *one* essence, hence *one* absolute self-presence, but also because there is only *one* self-utterance of the Father, The Logos. The Logos is not the one who utters, but the one who is uttered. And there is properly no *mutual* love between Father and Son, for this would presuppose two acts. (p. 106)

This I think is admirably clear. There is no mutual love: the Son does not, cannot love the Father, for this would mean that the Son is a "spiritual center of activity" distinct from the Father, which according to Rahner he cannot be. The anti-Social character of Rahner's trinitarianism is not in doubt, a fact that is underscored by a warning he issues about a "real danger in the doctrine of the Trinity, not so much in the abstract theology of the textbooks, but in the average conception of the normal Christian. This is the danger of a popular, unverbalized, but at bottom quite massive tritheism" (p. 42). (The "average Christians" who are threatened by this "massive tritheism" presumably cannot be the same ones who were earlier stated to be "almost mere 'monotheists'," but Rahner does not enlighten us concerning the different groups of believers involved.)

In view of the almost unavoidably misleading character of the term "person," Rahner asks whether some preferable alternative may be available. Like Barth, he settles on the expression, taken from the Cappadocians, *tropos hyparxeos*, which he prefers to translate "distinct manner of subsisting," rather than Barth's "manner (or mode) of being."[10] For Rahner as for Barth, this has the advantage of signifying a real distinction in the very being of God, while avoiding the tritheistic suggestions of the word "person." The further implications of this expression, however, remain to be explored.

IMPLICATIONS AND AFTERTHOUGHTS

According to both Barth and Rahner it is preferable to say, not that there are three "persons" in God, but that God exists in three *tropoi hyparxeos,* three "manners of being (or subsisting)," corresponding to Father, Son, and Holy Spirit. But what is the payoff for this move (over and above avoiding the suspicion of tritheism)? What further implications does it have for theology? One place we might think to look for an answer is to the original source of this terminology, the Cappadocian Fathers. However, they offer us no help with our question. The reason for this is that their use of the term, *tropoi hyparxeos,* is fundamentally different than the one found in Barth and Rahner. For them, the "manner of being" is an attribute *of each Person,* an attribute which distinguishes that Person from the other two. For instance, the Son's manner of being is that of *being begotten,* and the Spirit's manner of being is that of *proceeding.*[11] For these theologians, the *tropos hyparxeos* is not a designation of what each of Father, Son, and Holy Spirit *is,* but is rather the distinguishing attribute in virtue of which each is distinct from the other two. For Barth and Rahner, however, it is *God* who is the subject of all three *tropoi hyparxeos;* accordingly, for them the expression has to carry a burden—that of explaining the sense in which each is a *hypostasis*—that it was never designed by the Cappadocians to bear. Accordingly, the use of the expression by Barth and Rahner gains no authority or sanction from the ancients from whom the terminology is derived.

In Rahner's book on the Trinity, resources for answering this question are rather slim. Although he is insistent on grounding the doctrine of the Trinity in salvation history, he actually has rather little to say about specific biblical texts. He concludes the book with the assertion that "the real doctrine of the Trinity is presented in Christology and in pneumatology" (p. 120), inviting us to look at treatises on those topics for further enlightenment. Barth, on the other hand, concludes his presentation of the Trinity with three chapters, one

---

[10] Thus the title of this chapter is slightly inaccurate in attributing "mode of being" to Rahner as well as to Barth. The change, however, seems to be of only minor significance.

[11] See Lewis Ayres, *Nicaea and its Legacy* (Oxford: OUP, 2004), 210–22, 359. Presumably the Father's manner of being is that of being unbegotten, though this is never actually said.

each on God the Father, God the Son, and God the Holy Spirit. These chapters are especially helpful for our present question.[12]

One thing that may strike us as we peruse these chapters is that the grounds on which the doctrine of the Trinity is based seem to have shifted. No longer are we dealing with a general pattern of Revelation, Revealer, and Revealedness; instead, the whole discussion revolves around the one man, Jesus Christ, in his relationship with the heavenly Father. Furthermore, what is said concerning Jesus could never be extended to cover the whole field of biblical revelation. It is God the Father—the *trinitarian* Father—whom Jesus obeyed, to whom he prayed, and whom he declared to us as *our* Father (see p. 422). Of Jesus himself it is said, "Jesus Christ, as him who reveals the Father and reconciles us with the Father, is the Son of God" (p. 474). Furthermore, "Jesus Christ, the Son of God, is God Himself, as God his Father is God Himself" (p. 474). It is hard to avoid the impression that in saying these things Barth has violated his earlier insistence that the trinitarian distinctions are not directly present in the distinctions in revelation, but are only analogically indicated by them. The argument presented in these chapters hinges on the assumption that the trinitarian Fatherhood and Sonship are *directly present* in the relationship between Jesus and his Father in heaven.[13] But if this is so, then the personal relationship between Jesus and the Father is a relationship *between God the Father and God the Son*. And this, of course, is the key exegetical point on which a Social (or pro-Social) doctrine of the Trinity is based.

It will be helpful to look at some of the uses made of the doctrine of the Trinity by Barth elsewhere in his dogmatics. In his discussion of the love of God, he states, "As and before God seeks and creates fellowship with us, He wills and completes this fellowship in Himself. In Himself He is Father, Son and Holy Spirit and therefore alive in His unique being with and for and in another.... He does not exist in solitude but in fellowship."[14] How are we to understand this fellowship, if it is not a fellowship between *persons*? But a still more striking passage occurs in Barth's treatment of the doctrine of reconciliation. Here Barth discusses the difficulty for our doctrine of God, involved in the suffering and obedience of Christ. He asks,

> Is it a fact that in relation to Jesus Christ we can speak of an obedience of the one true God Himself in His proper being? ... We have not only not to deny but actually to affirm and understand as essential to the being of God, the offensive

[12] Claude Welch, *The Trinity in Contemporary Theology* (London: S.C.M. Press, 1953), 173, suggests that it may be in these chapters that we should look for the "already completed proof" of the doctrine of the Trinity referred to earlier. Barth does not specifically say this.

[13] As we saw in Part I of this book, that assumption lies at the heart of the trinitarian exegesis of the Church Fathers (see Ch. 9); these chapters make it clear that Barth does not in the end wish to distance himself from them on this crucial point.

[14] *Church Dogmatics*, ii/1. *The Doctrine of God*, tr. T. H. L. Parker *et al.* (Edinburgh: T. & T. Clark, 1957), 275.

fact that there is in God Himself an above and a below, a *prius* and a *posterius*, a superiority and a subordination.[15]

In explaining the possibility of this, Barth tells us that

> In order not to be alone, single, enclosed within Himself, God did not need co-existence with the creature. He does not will and posit the creature neces-sarily, but in freedom, as the basic act of His grace.... For everything that the creature seems to offer Him—its otherness, its being in antithesis to Himself and therefore His own existence in co-existence—He has also in Himself as God, as the original and essential determination of His being and life as God.... [N]ot in unequal but equal, not in divided but in the one deity, God is both One and also Another, His own counterpart, co-existent with Himself. We can say this quite calmly: He exists as a first and as a second, above and below, *a priori* and *a posteriori*.[16]

By this time the claim that the divine "modes of being" are something other than *persons* has worn very thin indeed. Cyril Richardson observes that, for Barth, "Personality in our sense, being an 'I', is to be attributed to the whole Trinity, not to the modes of God's being." But if the Father and Son "are only modes of God's being, how can they love each other? If the 'I' belongs to the Trinity rather than to the modes, how can we speak of their mutual relations of love?"[17] How indeed?

This material strongly suggests that, as his theology continued to develop, Barth began to have afterthoughts concerning his denial that Father, Son, and Spirit are persons in something approximating our modern understanding of that notion. Or perhaps it is more accurate to see him as attempting to straddle the divide between affirming that God, the Trinity, is one and only one person, and recognizing Father, Son, and Holy Spirit as each genuinely a distinct per-son. His denial that the latter is the case becomes difficult if not impossible to sustain, in the light of statements such as the ones quoted above.

But what of Rahner? As already stated, his short book on the Trinity gives us much less to go on. But there is at least one important statement of his that gives us pause; it seems to indicate, if not an afterthought on his part, at least a difficulty in maintaining his denial that the trinitarian Three are genuinely persons. In his account of "God's threefold relation to us in the order of grace," he states,

> The Father gives himself to us too as *Father*, that is, precisely because and inso-far as he himself, being essentially with *himself*, utters himself and *in this way* communicates the Son as his own, personal self-manifestation; and because and insofar as the Father and the Son (receiving from the Father), welcoming each

---

[15] *Church Dogmatics*, iv/1. *The Doctrine of Reconciliation*, tr. G. W. Bromiley (Edinburgh: T. & T. Clark, 1956), 200–1.
[16] *Church Dogmatics*, iv/1. 201–2.　　　[17] Richardson, *Doctrine*, 106.

other in love, drawn and returning to each other communicate themselves *in this way,* as received in mutual love, that is, as Holy Spirit. (p. 35)[18]

As so often with Rahner the dialectic is complex, but it is hard not to see in his assertion that Father and Son *welcome each other in love* a direct contradiction of his later assertion that "there is properly no *mutual* love between Father and Son" (p. 107). But if there is an inconsistency here it is a welcome inconsistency, one that reveals the great difficulty that is encountered if theology really wishes to rid itself of the mutual love between the Persons of the Trinity.

---

[18] Rahner here reflects the "Augustinian" theme of the Spirit as the bond of love between Father and Son, a theme which does have a tendency to depersonalize the Spirit. (The same seems to be true at times of Barth as well.)

13

Moltmann and Zizioulas:
Perichoresis and Communion

From Barth and Rahner, two pioneers of the revival of trinitarian theology, we turn to two more recent contributors to that revival, Jürgen Moltmann and John Zizioulas. Both of them hold to decidedly Social trinitarian views, in sharp contrast to the "two Karls." As with Barth and Rahner, we will focus especially on the "three-in-oneness problem" which is the main topic of the present work.

The importance of the doctrine of the Trinity for Moltmann is evident in one of his earlier books, *The Crucified God*.[1] In an introductory essay he tells of his experience in a prison camp during the Second World War, and states, "Shattered and broken, the survivors of my generation were then returning from camps and hospitals to the lecture room. A theology which did not speak of God in the sight of the one who was abandoned and crucified would have had nothing to say to us then."[2] But if it was indeed God who was crucified, this raises the question of the Trinity. Moltmann asks, "if we are to understand the 'human', the 'crucified' God, must we think of God in trinitarian terms? And conversely, can we think of God in trinitarian terms if we do not have the event of the cross in mind?"[3] Answering his own questions, he states,

> The place of the doctrine of the Trinity is not the 'thinking of thought' but the cross of Jesus. 'Concepts without perception are empty' (Kant). The perception of the trinitarian concept of God is the cross of Jesus. 'Perceptions without concepts are blind' (Kant). The theological concept for the perception of the crucified Christ is the doctrine of the Trinity. The material principle of the doctrine of the Trinity is the cross of Christ. The formal principle of knowledge of the cross is the doctrine of the Trinity.[4]

---

[1] Jürgen Moltmann, *The Crucified God*, tr. R. A. Wilson and John Bowden (New York: Harper & Row, 1974).
[2] Moltmann, *Crucified God*, 1.   [3] Moltmann, *Crucified God*, 236.
[4] Moltmann, *Crucified God*, 240–1.

There follows an examination of New Testament passages in which Christ is described as "delivered up" (*paradidonai*) to the Cross by his Father. Moltmann summarizes:

> If the cross of Jesus is understood as a divine event, i.e. as an event between Jesus and his God and Father, it is necessary to speak in trinitarian terms of the Son and the Father and the Spirit. In that case the doctrine of the Trinity is no longer an exorbitant and impractical speculation about God, but is nothing other than a shorter version of the passion narrative of Christ in its significant for the eschatological freedom of faith and the life of oppressed nature.[5]

That is powerfully stated, but for further clarification concerning the Trinity we must turn to a later book, *The Trinity and the Kingdom*.[6]

Moltmann's exposition of the Trinity begins with a lengthy chapter on "The Passion of God," in which he addresses, and rejects, the tradition of divine impassibility; he also develops various ways in which modern writers have depicted the sufferings of God. In the following chapter on "The History of the Son," he deploys the New Testament testimony concerning Jesus and his relationship with his Father as the source and foundation for trinitarian doctrine. (In this, as we have already seen, he is very much in agreement with the Church Fathers' approach to the Trinity.) Following up on the note struck in *The Crucified God*, the surrender of the Son to death and the passion of Jesus play a central role here. For our present purposes, however, the most important material is found in the chapter titled "The Mystery of the Trinity." The chapter begins with "A Criticism of Christian Monotheism." ("Monotheism" as used by Moltmann is virtually equivalent to unitarianism.) Arianism and Sabellianism are both cited as examples of "Christian Monotheism"; Tertullian is presented as having developed the idea of the Trinity, but in an imperfect and ambiguous form. Interestingly, both Barth and Rahner come in for serious criticism, for in effect identifying God in his unity as the "absolute subject," and denying the reality of the three distinct Persons. In this Barth's "Idealist heritage" betrays itself—a charge that must surely have caused Barth to stir indignantly in his grave!

> The reason for the difficulties Barth gets into here with his acceptance of the Idealistic reflection Trinity of the divine subject, is that he puts the divine lordship before the Trinity and uses the 'doctrine of the Trinity' to secure and interpret the divine subjectivity in that lordship. That is why Barth presents the 'doctrine of the Trinity' as Christian monotheism and argues polemically against a 'tritheism' which has never existed. That is why he uses a non-trinitarian concept of the unity of the one God—that is to say, the concept of the identical subject. (pp. 143–4)

---

[5] Moltmann, *Crucified God*, 246.

[6] Jürgen Moltmann, *The Trinity and the Kingdom: The Doctrine of God*, tr. Margaret Kohl (Minneapolis: Fortress Press, 1993; originally publ. by Harper & Row, 1981). Page references in this chapter are to this volume.

Karl Rahner, according to Moltmann, "developed his doctrine of the Trinity with an astonishing similarity to Barth and almost the same presuppositions" (p. 144). When Rahner states that we cannot, in view of our modern conception of person, speak of three divine persons,

> What he describes is actually extreme individualism: everyone is a self-possessing, self-disposing centre of action which sets itself apart from other persons. But the philosophical personalism of Hölderlin, Feuerbach, Buber, Ebner, Rosenstock and others was designed precisely to overcome this possessive individualism: the "I" can only be understood in the light of the "Thou"—that is to say, it is a concept of relation. Without the social relation there can be no personality. (p. 144)

Given this more adequate conception of personhood, Moltmann thinks, we need not hesitate to affirm that there are three Persons in the Godhead. Rahner, however, fails to see this: Moltmann quotes him as saying, "The one and the same God is given for us as Father, Son-Logos and Holy Spirit, or: the Father gives us himself in absolute self-communication through the Son in the Holy Spirit" (p. 147).[7] Moltmann continues,

> In this last formulation it becomes clear that Rahner transforms the classical doctrine of the Trinity into the reflection trinity of the absolute subject; and the way he does this is plain too. The "self-communication" of the Absolute has that differentiated structure which seems so similar to the Christian doctrine of the Trinity. But in fact it makes the doctrine of the Trinity superfluous. The fact that God gives us himself in absolute self-communication *can* be associated with Father, Son, and Spirit but it does not have to be. On the other hand what is stated biblically with the history of the Father, the Son and the Spirit is only vaguely paraphrased by the conception of God's self-communication. (p. 147)

Building upon these reflections, Moltmann goes on to consider the question of the unity of God. According to him,

> The early creeds, which set the trend for tradition, remain ambivalent where the question of God's unity is concerned. The Nicene Creed with its use of *homoousios* as keyword, suggests a unity of substance between Father, Son and Spirit. But the Athanasian Creed, with the thesis *"unus Deus"*, maintains the identity of the one divine subject.[8] In the first case the threeness of the Persons is in the foreground, while the unity of their substance is in the background. In the second case the unity of the absolute subject is in the foreground, and the three Persons recede into the background. The first case is obviously open to the charge of tritheism; the second case to the reproach of modalism.... If the biblical testimony is chosen as point of departure, then we shall have to start from the three Persons of the history of Christ. If philosophical logic is made the starting point, then the enquirer proceeds from the One God. (p. 149)

---

[7] The reference is to Rahner's *Grundkurs des Glaubens* (Freiburg: Herder, 1976), 141.

[8] Here and elsewhere, I cite Moltmann's interpretations of ancient and contemporary sources without necessarily endorsing them.

In the light of all this, it comes as no surprise when Moltmann states that "it seems to make more sense theologically to start from the biblical history, and therefore to make the unity of the three divine Persons the problem, rather than to take the reverse method" (p. 149). This does not mean, however, that he endorses the Nicene doctrine of the "one divine substance." On the contrary, he takes the issue of divine unity in quite a different direction:

> The unity of the Father, the Son and the Spirit is then the eschatological question about the consummation of the trinitarian history of God. The unity of the three Persons of this history must consequently be understood as a *communicable* unity and as an *open, inviting unity, capable of integration*. The *homogeneity* of the one divine substance is hardly conceivable as communicable and open for anything else, because then it would no longer be homogeneous. The *sameness* and the identity of the absolute subject is not communicable either, let alone open for anything else, because it would then be charged with non-identity and difference. Both these concepts of unity ... are exclusive, not inclusive. If we search for a concept of unity corresponding to the biblical testimony of the triune God, the God who unites others with himself, then we must dispense with both the concept of the one substance and the concept of the identical subject. All that remains is: the unitedness, the at-oneness of the three Persons with one another, or: the unitedness, the at-oneness of the triune God. (pp. 149–50)

This is, to say the least, a bold move—not that we should expect anything less than boldness from Moltmann. The notion of unity as "open and communicable" is clearly aimed at the idea that God's purpose is to unite us human beings with God; thus the reference to eschatology. But there is here at least a strong suggestion that the unity of Father, Son, and Holy Spirit will itself not be complete until that eschatological unity becomes a reality. In any case, it is clearly stated that there is no "unity of substance"; *all that remains* of the divine unity is the "at-oneness" of the three Persons—that is, the *personal union and communion* between Father, Son, and Holy Spirit. The divine unity, says Moltmann, "must be perceived in the *perichoresis* of the divine Persons. If the unity of God is not perceived in the at-oneness of the triune God, and therefore as a *perichoretic* unity, then Arianism and Sabellianism remain inescapable threats to Christian theology" (p. 150).

The logic here is powerful, but the conclusion may give us pause. Moltmann exploits the idea, already present in the ancient Fathers and indeed in the New Testament, that we human beings are to be drawn into the relationship of love and communion that exists between the Father and the Son within the Trinity. He infers from this, however, that the unity of Father, Son, and Holy Spirit cannot be anything that is not, in principle, open to human beings—or, for that matter, to angels, or to aliens if such there be. But is this sort of unity sufficient, all by itself, to constitute the unity of *God*? The human beings who will share in the eschatological *perichoresis* will come from all different sources and conditions of life; could this be true also of Father, Son, and Holy Spirit?[9] If not, then why not?

More light is thrown on these questions by the later section on "The Immanent Trinity." Here Moltmann offers an additional explanation of the notion of *perichoresis*:

> John Damascene's profound doctrine of the eternal *perichōrēsis* or *circumincessio* of the trinitarian Persons ... grasps the circulatory character of the eternal divine life. An eternal process takes place in the triune God through the exchange of energies. The Father exists in the Son, the Son in the Father, and both of them in the Spirit, just as the Spirit exists in both the Father and the Son. By virtue of their eternal love they live in one another to such an extent, and dwell in one another to such an extent, that they are one. It is a process of most perfect and intense empathy. (pp. 174–5)

Perhaps surprisingly, in view of what was said earlier, Moltmann also affirms the doctrine of the eternal generation of the Son, and the eternal procession of the Holy Spirit:

> In respect of the constitution of the Trinity the Father is the 'origin-without-origin' of the Godhead. According to the doctrine of the two processions, the Son and the Spirit take their divine hypostases from him. So in the constitution of the Godhead *the Father* forms the 'monarchial' unity of the Trinity. (p. 177)

However, he goes on to say,

> But in respect of the Trinity's inner life, the three Persons themselves form their unity, by virtue of their relation to one another and in the eternal perichoresis of their love. They are concentrated in *the eternal Son*. This is the perichoretic unity of the Trinity.
>
> Finally, the mutual transfiguration and illumination of the Trinity into the eternal glory of the divine life is bound up with this. This uniting mutuality and community proceeds from *the Holy Spirit*.
>
> The unity of the Trinity is constituted by the Father, concentrated round the Son, and illumined through the Holy Spirit. (pp. 177–8)

These thoughts, it seems to me, convey a somewhat different picture of the divine unity than one would receive from the earlier sections taken by themselves. The doctrine of *perichoresis*, while still important, does not have to carry by itself the whole burden of the unity of God—a task for which it is arguably insufficient. And the "openness" of the divine *perichoresis* does not mean that human beings, and other creatures, are able to be united with God in exactly the same way that the Persons are united with one another. It cannot be the case, for example, that the author and the reader

---

[9] Here we might think of Mosser's suggestion (Ch. 3 above) that it is Mormonism that offers a "fully Social trinitarianism."

of this book can come to be "eternally generated" from God the Father. In the light of all this, it seems that Moltmann has a stronger conception of divine unity than one might otherwise have supposed. Accordingly, he is not without resources with which to contest the charge of tritheism that has been brought against him.

Nevertheless, there are things he says that may cause us to wonder. When, in his criticisms of Barth and Rahner, he denies that "Christian tritheism" is a problem at all, he dismisses all too easily a charge that, in fact, he needs to seriously address. His apparent desire to eliminate all talk of the divine substance may also give us pause—though to be sure, he is not alone in that desire. Has Moltmann forgotten that in the ancient Church it was the Homoian Arians—representatives of the "Christian monotheism" that he detests—who wished to ban all mention of substance (*ousia*) in relation to God?[10] Their inability to succeed in this can perhaps stand as a reminder that, whether we are happy to address them or not, metaphysical questions are bound to arise and to demand our attention. Moltmann, however, shows little interest in metaphysical inquiry, except where it can be related to practical social and political concerns. (His objection to "monotheism" is in part due to its alleged connection with political monarchy and domination.) All things considered, I believe that even Social trinitarians who are inclined to sympathize with some of Moltmann's trinitarian views will agree that his version of the doctrine is a work in progress, needing considerable additional clarification.[11]

JOHN ZIZIOULAS

John Zizioulas's seminal work, *Being as Communion*,[12] does not initially present itself as a treatise on the doctrine of the Trinity. Perhaps it could be described most perspicuously as a treatise on theological anthropology, considering the nature of human beings with special reference to their existence and participation in the Church. The subtitle, "Studies in Personhood and the Church," tells the story. However, the anthropological thesis is developed against the background of ancient trinitarian thought, particularly the resolution of the trinitarian controversy achieved by the Cappadocian Fathers in the late fourth century. It soon came to be recognized that Zizioulas's

[10] In the Second Creed of Sirmium, AD 357; see R. P. C. Hanson, *The Search for the Christian Doctrine of God* (Grand Rapids, MI: Baker Books, 2005), 343–7.

[11] For further discussion of Moltmann's views, see McCall, *Which Trinity?*, 156–74; also Thompson, *Modern Trinitarian Perspectives*, 61–3.

[12] John D. Zizioulas, *Being as Communion: Studies in Personhood and the Church* (Crestwood, NY: St Vladimir's Seminary Press, 1985). Page references are to this book.

account of that history implies a distinctive trinitarian theology, and he has become an acknowledged leader of Social trinitarianism. In his Introduction he states,

> the discussion of the being of God leads patristic thought to the following theses, which are fundamentally bound up with ecclesiology as well as ontology:
>
> (a) There is no true being without communion. Nothing exists as an "individual" conceivable in itself. Communion is an ontological category.
>
> (b) Communion which does not come from a "hypostasis," that is, a concrete and free person, and which does not lead to "hypostases," that is concrete and free persons, is not an "image" of the being of God. The person cannot exist without communion; but every form of communion which denies or suppresses the person is inadmissible. (p. 18)

These theses immediately alert us both to the kind of anthropology Zizioulas intends to present, and to the connection of that anthropology with trinitarian theology.

Zizioulas's historical narrative is both complex and controversial. We cannot present it here in full detail, nor will we enter deeply into the controversy concerning its historical accuracy. (I will note, however, that it is hard to avoid the impression that quite a bit of modern content has been injected into the ancient narrative.) By way of a brief summary, the starting point is the fundamental *monism* of Greek philosophy:

> Ancient Greek thought remained tied to the basic principle which it has set itself, the principle that being constitutes in the final analysis a unity in spite of the multiplicity of existent things because concrete existent things finally trace their being back to their necessary relationship and "kinship" with the "one" being, and because consequently every "differentiation" or "accidence" must be somehow regarded as a tendency towards "non-being," a deterioration of or "fall" from being. (p. 29)

This unity means that God, if there is a God, must himself be part of the cosmos rather than standing over against it: "He too is bound by ontological necessity to the world and the world to him" (pp. 29–30). Furthermore, "in such a world it is impossible for the unforeseen to happen or for freedom to operate as an absolute and unrestricted claim to existence" (p. 30). This means that when man, as portrayed in Greek tragedy, "strives to become a 'person', to rise up against this harmonious unity which oppresses him as rational and moral necessity" (p. 32), he is bound to fail. "His freedom is circumscribed, or rather there is no freedom for him—since a 'circumscribed freedom' would be a contradiction in terms—and consequently his 'person' is nothing but a 'mask' [Greek, *prosopon*], something which has no bearing on his true 'hypostasis,' something without ontological content" (p. 32). There is, then, no proper concept of a *person*; both *prosopon*, in Greek, and *persona*, in Latin, express "the role which one plays in one's social or legal relationships, the moral or 'legal' person which either collectively or individually has nothing to do with the *ontology* of the person" (p. 34).

In order to arrive at a viable concept of the person, two changes were necessary: "(a) A radical change in cosmology which would free the world and man from ontological necessity; and (b) an ontological view of man which would unify the person with the *being* of man, with his permanent and enduring existence, with his genuine and absolute identity." Zizioulas continues, "The first of these could only be offered by Christianity with its biblical outlook. The second could only be attained by Greek thought with its interest in ontology. The Greek Fathers were precisely those who could unify the two" (p. 35).

Here in brief is how the transformation came about. The Cappadocian Fathers took the word *hypostasis,* which formerly had been synonymous with *ousia,* indicating the "being" which was central for Greek thought, and fused it with *prosopon,* indicative of the individual in his or her various relationships (see p. 87). In doing this, they created the concept of a *person,* as we have understood that notion ever since. The implications of this shift were momentous:

> (a) The person is no longer an adjunct to a being, a category which we *add* to a concrete entity once we have first verified its ontological hypostasis. *It is itself the hypostasis of the being.* (b) Entities no longer trace their being to being itself—that is, being is not an absolute category in itself—but to the person, to precisely that which *constitutes* being, that is, enables entities to be entities. In other words from an adjunct to a being (a kind of mask) the person becomes the being itself and is simultaneously—a most significant point—*the constitutive element* (the "principle" or "cause") of beings. (p. 39)

This shift, however, was only possible because of two other changes, both of them occurring within Christian theology. The first of these was the doctrine of creation *ex nihilo,* which "made being—the existence of the world, existent things—*a product of freedom....* [W]ith the doctrine of creation *ex nihilo* the 'principle' of Greek ontology, the 'archē' of the world, was transposed to the sphere of freedom. That which exists was liberated from itself; the being of the world became free from necessity" (pp. 39–40). The second was a particular conception of what the *unity of God* consists in: "Among the Greek Fathers, the unity of God, the one God, and the ontological 'principle' or 'cause' of the being and life of God does not consist in the one substance of God but in the *hypostasis,* that is, *the person of the Father....* Thus, when we say that God 'is', we do not bind the personal freedom of God—the being of God is not an ontological 'necessity' or a simple 'reality' for God—but we ascribe the being of God to his personal freedom" (pp. 40–1).

So far, all this may seem reasonably clear. Zizioulas has offered a compelling (if far from uncontroversial) narrative concerning ancient trinitarian thought, a narrative which portrays the emergence of the concept of a *person* as we now understand it. And it seems fairly clear what sort of trinitarian doctrine the narrative will support. It will be a Social trinitarianism, in which the Father, Son, and Spirit are "persons" in a sense that is at least strongly analogous with our ordinary usage of the word "person," and in which their communion with one another will receive heavy emphasis. This view will, of course, be liable to the sorts of challenges that are customarily directed at Social doctrines of the Trinity: Is it biblically well-founded? Is it faithful to the tradition? Will the historical narrative stand up to critical scrutiny? Does the view permit an adequate conception of the unity of God? And so on. But so far, there is nothing here that seems particularly radical.

Radical implications do emerge, however, when we probe the notion of the freedom that Zizioulas attributes to the Father.[13] He states,

> The fact that God owes His existence to the Father,[14] that is to a person, means (a) that His "substance," His being, does not constrain Him (God does not exist because He cannot but exist), and (b) that communion is not a constraining structure for His existence (God is not in communion, does not love, because He cannot but be in communion and love). The fact that God exists because of the Father shows that His existence, His being, is the consequence of a free person; which means, in the last analysis, that not only communion but also *freedom*, the free person, constitutes true being. True being comes only from the free person, from the person who loves freely—that is, who freely affirms his being, his identity, by means of an event of communion with other persons. (p. 18)

This, I submit, is truly radical. "God does not exist because he cannot but exist." If this means anything, it means that it is *really possible* for God *not* to exist—which means, in effect, for God to commit suicide. Furthermore, "God is not in communion, does not love, because He cannot but be in communion and love." This means (and Zizioulas is quite clear about this) that the *existence of the Son and the Holy Spirit* is contingent upon the Father's free decision to give being to the Son and the Spirit; had he decided otherwise, he could have existed in solitary splendor. Furthermore, I think we have to conclude that *it is even now possible* for the Father to cease to love, to cease to sustain the existence of the Son and the Spirit, and even for the Father himself to cease to exist. (If not, then the "freedom of God" Zizioulas prizes so highly would be

---

[13] The critique which follows is indebted to the discussion in Thomas McCall, *Which Trinity?*, 197–215.

[14] Apparently "God" here refers to the Father, so "God owes His existence to the Father" is equivalent to "the Father owes His own existence to Himself." If on the contrary we took "God" here to refer to the entire Trinity, we would have the Trinity as the referent of singular pronouns and the subject of singular verbs in a way that is not found elsewhere in Zizioulas's treatise. At *Being as Communion*, 89, Zizioulas points out that in the Bible, "God = the Father."

compromised; this freedom may have existed in some realm outside of time, but it has long since been annulled by his decisions to exist, to love, and so on.) One is led to wonder what is the ground for Zizioulas's confidence (for I am sure he *is* confident about this) that the Father will not, even now, decide to reverse his former decisions and bring all existence to a close in a catastrophic divine murder-suicide? The answer to this *cannot* be that God, who is a loving God, could never do such a thing. For it is precisely Zizioulas's claim that the "nature of God," which of course includes his love, is *not* a constraint on the Father's decision-making, but is itself rather the result of his decisions.

We are led to ask, what has prompted Zizioulas to attribute such a radical and comprehensive freedom to the Father? I believe we get a clue to his answer when he states, "The ultimate challenge to the freedom of the person is the 'necessity' of existence" (p. 42). He goes on to cite Dostoevsky's Kirilov to the effect that the only way to demonstrate true freedom is to put an end to one's life in suicide. Otherwise, "how can a man be considered absolutely free when he cannot do other than accept his existence?" (p. 42). Indeed, the ability to negate one's own existence is an essential component of freedom; that is why this ability cannot be denied to God. But there is an alternative, the alternative that is actually exercised by the Father, namely to affirm and exercise the *love* in which he generates, and has communion with, the Son and the Holy Spirit.

> All this means that personhood creates for human existence the following dilemma: either freedom as love, or freedom as negation. The choice of the latter certainly constitutes an expression of personhood—only the person can seek negative freedom—but it is a negation nevertheless of its ontological content. For nothingness has no ontological content when the person is seen in the light of trinitarian theology. (p. 46)

This conception of freedom, however, comes at a heavy price. Consider Zizioulas's claim, cited above, "There is no true being without communion. Nothing exists as an 'individual' conceivable in itself. Communion is an ontological category." We now see that this is not a fundamental truth, as we may previously have assumed—at least, it is not the *most* fundamental truth. The *most* fundamental truth is the existence of the Father as a radically free person, a person who could have negated his own existence, with the consequence that there would be *nothing at all*—or (and this was the option that was actually taken) could have elected to live in loving communion with the Son and the Holy Spirit. Only *consequent upon* this initial, and all-important, decision is it the case that "there is no true being without communion." This is true, that is to say, contingent not only on that initial decision, but on the *continuance* of that decision on the Father's part, for inasmuch as he continues to be radically free, it remains the case that he could at any moment make any one of a number of decisions that would negate the ontological status of love and communion. (For instance, he could decree that all-out egoism rather than love would henceforth receive his approbation and support.) We can still say, if we like, that it is God's nature to be loving and good. But this is a "nature" which is eternally up for grabs, subject to change without notice for any or no reason. This, I submit, is not the God of the Christian tradition.

Nor is it the God of the Greek Fathers. For both Athanasius and the Cappadocians, God the Father wills the existence of the Son and the Holy Spirit. But this willing is not a choice between open alternatives, as though he could equally well have refrained from bringing about the existence of the other two Persons. Rather, it is a consequence of his nature as holy love. God's nature—*what God is*—is not something chosen arbitrarily, but rather something fundamental. Strangely, Zizioulas himself states that "The *homoousion* presupposes that *ousia* represents the ultimate ontological category" (p. 89n.). He contends that "Athanasius' relational notion of substances becomes through the creative work of the Cappadocians an ontology of personhood" (p. 89n.). Perhaps so—but even if this is correct, he surely cannot mean to be claiming that the Cappadocians rejected the *homoousion*. But precisely the *homoousion* is imperiled, if the existence of Son and Spirit depends on the Father in such a way that (a) the Father might never have willed their existence at all, and (b) the Father could at any moment annul the existence of both Son and Spirit. It is perfectly clear that, given that assumption, the Son and the Holy Spirit cannot have the same nature as the Father; in particular, they cannot be omnipotent, as he is. (Unless, to be sure, they also have the power to annul the existence of the Father and of each other. But in that case, none of the three will be omnipotent, as is shown by the following question: Does each of the three Persons have the power to resist annihilation, should another Person attempt to annihilate him?) On these assumptions, one theological disaster follows after another.

It seems clear that the source of this doctrine of freedom is not the Greek Fathers, but rather modern existentialism. In Zizioulas's account of the relation between divine freedom and the divine nature, one hears an echo of Sartre's "existence precedes essence." I don't mean to claim that there is direct dependence on Sartre; I have no evidence that this is the case. But the influence of existentialist modes of thought is clear enough; for this see the references in the text to Dostoevsky and to Heidegger (see p. 45n.). I submit that for the Greek Fathers the idea that the Father might have "chosen" not to be God, not to be holy and loving, not to have caused the existence of the Son and the Holy Spirit, would have been unintelligible.

It must be acknowledged that in this critique I have passed by a good deal of Zizioulas's subtle and complex dialectic. To discuss all that in detail would consume far more space than is available here. Nor have I even begun to explore his applications of trinitarian doctrine to soteriology, ecclesiology, and other aspects of Christian doctrine. But with regard to the central problem of the divine three-in-oneness, I believe the results are clear. The doctrine of radical divine freedom has got to go; once that has been done, many other possibilities remain open.

AFTERTHOUGHT AND TRANSITION

For all that has been said here, Moltmann and Zizioulas remain major figures of recent trinitarian thought. If we conclude that the best approach to the doctrine lies in some form of Social trinitarianism, many aspects of their views should prove helpful. Nevertheless, problems do remain. It can be argued that Moltmann faces serious difficulties because of his attempt to use the same concept of *perichoresis* to express both the union of the trinitarian Persons with one another, and their union with created persons. I have pointed out that Zizioulas's conception of absolute divine freedom leads to many difficulties; not least, it threatens to undermine even his cherished notion of "being as communion." Beyond this, it seems clear that neither of them has produced an accounting of the divine three-in-oneness that is equal in its depth and precision to what was achieved in the late fourth and early fifth centuries, by the Cappadocians and Augustine, let alone to what was done in the medieval period. If we do wish to get a better grip on this crucial topic, it may be that the best we can do is to turn to recent work on the Trinity by analytic philosophers.

14

Leftow: God Living Three Life-Streams

As we move from theologians such as Barth, Rahner, Moltmann, and Zizioulas to the writings of philosophers on the Trinity, changes of style and approach become evident. The philosophers we will be considering do not, in general, construct a broad case for the doctrine of the Trinity from scripture and tradition. Instead, they tend to take one or more traditional formulations of the doctrine as a starting point, and proceed from there to argue for the possibility of the doctrine as they construe it. They also, unsurprisingly, devote considerably more attention to the philosophical implications of saying that God is three Persons in a single divine nature—however they understand those concepts. As indicated in Chapter 11, the progression will be generally from views that are less sympathetic to those that are more sympathetic to Social trinitarianism.

The first philosopher to be addressed is Brian Leftow, a critic of Social trinitarianism[1] who puts forward what he terms "a Latin Trinity," or LT.[2] Leftow begins his exposition with quotations from the Athanasian Creed, the Creed of the Council of Toledo, and Aquinas. The latter wrote,

> among creatures, the nature the one generated receives is not numerically identical with the nature the one generating has ... But God begotten receives numerically the same nature God begetting has. (p. 305)[3]

---

[1] See Brian Leftow, "Anti Social Trinitarianism," in S. T. Davis, D. Kendall, and G. O'Collins (eds), *The Trinity: An Interdisciplinary Symposium on the Trinity* (Oxford: OUP, 1999), 203–49.

[2] Brian Leftow, "A Latin Trinity," *Faith and Philosophy*, 21/3 (July 2004), 304–33. Page numbers in the text refer to this article. An earlier (and longer) version of this critique may be found in "A Leftovian Trinity?," *Faith and Philosophy*, 26/2 (2009), 154–66. For further discussion, see Leftow's "Time-Travel and the Trinity," *Faith and Philosophy*, 29/3 (July 2012), 313–2; also my "Dancers, Rugby Players, and Triniarian Persons," 325–33, and Leftow's "On Hasker on Leftow on Hasker on Leftow," 334–9, both in that same issue. Leftow returned to the task of trinitarian theorizing in "Modes without Modalism," in P. van Inwagen and D. Zimmerman (eds), *Persons: Human and Divine* (Oxford: Clarendon Press, 2007), 357–75. This article presents essentially the same understanding of trinitarian doctrine as "A Latin Trinity," with additional metaphysical elaboration.

[3] The reference is to the *Summa Theologiae* Ia.39.5 ad 2.245a; Leftow's tr.

Leftow explains Thomas's talk of "natures" in terms of "tropes":

> Abel and Cain were both human. So they had the same nature, humanity. Yet each also had his own nature, and Cain's humanity was not identical with Abel's....On one parsing, this is because while the two had the same nature, they had distinct tropes of that nature. A trope is an individualized case of an attribute. Their bearers individuate tropes: Cain's humanity is distinct from Abel's just because it is Cain's, not Abel's.[4]

He then continues,

> With this term in hand, I now restate Thomas' claim: while both the Father and Son instance the divine nature (deity) they have but one trope of deity between them, which is God's. While Cain's humanity ≠ Abel's humanity, the Father's deity = the Son's deity = God's deity. But bearers individuate tropes. If the Father's deity is God's this is because the Father *just is* God: which last is what Thomas wants to say. (p. 305)

Leftow recognizes, however, that this poses a problem for his view:

> On LT, then, there clearly is just one God, but one wonders just how the Persons manage to be three. If the Father 'just is' God, it seems to follow that
>   (1) the Father = God.
>   If 'each single Person is wholly God in Himself', and both Son and Father have God's trope of deity, it seems also to follow that
>   (2) the Son = God.
>   But then since
>   (3) God = God,
>   it seems to follow that
>   (4) the Father = the Son,
>   and that on LT, there is just one divine Person. (p. 305)

Leftow goes on to explain why it seems impossible for a trinitarian doctrine to reject either or both of (1) and (2) and remain orthodox. (1) of course, is the view he has attributed to Thomas, and is the cornerstone of LT. As regards (2), he says, "Everything is either God, an uncreated object distinct from God or a creature" (p. 306). So if (2) is rejected, the only alternatives are that the Son is an uncreated object distinct from God, or that he is a creature, both clearly options Leftow would reject. He seems, then, to be firmly committed to the truth of both (1) and (2). For convenience, I will label (1)–(4) as the One Person Argument; finding a satisfactory answer to this argument becomes a major part of Leftow's agenda.

An important role is played in the exposition and defense of LT by an extended example featuring the Radio City Music Hall Rockettes:

> You are at Radio City Music Hall, watching the Rockettes kick in unison. You notice that they look quite a bit alike. But (you think) they must just be made up

---

[4] As was noted in Part I, I believe Leftow's rephrasing in terms of tropes is genuinely helpful, and I have adopted it in my own formulation of the issues concerning the Trinity.

to look that way. After all,...they certainly seem to be many different women. But appearances deceive. Here is the true story. All the Rockettes but one, Jane, called in sick that morning. So Jane came to work with a time machine her nephew had put together for the school science fair. Jane ran on-stage to her position at the left of the chorus line, linked up, kicked her way through the number, then ran off. She changed her makeup, donned a wig, then stepped into her nephew's Wells-o-matic, to emerge in the past, just before the Rockettes went on. She ran on-stage from a point just to the right of her first entry, stepped into line second from the chorus line's left, smiled and whispered a quip to the woman on her right, kicked her way through the number, then ran off. She then changed her makeup again...Can one person thus be wholly in many places at once? The short answer is: she is in many places at the same point in *our* lives, but not the same point in *hers*. If Jane travels in time, distinct segments of her life coincide with the same segment of ours. To put this another way, Jane's personal timeline intersects one point in ours repeatedly. (p. 307; second ellipsis in original)

Now, however, it becomes possible to construct an analogue for the One Person Argument (call this the One Rockette Argument):

in this story, there is among all the Rockettes just one trope of human nature. All tropes of human nature in the Rockettes are identical. But consider this argument:

1a. the leftmost Rockette = Jane.
2a. the rightmost Rockette = Jane.
3a. Jane = Jane.
So,
4a. the leftmost Rockette = the rightmost Rockette.

The argument appears sound, but doesn't shorten the chorus line. There is just one substance, Jane, in the chorus line. But there *is* also an extended chorus line, with many of *something* in it. Many what, one asks? Some philosophers think that Jane is a four-dimensional object, extended through time as well as space—that not Jane's life but Jane herself has earlier and later parts. If this is true, each Rockette is a temporal part of Jane. If (as I believe) Jane has no temporal parts, then not just a temporal part of Jane, but Jane as a whole, appears at each point in the chorus line, and what the line contains many of are segments or episodes of Jane's life-events.... What you see are many dancings of one substance.... Each Rockette is Jane. But in these many events, Jane is there many times over. (pp. 307–8)

And "If God as the Persons is relevantly like Jane as the Rockettes, then just as (1a)–(4a) did not shorten the chorus line, (1)–(4) do not collapse the Trinity" (p. 316). The One Person Argument, in other words, is "sound but irrelevant" (p. 316). We shall consider Leftow's reasons for these claims after we've examined some other features of his position.

At this point we need to examine the positive explanation Leftow gives concerning the nature of the trinitarian Persons. Here is what he says:

Suppose, then, that God's life has the following peculiar structure: at any point in our lives, three discrete parts of God's life are present. But this is not because one life's successive parts appear at once. Rather, it is because God always lives His life in three discrete strands at once, no event of His life occurring in more than one strand and no strand succeeding another. In one strand God lives the Father's life, in one the Son's, and in one the Spirit's. The events of each strand add up to the life of a Person. The lives of the Persons add up to the life God lives *as* the three Persons. There is one God, but He is many in the events of his life, as Jane was in the chorus line: being the Son is a bit like being the leftmost Rockette. (p. 312)

In a note, Leftow further clarifies this by stating that the strands do not have in common "any events composing His conscious life or involving His agency" (p. 330 n. 22). Furthermore, "every event in God's life is part of the Father-Son-Spirit chorus line; God does not live save as Father, Son and Spirit.... God's life always consists of three other things which count as entire ongoing lives" (p. 312).

But how is this multiplication of life-strands in God possible? To answer this, Leftow draws yet again on the Rockette story. What makes that story work, he tells us, is "the causal relations between her life-segments. These are segments of one individual's life not because they succeed one another in a timeline but because the right causal relations link them" (p. 313). But then "we can suppose that causal relations do the like without succession in the Trinitarian case: that is, we can suppose that causal relations between the event-streams involved are what make them all streams within one individual's life" (p. 314). These causal relations consist in the eternal "begetting" of the Son by the Father, and the eternal "spiration" of the Spirit from Father and Son. (Leftow observes that "Nobody has ever claimed to explain how these work, so I'm at no disadvantage if I do not either" (p. 314).) Leftow goes on to offer some fascinating reflections concerning the nature of the Persons and the distinction between them:

> If one asks what sort of persons the Persons are, on this account, the right answer is that they are whatever sort God is—the Persons just *are* God, as the Latin approach will have it.... Just as Jane has her own thoughts while she is the left- and rightmost Rockettes, God has His own thoughts as Father and Son. But just as Jane does not think her leftmost thoughts at the point in her life at which she is rightmost, God does not think His Father-thoughts at the points in His life at which He is Son. Just as Jane can token with truth "I am the leftmost Rockette" and "I am the rightmost," God can token with truth "I am the Father" and "I am the Son." But just as Jane cannot token both claims with truth at the same points in her life, God cannot token with truth "I am the Son" at points in His life at which He is Father. Just as Jane at the leftmost spot on the chorus line has no internal access to and is not thinking the thoughts she thinks at the rightmost spot, God as Father has no internal access to and is not thinking the thoughts of God as Son. So the Son is as distinct from the Father as the leftmost Rockette is from the rightmost, and the

Son's mind is as distinct from the Father's as the leftmost's is from rightmost's. (pp. 314–15)[5]

At this point we must guard against a misunderstanding of Leftow's view. It would be a mistake to suppose that, on his account, there are three distinct persons, Father, Son, and Holy Spirit, each of whom is the subject of one of the three "strands" in the divine life. To think that would be to overlook his assertion that the Persons "just *are* God"—that is, are identical with God. Rather, there is just *God,* who *as* Father thinks one series of thoughts, *as* Son thinks another series of thoughts, and *as* Spirit thinks yet a third series of thoughts. There are three "strands of divine life" but just *one* person who is living all three of these strands, namely God. The three trinitarian Persons, then, are God-*as*-Father, God-*as*-Son, and God-*as*-Holy Spirit. To repeat—and this is a point Leftow hammers home time after time—there is just *one* being involved, namely God.

Now that we have all this before us, it seems that Leftow's view presents an intriguing combination of elements from both Social trinitarianism and modalism. He has affirmed that, in the one life of God, there are three distinct strands of conscious experience, associated with Father, Son, and Holy Spirit. Social trinitarians will applaud this result, and will be most interested in seeing how Leftow has arrived at it and justified its possibility. But then he adds to this that there is really only *one* subject of this three-fold life, namely the very strange person we know as "God." It would certainly seem that this is a form of modalism; Father, Son, and Holy Spirit are each different *personae*—different "personations," we might say—in which the one person who is God lives his life. To be sure, the distinction of the "modes" is unusually rich in this case; most classical forms of modalism would not have postulated three wholly discrete streams of experience to correspond to the different modes. But each of the Persons "*just is*" God; there is just this one being experiencing in these different strands.

Social trinitarians will undoubtedly feel that the assertion that each of the three Persons is identical with the one person who is God undermines much of the promise that seemed to emerge from the recognition of three discrete strands of divine experience. In commenting on the Rockettes case, Leftow points out that something like personal relationships might be possible among the Rockettes, even if each of them is in fact Jane. She

has genuine interpersonal relations with herself in her other roles. She leans on herself for support, smiles to herself, talks (and talks back) to herself. The talk

---

[5] A referee observed that "the big disanalogy is that Jane-on-the-left and Jane-on-the-right do not exist at simultaneous points in Jane's life but (ignoring timelessness) the Trinitarian Persons do exist at simultaneous points in their lives." This is indeed an important difference; in order to bridge the gap Leftow must consider the different episodes in Jane's life and the different strands of experience in God's life as analogous; both constitute "points" in their respective lives. If one finds this analogy unconvincing, the story about Jane contributes rather little to our understanding of the doctrine of the Trinity.

may even be dialogue in the fullest sense. In changing makeup, wig, etc., Jane might well forget what she said when she was leftmost in the line, and so a remark she hears when she is one in from the left might well surprise her, and prompt a response she did not anticipate. (p. 308)

(He observes, however, that it is difficult to see how one trinitarian Person could surprise another.) All well and good, to be sure; clearly the possibility of personal relationships between the trinitarian Persons is one of the main advantages claimed for Social trinitarianism. But there seems to be something lacking in Jane's case. Suppose, for instance, that the rightmost Rockette, as she is leaving the stage, trips over a bouquet that has been carelessly tossed onto the stage by an admirer; falling, she suffers a nasty bruise. Without doubt, the other Rockettes (at least the ones nearby when she falls) will be full of sympathy at this untoward occurrence. They will gather around her, gently help her to her feet and back to the dressing room, say comforting things to her, summon medical help if needed, and so on. After all, each of them knows that it is *she herself* who has fallen; even if she isn't suffering the pain at that very moment, she soon enough will be. (But won't she be able to avoid the bouquet, now that she knows it is there? No, she won't, but I'll leave it to the friends of time travel to explain why not.) Still, there seems to be something qualitatively different between sympathizing *with oneself,* even with oneself during a different life-segment or in a different life-strand, and sympathizing with another person. The idea that the Persons of the Trinity love and commune with each other loses much of its appeal if it is all just a matter of the one person, namely God, loving and communing with himself. To be sure, it could be argued that judgments such as this one are misplaced—that even if they do hold where human relationships are concerned, they are inappropriate and incorrect when applied to the divine Persons. Most Social trinitarians, however, will undoubtedly respond with disappointment to this "self-relationship" model. Admittedly, the inherent attractiveness of the idea of love and communion between the trinitarian Persons is not by itself a sufficient grounding for a Social doctrine of the Trinity. But once one has done the hard conceptual work needed to secure the existence of three distinct strands of divine conscious experience, it seems a shame to spoil the effect by insisting that the relationships involved are all the relations of a single person to himself.

At this point, however, we need to consider Leftow's response to the One Person Argument. His attitude towards that argument, as well as to the One Rockette Argument, is complex and potentially confusing. On the one hand (as we've already noted), he says several times that these arguments are sound, but irrelevant; they do no damage to his position. But he also spends a considerable amount of time in discussing alternative readings of the arguments and contending that these alternative versions are *not* sound. So we need to get a grip on these different readings of the arguments. On what I shall term the "standard reading" of the arguments, '=' is interpreted to mean strict identity; it is governed by Leibniz's Law, sometimes known as the "indiscernibility of identicals," which states that, if x is identical with y, then anything true of x is true of y, and vice versa. Furthermore, the items flanking the identity sign are to be understood as *rigid designators*; they designate one and the same object in all situations. For instance, suppose we were to say, "The 44th President of the United States lived in Indonesia." US Presidents don't live in Indonesia, they reside in Washington, DC. But having fixed the reference of "44th President" to Barack Obama, we can refer to him as such throughout his life, even though he was not then President. The expression "44th President," *rigidly designates* Obama. Now as I've said, Leftow devotes considerable attention to "non-standard" readings of the One Person Argument in which the terms do not designate rigidly.[6] But please note: *Only the standard reading of the argument plays a role in the present discussion.* If Leftow proves to be right in his claim that the arguments so understood, even if sound, pose no threat to his position, we will make no attempt to raise difficulties based on the alternative readings. If on the other hand the standard reading is *not* innocuous, that will provide quite enough to occupy us without considering the alternative readings.

We will say no more here about the One Rockette Argument, which raises fascinating issues of its own that are not essential to our consideration of Leftow's view of the Trinity. Leftow's problem with the One Person Argument concerns, of course, the conclusion

(4) the Father = the Son,

a conclusion which is heretical by any orthodox trinitarian standard. Leftow, however, maintains that the "real force" of (4) is captured by

(4*) the substance who is the Father = the substance who is the Son,

the substance in question being simply God. On this interpretation, then, (4*) states simply that God = God, which no one can reasonably disagree with. Now, one's initial inclination is to object to this: what (1)–(3) entail is not (4*), but simply

(4) the Father = the Son.

This is perfectly clear and unambiguous; it states that the Son, the second trinitarian Person, is identical with the Father, the first trinitarian Person—a

---

[6] Strangely, Leftow thinks that he can interpret the statement, "Jane = the leftmost Rockette," in such a way that "leftmost Rockette" is non-rigid (it refers to Jane only while she is playing that role), yet '=' still signifies strict, Leibnizian identity. (See "Time-Travel and the Trinity.") But this is impossible. If "leftmost Rockette" is non-rigid, the statement "Jane = the leftmost Rockette," will be contingent; it will be true while Jane occupies the role in question, and false otherwise. But statements of strict identity must be necessarily true—at least, they must be true in any situation in which the object in question (i.e. Jane) exists. A thing cannot exist and fail to be identical with itself.

conclusion that is quite straightforwardly heretical. It is hard to see how one can legitimately assert that (4) does not mean what it very clearly says, but expresses instead the different proposition (4*).[7] If in formulating the argument (1)–(4) Leftow intended propositions different from the ones those formulas ordinarily express, he ought to have given us those other propositions from the start. Nevertheless, he continues to insist that (4), as he uses it, does *not* state the heretical proposition that the Father and the Son are identical with each other, but rather some other proposition; another suggested candidate is

> (4b) The God who is in some life the Father is also the God who is in some life the Son.[8]

We do not, however, find (at least, *I* don't find) any explanation of just how the formula (4) manages to express *that* proposition rather than the one (4) would most naturally be taken to express. Nor is there an explanation as to why the intended proposition was initially expressed in terms of the (at least) seriously misleading formula (4).

At this point I wish to propose a "friendly amendment" to Leftow's position—a way of describing the Trinity as he understands it that avoids some of the difficulties noted thus far. The urgent problem is that of avoiding the conclusion of the One Person Argument,

> (4) the Father = the Son.

Leftow thinks this conclusion is innocuous, but this can be so only if the words are given a novel interpretation, and it is not clear just what that interpretation is supposed to be. Taking the words in their ordinary sense the problem is real, and cannot be avoided so long as we assume a relation of identity to hold between God and the Father, and between God and the Son. So long as these assumptions are maintained, the entailment of (4) will go through.

What we need, then, is some way to understand "the Father is God," that does not posit strict identity between the items in question, and thus steers clear of the One Person Argument.[9] The Father, let us say, is identical with *God-living-the-Father-life-strand*, and so also with the Son and the Spirit. The hyphens are essential here; the referent of the expression is not God *simpliciter* but rather what we might term a *Personal aspect* of God; that is to say, God

---

[7] If anyone questions whether these are distinct propositions, notice that one can affirm (4) without subscribing to any kind of substance metaphysic. If the propositions are in fact logically equivalent, this is something that needs to be argued for—but this means they cannot be the very same proposition.

[8] See "On Hasker on Leftow on Hasker on Leftow."

[9] Another possibility, but one Leftow has explicitly rejected, states that each Rockette is a temporal part of Jane (see "A Latin Trinity," 307–8); apparently the trinitarian parallel would be to say that each Person is a Personal part of God. Whatever its other merits, this also would have the advantage of avoiding the One Person Argument.

insofar as he is living the Father-life-strand and not the Son-life-strand or the Spirit-life-strand.[10] So we do not get

   (1) the Father = God,

but rather

   (1′) the Father = God-living-the-Father-life-strand,

and similarly,

   (2′) the Son = God-living-the-Son-life-strand.

As a result, the One Person Argument does not get off the ground.[11] In fact, this rephrasing is suggested by something Leftow himself has said: "Each Person is just God, but God at a particular point on his personal timeline—God when He is living as the Father, as the Son, etc."[12] That is exactly what (1′) says, and it completely avoids the One Person Argument. It seems to me, in view of this, that replacing (1) with (1′) represents a substantial improvement.

   All this leads us to conclude that Leftow's LT thus modified is not formally heretical, as the unmodified version appeared to be from our earlier considerations. That is not to say, however, that all of the objections to the view have been avoided. There is, for instance, the very peculiar character of the personhood of God, as a single person who simultaneously enjoys three discrete, and mutually inaccessible, life-strands of experience. Still, this may not be viewed as an overly serious problem; the trinitarian nature of God, it may be said, should be expected to be mysterious and even peculiar.[13] More serious, at least in the eyes of some, is the aroma of modalism that still hangs around the proposal.[14] Earlier we noted Leftow's assertion that

[10] But does this really solve the problem? One referee comments: "This seems to me to refer to (the) God under the aspect of one life-strand. In that case, the reference of 'Father', 'Son', and 'Spirit' is still (the) God, though the senses of the designators differ." This however is incorrect. If we ask, "Does God-living-the-Father-life-strand also live the Son-life-strand?," the answer is No, whereas if we asked that question concerning God (simpliciter), the answer would be Yes.

[11] Similarly, (1a) is replaced by: (1a′) The leftmost Rockette = Jane-during-the-interval-t_n-to-t_{n+m}. (Here "n" and "n+m" represent indices on Jane's personal timeline—different indices, of course, for each Rockette.) This secures the result that each Rockette is "just Jane," but avoids the One Rockette Argument.

[12] "On Hasker on Leftow on Hasker on Leftow."

[13] But perhaps no one else has supposed it was peculiar in just this way. Leftow, by terming his view "Latin Trinitarianism," associates it with the traditional view associated with Augustine and Aquinas. According to medieval scholar Richard Cross, however, Leftow's "version of Trinitarianism is itself novel" ("Latin Trinitarianism," in McCall and Rea, *Philosophical and Theological Essays*, 213).

[14] In the final section of his paper, titled "The Menace of Modalism," Leftow defends his LT from the charge that it is a version of modalism. He cites several definitions of modalism from theological dictionaries, and insists that on these definitions, LT doesn't qualify. I don't disagree with this; modalism is standardly considered a heresy, and I have not claimed that LT (once it has been modified to avoid the One Person Argument) is heretical. I do think, however, that it has a modalist "flavor or aroma," and in support I adduce the points made in the text. Readers are invited to consider for themselves whether this "flavor" renders the view less plausible and attractive.

Just as Jane can token with truth "I am the leftmost Rockette" and "I am the rightmost," God can token with truth "I am the Father" and "I am the Son." But just as Jane cannot token both claims with truth at the same points in her life, God cannot token with truth "I am the Son" at points in His life at which He is Father. (p. 315)

But here a distinction seems to be called for. When Jane is at the left end of the line, she cannot truthfully say, "I am the rightmost Rockette," if she means by that, *"I am now (in this segment of my personal timeline) performing the role of the rightmost Rockette."* She can, however, state in perfect truthfulness, *"I am the person who now (in the public timeline) is performing the role of the rightmost Rockette."* Similarly, God as Father cannot truthfully say, "I am the Son," if he means by that, *"I am now (in this life-strand) experiencing the Son-life-strand."* He can, however, say truthfully that *"I am the person [not, the trinitarian Person] who experiences the Son-life-strand."* He cannot say, "I, the Father, suffered and died on the cross." But he can say, "I am the person who, *as the Son,* suffered and died on the cross." The difference between the Persons is a good deal less pronounced than many have supposed it to be. In the Gospels, we have the spectacle of God-as-Son *praying to himself,* namely to God-as-Father. Perhaps most poignant of all (and this should be no surprise) are the words of abandonment on the Cross: "My God, why have you forsaken me?" On the view we are considering, this comes out as *"Why have I-as-Father forsaken myself-as-Son?"* To some of us, this just doesn't seem to be what the Gospels are saying.

If these objections strike you as formidable, then you will not find Leftow's LT to present an attractive or plausible account of the Trinity. Unlike the One Person Argument, the objections sketched above can't be avoided by any minor modification; they are integral to Leftow's trinitarianism. Nevertheless, the view overall is not entirely without promise. The idea that a single divine substance can be the locus of three distinct streams of consciousness—indeed, of three *minds*[15]—is one we may, in the end, be happy to avail ourselves of.

---

[15] Recall: "the Son's mind is…distinct from the Father's" (p. 315).

15

Van Inwagen: The Trinity and Relative Identity

One of the more impressive analytic contributions to the trinitarian discussion is Peter van Inwagen's essay, "And Yet They are Not Three Gods, But One God."[1] Van Inwagen begins with an eloquent account of the importance of the doctrine of the Trinity for Christian faith and life. He also acknowledges the force of the logical challenge brought against the doctrine:

> Must not Jew and Muslim and unbeliever join in demanding of us that we disclose the ill-concealed secret of all the Christian ages: That we are mere polytheists? Or if we are not mere polytheists, then are we not something worse: polytheists engaged in a pathetic attempt to remain loyal to the God of Israel through sheer force of reiterated logical contradiction? For do we not say all of the following things? There is one divine Being, but there are three distinct Persons, each of whom is a divine Being; and the one divine Being is a Person, though not a fourth Person in addition to those three; nor is he any one of the three. (p. 218)

Van Inwagen's initial response to this challenge is to remind us that the doctrine has always been described as a mystery, and "If one is unable to answer satisfactorily questions posed by a mystery—well, what should one expect?" (p. 218). Furthermore, "As to alleged demonstrations of contradiction—well, our faith is: There is some way to answer these demonstrations, whether or not we can understand it" (p. 219). So if we are unable to answer the challenges to the doctrine, then we ought simply to continue to accept the doctrine as a mystery in spite of the challenges. To be sure, nonbelievers in the Trinity will take this as evidence that the doctrine is incoherent and not worthy of belief. But perhaps even they can be brought to acknowledge that "If the Holy Spirit really existed and had led the mind of the Church to the doctrine of the Trinity, *then* might not the Trinitarian be in a position analogous to that of

---

[1] In T. Morris (ed.), *Philosophy and the Christian Faith* (Notre Dame, IN: University of Notre Dame Press, 1988), 241–78; repr. in McCall and Rea, *Philosophical and Theological Essays*, 217–48. Page references in this chapter are to the latter volume.

the physicist to whom nature had revealed the doctrine of the [wave-particle] Duality?" (p. 220).

He admits, however, that "I could not help being disappointed as a philosopher if there were no good, humanly accessible replies to the pointed questions raised by the doctrine of the Trinity" (p. 220). Because of this, he has written an essay whose "main purpose is to explore one way of responding to those questions." But he adds,

> I should say, first, that I do not endorse the way of looking at the Trinity I shall ask you to consider, but I do think it is worth considering.... I should say, secondly, that I do not propose to *penetrate* the mystery of the Trinity. I propose to state the doctrine of the Trinity ... in such a way that it is demonstrable that no formal contradiction can be derived from the thesis that God is three persons and, at the same time, one being. I do not propose to *explain* how God can be three persons and one being. (pp. 220–1).

These qualifications need to be kept in mind as we examine van Inwagen's presentation of the doctrine.

The key to his presentation is to be found in the philosophical doctrine of "relative identity," a doctrine proposed by Peter Geach.[2] It should be said at the outset that van Inwagen's presentation of his solution is quite detailed and technical. Much of this technical discussion will not be rehearsed here. Instead, I shall attempt to convey the central ideas of his treatment in a way that will make them accessible to as broad a readership as possible; those who want the details are advised to seek them in van Inwagen's own presentation. In any case, the questions raised and the criticisms that will be made do not hinge on the omitted technical details. With these cautions in mind, we can proceed.

We begin by recalling the classical, non-relative concept of identity. I am speaking, of course, of *numerical* identity, not of qualitative identity, such as that of two "identical" new pennies. Numerical identity is a relation each thing has to itself, and only to itself—as Joseph Butler said, "Every thing is what it is, and not another thing." So stated, the notion may seem trivial, but it is anything but that. For one thing, identity statements may be quite informative: when the same object has been encountered under a different name, or under different circumstances, it may be far from obvious that the two items thus encountered are one and the same. (Clark Kent is, in fact, identical with Superman, but his fellow-workers at the *Daily Planet* are unaware of this fact.) Another important feature of identity is what is sometimes called "Leibniz's Law," also referred to as the "indiscernibility of identicals": If x and y are identical, then anything that is true of x is also true of y, and vice versa. (It is true

---

[2] See "Identity," and "Identity—A Reply," in Peter Geach, *Logic Matters* (Oxford: Basil Blackwell, 1972), 238–49; and "Ontological Relativity and Relative Identity" in M. K. Munitz (ed.), *Logic and Philosophy* (New York: NYU Press, 1973).

of Clark Kent that he sometimes flies through the air in a colorful costume with an "S" emblazoned on his chest, and it is true of Superman that he is consumed with unfulfilled love for Lois Lane.)

And now for relative identity. The proponents of relative identity typically contend that the classical, Leibnizian notion of identity rests on a mistake: the failure to notice that "identity" is always *relative to a kind*—to a "sortal," as philosophers are wont to say. So the perspicuous way to talk about identity is not in statements such as "Samuel Clemens is identical with Mark Twain," but rather in statements like "Samuel Clemens is *the same man as* Mark Twain." Sometimes the sortal may be understood rather than expressed, but it must always be there in the background, if the identity statement is to make sense. The importance of this lies in the fact that a pair of items may be identical relative to one sortal, but non-identical relative to another. As a possible example (one taken from the literature on relative identity), van Inwagen considers a situation in which a lump of clay has been formed by a potter into a vase. Applying relative identity to this case, one might say that the vase and the lump of clay are identical relative to the sortal, *quantity of matter*, but the vase and the lump are not identical relative to the sortal, *items less than one hour old*. (The vase has just been formed, but the lump of clay has existed for a long time.) But while this example illustrates the idea of relative identity, van Inwagen does not himself endorse it, because there are other, perfectly good ways of describing the situation that need not involve relative identity. For instance, one can say that there is nothing there but the lump of clay, which always remains identical with itself, but which has temporarily become vase-shaped.

Now with this in place (and with apologies to van Inwagen for the many important technical details that have been omitted), we are ready for the application to the Trinity. We can say, in effect,[3] that "The Father is the *same Being* as the Son, but the Father is not the *same Person* as the Son." And this having been said, we are able to go on and reconstruct the entire doctrine of the Trinity. Van Inwagen gives the appropriate relative-identity formulations of the following trinitarian assertions, among others:

(1) There is (exactly) one God.

(2) There are (exactly) three divine Persons.

(3) There are three divine Persons in one divine Being. (p. 243)

He proceeds to show how statements about the "begetting" of the Son and the "procession" of the Holy Spirit can be expressed in terms of relative identity. And he goes on to prove that, within the system of relative-identity logic, no contradiction can be derived from any of the trinitarian statements.

---

[3] Only "in effect," because the accurate statement of this idea in the logic of relative identity involves complications that are not addressed in the present discussion.

But what of "absolute" or classical identity? Van Inwagen observes that "it seems to be the consensus among the friends of relative identity that classical identity does not exist" (p. 232). However, he prefers to take no position on the question: "In the sequel...I shall neither assume that classical identity exists nor that it does not exist" (p. 233). (As we shall see later on, this indecision creates a problem for van Inwagen's view.)

One final question is, where does van Inwagen stand with regard to the antithesis between Social and anti-Social theories of the Trinity? So far as his formal theory is concerned, the answer must be that the theory takes no stand on the question. For in stating the theory he introduces "is the same being as" and "is the same person as" as *undefined predicates*—that is, the theory itself says nothing about their meaning: in particular, it does not answer the question, "What is a trinitarian Person?" But when we turn to his interpretive remarks, a clearer answer seems to emerge. In his opening remarks he states that, of the two main trinitarian heresies modalism and tritheism, "it is Tritheism that I shall risk" (p. 223). He quickly dismisses the claim (made universally by anti-Social trinitarians) that "'person' in Trinitarian theology does not mean what it means in everyday life or in the philosophy of mind or even in non-Trinitarian applications of this word to God" (p. 224). Near the end of his paper, he asks, "Have I fallen into Tritheism?" (p. 246). He observes that "Perhaps the most objectionable—I do not say the only objectionable—feature of polytheism is that if one believes that Zeus and Poseidon are real and are two divine beings and two divine persons, one must admit that one has no guarantee that Zeus and Poseidon will not demand contrary things of one" (p. 246). He answers this by explaining how, within his relative-identity formulation of the doctrine, the danger of conflicting demands by the trinitarian Persons can be ruled out. But the fact that such conflicts are even conceptually possible suggests that, for him, the trinitarian Persons are indeed "distinct centers of knowledge, will, love, and action." Does this mean, then, that van Inwagen must be classified as a Social trinitarian? We need to recall, at this point, that van Inwagen himself *does not endorse* his relative-identity formulation of the doctrine of the Trinity. He presents this formulation as a defensive strategy, seeking to show that the doctrine can be formulated in a way that is not contradictory. He does not, however, commit himself to the correctness of the formulation, and this refusal to commit may also apply to the remarks about the Persons cited above. Fortunately, however, van Inwagen has made additional statements in correspondence that clarify the situation, and permit us to affirm that, in the sense of "Social trinitarian" assumed throughout the present work, van Inwagen is indeed a Social trinitarian.[4]

---

[4] His remarks include the following: "I'd say that 'person' is the concept marked out by pronouns like 'he', 'she', (as opposed to 'it'), 'who' (as opposed to 'which' and 'that'), and 'someone' (as opposed to 'something'). Alternatively, a person is something that can be addressed—a person is a 'thou'.... If you want a Chisholm-style definition: x is the same person as y $=_{df}$ x is someone and y is also someone—but not someone else. So, I would say, for example, that the Father is someone

CRITICISM AND ASSESSMENT

Has van Inwagen solved the logical problem of the Trinity? Before we answer in the affirmative, we need to consider some objections to his relative-identity treatment of the doctrine—objections which may be at least partly responsible for his unwillingness to endorse his own proposal. For our purposes, there are five such objections that stand out.

(1) Relative identity is rejected by most logicians

While relative identity has distinguished defenders, it is also true that a strong majority of philosophers and logicians who have considered the matter do not support the notion. According to the majority, classical identity is a perfectly clear, and extremely useful, notion, one that does not need to be replaced by relative identity. They would say, furthermore, that the relative-identity assertion "Samuel Clemens is *the same man as* Mark Twain" is equivalent to "Samuel Clemens is a man, Mark Twain is a man, and Samuel Clemens = Mark Twain," where '=' expresses classical identity. But if relative-identity statements are treated this way, the notion of relative identity becomes superfluous, since it will never be the case that two items are identical relative to one sortal but distinct relative to another sortal.

Now, the fact that relative identity is unpopular does not mean that it must be abandoned; there are many situations in which it is perfectly reasonable and appropriate for a philosopher to maintain a view that the majority of her colleagues reject. (Belief in the existence of God would seem to be an example of this!) On the other hand, if one is engaged in the defense of a contested belief such as the doctrine of the Trinity, it would certainly be more helpful if the defense could be conducted in terms of concepts that are themselves widely accepted as coherent and philosophically useful. This point is underscored by the second objection, as follows.

(2) Relative identity has no useful application outside of theology

This at any rate is van Inwagen's view; he states, "As far as I am able to tell, RI-logic has no utility outside Christian theology" (p. 234). We have already seen that he declines to endorse the example of the vase and the lump of clay, and he is similarly unimpressed with other examples that have been proposed

and the Son is also someone—but someone else. I would also say that the Father is a 'thou' to the Son and the Son is a 'thou' to the Father (that is, each can address the other: 'Thou art my beloved son, and this day have I begotten thee'; 'Why hast thou forsaken me?').... If these statements make me a Social Trinitarian, so be it" (from private correspondence).

in the natural world. But if this is so, one is in the position, not only of advocating a variant logic which has little support among logicians generally, but of advocating it when its *only* useful application is precisely to the theological doctrines one is seeking to defend. In such a situation, it is difficult to avoid the suspicion that one is engaging in special pleading. Aware of this, van Inwagen avails himself of a parallel with "quantum logic," a variant logic some have advocated as a way of dealing with the wave-particle duality in quantum mechanics, in order to avoid the apparent contradiction involved in saying that the same entity is both a wave and a particle. The experimental results seem to assure us that the wave-particle duality is a reality, and if so then a modified logic may be the best way to account for it. In the same vein, if one is confident that the Church has received divine guidance in its adherence to the doctrine of the Trinity, a novel type of logic that enables one to state that doctrine without contradiction is worthy of serious consideration.

This may well be true, but there is another possibility that van Inwagen does not consider. One might suppose that, whereas the experimental phenomena indicating wave-particle duality are real and are not to be denied, the theory describing those phenomena may be in an imperfect state which needs to be improved upon; one would then hope that the apparent contradiction would disappear without our having to take the drastic step of modifying our logic.[5] The parallel supposition with regard to the Trinity would be this: The revelation of God in Jesus Christ, upon which the doctrine of the Trinity is ultimately based, is true and reliable. But the formulations of the doctrine which created the contradictions van Inwagen is concerned with need to be (and, one would hope, can be) improved in such a way as to remove the contradictions without invoking a variant form of logic.

The third objection is best stated in the form of a question.

(3) Does relative identity enable us to understand the doctrine of the Trinity?

Or perhaps better, *to what extent* does relative identity enable us to understand the doctrine? This question picks up from van Inwagen's admission that he does not intend to "penetrate" the doctrine or to "explain" how it is that God can be three Persons but only one Being. But putting it this way may still understate the difficulty. Take the key assertion, "The Father is the *same Being* as the Son, but the Father is not the *same Person* as the Son." As I consider that sentence, I can in one sense understand it; that is, I understand the individual words,

---

[5] For what it is worth, it is my impression that at the present time, a quarter-century after van Inwagen's paper was written, there is considerably less interest than there was then in a revised system of logic by which to account for quantum mechanics.

and I can see that the words are assembled in a way that conforms to the rules of grammar. But when I try to conceive of the state of affairs the sentence affirms to exist, I draw a blank. I simply do not grasp what the relation between the Father and the Son is supposed to be, according to this sentence. To the extent that sentences such as this are central, on the relative-identity formulation, to the doctrine as a whole, I cannot really say that I understand the doctrine as so formulated—though I do understand *some* of the sentences involved in the doctrine. (For instance, "The Son is a person.") So if the RI-formulation of the doctrine is the correct one, there may well be some doubt as to whether it is even *possible* for me to believe the doctrine, since I cannot believe propositions that I am unable to grasp. (To be sure, I could still believe, on authority, that *the Church's doctrine of the Trinity is true*. But this does not seem to be enough; more than this, I should think, is expected of us.)

This objection is certainly not conclusive. Someone else may be able to understand what I find myself unable to understand; we sometimes need to be reminded that the inference from "I don't understand so-and-so" to "So-and-so is unintelligible" is invalid. Or it could be that I am being too fastidious in what I require in order to say that I "understand" the doctrine of the Trinity. Nevertheless, the objection seems to me to have some force, and I record it here in case others might find themselves in a similar situation.

One of the more astute critics of relative-identity trinitarianism is Michael Rea. In order to formulate his criticisms, he first divides relative-identity trinitarians into two camps, depending on their attitude towards two key principles:

> (RI1) States of affairs of the following sort are possible: x is an F, y is an F, x is a G, y is a G, x is the same F as y, but x is not the same G as y.
> (RI2) Either absolute (classical) identity does not exist, or statements of the form "$x = y$" are to be analyzed in terms of statements of the form "x is the same F as y" rather than the other way around.[6]

What Rea terms the "pure" RI strategy for the Trinity embraces both of these principles. (He observes that a doctrine that fails to affirm (RI2)—i.e. a doctrine in which absolute identity exists and does not need to be defined in terms of something else—is not really a doctrine in which *identity* is relative, though such a doctrine may recognize "sameness relations" other than identity.) On the other hand, the "impure" RI strategy affirms (RI1) but not (RI2); thus, it allows that classical identity does exist and does not need to be defined in terms of relative identity. However, it insists that "the relations expressed by 'is God' and 'is distinct from' in [the doctrine of the Trinity]

---

[6] From Michael C. Rea, "The Trinity," in T. P. Flint and M. C. Rea (eds), *The Oxford Handbook of Philosophical Theology* (Oxford: OUP, 2009), 417.

are relations like *being the same God as* and *being a distinct Person from*, respectively."[7] Having thus divided the field of RI trinitarians, Rea proceeds to offer one criticism of each strategy; these are the fourth and fifth in our series of objections.

(4) Criticism of the impure strategy

Any RI-trinitarian is going to want to say that

(Q) The Son is not the same Person as the Father, but the Son is the same Being as the Father.

Rea argues, however, that if absolute identity exists, it is highly plausible that

(P) If x and y are non-identical, then x is not the same being as y.

In support of this, he states that "'Being' is plausibly the most general sortal, on a par with sortals like 'entity', 'thing', and 'object'. Thus, 'x is (absolutely) distinct from y' seems to be synonymous with 'x is not the same being (thing, entity, object) as y.' If this is right, then P is analytic."[8] This, however, entails that the RI-trinitarian assertion Q is necessarily false; since Father and Son are distinct Persons, they cannot be absolutely identical, and if they are absolutely distinct, then (according to P) they cannot be the same being.[9]

Now a "pure" RI-theorist can resist this argument; she might point out that "nonidentical" in P (symbolized by "$x \neq y$") is the negation of classical identity, which on her view does not exist; thus P fails to express a genuine assertion and should be rejected. But the "impure" RI-theorist, who does not reject classical identity, cannot take this line.[10] There is, however, another tack that might be taken by the impure theorist: he might provide a story that enables us to understand "x is the same being as y" in a way that is not inconsistent with "x is (absolutely) distinct from y." Rea's conclusion, therefore, is not that the impure strategy is necessarily doomed to failure, but rather that, in order for it to succeed, "some such story is needed and has not so far been offered by anyone who wishes to pursue the impure RI strategy."[11]

---

[7] Michael C. Rea, "Relative Identity and the Doctrine of the Trinity," *Philosophia Christi*, 5 (2003), 431–46; repr. in McCall and Rea, *Philosophical and Theological Essays*, 249–62; quotation from p. 255 in the latter volume.

[8] Rea, "Relative Identity," in McCall and Rea, *Philosophical and Theological Essays*, 258.

[9] As with van Inwagen, I am simplifying Rea's argument considerably. My apologies to the author for this; unsatisfied readers are urged to consult the original article.

[10] This is what I had in mind by saying that van Inwagen's failure to take a stand on the existence of classical identity creates a problem for him.

[11] Rea, "Relative Identity," in McCall and Rea, *Philosophical and Theological Essays*, 259. In the next chapter, we shall see that Rea and Jeffrey Brower have undertaken to tell such a story, and thereby to rescue the impure RI strategy.

(5) Criticism of the pure strategy

Rea's criticism of the pure strategy is not that it is logically inconsistent, but rather that it seems to presuppose an "antirealist metaphysic" whose acceptance would be "catastrophic." This worry is illustrated by a quotation from Michael Dummett, who is concerned about the interpretation of the logical variables (expressions such as "x" and "y," representing individual objects) presupposed by Geach's theory of relative identity. Dummett states,

> [I]t seems that Geach means us to picture that over which the variables range as an amorphous lump of reality, in itself not articulated into distinct objects. Such an articulation may be accomplished in any one of many different ways; we slice up reality into distinct individual objects by selecting a particular criterion of identity.[12]

The reason for this lies in Geach's insistence that identity statements only make sense if we have first specified the sortal concept in relation to which identity is being asserted. The point is bolstered by quotations from Nicholas Griffin, another relative-identity theorist, and from Geach himself. Finally, Rea offers an example to illustrate both the problem and its seriousness:

> Imagine two theories: one, T_1, which includes the sortal "lump of clay" but no artifact sortals (like "statue" or "bowl"), and another, T_2, which includes the sortals "lump of clay," "statue," and "bowl," and, furthermore, treats statues and bowls that have been made from the same lump of clay as distinct items. Now suppose a T_1-theorist and a T_2-theorist watch a sculptor take a lump of clay and make first (what the T_2-theorist would call) a statue, then a bowl. By the lights of the T_1-theorist, the sculptor does not manage to generate or destroy anything. What the T_2-theorist might call "the statue" and "the bowl" are identical. By the lights of the T_2-theorist, however, statue and bowl are distinct. But, obviously, *both* cannot be right. Thus, we have a problem. One way out is to say that identity is theory-relative: the bowl and statue are the same lump of clay; they are not the same bowl or statue; and there is simply no fact about whether they are absolutely identical or distinct. But if we do say this (taking very seriously the claim that there is *no* theory-independent fact about *what* there is or about how many things there are in the various regions occupied by what the T_1-theorist calls the "lump of clay"), then we commit ourselves to the view that the very existence of things like statues, bowls, and lumps of clay depends upon the theories that recognize them. This is antirealism.
>
> Many philosophers are attracted to antirealism, but accepting it as part of a solution to the problem of the Trinity is disastrous. For clearly orthodoxy will not permit us to say that the very existence of Father, Son, and Holy Spirit is a *theory-dependent* matter. Nor will it permit us to say that the distinctness of the divine Persons is somehow relative to our ways of thinking and theorizing.[13]

---

[12] Michael Dummett, *Frege: Philosophy of Language* (London: Harper & Row, 1973), 563; quoted by Rea, "Relative Identity," in McCall and Rea, *Philosophical and Theological Essays*, 254.

[13] Rea, "Relative Identity," in McCall and Rea, *Philosophical and Theological Essays*, 260.

It is time to sum up. At this point I have to confess that, while van Inwagen's development of RI-trinitarianism is elegant and technically admirable, I do not find it at all persuasive as a solution to the logical problem of the Trinity. It seems to me that I do perfectly well understand statements involving classical identity, and I feel no need to replace this with a version of relative identity. I am not certain whether the pure RI strategy must commit one to antirealism, as Rea suspects; certainly he is right that a "solution" to the problem of the Trinity that involves antirealism about the divine Persons is completely unacceptable. Rea's criticism of the impure strategy is likewise compelling, but there is the possible way out that Rea suggests: perhaps a way can be found to understand "x is the same being as y" that does not commit us to holding that x and y are identical. Since Rea's version of this strategy is the topic of the next chapter, I shall say no more about it here.

16

Brower and Rea: Sameness in Number without Identity

The solution to the logical problem of the Trinity advanced by Jeffrey Brower and Michael Rea[1] develops directly out of Rea's critique of relative-identity trinitarianism, which I examined in the previous chapter. As we saw, relative-identity trinitarians affirm that

> (Q) The Son is not the same Person as the Father, but the Son is the same Being as the Father.

Rea divides relative-identity trinitarians into two camps, depending on whether or not they recognize classical or "absolute" identity without requiring that it be defined in terms of relative identity—i.e. whether or not they affirm:

> (RI2) Either absolute (classical) identity does not exist, or statements of the form '$x = y$' are to be analyzed in terms of statements of the form 'x is the same F as y' rather than the other way around. (Rea, p. 417)

Those who affirm (RI2), and thus deny the independent existence of classical identity, are termed "pure" RI-strategists, while those who accept classical identity along with relative identity are "impure" RI-strategists.

As we have seen, Rea rejects (RI2), and with it the pure RI-strategy for the Trinity. This rejection is partly because he simply doesn't find the arguments against classical identity convincing. But also, and more importantly, he is convinced that the pure strategy commits its adherents to an antirealist metaphysic that is incompatible with trinitarian orthodoxy. It just will not do to say that the existence of Father, Son, and Holy Spirit is dependent on our theorizing!

---

[1] Jeffrey E. Brower and Michael C. Rea, "Material Constitution and the Trinity," *Faith and Philosophy*, 22/1 (Jan. 2005), 57–76, referenced with "Brower and Rea" and page numbers; and Michael C. Rea, "The Trinity," in Flint and Rea, *Oxford Handbook of Philosophical Theology*, 403–29, referenced with "Rea" and page numbers.

Not that the impure strategy is home free. That strategy is threatened by the apparent plausibility of

(P) If x and y are non-identical, then x is not the same being as y.[2]

If (P) holds, then (Q), the key assertion of relative-identity trinitarianism, is doomed: since the Son is not the same Person as the Father, he cannot be identical with the Father and cannot be the same Being as the Father. In order to save (Q), then, the impure RI-strategist must find a way to undermine (P). And the way to do that, Rea suggests, is to provide a meaning for "is the same being as" which does not entail that if x and y are the same being they must be identical. This, then, is the task Brower and Rea have undertaken in their own proposal.

Rea begins his exposition by setting out the problem for trinitarian theology for which his and Brower's model provides the solution. He then proffers relative-identity trinitarianism as the solution to that problem. Finding that the relative-identity solution still leaves us with unresolved mystery, he turns to the problem of material constitution for further insight. But material constitution, according to Brower and Rea, is best understood in terms of the Aristotelian notion of "sameness in number without identity." We will need to follow these developments in some detail.

Rea begins by setting out the "three central tenets" of the doctrine of the Trinity:

(T1) There is exactly one God, the Father almighty.
(T2) Father, Son, and Holy Spirit are not identical.
(T3) Father, Son, and Holy Spirit are consubstantial (Rea, p. 405).

He then presents an argument purporting to show that these tenets generate a contradiction. The key assumption of that argument is

(P1) Necessarily, if x and y are not identical then x and y are not numerically the same substance.

But (P1) can be rejected if we embrace the doctrine of relative identity, as formulated in the principle:

(RI1) States of affairs of the following sort are possible: x is an F, y is an F, x is a G, y is a G, x is the same F as y, but x is not the same G as y. (Rea, p. 417)

Rea notes, however, that (RI1) by itself creates a problem for the understanding of statements about sameness. We cannot, given (RI1), interpret sameness statements in terms of identity, but if not we need some other way to understand such statements, which (RI1) does not supply. In order to meet this need, Rea turns to the notion of constitution. He imagines that a contractor has

---

[2] Rea, "Relative Identity," in McCall and Rea, *Philosophical and Theological Essays*, 258.

fashioned a stone so that it is at once a supporting pillar for a building and a statue. We have, then, both a statue and a pillar. But it would be strange to say that the contractor has made two material objects that are simply located in exactly the same spot at the same time—though Rea acknowledges that some philosophers do in fact say just that. Still, the pillar and the statue are not identical, as is shown by the fact that it would be possible to destroy the statue (e.g. by chipping away all the distinctive features that make the statue recognizable as such) without thereby destroying the pillar. Rea concludes,

> Thus, what we want to say is that the statue and the pillar are *the same material object*, even though they are *not identical*. If we do say this, we are committing ourselves to (RI1). But we can make (RI1) intelligible by adding that all it means to say that two things are the same material object at a time is that those two things share all the same physical matter at that time. (Rea, p. 418)

In thus appealing to the notion of constitution, Rea has in mind a particular solution of the problem of material constitution.[3] For further elucidation on this point we turn to the earlier article on the Trinity jointly authored by Rea along with Jeffrey Brower. According to Brower and Rea, the problem of material constitution arises because we have strong intuitions that support

> (MC) In the region occupied by a bronze statue, there is a statue and there is a lump of bronze; the lump is not identical with the statue (the statue but not the lump would be destroyed if the lump were melted down and recast in the shape of a disc); but only one material object fills that region. (Brower and Rea, p. 62)

If we are to honor this intuition, we need to make sense of the idea that the statue and the lump are one material object—i.e. they are "one in number"—yet not identical. For help with this they turn to Aristotle's doctrine of "accidental unities." Aristotle's ontology includes entities some have termed "kooky"; an example of such an entity is seated-Socrates. They write,

> Seated-Socrates is an 'accidental unity'—a unified thing that exists only by virtue of the instantiation of an accidental (non-essential) property (like seatedness) by a substance (like Socrates).... Accidental sameness, according to Aristotle, is just the relation that obtains between an accidental unity and its parent substance. (Brower and Rea, p. 60)

Seated-Socrates and Socrates *simpliciter* are not the same in all respects—the latter, but not the former, sometimes stands or walks—but they nevertheless

---

[3] Interestingly, Rea's exposition does not include the word "constitution." On his view, however, whenever two objects are each composed at a time by all of the same parts, they mutually constitute one another. The point of Rea's solution is that it denies the identity of objects that constitute each other (thus resolving the "problem of material constitution," which arises when identity is asserted), but avoids recognizing co-located material objects, which Rea (along with many others) regards as extremely counter-intuitive. (See Michael Rea, "The Problem of Material Constitution," *Philosophical Review,* 104 (1995), 525–52.)

count as one object; it would be absurd to suppose that Socrates creates a whole new object just by sitting down.

Brower and Rea acknowledge that we might well be reluctant to admit objects such as seated-Socrates into our ontology. But, they add,

> [W]e (fans of common sense) believe in many things relevantly *like* seated-Socrates. That is, we believe in things that are very plausibly characterized as hylomorphic compounds whose matter is a *familiar material object* and whose form is an accidental property. For example, we believe in fists and hands, bronze statues and lumps of bronze, cats and heaps of cat tissue, and so on.... This last point is important because the things we have listed as being relevantly like accidental unities and their parent substances are precisely the sorts of things belief in which gives rise to the problem of material constitution.... Socrates and seated-Socrates are, as [Aristotle] would put it, *one in number* but not *one in being.* They are distinct, but they are to be counted as one material object. (Brower and Rea, p. 61)

And this, they claim, provides a solution to the problem of material constitution, a solution that can be applied to the statue and the pillar. So we can say that "the statue and the pillar are numerically the same substance, even though they... would not share the same form, or nature. They would be numerically the same substance, one material object, but different form-matter compounds. They would be the same without being identical" (Rea, p. 419).

To amplify this further, note that each of the statue and the pillar is a form-matter compound; in each case the same underlying matter is configured by a different form.

> This gives us two compounds, a statue and a pillar. Each is *a* substance. Thus, the statue and the pillar are emphatically *not* mere aspects of a common substance.... Furthermore, each is distinct from the other. But they are, nevertheless, the *same* substance.... You might think that if there is just one substance, then we ought to be able to ask whether *it*—the one substance—is essentially a mere statue or a mere pillar (or perhaps essentially a statue-pillar). But this thought is incorrect. On the present view, terms such as 'it' and 'the one substance' are ambiguous: they might refer to the statue, or they might refer to the pillar. For again, statue and pillar are distinct, though not distinct *substances*.... On the view I am defending, if x and y share the same matter in common, and x is a primary substance and y is a primary substance, then x and y are the *same* primary substance, despite being different matter-form compounds. (Rea, p. 419)

With all this in place, we can proceed to the application to trinitarian doctrine:

> In the case of the divine persons, we have three properties—*being the Father, being the Son, and being the Spirit* ... all had by something that plays the role of matter. (It can't *really* be matter, since God is immaterial. Suppose, then, that it is the *divine substance,* whatever that is, that plays the role of matter). Each

divine person is *a* substance; thus, they are not mere aspects of a common substance. Furthermore, each is distinct from the other.... But they are nevertheless the *same* substance... Since Father, Son, and Holy Spirit count, on this view, as numerically the same substance *despite their distinctness,* [(P1)] is false, and the problem of the Trinity is solved. (Rea, pp. 419–20)

But what exactly is the "divine substance," which on this view plays the role of matter in the doctrine of the Trinity? The answer is that it is the divine nature, but Rea declines to take a position concerning what exactly a nature is, except that it must allow the divine Persons to be "concrete particular non-properties" (Rea, p. 420).

Before proceeding to the evaluation of this proposal we need to ask, where do Brower and Rea stand on the issue of Social versus anti-Social trinitarianism? As with van Inwagen, their formal theory is neutral on the issue. If we attend to other things they say, however, it becomes evident that they are decidedly opposed to Social trinitarianism.[4] Unlike van Inwagen, however, they really do not tell us what they understand a trinitarian Person to be, other than the rather opaque characterization cited in the previous paragraph: the Persons are "concrete particular non-properties."[5] So if we were to accept their resolution of the logical problem of the Trinity, a good deal more would still be needed for a complete doctrine.

So much for exposition; the task remaining for us is assessment. As we've seen, the solution to the problem of the Trinity is found in relative identity, which is then explained in terms of constitution, which in turn is explained by the Aristotelian notion of sameness in number without identity. In view of this, we had best begin our evaluation by looking at the latter notion.

At this point, however, I wish to suggest that Brower and Rea's view of the constitution relation may be less closely connected with Aristotle's ideas than they imply. Look again at their list of "Aristotle-like" examples: "fists and hands,

---

[4] This, then, is the one exception to the organizing principle stated earlier—that we will progress gradually towards views that are more friendly to Social trinitarianism. It will be obvious why van Inwagen's proposal, which leans towards Social trinitarianism, needed to be discussed before Brower and Rea. For Brower and Rea's opposition to Social trinitarianism, see Jeffrey Brower, "The Problem with Social Trinitarianism: A Reply to Wierenga," *Faith and Philosophy,* 21/3 (July 2004), 295–303; also Rea, "Relative Identity," 250, and "The Trinity," 412–16. For a critique of Brower and Rea, see my "Constitution and the Trinity: The Brower–Rea Proposal," *Faith and Philosophy,* 27/3 (July 2010), 321–8.

[5] A bit more is said about the Persons in the earlier Brower–Rea article, but it is unclear to me whether it clarifies matters. They reject any account of the doctrine of the Trinity that does not satisfy the requirement that "(D3) It is consistent with the view that God is an individual rather than a society, and that the Persons are not parts of God" (p. 59). This seems to be a clear repudiation of Social views as understood in the present volume. However, they attach a note at this point which reads in part, "Note that the point of D3 isn't to deny that the Persons compose a society. Of course they do, if there are genuinely three Persons. Rather, the point of D3 is to deny both that the name 'God' refers to the society composed of three Persons and that the Persons are proper parts of God" (p. 75 n. 7). Readers must make what they can of what this tells us about the Brower–Rea view of the Persons.

bronze statues and lumps of bronze, cats and heaps of cat tissue." Of these three, I submit that only fists and hands are relevantly similar to Socrates and seated-Socrates. And on the other hand, fists and hands are not the sort of examples that are normally used in setting out the problem of material constitution. *That* problem is typically illustrated by examples similar to the other two mentioned here—bronze statues and lumps of bronze, cats and heaps of cat tissue. The difference between these two sorts of cases is that a fist is simply a hand characterized by the accidental property, *being clenched,* just as seated-Socrates is simply Socrates himself, characterized by the accidental property, *being seated.* But it is extremely implausible that *being a statue* and, more importantly, *being a cat* are mere accidental properties, instantiated respectively by a lump of bronze or a heap of cat tissue. When a cat is run over by a car, something of significance is destroyed; it's not just a matter of a certain substance (namely, the heap of cat tissue) losing an accidental property. It is for this reason that many of us find ourselves with problematic intuitions such as are expressed in Brower and Rea's (MC) quoted above. I myself have no such intuitions in the case of hands and fists, and I suspect that many readers will agree with me about this. If this is correct, then Aristotle's accidental unities are not relevantly similar to the cases that are paradigmatic for the problem of material constitution.[6]

This, however, is a relatively minor point; the more important question is whether the Brower–Rea notion of constitution, however derived, does provide an illuminating solution to the problem of the divine Trinity in unity. Unfortunately, I don't believe this is the case. To see why not, let us look at Rea's answer to the suggestion that "if there is just one substance, then we ought to be able to ask whether *it*—the one substance—is essentially a mere statue or a mere pillar (or perhaps essentially a statue-pillar)." He responds by saying that "On the present view, terms such as 'it' and 'the one substance' are ambiguous: they might refer to the statue, or they might refer to the pillar." Surely, however, this is unsatisfactory as applied to trinitarian doctrine. It will hardly do to be told that Father, Son, and Spirit are the "same substance" in that the expression "the one divine substance" is ambiguous and can be used to refer to any one of the three! If it is the fact that there is only one divine substance that guarantees monotheism, it is not acceptable that there are three different, but equally good, candidates for that one substance. What is needed is that there should be *one thing only* to which "the divine substance" refers, not that the expression can be used, ambiguously, to refer to any of three different things. But the remark about ambiguity is not an accidental misstatement; it is forced

[6] Alexander Pruss gives additional reasons for questioning whether the Brower–Rea view really is significantly similar to Aristotle's ideas. See his "Brower and Rea's Constitution Account of the Trinity," in McCall and Rea, *Philosophical and Theological Essays,* 314–25, esp. 317–19.

by the logic of the position. There is, we are told, only one substance. *What is* this one substance? It can't be (merely) a statue, because if it were the substance would be destroyed if the features of the statue were obliterated. It can't be (merely) a pillar, because if it were nothing would be destroyed by defacing the statue. It can't be both at once; if it were, then in the situation described it would both be destroyed and not be destroyed. So it is unavoidable that "the one substance" is ambiguous. But such ambiguity is a poor foundation for trinitarian doctrine.

This point can be brought out even more clearly by considering a different version of the problem of the Trinity. Recall Rea's initial formulation of the central tenets of trinitarian doctrine:

(T1) There is exactly one God, the Father almighty.
(T2) Father, Son, and Holy Spirit are not identical.
(T3) Father, Son, and Holy Spirit are consubstantial. (Rea, p. 405)

(T1) apparently amounts to:

(T1′) For some x, x is God, and x = the Father, and for all y, if y is God $y = x$.

(T2) clearly entails

(T2′) the Father $\neq$ the Son

from which it follows that

(T4) the Son is not God,

a heretical conclusion that apparently follows directly from two of Rea's three "central tenets," without any assistance from (P1). Rea could reply to this by claiming that "God" as used here is ambiguous, in that it can refer to any of several items. It would then be true after all that "the Son is God," but "God" has a different referent here than it does in (T1′). Adding subscripts to disambiguate, we have both

(T1*) the Father is God$_F$
(T4*) the Son is God$_S$

and the conjunction of these is consistent with

(T2′) the Father $\neq$ the Son.

But the conjunction of (T1*), (T4*), and (T2′) entails

(T5) God$_F$ $\neq$ God$_S$

It is hard to avoid the conclusion that we have here a straightforward affirmation of two Gods—in other words, polytheism.

It might be objected, however, that this argument begs the question by ignoring Brower and Rea's redefinition of the number concepts.[7] They acknowledge that their account is incompatible with the standard definitions of number concepts in terms of identity, such as, "There is exactly one $F =_{def} \exists x$ (Fx & (y) (Fy iff $y = x$))."[8] (And this definition is assumed in my rephrasing above of (T1) as (T1').) They contend, however, that these definitions are wrong; number concepts should instead be defined in terms of numerical sameness, of which identity is one species (see Brower and Rea, pp. 62–3).[9] If (T1) is interpreted in terms of the revised number concepts, it comes out as

(T1″) For some x, x is God, and x = the Father, and for all y, if y is God y is the same God as x.

And since the Son is, in their view, the same God as the Father, it does not follow that the Son is not God.

There are two things that can be said about this. First of all, this move simply brings out once again the same point that was made just above: we now have *two distinct items,* the Father and the Son, each of whom is said to be "*the one and only God.*" Speaking only for myself, I have to say that this doesn't sound much like monotheism! (In fact, I am not sure that it makes sense.) But secondly, the redefinition of the number concepts for this purpose should strike us as problematic. The standard definitions of the number concepts in terms of identity have seemed extremely plausible and intuitive to a great many philosophers over a considerable period of time. To replace these definitions would seem to require more justification than is provided by the desire to support a particular solution to the admittedly puzzling problem of material constitution. Furthermore, it arouses one's suspicions if a person, challenged by the accusation that he has "too many" of something, responds by redefining the number concepts so that the excess number is reduced. (Suppose a man accused of bigamy were to explain that, while he admittedly is married to each of two women, he has devised a new method of counting such that the two women "count as" one and the same wife!)

But finally, it is precisely the application of these concepts to the doctrine of the Trinity that causes the greatest concern. Probably no one cares greatly (possibly excepting a few metaphysicians) whether the statue and the pillar count as one object or as two. But for the Trinity what is at stake is monotheism itself, and that is no small matter. In the classical formulation of the doctrine, the Persons are three but monotheism is guaranteed by the fact that the divine nature or substance is one. Just for this reason, explanations that "divide the

---

[7] My thanks to Joseph Jedwab for clarifying this point for me.

[8] "There is exactly one F if and only if there is something, x, which is F and anything is F if and only if it is identical with x."

[9] i.e. "There is exactly one F if and only if there is something, x, which is F and anything is F if and only if it is the same in number with x."

substance" are unacceptable. But that is what the Brower–Rea proposal does; it is precisely such expressions as "the divine substance," or indeed "God," that are rendered ambiguous by their proposal, as I have pointed out in the preceding paragraphs. In order to disambiguate, we can employ subscripts or some other form of notation. But once we have done this, we have *three distinct items* each of which is said to be "*the* divine substance" or "*the* one and only God." It is then, I submit, too late to resolve the problem by proposing a revision of the number concepts such that the three individuals "count as" one.[10]

Our problem, then, is how to avoid making such terms as "the divine substance" and "God" ambiguous, as they are on the Brower–Rea view. What we need in order to avoid this, I suggest, is a different account of the relation that obtains between, on the one hand, the statue and the parcel of matter that constitutes it, and on the other hand between the Father and "the one and only God." It can't be identity, because we then should have both "the statue = the parcel of matter" and "the pillar = the parcel of matter," from which immediately follows the false proposition, "the statue = the pillar." And the same applies, *mutatis mutandis,* to the relation between each of the trinitarian Persons and the divine nature or substance. If we can clarify the relation in this way, we will no longer need to hold that "the one divine substance" is ambiguous.

My proposal is that the notion of constitution does have an important role to play here, although it needs to be understood in a somewhat different way than we have seen with Brower and Rea. At this point I will sketch this out briefly as it applies to the pillar–statue; the application to the Trinity will be worked out in Part III below. We begin with their other example, the lump of bronze and the statue. The lump, we want to say, is a material object, and so is the statue; furthermore, the lump is not identical with the statue, yet there is only one material object there. Clearly, we have a problem. But we need to ask, where does the problem come from? The idea that the statue "just is" the mass of bronze, and also the idea that there is only one material object present, have the solid endorsement of common sense. On the other hand, the fact that the statue is not identical with the lump is a deliverance of modal logic; their non-identity follows from their different persistence conditions. Now it just so happens that the human brain is not hard-wired for modal logic; apparently the need to solve metaphysical puzzles such as this one has never exerted a strong selection pressure on the human genome. The result of this is that sometimes our instinctive reaction to various problem situations comes into conflict with principles we come to accept after reflection. So we have to accept that, as Brower and Rea have said, any solution to the problem at hand will be somewhat counterintuitive.

[10] For some additional, and quite interesting, criticisms of the Brower–Rea view, see Pruss, "Brower and Rea's Constitution Account." These criticisms will not be pursued here.

One intuition they are not willing to surrender, however, is the intuition that we have in the case of the statue–pillar only one material object. This intuition can be preserved, if we are willing to define "material object" in a way that corresponds with Rea's assertion that "all it means to say that two things are the same material object at a time is that those two things share all the same physical matter at that time" (Rea, p. 418). Guided by this, we can define "material object" as follows: a material object is a parcel of matter in the solid state, causally bound together.[11] This does capture, I think, the most important elements in our ordinary conception of a material object. A "material object" needs to be solid; we would not normally think of a mass of gas or liquid as a material object. And it needs to be causally bound. A set of chessmen sitting on a chessboard is not a single material object, because the pieces are not causally bound to the board, but a bronze casting of chessboard-and-chessmen, in a single piece, would be a material object. (Obviously, causal binding comes in degrees, and context may determine how close it needs to be for there to be a single object. In some contexts, a sand dune may well count as a material object, in spite of the fact that the grains of sand are piled loosely on one another.[12])

But what of the pillar and the statue? My proposal is that we should say that each of them "is" the piece of marble, where the "is" represents not identity but rather *constitution*—each of the pillar and the statue is *constituted by* the chunk of marble. And we can also say that the piece of marble "is" the pillar, and "is" the statue, where "is" expresses the fact that the marble *constitutes* both pillar and statue. (Unlike Rea, but in agreement with some other constitution theorists, I take constitution to be an asymmetrical relation.[13]) And this, I think, gives us almost everything we want, perhaps with this exception: when we say that the pillar "is" a material object, what we shall mean is not that it is identical with such an object but rather that it *is constituted by* a material object, namely by the piece of marble. So much, then, for the pillar–statue; the application to the Trinity will be made presently.

---

[11] Dale Tuggy has pointed out to me that this definition entails that there can be no simple material object. I'm inclined to think this is acceptable. Our ordinary idea of a material object is of something that is perceptible to the senses (in particular, the sense of touch), and it is pretty obvious to common sense that such objects are not simple, i.e. absolutely indivisible. But if the entailment is found to be a problem, we can revise the definition as follows: "a material object is a parcel of matter in the solid state, either simple or causally bound together."

[12] Notice that this definition does not by itself commit us to any particular solution to the problem of material constitution; it is compatible with various solutions to that puzzle, including the one that states that the statue and the lump are identical.

[13] Rea acknowledges that the relation is more commonly taken to be asymmetrical. (See "Problem of Material Constitution," p. 527 n. 5.)

17

Craig: A Soul with Multiple
Sets of Faculties

In William Lane Craig we encounter for the first time a philosopher who explicitly identifies himself as a Social trinitarian.[1] Craig begins his presentation with a brief review of biblical materials relevant to the Trinity, followed by a concise summary of the historical development of the doctrine. He then reviews the recent trinitarian debate among philosophers, and identifies his own view as "Trinity monotheism," a version of Social trinitarianism that identifies the "one God" of scripture and tradition with the Trinity. Craig goes on to address a criticism of Trinity monotheism by Brian Leftow, who wrote as follows:

> Either the Trinity is a fourth case of the divine nature, in addition to the Persons, or it is not. If it is, we have too many cases of deity for orthodoxy. If it is not, and yet is divine, there are two ways to be divine—by being a case of deity, and by being a Trinity of such cases. If there is more than one way to be divine, Trinity monotheism becomes Plantingian Arianism.[2] But if there is in fact only one way to be divine, then there are two alternatives. One is that only the Trinity is God, and God is composed of non-divine persons. The other is that the sum of all divine persons is somehow not divine. To accept the last claim would be to give up Trinity monotheism altogether.[3]

Craig's initial response to this complex dilemma is to embrace the alternative Leftow terms "Plantingian Arianism." (Craig remarks that it is uninformative to be told that this is "the positing of more than one way to be divine"; "what we want to know is why the view is objectionable" (p. 590).) As we would expect,

---

[1] J. P. Moreland and William Lane Craig, *Philosophical Foundations for a Christian Worldview* (Downers Grove, IL: InterVarsity, 2003), ch. 29, "The Trinity," pp. 575–95 (Craig is primarily responsible for the material on the Trinity); repr. in part as William Lane Craig, "Toward a Tenable Social Trinitarianism," in McCall and Rea, *Philosophical and Theological Essays*, 89–99. Page references in the text of this chapter are to the former volume.

[2] The reference is to Cornelius Plantinga, Jr., not to Alvin Plantinga.

[3] Leftow, "Anti Social Trinitarianism," 221.

he rejects the notion that the Trinity is a fourth instance of the divine nature. But nor does he accept that "God [i.e. the Trinity] is composed of non-divine persons"; the Persons are indeed divine. He explains,

> The persons of the Trinity are not divine in virtue of instantiating the divine nature. For presumably *being triune* is a property of the divine nature (God does not just happen to be triune); yet the persons of the Trinity do not have that property. It now becomes clear that the reason that the Trinity is not a fourth instance of the divine nature is that there are no other instances of the divine nature. The Father, Son and Holy Spirit are not instances of the divine nature, and that is why there are not three Gods. The Trinity is the sole instance of the divine nature, and therefore there is but one God. (p. 590)

This of course raises the question: In what sense *are* the Persons divine, if they are not instances of the divine nature? Craig approaches this question by pointing out that

> a cat's DNA or skeleton is feline even if neither is a cat. Nor is this a sort of downgraded or attenuated felinity: A cat's skeleton is fully and unambiguously feline. . . . Now if a cat is feline in virtue of being an instance of the cat nature, in virtue of what is a cat's DNA or skeleton feline? One plausible answer is that they are parts of a cat. This suggests that we could think of the persons of the Trinity as divine because they are parts of the Trinity, that is, parts of God. Now obviously, the persons are not parts of God in the sense in which a skeleton is part of a cat; but, given that the Father, for example, is not the whole Godhead, it seems undeniable that there is some sort of part–whole relation obtaining between the persons of the Trinity and the entire Godhead. (p. 591)

He goes on to insist that

> Far from downgrading the divinity of the persons, such an account can be very illuminating of their contribution to the divine nature. For parts can possess properties which the whole does not, and the whole can have a property because some part has it. Thus, when we ascribe omniscience and omnipotence to God, we are not making the Trinity a fourth person or agent; rather, God has these properties because the persons do. Divine attributes like omniscience, omnipotence and goodness are grounded in the persons' possessing these properties, while divine attributes like necessity, aseity and eternity are not so grounded. With respect to the latter, the persons have these properties because God as a whole has them. (p. 591)

Here, then, we have Craig's solution to the logical problem of the Trinity. Briefly stated: The Persons are not identical with God (that is, with the Trinity); nor are the Persons Gods. The Persons are divine in virtue of being (in an appropriate sense) parts of God; some of the traditional divine attributes are ascribed to God because they are in the first instance attributes of the Persons, while others are ascribed to the Persons because they are in the first instance attributes of God.

He notes, however, that "All of this still leaves us wondering, however, how three persons could be parts of the same being, rather than be three separate beings" (p. 593). That is to say, we would like to be able to form some sort of positive conception of the relation between the trinitarian Persons, rather than having to accept some merely formalistic solution to the logical problem. As a possible analogy, Craig cites the three-headed dog Cerberus from Greco-Roman mythology. We suppose that "Cerberus has three brains and therefore three distinct states of consciousness of whatever it is like to be a dog" (p. 593). We could name these three centers of consciousness Rover, Bowser, and Spike. They could even come into conflict with one another, though in order for Cerberus to be biologically viable there must be a considerable degree of coordination. Now as the situation has been described,

> Despite the diversity of his mental states, Cerberus is clearly one dog. He is a single biological organism having a canine nature. Rover, Bowser and Spike may be said to be canine, too, though they are not three dogs, but parts of the one dog Cerberus.... Although the church fathers rejected analogies like Cerberus, once we give up divine simplicity, Cerberus does seem to represent what Augustine called an image of the Trinity among creatures. (p. 593)

This analogy is not, however, entirely satisfactory: "suppose Cerberus were to be killed and his minds survive the death of his body. In what sense would they still be one being?... Since the divine persons are, prior to the Incarnation, three unembodied minds, in virtue of what are they one being rather than three individual beings?" (p. 593). In order to resolve this problem, Craig invites us to reflect on the nature of the soul, which he takes to be an immaterial substance. He then reasons,

> Now God is very much like an unembodied soul; indeed, as a mental substance God just seems to be a soul. We naturally equate a rational soul with a person, since the human souls with which we are acquainted are persons. But the reason human souls are individual persons is because each soul is equipped with one set of rational faculties sufficient for being a person. Suppose, then, that God is a soul which is endowed with three complete sets of rational cognitive faculties, each sufficient for personhood. Then God, though one soul, would not be one person but three, for God would have three centers of self-consciousness, intentionality and volition, as social trinitarians maintain.... God would therefore be one being that supports three persons, just as our own individual beings each support one person. Such a model of Trinity monotheism seems to give a clear sense to the classical formula, "three persons in one substance". (p. 594)

In concluding his exposition, Craig points out that his model does not feature (though it does not preclude) the derivation of one person from another—i.e. the eternal generation of the Son and procession of the Holy Spirit. From his standpoint, however, it is "all for the better" that the relations of origin are not entailed by his version of the doctrine. "For although creedally affirmed, the doctrine of the generation of the Son (and the procession of the Spirit) is a relic of Logos Christology which finds virtually no warrant in the biblical text and introduces a subordinationism into the Godhead which anyone who affirms the full deity of Christ ought to find very troubling" (p. 594).

CRITIQUE AND EVALUATION

Craig's account of the Trinity consists of two parts: there is the formal theory, and there is the model. The formal theory states that there is one God, the Trinity, which alone instantiates the divine nature. The three Persons, Father, Son, and Holy Spirit, do not instantiate the divine nature, because that nature includes the property, *being triune,* which is not instantiated by any of the Persons. The Persons, rather, are divine in virtue of being in the appropriate way *parts* of God. The model, on the other hand, portrays God as a soul endowed with three sets of faculties, each sufficient for personhood. It should be noted that the theory and the model are to some extent separable: one could embrace the theory without the model, or the model without the theory, though both must be combined to give us Craig's overall view of the doctrine.

The most assiduous critic of Craig's Trinity monotheism is Daniel Howard-Snyder; most though not all of his criticism is directed at Craig's formal theory.[4] In particular, he criticizes the claim that the Persons are divine in virtue of being parts of God. He raises two related questions:

1. What sort of part–whole relation is involved here?
2. Is the sense in which, according to the theory, the Persons "are divine" sufficient to satisfy what is intended by Christians when they say that each of Father, Son, and Holy Spirit "is God"?

The first question arises because it is evident that not just any part–whole relation will do the job. For example, an atom of iron, present in one of Felix's red-blood cells, is a "part" of Felix, but the atom is not "feline" in any meaningful sense; in fact, it is indistinguishable from any other atom of iron anywhere else in the universe. Craig, mindful of this, suggested to Howard-Snyder that a cat's skeleton or DNA are "fully feline" because they are *distinctive of the species*—neither the skeleton nor the DNA could belong to anything that is

---

[4] See Daniel Howard-Snyder, "Trinity Monotheism," *Philosophia Christi,* 5/2 (2003), 375–403; repr. in McCall and Rea, *Philosophical and Theological Essays,* 100–25. Page references to the text in this chapter are to the latter volume. For Craig's rejoinder, see "Trinity Monotheism Once More: A Response to Daniel Howard-Snyder," *Philosophia Christi,* 8/1 (2006), 101–13, and "Another Glance at Trinity Monotheism," in McCall and Rea, *Philosophical and Theological Essays,* 126–30.

not a cat (see p. 110). Similarly, Father, Son, and Holy Spirit are "distinctive of deity" in that none of them could be part of anything other than God, the Holy Trinity. Howard-Snyder, however, doubts that this is sufficient, but to see why it may not be we need to go on to his second question.

The second question arises because, while we are told that Father, Son, and Spirit are each "divine," they cannot be divine in the same sense in which God, the Trinity, is divine. The Trinity is divine in virtue of instantiating the divine nature, but we are told explicitly that the Persons do not instantiate the divine nature. So they must be divine in some derivative sense, and the question arises whether this sense is sufficient to satisfy what is meant when Christians say that each of the Persons "is God." (Howard-Snyder terms this the "diminished divinity problem.") In terms of the cat analogy, that Felix is a cat means that there are certain appropriate ways in which his owner needs to relate to him: he must be given food, water, and shelter, he should be played with from time to time, have his litter box cleaned, and so on. However, no one would think of doing these things with Felix's skeleton or with his DNA. Now when Christians say, for example, that "Christ is God," one of the important things they have in mind is that Christ is *worthy of worship*—but is the mere fact that Christ is "part of God"—even a distinctive part—sufficient to guarantee this? Howard-Snyder suspects that it may not be; as a possible counterexample he suggests a proper part which is a "faculty" of a divine Person—for instance, the Father's affective faculty. But, he says, this faculty "fails to exemplify the properties of omnipotence, omniscience, and unsurpassable moral goodness... [and] is not worthy of worship" (p. 114). He acknowledges that Craig might deny that the Father has proper parts, but he says it is a consequence of Craig's position that "if He did, they would be omnipotent, omniscient, morally perfect, and worship-worthy; however, this counterpossible proposition is false" (p. 114).[5]

It is somewhat unclear to me whether this criticism of Craig's theory is effective. Perhaps it would be fair to say that Craig has failed to make it clear that the sort of "parthood" that he has in mind is sufficient for full divinity, in the sense of being worthy of worship. It may be, however, that Howard-Snyder has himself satisfied this need for Craig, without being aware of having done so. Howard-Snyder imagines

> what it would be like for someone alien to Trinitarianism to hear for the first time that God is composed of three distinct Persons. Our alien might naturally wonder whether the Persons are fully divine and, if so, how that could be....If he were answered that the Persons are, indeed, fully divine, because they are proper parts of God, he would rightly remain puzzled. After all, he might say, something's being a proper part of God would not logically suffice for its being

---

[5] He acknowledges that the reader's response to this may depend on "how sympathetic you are to false counterpossibles."

fully divine; would it not have to be a proper part that was a *person* as well? "Well, of course!" we might reply; we were taking it for granted that the Persons are persons. Our alien might still remain puzzled, however. After all, he might say, something is a person just in case it has powers of rationality, volition, and so on that are sufficient for personhood, but something's being a proper part of God that possesses any old powers of rationality, and so forth, is not logically sufficient for its being fully divine. Would it not have to possess the *appropriate* powers of rationality, and so forth, those that are logically sufficient for being fully divine? "Well, of course!" we might reply; we were taking it for granted that the Persons were persons who had the appropriate powers of rationality, and so on. (p. 115)

Howard-Snyder thinks the alien should now admit that "*being a proper part of the Trinity 'as a whole' that possesses powers of rationality, volition, and so forth, that are logically sufficient for full divinity* is, indeed, logically sufficient for being fully divine" (p. 115). However, the alien should not be satisfied with this answer, because the question was "not only *whether* the Persons are fully divine but also, if so, *how that could be*, given that they do not exemplify the divine nature. The new explanans sheds no light on that question; moreover, the part of it that has to do with being a proper part is explanatorily idle" (p. 115).

Our alien's dissatisfaction is understandable, but Howard-Snyder seems unaware that he has created the dissatisfaction himself by the way he has formulated the answer given to the alien. By stipulating that the powers of rationality and volition possessed by the Persons are "logically sufficient for full divinity" he has trivialized the answer and drained away its explanatory power.[6] Suppose, however, we reformulate the answer in this way: *each Person is a proper part of the Trinity "as a whole" that possesses powers of rationality, volition, and so forth such that the Person is omnipotent, omniscient, and morally perfect.* Should our alien not be satisfied with this answer? I do believe that the answer captures much, perhaps all, of what is meant when Christians say that each of the Persons is "fully God." Perhaps, though, our alien will still be wondering what the Person's being a proper part of the Trinity contributes to the explanation. If so, the answer might well be that *only* a person who is a proper part of the Holy Trinity could have the sorts of powers enumerated; these powers are, in fact, unique to and definitive of the divine Being that is the Trinity.[7]

---

[6] If the explanation we are given for p's being true is that p and q are both true, q makes no contribution to the explanation; it doesn't matter *what* q may be.

[7] Craig comments: "As for Howard-Snyder's complaint that *what* makes the persons divine is not their being part of the Trinity but their possessing the properties of divinity, one could either just agree with him on that score or one could insist that their being members of the Trinity is explanatorily prior to their possessing such properties." "Trinity Monotheism Once More," 111–12. And see pp. 110–13 for Craig's interesting discussion of parthood in relation to the Trinity.

At this point it must be left to the reader to judge whether the answers that have been given to Howard-Snyder's objections are adequate.[8] However, there is another difficulty with Craig's theory that has not so far been addressed. What he identifies as "the divine nature" simply is not the same as what the Church Fathers referred to by that designation. For them, the divine nature was not something unique to the Trinity as a whole, including the property, *being triune*. Rather, it was the common essence of Father, Son, and Holy Spirit. Anyone thinking of the divine nature in Craig's terms is going to have considerable difficulty with such expressions as "from the essence of the Father" (from the creed of the Nicene council)—not to mention, of course, *homoousios* itself. At the very least, such a person will have a lot of tricky translation work to do, in order to match up the patristic formulas with the ones sanctioned by Craig's theory—a task which has not been attempted here. I believe, therefore, that it may be wiser for us to try to arrive at some formulation which meshes better with the things said by the pro-Nicene trinitarians we have taken as our starting point in this study.[9]

We turn to Craig's model for the Trinity, God as a soul with three sets of faculties. Once again, we note that this model is to some degree independent of the theory discussed above, so we are free to consider it on its own merits.[10] Howard-Snyder's objections to the model are objections to Social trinitarianism as such; he finds it unacceptable that God, the Trinity, is not a single person. For the time being we will postpone the discussion of those objections. There are, however, two points that can be made concerning the model without engaging those broader questions about Social trinitarianism. First of all, it is infelicitous to say that the soul which is God is "endowed with three complete sets of rational *cognitive* faculties." As Brian Leftow has pointed out,[11] if "cognitive" is taken strictly it excludes volitional and affective faculties, which cannot be what was intended. (Other things Craig says make that clear.) This however is easily remedied: we need only omit the word "cognitive," and speak simply of "three complete sets of rational faculties."

---

[8] By no means, however, have all of the objections been dealt with. That would not be possible in the space available here; readers should consult Howard-Snyder's article, and Craig's replies, for much additional material.

[9] Craig might say that, as a Protestant, he is more concerned to be biblically orthodox than to be creedally orthodox. Still, he is not indifferent to the traditional formulations, as seen by his approval (seen earlier) of the formula, "three persons in one substance."

[10] Craig underscores this independence when he writes, in his reply to Howard-Snyder, "The strength of our proposal lies in the fact that it does not rest content with a merely formulaic understanding of the Trinity. Rather we try to offer a model that actually shows how the Father, Son, and Holy Spirit can be three persons in one substance.... [W]hether the persons mentioned in the model ought to be characterized as parts of God is quite incidental to the proposal and may be left to mereologists to decide. The issue of parthood arose only as a suggested way of explaining why the persons are divine." "Trinity Monotheism Once More," 101.

[11] See Brian Leftow, "Two Trinities: Reply to Hasker," *Religious Studies,* 49 (2010), 441.

A second, and less obvious, point is that the talk of "faculties" is not meant to commit the model to a faculty psychology; Craig states, "I'm open to talk of 'faculties' as just a manner of speaking."[12] (So we won't have faculties as "proper parts" of God, as was assumed in one of Howard-Snyder's objections.) What is essential is that there are in God three streams of conscious life, each endowed with the aptitudes for cognitive, affective, and volitional mental states.

At this point, however, the picture should begin to look familiar. Craig's picture of there being in God three such streams of conscious life seems remarkably similar to Leftow's picture of "God living three life-streams." The two pictures are not the same, of course. In Craig's model each life-stream is that of a distinct person, whereas for Leftow all three are the "lives" of a single person. They are, however, similar in that in each case there is a single divine substance that supports three different streams of conscious experience. Anyone who finds the general picture attractive must choose between the two, no doubt on the basis of theological reasons supplemented by considerations of general plausibility. There does not, however, seem to be any discernible reason why one of the two is more likely than the other to be metaphysically possible; it does not seem that there is a plausible way to rule out one proposal as impossible while regarding the other as viable.[13] With regard to their prima facie possibility, this Social model and a leading anti-Social model are on a par with each other.

Finally, a little should be said here about Craig's rejection of the relations of origin between the divine Persons. I personally find it remarkable that a person as concerned with orthodoxy as Bill Craig is should be willing to dismiss casually a doctrine that is expressed six times and in six different ways in the Nicene Creed.[14] The claim that this represents "a relic of Logos Christology which finds virtually no warrant in the biblical text" is also quite surprising. Craig associates Logos Christology with the apologists of the second century, and attributes it to the influence of Philo. In fact, however, "Logos Christology" has a continuous record beginning (for Christians) with the Fourth Gospel and continuing throughout almost all later trinitarian reflection. Ironically, the assertion that the "begetting" of the Son was a sign of metaphysical inferiority was one of the main contentions of fourth-century Arians such as Eunomius—not, one would think, good company for a contemporary trinitarian! Finally, the rejection of the relations of origin poses serious problems for trinitarian metaphysics; this topic, however, will be postponed until Part III.

---

[12] Private communication.

[13] If one of the proposals is correct, the other will in fact be metaphysically impossible; we should not suppose that God chooses whether to be one person or three. But this necessity and impossibility are hidden from us; they cannot be used to argue for or against either position.

[14] Christ is "The only-begotten Son of God, begotten from the Father before all ages, light from light, true God from true God, begotten not made"; the Spirit "proceeds from the Father." Tr. from J. N. D. Kelly, *Early Christian Creeds* (London: Longmans, Green & Co., 1960), 297–8.

18

Swinburne: Created Divine Persons

For Richard Swinburne, the most pressing question concerning the Trinity is whether there could be more than one divine individual.[1] This amounts to asking whether there could be two individuals having the properties of being "necessarily perfectly free, omniscient, omnipotent, and existing of metaphysical necessity" (p. 171). Swinburne admits that "an initial gut reaction" to his question is "No," for "Would not the omnipotence of one such individual be subject to frustration by the other individual and so not be omnipotence?" (p. 171). He sets out, however, to show that this initial reaction is mistaken. In order to see this, we need to consider briefly the nature of omnipotence. The omnipotence of a divine person[2] is defined as "the power to do anything logically possible, if he so chooses"; this Swinburne terms *compatibilist power*, by analogy with the "power to do otherwise" as understood according to some compatibilist theories of free will. However, a divine person's *absolute power* is "the power to choose and do, and that is limited not merely by logical possibilities but by perfect goodness" (p. 171). Clearly, the "power" of a divine person to do something incompatible with perfect goodness is a power that can never be exercised, so in considering possible conflicts of will between divine persons we need only consider their absolute power.

So, how might such conflicts be supposed to occur? There cannot be any conflict over actions that are either morally required or morally impermissible; about such actions perfectly good individuals will necessarily be in agreement. Any conflicts, then, must concern actions that are morally good but not morally required. Even here, however,

> Since each would recognize the other as having the divine properties, including perfect goodness, it is plausible to suppose that each would recognize a duty not

[1] See Richard Swinburne, *The Christian God* (Oxford: Clarendon Press, 1994), 170; ch. 8 of this book is repr. in McCall and Rea, *Philosophical and Theological Essays*, 29–37. In an earlier article, Swinburne posed the question by asking, "Could there Be More than One God?," *Faith and Philosophy*, 5/3 (July 1988), 225–41. A somewhat simpler exposition (but with no difference of content) will be found in Richard Swinburne, *Was Jesus God?* (Oxford: OUP, 2008), 28–38. Page references in this chapter are to *The Christian God*.

[2] Since Swinburne regards "person" as essentially univocal as between divine and human persons, the capital for "Person" will not be used in this chapter.

to prevent or frustrate the acts of the other…If the second individual creates a universe which the first individual by himself would not have chosen to create, there would be wrong in the first individual attempting to prevent or frustrate this creative work; on the contrary, it would be good that he should give it his backing. (p. 172)

It follows that conflict could only arise "where each tried to do an act compatible with his perfect goodness but incompatible with the act which the other was trying simultaneously to do" (p. 172). (As an example, Swinburne supposes that the two divine individuals might each settle on a different direction for the revolution of the earth about the sun.) If this were to occur, we would have a literal example of an irresistible force opposed by an immovable object, a paradoxical situation which must be ruled out if both divine persons are to be omnipotent.

It also follows that "There could not be two divine individuals unless there was some mechanism to prevent interference and the mechanism could not limit their power in the compatibilist sense, only in the absolute sense (by making it no longer good to do acts of a certain sort)" (p. 172). This mechanism, Swinburne supposes, would take the form of rules for distributing power—i.e. rules determining for each divine individual a sphere of activity in which he has primary authority, and in which his wishes should prevail in the event of a conflict of preferences. But how are such rules to be arrived at? "[T]here is nothing to guarantee that at the moment at which [one divine individual] draws up a proposal for distributing power, the other divine individual might not draw up a different proposal; and even with the best will in the world, only luck could prevent an actual collision of wills" (p. 172). We therefore conclude that "Only if one lays down what the rules are, and his decision is accepted because he has the authority to lay down the rules, will the collision necessarily be avoided" (p. 173).[3] This authority, however, must be based on some other, previously existing, difference between the two divine individuals; this difference is to be found in the fact that one of the individuals is for the other the "source of being." And so we find the solution to our dilemma:

Such unity of action could be secured if the first individual solemnly vows to the second individual in causing his existence that he will not initiate any act (of will) within the second individual's allocated sphere of activity. So, although the first divine individual retains his omnipotence, it is…limited by his inability to do other than what is perfectly good, and in virtue of this promise this limitation will ensure that he does not frustrate the actions of the second divine individual. Conversely, although all power is given to the second individual, it comes with a request that it should not be exercised in a certain way. The overall goodness of conformity to that request (and not to conform would be not to conform to

[3] I am not sure that this is, in fact, the only way in which the collision can be avoided. For another suggestion, see the following chapter, on Yandell.

a reasonable request from the source of his being and power) will ensure that, although omnipotent, the second individual cannot frustrate any action of the first individual. The sharing of divinity could (logically) only occur subject to some restriction preventing mutual impediment of action. I have presented a highly fallible human judgement as to what the best such mechanism...would be. (pp. 174–5)

Swinburne's solution to this problem presupposes, of course, that one divine individual is the source of being for the others. But this, he argues, is necessary in any case, otherwise we would have two ultimate sources of being, which conflicts with the conclusion of the arguments for the existence of God. (And we may add that a metaphysic which recognizes two ultimate sources of being is evidently deficient as regards the theoretical virtue of simplicity.) He argues that one divine individual can derive his existence from another, so long as the derivation is inevitable. That this would be inevitable (assuming it to be possible) is guaranteed, because it would be a good thing for the first divine individual, G_1, to bring about the everlasting existence of the second divine individual, G_2, and so G_1 would have overriding reason to do so.[4] And on the other hand, it would be a good thing for G_2 to permit the everlasting existence of G_1, and so G_2 would have overriding reason to do this. (Since Swinburne thinks that the existence of divine persons is not logically necessary, it lies within the compatibilist power of a divine person to bring to an end the existence of another divine person, or even to bring to an end his own existence. But since doing either of these things would be morally bad, these actions do not lie within the absolute power of a divine person; we need not, then, be concerned about the end of everything in a catastrophic divine murder-suicide![5])

But would it in fact be the case that the first divine individual would have overriding reason to bring about the existence of a second and a third divine individual, so that his doing so is inevitable and necessary? Swinburne replies,

I believe that there is overriding reason for a first divine individual to bring about a second divine individual and with him to bring about a third divine individual, but no reason to go further. If the Christian religion has helped us, Christians and non-Christians, to see anything about what is worthwhile, it has helped us to see that love is a supreme good. Love involves sharing, giving to the other what of one's own is good for him and receiving from the other what of his is

---

[4] Swinburne considers at some length a difficulty that would result if divine individuals have "thisnesses" (haecceities), attributes which are unique to an individual and make it the individual that it is. I shall join Swinburne in assuming that a divine individual does not have a thisness, so this topic will not be pursued here.

[5] As we saw earlier (Ch. 13 above), for Zizioulas the power of the Father is not limited by the divine nature, not even by perfect goodness. So for him, the destruction of the other two divine persons, and even the Father's self-destruction, lies within the Father's "absolute power."

good for one; and love involves co-operating with another to benefit third parties. This latter is crucial for worthwhile love.... Love must share and love must co-operate in sharing. The best love would share all that it had. A divine individual would see that for him too a best kind of action would be to share and to co-operate in sharing.... So the love of a first divine individual G_1 would be manifested first in bringing about another divine individual G_2 with whom to share his life, and the love of G_1 or [sic] G_2 would be manifested in bringing about another divine individual G_3 with whom G_1 and G_2 co-operatively could share their lives. (pp. 177–8)

And now, since each of the divine individuals is able both to love each of the others, and to share with each of the others in love for the third, there is no need for the series to go further. Swinburne concludes that "the simplest sort of God to whom arguments lead inevitably tripersonalizes, to coin a word" (p. 191). (Thus, the doctrine of the Trinity is initially put forward as a conclusion of natural theology! This is a bold claim, though not so bold as Anselm's claim to have demonstrated the incarnation through natural reason. Swinburne goes on to say, "What I have presented as a priori a marginally more probable account of the divine nature than any other, becomes enormously more probable if backed up by revelation" (p. 191).)

Swinburne considers what was meant, in the creeds and traditions of the Church, by the claim that there is only one God. He writes, "If 'there is only one God' meant 'there is only one divine individual', then the doctrine of the Trinity would be manifestly self-contradictory.... [But] no person and no Council affirming something which they intend to be taken with utter seriousness can be read as affirming an *evident* contradiction" (p. 180). In denying tritheism, "I suggest that they were denying that there were three *independent* divine beings, any of which could exist without the other; or which could act independently of each other" (p. 180). He goes on to summarize the kind of unity possessed by the Trinity as he conceives of it:

On the account which I have given, the three divine individuals taken together would form a collective source of the being of all other things; the members would be totally mutually dependent and necessarily jointly behind each other's acts. This collective would be indivisible in its being for logical reasons—that is, the kind of being that it would be is such that each of its members is necessarily everlasting, and would not have existed unless it had brought about or been brought about by the others.... It is they, however, rather than it, who, to speak strictly, would have the divine properties of omnipotence, omniscience, etc.; though clearly there is a ready and natural sense in which the collective can be said to have them as well. If all members of a group know something, the group itself, by a very natural extension of use, can be said to know that thing, and so on. Similarly this very strong unity of the collective would make it, as well as its individual members, an appropriate object of worship. The claim that "there is only one God" is to be read as the claim that the source of being of all other things has to it this kind of indivisible unity. (pp. 180–1)

Swinburne goes on to explain that the claim that each of the individuals is "God" is to be understood as "the claim that each is divine—omnipotent, perfectly good, etc. Each such being would be an all-perfect source of all things—what more could councils intelligibly mean by that claim that an individual is God?" (p. 181).

SWINBURNE AND THE TRINITARIAN TRADITION

Any attentive reader of Swinburne's work must admire the logical clarity which he achieves in writing on topics for which such clarity has often been in short supply. Furthermore, he has managed to retrieve, in his own idiom, a great deal of the traditional doctrine of the Trinity.[6] In his earlier article, to be sure, there are locutions which are bound to grate on the ears of the traditionally minded—most notably, his references to the Son and the Spirit as "the second God" and "the third God." (Sarah Coakley notes the "embarrassingly tritheistic overtones" of this language.[7]) In *The Christian God*, however, such verbal occasions of offense have for the most part been eliminated. Nevertheless, there is room for further inquiry with regard to the question: To what extent does Swinburne succeed in affirming the traditional, orthodox doctrine of the Trinity?

It is interesting in this connection to compare Swinburne's doctrine with that of William Craig. On the one hand, it is clear that the "unity of nature" affirmed by Swinburne is the unity of an abstract, universal essence; in the terminology we have adopted, for each divine person there is a distinct trope of the divine nature. For Craig, on the other hand, the "one soul" which is God plays the role of the singular, concrete divine nature common to the three persons which (we have argued) is characteristic of the trinitarian tradition. In this respect, then, Craig is closer to the tradition than is Swinburne. (I suspect Swinburne would find the attribution to the three persons of a single concrete nature to be unintelligible or logically incoherent.) On the other hand, however, Swinburne does affirm the derivation of the Son and the Spirit from the Father, a central element of the tradition which Craig, as we have seen, is prepared to jettison. In that respect, then, Swinburne is closer to the mainstream than Craig. But a question arises here: Just what is Swinburne's understanding of this derivation? In *The Christian God*, we learn only that the Father is the "source of being" for the other persons, that he is their "cause," and that he

---

[6] It is clear that this is a matter of some importance for Swinburne; pp. 180–91 of *The Christian God* are devoted to a discussion of "The Traditional Doctrine" and its relation to Swinburne's formulations.

[7] Sarah Coakley, "'Persons' in the 'Social' Doctrine of the Trinity: A Critique of Current Analytic Discussion," in Davis *et al.*, *The Trinity*, 127.

"brings about" their existence. But just what is involved, we may wonder, in his doing this?

One place we might look for further information on this topic is Swinburne's earlier article, "Could there Be More than One God?" There he wrote,

> The creation of the second God by the first of which I am speaking is an everlasting creation; at each moment of endless time the first God keeps in being the second God. How in that case is the creation to be done? *Ex nihilo?* No. For that would not create a God. For to be God, as we saw earlier, a being has to be necessary—it has to be no accident that he exists rather than some qualitatively identical individual with his powers. God could create out of the blue one of any number of possible beings. Yet however much power one had, he would not be almighty because he would not be a necessary being.[8] But if it is an overall best act that a solitary God share his essential almightiness, the only way in which this can be done is if he creates as a separate God what is God anyway, i.e., if he divides himself. The creation being everlasting, this is to be read as: he creates as a separate God what, but for his creative action, would be himself.[9]

This passage seems to contain an answer to our question, but it may also leave us puzzled: If this is indeed the answer to a question that was left unanswered in *The Christian God,* why was it not repeated (unlike much else in the article) in the later work?

Fortunately, Professor Swinburne has kindly consented to clarify this situation by responding to my queries. He states: "in chapter 8 of *The Christian God,* I dropped the claim that the Son and the Spirit can only be 'created' if the Father 'divided himself'. I can't see any need for that requirement, and in any case I doubt that it makes any sense to talk of a non-physical being dividing itself—division only applies to extended and so physical substances."[10] He also says, "I avoid talk of the Father 'creating' the other members of the Trinity in the book, in deference to the normal usage of the Fathers and scholastics that 'creates' only applies to the bringing about of something finite by an act of will." Does this mean, then, that the Son and the Spirit are brought into being *ex nihilo?* In response to this question, Swinburne states, "I'd prefer to say that the Son and the Spirit were 'brought about, but not brought about out of anything', rather than that they were 'brought about from nothing'. The phrase '*ex nihilo*' caused a lot of trouble in the Middle Ages, when creation of

---

[8] Apparently the thought here is that if God (i.e. the Father) were to create *ex nihilo* persons with the attributes of omnipotence, omniscience, etc., God would freely choose which of a number of "possible individuals" of this sort to create. The existence of the ones actually created would not, then, be necessary, and so those created individuals would not be Gods, regardless of their other attributes. As we shall see, Swinburne later came to rethink this assumption.

[9] "Could there Be More than One God?" 232.

[10] This and the following quotations are from private emails; my thanks to Richard Swinburne for permitting me to use them here.

the universe *ex nihilo* was understood by some as if being brought about from some pre-existing thing, 'nothing'."[11]

Once again, this is admirably clear, and it puts the "bringing about" of the existence of Son and Spirit in a considerably different light than what would appear from the quotation taken from the earlier article. The talk of the Father "dividing himself," while certainly not without problems, seems fairly close to the traditional doctrine of the eternal generation of the Son and procession of the Spirit. To say, on the other hand, that they were "brought about, but not brought about out of anything" (and surely, this is the proper and correct meaning of the phrase, *ex nihilo*), really does seem to amount to saying that the Son and Spirit are created.[12] It is true that this creation is "necessary," in the sense explained above, but that does not seem a sufficient reason to refuse to use the word "created." (In Leibniz's scheme the existence of the "best possible world"—and therefore, of all the individuals comprised in that world—is necessary in exactly this sense; it is required by the divine goodness. But that did not lead Leibniz to deny that God *creates* the denizens of that world.) It is certainly true that "deference to normal usage" would prompt us to refrain from saying that the Son and the Spirit are created. But in a philosophical investigation such as this one "normal usage" should not be allowed to keep us from saying things that are clearly implied by other claims that are being made; as I am sure Swinburne would agree, diplomacy and philosophy are different language games! I therefore respectfully suggest that Swinburne's view of the Trinity does imply that the Son and the Holy Spirit are created, even though they are beings of a very different sort than all the other individuals that God has created.

If this is correct, however, it opens a significant breach between Swinburne and the main trinitarian tradition. Probably this breach is even more serious than the one occasioned by calling the Son and the Spirit the "second God" and the "third God." That rift could be closed—and was closed by Swinburne—simply by ceasing to use the questionable terminology, but this one arises because of fundamental commitments of his position. To bring this out, I would call our attention to certain features of the Arian controversy. One of the factors which helped to precipitate that controversy was the rise, during the third century, of a recognition of a sharp division between God, the Creator, and everything else in existence, all of which is created by God.

---

[11] When he wrote the book, Swinburne no longer believed that the Son and the Spirit would have "thisnesses" even if, as he now supposes, they were "brought about, but not brought about out of anything." So the difficulty previously noted no longer applies.

[12] Interestingly, in the earlier article Swinburne does speak of the Son and the Spirit as "created" (see "Could there Be More than One God?" p. 233), though it would have seemed he could have avoided saying this by appealing to the division by the Father of his own substance. It is harder to see how his later view can consistently avoid the language of creation. For a similar criticism, see Brian Leftow, "Anti Social Trinitarianism," in McCall and Rea, *Philosophical and Theological Essays*, 82–4.

Methodius of Olympus took the lead in emphasizing this division; he attacked Origen's doctrine of an "eternal creation" and "insisted on a punctiliar eruption of creation from nothing into existence. God alone was unbegotten, sole existent, uniquely prior to everything that came to be through him."[13] This new emphasis may well have been part of what pushed Arius and his followers to insist on the status of the Logos as a created being, whereas earlier subordinationists had often been vague on this point. For Arius, Asterius, and Eunomius it was of paramount importance to maintain the absolute distinction between God, the Unbegotten, and everything else. At the same time, however, they were forced to compromise this distinction by affirming that the Logos was both a creature and himself a creator—the latter both because of scripture, which attributes creation to Christ, and because of the structural requirements of their own system.[14] This compromise was in turn exploited against the Arians by the followers of Nicaea: since the Son-Logos is recognized as Creator, he must be unequivocally divine rather than being in any sense himself a creature.[15]

In a certain way, Swinburne finds himself aligned with the Arian side in this controversy. Not that Swinburne is an Arian! He fully supports the Nicene doctrine that Father, Son, and Spirit are *homoousios*—i.e. fully divine, sharing in all of the essential divine attributes (see *The Christian God*, 185–6). But he is in agreement with the anti-Nicenes in blurring the fundamental distinction between creatures and the Creator. He does this, not by making the Creator less than fully divine (as the Arians did), but by allowing that the Creator, the Son-Logos, was himself created *even though fully divine*. None of the ancient Fathers, I believe, would have accepted that a person could be both fully divine ("true God," as they would say) and created, even in the special sense in which, according to Swinburne, the Son and the Spirit are created. Nor, I believe, would they have accepted that a divine person could conceivably be annihilated, even by divine "compatibilist power." If we are reluctant (as I think we should be) to breach the Creator–creature distinction in this way, then we will also be reluctant to accept Swinburne's doctrine of the Trinity as a satisfactory solution to the problems of trinitarian theology.

---

[13] Khaled Anatolios, *Retrieving Nicaea*, (Grand Rapids MI: Baker Academic, 2011), 39; cf. Ayres, *Nicaea*, 29.

[14] Anatolios characterizes the anti-Nicene or Arian position thus: "Jesus Christ, inasmuch as he is scripturally designated even in his exalted titles as deriving his being from the Father, enjoys a precedence that is still within the realm of creation and inferior to the Unbegotten and unoriginated God. But inasmuch as he is also scripturally characterized as Creator, then he must be conceived, in his divinity, as created Creator." *Retrieving Nicaea*, 288.

[15] *Retrieving Nicaea*, 80–1, and esp. 288: "In ruling out the notion of a created Creator...Nicene theology instituted a strict and unqualified demarcation between the eternal perfection of divine being and the contingency of creation from nothing, as well as its global status of servitude."

19

Yandell: The Trinity as a Complex Bearer of Properties

The last in our series of philosophers' readings of the doctrine of the Trinity comes from Keith Yandell.[1] He begins by listing seven claims, each of which is entailed by the doctrine of the Trinity:

(1) The Father is God.

(2) The Son is God.

(3) The Holy Spirit is God.

(4) The Father is not the Son.

(5) The Son is not the Holy Spirit.

(6) The Father is not the Holy Spirit.

(7) There is one God. (p. 152)

If the "is" of (1)–(3) is read as the "is" of identity, we immediately get several contradictions. For instance, (1) and (2) jointly entail the negation of (4), and (4)–(6) together with (7) entail the negation of the conjunction of (1)–(3). These contradictions, Yandell tells us, provide "an excellent reason not to read the 'is' of (1)–(3) as the 'is of identity'" (p. 152). Instead, he invites us to suppose that

> there is a set G of properties such that if something has all of the members of G, that is necessary and sufficient for being God or having the divine nature. Then (1) says that the Father possesses all the members of G, and (2) and (3) say that the Son and the Holy Spirit possess all the members of G as well. This leaves us with three persons having the divine nature. How can this be reconciled to (7), the statement of monotheism? (p. 152)

So even if we avoid the initial contradictions by declining to read the "is" of (1)–(3) as the "is" of identity, we are left with a problem concerning (7). Nor

---

[1] The principal source is Keith Yandell, "How Many Times does Three Go into One?" in McCall and Rea, *Philosophical and Theological Essays*, 151–68. (Page references in this chapter are to this essay.) An earlier article is "The Most Brutal and Inexcusable Error in Counting? Trinity and Consistency," *Religious Studies*, 30 (1994), 201–17.

is this the only remaining problem. There is a classic philosophical doctrine, the Identity of Indiscernibles, which Yandell states as follows: "For all X and Y, and any property Q, if X has Q if and only if Y has Q, then X=Y. Given this, if the Father, the Son, and the Holy Spirit all possess all the members of G, then they are numerically identical. But then (4)–(6) are false" (p. 152).[2]

Yet another problem lurks, which is introduced by a quotation from Augustine:

> There are the Father, the Son, and the Holy Spirit, and each is God, and at the same time all are one God and each of them is a full substance, and at the same time all are the same substance.[3]

Yandell comments:

> It seems natural to talk about the Father as a substance, the Son as a substance, and the Holy Spirit as a substance. Each is biblically described as an agent, an initiator of actions for purposes, as possessing intelligence and will. The term "person" seems to fit nicely, and persons, at least for common sense, and lots of philosophers, are substances. It does not seem natural to speak of three persons as "all…the same substance."…How is it possible that each person is a substance, and the Trinity is also a substance? Is the Trinity a composite substance? (p. 153; first ellipsis in original)

Yandell proceeds to consider a way out of these difficulties we have already taken account of, the doctrine of relative identity. He argues to the conclusion that "identity can neither be relativized nor be contingent" (p. 157). Nor, he goes on to argue, can any form of subordination within the Trinity be accepted as a solution to the difficulties. What then is left? He concludes his essay by offering "an extremely elementary sketch of two possible ways of seeing trinity-in-unity in a Christian view of God" (p. 162). These "two ways" are built around different ways of understanding the nature of and relationship between properties and individuals, ways that trace all the way back to Plato and Aristotle. Yandell acknowledges the complexity of the issues involved, and states, "I can only hope to be as accurate as a very general sketch allows. I will not defend one account against the other, or against competitors. Thus what we have here is suggestive rather than definitive" (p. 162).

The two ways in question are differentiated by their respective views of properties. On the "properties as universals" view (PAU), properties are indeed

---

[2] There are two problems here. First, Yandell actually calls this principle the "Indiscernibility of Identicals," but this is a mistake. The principle of the Indiscernibility of Identicals states that "For all X and Y, if X = Y, then for any property Q, X has Q if and only if Y has Q." This principle simply does not apply here, since Yandell has already rejected the view that the Persons of the Trinity are identical. Furthermore, the Identity of Indiscernibles could apply only if the members of G are the only properties possessed by any of the trinitarian Persons. As we shall see, something similar to this does seem to be Yandell's view, but nothing to that effect has been stated thus far.

[3] Augustine, *On Christian Doctrine*, tr. G. W. Robertson (Indianapolis: Bobbs-Merrill, 1958), 10; quoted at Yandell, "How Many Times?" p. 153.

universals that are instantiated by individuals. On the "embedded property view" (EPV), there are no universals, and

> each property is "embedded in" its "owner". The phrase "embedded in" is to be at least partly understood in this manner: property Q is embedded in item X only if (i) X has Q, (ii) Q exists only insofar as it is a property of X, (iii) X's having Q is not due to X's being in any relation to (instantiating) a universal. For EPV, every property is bearer-specific, not something that can have many instances though, depending on the property, it may resemble other properties. (p. 164)

It is clear from his exposition that Yandell favors the EPV, but as things turn out either view of properties allows for the formulation of a coherent doctrine of the Trinity. The trinitarian payoff for the two views of properties comes in their respective views concerning individuation. "If one accepts EPV, one can offer the suggestion that the bottom line of individuation is reflected in a basic category of a metaphysics where neither 'substance' nor 'property' plays that role, and 'bearer-with-property' does. Bearers of properties, for EPV, are not composed of properties, but cannot exist without some" (p. 165). And on the other hand, "For PAU, the bottom line is bearer-of-property-instantiations and universals (instantiated or not). But each instantiation is owned and could not be owned by any other item than the one that does own it" (pp. 165–6). One might put this by saying that, on either of these views, *individuation is primitive,* and need not be explained by anything else (for instance, by the possession of some unique property or combination of properties). Because of this, the Persons of the Trinity can be distinct (as the doctrine requires them to be) even though each Person has all and only the same essential properties, namely the members of G. As Yandell states, "taking the notion of a bearer-of-properties, in one or other of the senses sketched, as a primitive category in an ontology, will give numerical distinction incapable of, and so needing no, further individuation in terms of other sorts of items of which property-bearers are composed" (p. 168).[4]

Yandell concludes that, on either of the schemes he has explained, "(1)–(6) are a consistent set of propositions. They say that the divine nature is had by each of three bearers-of-property-instantiations, or each of three bearers-of-embedded-properties. That leaves (7), the assertion of monotheism" (pp. 166–7). Finally, then, in the last two pages (!) of his article, Yandell addresses the theme of the unity of God.

---

[4] The upshot of this is that Yandell rejects the Identity of Indiscernibles. This principle continues to be controversial, though most philosophers seem to have accepted some version of it. (Properties of *a*, such as *being identical with a* and *being distinct from b*, presuppose individuation; they can't be used to explain it.)

Yandell begins his account of God's unity by setting out four propositions that are at least implicitly included in the doctrine of the Trinity:

> (T1) For any Trinitarian person P, it is logically impossible that P exist and either of the other Trinitarian persons not exist.
> (T2) For any Trinitarian person P, it is logically impossible that P will what is not willed by the other Trinitarian persons.
> (T3) For any Trinitarian person P, it is logically impossible that P engage in any activity in which the other Trinitarian persons in no way engage.
> (T4) The persons of the Trinity have complete non-inferential awareness of one another. (p. 167)[5]

After a brief discussion of these propositions, Yandell concludes simply, "(T1)–(T4) defines oneness of the three" (p. 167). He goes on to consider the problem created by Augustine's dual use of "substance." That term, however, is deemed unsuitable in view of its complex and potentially confusing history of use. He says, "I propose that either notion of property or property-bearer, insofar as otherwise in order, will do the job for which the double use of 'substance' was intended. The Trinity is a bearer of some properties that are not properties of the persons. *Being Trinitarian* and *being 'all there is' to God* are two such properties" (p. 168). So both the Trinity as a whole and each of the Persons is a bearer-of-properties; what Augustine called a "substance." Yandell concludes his exposition by stating, "if part of what it means [to say there is one Trinitarian God] is what is sketched here, and that part is logically consistent, then we have a sketch of a doctrine of the Trinity that meets the opening challenges. That would be a good beginning on a trip toward a goal we can't reach" (p. 168).

REMAINING QUESTIONS

As we begin our evaluation, I would agree that Yandell has succeeded in stating "part of what it means to say there is one Trinitarian God," and has done so in a clear, rigorous and formal fashion that is logically consistent. As he would readily admit, many more questions remain to be addressed. I propose to follow up some questions regarding his "Oneness Factors" (p. 167); principally about the claims (T1)–(T4), which according to him "define oneness of the three." These claims, of course, are not unique to Yandell; indeed virtually any of the major trinitarian thinkers we have considered could endorse them, perhaps

---

[5] It should be noted that Yandell seems to be a bit more tentative concerning (T2) and (T3) than he is concerning the other two propositions. Clearly, (T2) and (T3) need to be handled carefully in the context of the incarnation, to allow for actions of the incarnate Son that are not, in the same way, actions of the Father and the Holy Spirit. (I assume that (T4) also is taken to be necessary, though this is not explicitly stated.)

with minor variations. Those thinkers, however, had additional resources for affirming the divine oneness, resources that are not available to Yandell. All of the ancient writers on the doctrine affirmed the origin, in some way, of the Son and the Holy Spirit from the Father. I have argued, furthermore, that the pro-Nicene Fathers affirmed the numerical identity of the concrete divine nature, a nature that was possessed in common by Father, Son, and Spirit. Of the contemporary philosophers we have surveyed, Craig affirms the singular concrete divine nature (the "soul" which, in his view, is the one divine substance), while he abandons the relations of origin. Swinburne, on the other hand, rejects the singular concrete divine nature but affirms the relations of origin. Yandell, however, affirms neither of these traditional doctrines,[6] and so we have to ask: *Are (T1)–(T4), taken by themselves, sufficient to express the divine unity and guarantee monotheism?* I will argue that they are not sufficient for this.

Let us focus for the moment just on (T1), which states that no one trinitarian Person could exist without the other two, and ask the following question: Does the fact that (T1) is a necessary proposition constitute in itself a sufficient explanation for the fact stated by the proposition? There is a tendency to think that if a proposition is necessarily true, no further explanation for its truth is required. This tendency, I believe, comes from focusing on propositions that are analytic or conceptual truths. Suppose I say, comparing the height of three siblings, "If Peter is taller than Susan and Susan is taller than Edmund, Edmund can't be just as tall as Peter, as he claims." If you then ask for an explanation as to why my assertion is true, I can only conclude that you don't understand it—possibly, that you don't understand the expressions "taller than" or "just as tall as." But these sorts of considerations don't apply in the case of (T1). (T1) is not an analytic or conceptual truth;[7] pretty clearly, it falls in the vast and murky region of what Plantinga has termed "broadly logical necessity."[8] For truths such as this, even if they are in some sense necessary, it is far from obvious that no further explanation of their truth is required. Swinburne, for example, has given quite a careful explanation for the truth of (T1), as we saw in the last chapter. One may or may not agree with his explanation, but it would seem very strange to respond that it is out of order because the fact being explained neither requires nor admits of further explanation.

---

[6] For his rejection of the processions, see "How Many Times?" pp. 157–8 n. 8; his rejection of the singular concrete divine nature follows from his insistence that neither properties (on EPV) nor property-instantiations (on PAU) can be multiply owned.

[7] To be sure, (T1) can be made to be a conceptual truth, for instance by defining the expression "the Son" as meaning, "the Second Person of the Trinity, who eternally and necessarily co-exists with the Father and the Holy Spirit." But this trivializes the whole exercise, and leaves one open to the question, "Why do you suppose that the expression 'the Son', as you define it, refers to anything?"

[8] See Alvin Plantinga, *The Nature of Necessity* (Oxford: Clarendon Press, 1974).

It seems plausible, then, that the truth of (T1) does call for further explana-tion, even if it is admitted to be necessary. If so, however, the consequences for Yandell are serious. We have here a proposition of absolutely central and fun-damental importance, which is claimed to be both true and necessary, with no justification offered for either claim except that the proposition is implied by a doctrine one is trying to defend. Furthermore, it looks very doubtful that Yandell's theory, as he has expounded it, offers any resources at all for giving a further explanation for this alleged necessary truth. We might term such propositions *brute necessities*. Perhaps brute necessities are sometimes una-voidable, but it would be idle to pretend that they add anything to philosophi-cal understanding or enhance the credibility of a system of thought in which they are ensconced.

But the consequences for Yandell if (T1) does not require further explana-tion may be even worse. If (T1) does not require further explanation, this can only be because, in general, broadly logically necessary truths require no such explanation. But (T1)–(T4) are not the only broadly logically necessary truths in the vicinity. We also need to consider

(T5) Necessarily, the Father exists,
(T6) Necessarily, the Son exists, and
(T7) Necessarily, the Holy Spirit exists.[9]

Following our assumption with regard to (T1), the truth of (T5) *fully and com-pletely explains* the existence of the Father, and so also with the Son and the Spirit; no further explanation of their existence is possible or required. But from (T5)–(T7) the truth of (T1) follows immediately: since the existence of each Person is necessary and his non-existence impossible, it is obviously impos-sible for any of the three to exist without the other two. But here's the rub: (T1), understood in this way, *completely fails* to assert any significant metaphysical dependence of any trinitarian Person on either of the other two. Rather, each Person has his existence entirely "on his own"; they are "inter-dependent" only in the sense in which any necessary truth "depends" on any other, in that it is impossible for one to be true and the other false. In this sense, the tautol-ogy about the heights of the children cited above "depends on" the truth of the four-color theorem in topology, and vice versa—but clearly, this is not "dependence" in any intuitively meaningful sense. We have, rather, a situation in which, in Swinburne's words, Father, Son, and Holy Spirit are each "ulti-mate sources of being," which is surely intolerable both as trinitarian doctrine and as general metaphysics.

Now that we have seen this, we can also see that this untoward consequence is not to be evaded even if we go back to the earlier assumption that (T1) is

⁹ For Yandell's explicit endorsement of these claims, see "The Most Brutal and Inexcusable Error," 204.

indeed in need of further explanation. For it will still be true that (T5)–(T7) are all necessary truths, and that the truth of (T1) follows from their conjunction. So it may very well be that the needed further explanation of (T1) comes by way of the explanations (whatever they may be) of the truth of (T5)–(T7), and it remains true that Father, Son, and Holy Spirit are each ultimate sources of being. Now, that this is the case does not of course *follow from* (T1). It is however true that it is *consistent with* (T1); it is in no way *ruled out* by (T1). But a proposition which fails to rule out such an obviously unacceptable and heretical interpretation certainly cannot stand as an adequate affirmation of the unity of God and of monotheism.

It might occur to us that a closer union of the Persons will be forced if we consider (T2)–(T4) as well as (T1). This is not obviously correct, however. Each of the Persons is cognitively perfect and is therefore immediately (non-inferentially) aware of any state of affairs that obtains, including states of affairs involving the other Persons—so we have (T4) at no additional cost. Now, each Person, in virtue of bearing the properties in G, is morally perfect and in every other way excellent and admirable. It would then seem to follow, as Swinburne has argued, that each will recognize that is good to give his backing to, and participate in, the projects initiated by each other Person, projects which will inevitably be good things to do. But suppose, as Swinburne thinks possible, the Persons were to settle independently on courses of action that, while each individually good, are incompatible with each other? In that case, each supremely good Person will recognize that it would be a *bad thing* for him to insist on his own preferences in disregard for the preferences of another divine Person; they will, then, find some mutually agreeable way to settle the differences. (Of course, if there were some compelling reason why one course of action is better than the other, there would not be the disagreement in the first place.) Even we faulty and defective human beings often manage to avoid serious conflict in such situations, at least when egotism and self-interest are not too seriously involved! None of this, however, requires us to recognize any closer *metaphysical* unity than that which has been sketched in the text; it can still be the case that each Person is an ultimate, independent source of being. I conclude, then, that the conclusion stated above has now been fully justified: Yandell's sketch of the doctrine of the Trinity, however excellent in other respects, fails to guarantee monotheism or to provide us with an adequate account of the unity of God.[10]

---

[10] I've argued that Yandell is in trouble whether or not the truth of (T1) requires further explanation. Does this mean that a system that affirms (T1) can't escape these difficulties? No, it does not. The solution must be, not merely to hold that (T1) requires further explanation, but actually to provide such an explanation, one that precludes the Persons' being "each ultimate sources of being." But it is very doubtful that Yandell's theory as he has presented it (without either relations of origin or a single concrete divine nature) provides him with resources to offer such an explanation.

20

What Have We Learned?

So what have we learned from our review of trinitarian options? To begin with, none of the candidates has turned out to be fully satisfactory. That can hardly be a surprise; if it were otherwise, this book would have developed very differently, or might not have been written at all. Nor should we conclude that the philosophers and theologians who crafted these versions of trinitarian doctrine were in any way bunglers or incompetent. The "three-in-oneness" problem of the Trinity is *really hard*; once we move beyond simply repeating traditional formulas, it is difficult indeed to find our way and avoid mistakes. Nevertheless, I believe there is much to be learned from the candidates we have surveyed, in terms both of errors to be avoided and constructive ideas that can be incorporated into a better solution.

The "modes of being/subsistence" proposal from Barth and Rahner is included because it represents the best-developed view of the Trinity that is clearly anti-Social, put forward by eminent theologians who intended to be thoroughly orthodox, and who did much to energize the recent resurgence of trinitarian thought. These men also exhibit some of the biblical and theological difficulties that result if one makes a resolute attempt to avoid a Social trinitarian understanding of the divine Persons. Moltmann and Zizioulas, on the other hand, present to us two different theological accounts of Social trinitarianism. Each of their accounts has significant strengths, but also evident weaknesses. I suspect, in fact, that the problems with their proposals go some ways towards accounting for the wariness about Social trinitarianism exhibited by some contemporary theologians and philosophers.

Leftow's "Latin trinitarianism" represents an ingenious attempt to combine the insistence on God as a single divine person with some elements that seem more at home in Social trinitarianism—three divine "life-streams," and something approaching personal relationships between the Persons. If that combination of elements is attractive to you, I suspect you will not easily find a better realization of it than Leftow has provided. Van Inwagen's relative-identity solution has an obvious appeal: it provides a way to accommodate the paradoxical language often found in trinitarian discourse (e.g. in Augustine or in the Athanasian Creed) while avoiding contradiction and logical incoherence.

For the reasons given, I don't find it an adequate solution (and for what it's worth, the majority of interested philosophers seem to agree with this), but readers must consider the matter and decide for themselves. Brower and Rea's "impure RI" strategy offers a way to reap the benefits of relative identity without incurring the cost of denying the existence of classical identity. It has been argued here that this strategy cannot succeed; once terms such as "the one God" and "the one divine substance" are admitted to be ambiguous, the claim of this version to be orthodox can no longer be sustained.

The relative-identity versions are neutral, so far as the formal theories go, on the issue of Social versus anti-Social trinitarianism; the philosophers who promote these versions can and do have their own views on the matter. The remaining three options, in contrast, are all clearly in the Social trinitarian camp, as Social trinitarianism has been defined here. As I have noted, Craig's doctrine of the Trinity comprises two relatively distinct parts: there is a formal theory, and there is a model that aims at providing a more adequate intuitive understanding of the doctrine. According to the formal theory, "God" as a noun most properly refers to the Trinity as a whole; the Persons, Father, Son, and Holy Spirit, "are God" or "are divine" in virtue of being the right sort of *parts* of the Trinity which is God. This theory does not fit easily with the traditional language of trinitarian discourse, and has other difficulties that may or may not be solvable. According to the model, we may think of God as a single "soul" with three "sets of faculties," each set subserving the life of one of the three Persons. An additional feature worthy of note is Craig's rejection of the doctrine of "relations of origin," which has characterized the entirety of the ancient and medieval trinitarian tradition. Swinburne's carefully crafted account restores the relations of origin, but rejects the single, concrete divine nature which figured in the traditional doctrine. In addition, his account of the origin of the Son and the Spirit really does seem to have the implication that these fully divine Persons were *created* by the Father. Finally, Yandell, like Swinburne, presents a carefully crafted logical structure for trinitarian doctrine. However, he rejects both the relations of origin (like Craig) and the unitary concrete divine substance (like Swinburne). I have argued that, in virtue of these two deviations from the trinitarian tradition, his view is unable (contrary to his own intentions) to provide even a minimally satisfactory account of the divine unity.

Since the constructive view to be presented here is a version of Social trinitarianism (that at least should be no surprise!), the ideas offered by Craig, Swinburne, and Yandell will be especially pertinent as we move forward. However, the other authors will make their own contributions, both by providing constructive suggestions and for their penetrating criticisms of Social trinitarianism, criticism that will help to guide and to sharpen the view that is offered. These matters will provide the substance of the third and final part of this book.

Part III

Trinitarian Construction

21

Constructing the Doctrine of the Trinity

The divine Trinity of Father, Son, and Holy Spirit is not constructed by anyone, not even by God. God does not construct the Trinity; God *is* the Trinity. The *doctrine* of the Trinity, however, is undeniably something constructed, as the history of that doctrine amply attests. This no more suggests that the Trinity is unreal, a product of human ingenuity, than the laborious and still far-from-complete construction of physical theories suggests that the realities of which they speak—galaxies, black holes, quarks, electrons, dark matter, and dark energy—are produced by the imagination of the scientists who theorize about them. In either case, it is our hope that our laboriously constructed interpretations capture something (but never everything) of the realities with which we are concerned.

To be sure, the parallel between the theories of physics and of theology can easily be carried too far. There is no intent here to advance the claim that theology is an empirical science in the same way as physics! Theology has its own sources on which it draws, the most important of which is divine revelation. No revelation, no theology—at least, no Christian theology. Furthermore, it is the audacious but indispensable Christian claim that the revelation in Christ is unique and unsurpassable. However, the process of reflection and, yes, of theorizing called forth by that revelation continues, not only throughout the earliest Christian centuries but today as well. And the present book represents, it is hoped, one more small step in that process. My intent in the following pages, then, is to theorize about the divine three-in-oneness in a way that brings us a step closer to comprehending that mysterious reality. In this chapter something will be said about the procedure for this enterprise, and some methodological assumptions that will guide us as we pursue it. I shall also take the time for some remarks about a particularly crucial metaphysical concept that is involved in our reflections—the concept of necessity. Finally, I shall look at an important statement that sketches out, in anticipation, the goal of trinitarian doctrine I shall be hoping to express.

PROCEDURE AND METHODOLOGY

One slightly unusual feature of the exposition here is that it presents the central issues of trinitarian doctrine in a series of clear-cut steps, showing at each juncture the decision that must be made in order to proceed with the construction of the doctrine. Those who demur from the view of the doctrine that emerges will be able to see clearly at what point(s) they feel obliged to part ways with us; those who are able to continue will gain a clear view of the steps by which the construction has proceeded. This process of construction will not necessarily follow closely the actual historical evolution of the doctrine of the Trinity, but neither are the two processes unrelated.

Some of the methodological assumptions we will be making should be already apparent from Part I. I do believe that the Holy Spirit has not left the Church without guidance as it sought to comprehend the nature of the God who had revealed himself. This does not imply infallibility; it does mean, however, that we ought to treat both the historical process of the development of doctrine and the results of that process with a great deal of respect. I have indicated my conviction that the pro-Nicene theologians of the late fourth century constitute for us an invaluable, indeed indispensable resource. They may not have got everything right, but if we were to conclude that they got the doctrine of the Trinity fundamentally wrong we would have little reason to persist in our own efforts at trinitarian theorizing.

These reflections lead naturally to the question of how far should we feel free to digress from the actual thought-structures of the ancient pro-Nicenes. Lewis Ayres, in *Nicaea and its Legacy,* comes very close to insisting that we must accept the particular exegetical strategies of the Fathers as our own guide in setting forth the doctrine of the Trinity.[1] It seems to me that we simply cannot do this; to ignore what we have learned since the fourth century about the interpretation of biblical texts is simply to disregard some of what we know (or with good reason believe) to be the truth, and this cannot be the right way to arrive at further truth. Furthermore, it overstates the fragility of the doctrine of the Trinity to suppose that the doctrine's viability is tied to the particular exegetical strategies of those who first framed the doctrine. A more plausible view, I suggest, is that the key conceptions that ground the doctrine are *over-determined* by the biblical text; what may be lost in one place by giving up a traditional reading can often be recaptured somewhere else. (And some deletions may have the effect of ridding us of unwanted baggage. Proverbs 8: 22, "The LORD created me at the beginning of his works," speaks of the divine Wisdom. Interpreted as referring to the Logos, this text provided much fuel for the Arians and occasioned much heart-searching among the orthodox. It

---

[1] I find it interesting in this connection that Ayres the historian shows no signs of deferring to the historical interpretations of the ancient chroniclers!

then comes as something of a relief to recognize that this passage simply has nothing to say about the doctrine of the Trinity!) Obviously, not everything in contemporary biblical scholarship can or should be taken on board without reservation. Often enough, one scholar's "assured results" are in the eyes of another precarious speculations. Furthermore, some modern approaches to interpretation are specifically designed to negate or neutralize the "high christology" that is fundamental for the doctrine of the Trinity. But the solution for these problems is not to be found in simply reverting to the exegetical strategies of some favored period in the past.[2]

If we cannot accept without question the biblical interpretations put forward by the ancient Fathers, still less can we grant canonical status to their favored philosophical constructions. They did the best they could with the philosophical resources they had at their disposal, and it remains for us to do the same with what is available to us today. (And in neither case is there any guarantee that the tools available will be sufficient to the task.) Where we find their constructions solid and reliable, we will appropriate them and extend them as best we can, but when we find them inadequate we will need to strike out on our own in new directions. (I have already argued that the doctrine of divine simplicity, which plays a central role in many construals of the doctrine, cannot be retained in its traditional form.) There is, I believe, a built-in bias here that influences many patristic scholars. Their training, naturally enough, focuses mainly on the historical and philological skills needed if one is to properly interpret ancient documents. Such philosophical training as they have tends to be concerned mainly with the ancient philosophies that constituted the philosophical resources that were available to the early theologians. In interpreting the Fathers, furthermore, they are rightly concerned first of all to make sense of the texts as they stand, giving a sympathetic interpretation to assertions which to us today might seem at first sight to be implausible or even untenable. And finally, most of them develop an attachment and a sense of alliance with at least some of the Fathers to whom they devote their careers. All of this leads to an entirely understandable reluctance to challenge the Fathers' philosophical views, especially those that were integral to their developed theologies.

All this, it must be acknowledged, is entirely natural and in many ways commendable, but it leaves a fundamental question unanswered: *Are the philosophical assumptions and claims made by the various Fathers in their accounts of the Trinity credible and defensible?* If they are, then there is work that needs to be done in warding off the challenges posed by more recent

---

[2] Once again, I cite Gerald O'Collins, *The Tripersonal God: Understanding and Interpreting the Trinity* (New York: Paulist Press, 1999) as an example of such a mediating approach. O'Collins interacts extensively with contemporary critical scholarship, yet finds in the biblical texts ample warrant for an orthodox doctrine of the Trinity. In the following chapter, we will see examples of contemporary scholarship that are extremely helpful for the task on which we are engaged.

philosophy. If they are not, then an even more challenging task awaits us: the task of reformulating, in our own philosophical idiom, the theological claims they set forth in terms of philosophical assumptions we can no longer adopt as our own. Fortunately, there are a few scholars who are well-versed both in the ancient sources and in the disciplines of contemporary philosophy, who are willing to call a spade a spade and apply critical insight to the assumptions of our theological predecessors. G. Christopher Stead comes to mind here, and Richard Cross may be another example. The present volume makes no claim to rival these scholars in their mastery of the ancient sources, but it can benefit from their critical insights as we seek to arrive at formulations that are viable for us today.

So we need to bring to our task the tools of contemporary philosophy, but we also need to exercise discretion in how those tools are employed. In one way, it shows respect to the ancients when we deal with them as if they were colleagues in our philosophy departments. This is certainly an improvement over treating their ideas as curiosities, which we take down off the shelf from time to time in order to admire their cunning craftsmanship, but otherwise leave lying unused. But neglecting the particular character of ancient theological language, and treating it as if it were written by our philosophical colleagues, can also lead to distortions. We need to acknowledge and respect the nature and limitations of trinitarian language, in particular its analogical character. It has repeatedly been the experience of those who sought to write concerning the Trinity that "words fail us"—that what needs to be expressed exceeds the limits of the language that is available. So language has to be bent, stretched, taken out of its normal context, and put to new uses, in order to convey the appropriate ideas concerning the divine Tri-unity. Language treated in this fashion is inevitably analogical in character; it shares some of its meaning with more customary uses of the expressions in question, but deviates from those uses in other respects. To some extent, it must be said, this feature of trinitarian language tends to be obscured by the apparent precision of creedal formulations. The creeds are definite because they are intended to furnish a norm for Christian teaching and belief, but any sense of scientific precision is belied once we begin to look more closely at the process by which they were formulated. Accepting the tradition, then, entails accepting the language of trinitarian belief *with its limitations*. The nature of trinitarian language requires, I believe, that we exercise restraint in our attempts to formalize this language and to employ it in the construction of systematic deductive arguments. Here, I am afraid, is where the shoe really begins to pinch so far as we analytic philosophers are concerned! We have a strong professional bias that impels us to make our own language as precise as it can possibly be, and to demand the same precision of others insofar as it lies in our power to do so. When confronted with vague and imprecise formulations we feel a powerful urge to disambiguate them, and if this cannot be done we are inclined to doubt whether the offending expressions have any meaning at all. We have by now got beyond the stage at which all religious language automatically comes under suspicion as being meaningless, but the urge to precision, and the corresponding urge to construct tight formal arguments, remains very much a part of our mindset.[3]

I am not decrying these tendencies; they serve a purpose and much good philosophy results from their being honored. I merely point out that the nature of trinitarian language, as briefly described above, places necessary limitations on the tendencies in question. Terms used in formal arguments must be constant in meaning in relevant respects in order for the arguments to be valid; otherwise we have the fallacy of equivocation. With analogical language, on the other hand, there is often a degree of ambiguity or vagueness concerning the intended meaning—that is, concerning how much of the original meaning is carried over in the analogy. This ambiguity tends to be covered up, however, if we replace the analogical term with a symbolic letter or logical formula, as is often done in constructing formal arguments. Another pitfall lies in the assumption we are prone to make that our existing philosophical vocabulary is adequate to express the concepts and make the distinctions that are needed for the doctrine of the Trinity. Christian thinkers in the early centuries who were struggling to think through the doctrine of God often found existing conceptions inadequate for their purposes; it would be hubristic for us to assume that, because our philosophical resources are greater than theirs, the same situation cannot arise for us. But what I am saying should not be over-interpreted. I am not putting up a sign saying to my fellow analytic philosophers, "Abandon hope, all you who enter here." I merely suggest that we tread a bit softly, and consider carefully whether our professional inclinations are serving or impeding the task of understanding trinitarian doctrine.[4]

THE NATURE OF NECESSITY

One of the most central concepts of metaphysics is the concept of *necessity,* with its related notions of possibility, impossibility, and contingency. In a general sense, the idea is clear enough: what is necessary is what *could not be otherwise.* What is possible is what *might be,* what is impossible is what *could*

[3] One reader states, "I think that it is good to avoid over-emphasizing the distance between 'the tools of contemporary philosophy' and the tools available to the pro-Nicenes (in some important ways, it seems that contemporary analytic work is closer to classical philosophy than either is to, say, a lot of what was prevalent in the 19th and 20th centuries)." I agree with this, yet I still think the warning contained in the text is needed.

[4] Some of the material in this and the preceding paragraphs is adapted from my "Has a Trinitarian God Deceived Us?," in T. McCall and M. C. Rea, *Philosophical and Theological Essays on the Trinity* (Oxford: OUP, 2009), 44–6.

not be, and the contingent is that which *might either be or not be.* But while the relationships between these notions are firmly fixed, the core meaning remains elusive. What precisely is meant by saying that a state of affairs—or, perhaps, a proposition—"could not be otherwise"? A little reflection will suffice to convince us that there are different senses of "necessary," so that what is necessary in one of these senses may be contingent in another sense. There is, for example, *causal necessity,* the necessity that pertains to a state of affairs that is causally necessitated, in that it is required by the "laws of nature" in conjunction with the situation that obtained at a previous time. The positions of the planets in the twenty-third century are, one assumes, causally necessitated by their positions today, conjoined with the laws of physics; that is what makes astronomical prediction possible. Causal necessity as such is, however, relatively unimportant for metaphysics, and in particular for the doctrine of the Trinity. (The standard conception of divine omnipotence entails that God, by working miracles, is able to *prevent* things that are causally necessary, and to bring about things that are causally impossible.) For metaphysics, and for theology, we are looking for a sense of necessity that is absolute, so that what is necessary *cannot be prevented,* not even by God. But how this notion of necessity should be spelled out, is very much a matter of controversy.

The present chapter is not the most appropriate forum in which to engage at length in this controversy. Rather, I will set out briefly two distinct senses of "necessary" that will be sufficient for the following exposition of trinitarian doctrine. These two senses will have the advantage that they will be widely recognized in the philosophical community, and thus unlikely to cause a great deal of controversy. There will be those who hold that there are other relevant sorts of necessity that are in play here. But I have no need either to agree or to disagree with them; the senses that will be outlined will be sufficient for my purposes.

The first of these senses is *conceptual necessity.* Conceptual necessity in turn comprises three subcategories. There are the recognized truths—the axioms and theorems—of well-recognized systems of logic and mathematics. Substitution-instances of modus ponens, for instance, are valid arguments, and their corresponding conditionals—propositions of the form, "If (p, and if p then q), then q"—are necessary truths. Controversies concerning these matters are not entirely unknown, but there is a large central area in which essentially universal agreement can be presumed. The second subcategory consists of conceptual truths that are not theorems of logic or mathematics, but can be seen to be true in virtue of the concepts involved in them. An example was given earlier: "If Peter is taller than Susan and Susan is taller than Edmund, Edmund can't be just as tall as Peter." The necessary truth of this hinges on the fact that the relational predicate "taller than" is transitive: If a is taller than b, and b is taller than c, then a is taller than c. That this predicate is transitive is not a theorem of logic, but it is a truth that will be recognized by anyone who has a grasp of the concept, "taller than." Of course many examples will be far more complex than this, and disagreement is not uncommon; sometimes it simply is not clear to us what is implied by some of the concepts we employ. Nevertheless, we do have here a relatively well-defined category of necessary truths.

A third subcategory of conceptual necessities comprises the "a posteriori necessary truths" championed by Saul Kripke. Kripke convinced many philosophers that "Hesperus = Phosphorus" and "Water is H_2O" are necessary truths, in spite of the fact that their truth cannot be established a priori, and their negations do not appear to be contradictory.[5] Because of these facts, it has seemed to many philosophers that the necessity in question must somehow inhere in the objective structure of the world, rather than being in any way dependent upon our concepts. The right way of dealing with these examples, I believe, is the one proposed by Alan Sidelle. According to Sidelle, the key to such situations lies in "analytic general principles of individuation" of the form

(x)(If x belongs to kind K, then if p is x's P-property, then it is necessary that x is p).[6]

The particular principle that applies to chemical kinds such as water, is

(x)(If x is a chemical compound, then if p is x's chemical structure, then it is necessary that x has p).[7]

This is an analytic or conceptual truth, because it is part of our concept of a chemical compound that the chemical structure of a substance is definitive of its chemical kind. Instantiating, this yields:

If water is a chemical compound, then if water's chemical structure is H_2O, it is necessary that water is H_2O.

When combined with the empirical information that the formula for water is indeed H_2O, this yields the desired modal conclusion: *Necessarily, water is H_2O.* This strategy, I submit, offers a plausible way to include Kripke's a posteriori necessary truths under the broad heading of conceptual necessities.[8]

There are, however, a good many putatively necessary truths that apparently do not fall into the category of conceptual necessities. Here are a few propositions that have been claimed to be such: "Every event has a cause." "Nothing comes from nothing." "God exists." "Anything that is conscious must have a body." "Moral responsibility requires alternative possibilities."

---

[5] Saul Kripke, "Naming and Necessity," in D. Davidson and G. Harman (eds), *Semantics of Natural Language* (Dordrecht: D. Riedel, 1972).

[6] Alan Sidelle, *Necessity, Essence, and Individuation* (Ithaca, NY: Cornell University Press, 1989), 34.

[7] See Sidelle, *Necessity,* 34 n. 20.

[8] A somewhat fuller discussion of these matters can be found in William Hasker, "Analytic Philosophy of Religion," in W. Wainwright (ed.), *The Oxford Handbook of Philosophy of Religion* (Oxford: OUP, 2005), 438–40.

And so on, and on...All of these are controversial, and none can plausibly be included in the category of conceptual necessities, barring something like, for instance, a successful ontological proof of God's existence. Yet a great many philosophers evince a strong conviction that one or another of these, or of the many more candidates that could be supplied, is a necessary truth—that it absolutely could not be otherwise. There is, however, no agreement as to how the necessity in question should be understood. Some speak of such propositions as "true in all possible worlds," but this merely invites the further question, in virtue of what are "possible worlds" possible? Many have followed Plantinga in terming such propositions "broadly logical necessary." Plantinga himself admits, however (and this is somewhat ironic, in a book titled *The Nature of Necessity*), that he can give no informative general characterization of such necessary truth.[9] Like obscenity, you know it when you see it—or not.

Here then is my proposal: I term a proposition *metaphysically necessary* if and only if *its truth is required by the fundamental structure of reality*. What is meant here by "the fundamental structure of reality" can best be illustrated by adverting to some of the great metaphysical systems that have arisen throughout history. For a Neoplatonist, the fundamental structure of reality would consist of the One and the series of necessary emanations flowing from it. For Spinoza, the fundamental structure is "god or nature," with everything that is implied thereby. For a Hegelian, it consists in the dialectical structure of reality, culminating in Absolute Spirit. For a Marxist, it consists of the materialist dialectic of both nature and history. For a contemporary materialist, it consists of the true, ultimate system of the laws of nature. (If the laws of nature vary, as some have supposed, in different segments of the "multiverse," then the fundamental structure would consist of the "meta-laws" that determine how this variation occurs.) For a theist, the fundamental structure of reality consists of the existence and nature of God. For a trinitarian theist, the doctrine of the Trinity is an integral part of the metaphysically necessary ultimate structure of reality.

Given this list of examples, it is clear that the appeal to such "metaphysically necessary truths" offers little promise of being polemically effective, at least among disputants whose worldview commitments are fundamentally different. It may be, of course, that persons who disagree about some aspects of the ultimate structure of reality will nevertheless have shared intuitions about other aspects, and these shared intuitions may provide a basis for discussion between them. Furthermore, it may sometimes be possible to show that a philosopher is implicitly committed to a principle that the philosopher has not explicitly affirmed. But our expectations concerning the agreement that will result from such discussion should be modest; this is one of the hard lessons we have learned from two and a half millennia of philosophy.

---

[9] See Alvin Plantinga, *The Nature of Necessity* (Oxford: Clarendon Press, 1974), 1.

Yet in spite of these disagreements my proposal should, I believe, elicit widespread agreement in several respects. Most philosophers, and just about all metaphysicians, will agree that there *is* a fundamental structure of reality; otherwise what would metaphysics be about? And it is hard to deny that propositions describing that ultimate structure are in a very meaningful sense "necessary." Nothing can deviate from the ultimate structure of reality, since there is nothing outside of reality that could be a source for such deviation. If reality is subject to change in certain respects—even radical and unpredictable change—then the possibility of such change is part of the ultimate structure of reality; the change is metaphysically possible, and the features subject to change are not metaphysically necessary. We might ask a critic, if the fundamental structure of reality is not "necessary" enough for you, what more does it take?

I acknowledge, nevertheless, that many philosophers may not be satisfied with this account of metaphysical necessity. For some, it is not enough that various states of affairs are entailed by the ultimate structure of reality; they must be "necessary" in some deeper, more fundamental sense. What this sense is remains obscure—perhaps, terminally obscure. Nevertheless, *I have no need either to agree or to disagree with this claim.* Anyone who wishes to make the claim is free to do so—accompanying it, one would hope, with some at least moderately illuminating explanation of the sense of necessity in question. If someone succeeds in doing this, another sense of necessity will have been added to the two that have been proposed here. As I've said, I have no need at this point either to agree or to disagree.

Another interesting possibility is that in the end metaphysical necessity may be reduced to, or may collapse into, conceptual necessity. This could happen in either of two ways. On the one hand, someone might produce a convincing proof, from universally acceptable premises, that the propositions said to be metaphysically necessary are in fact conceptually necessary. A successful ontological proof of the existence of God would be an example of this, were such proof available. (I suspect that it is not, but that is another story.) If such an endeavor were to be successful, it would show that my subdivision of (absolutely) necessary truth into subcategories is merely provisional, but would otherwise leave my proposal unaffected. The other possibility is that reality is either so malleable or so prolific that *no* conceptually possible state of affairs is such that it cannot possibly obtain. Perhaps David Lewis held such a view, and some of his followers may still hold it. Theists, and trinitarian theists in particular, will not accept this as being the truth, but it remains as a theoretical option.

Clearly, a great many more points remain to be discussed. But this is a subsection in a book on the Trinity, not a treatise on the philosophy of logic, so enough will have to be enough. For our task of trinitarian theorizing, it should be sufficient.

THE GOAL OF OUR THEORIZING

As we proceed in our construction of trinitarian doctrine, it will be helpful to have before us a concise summary of the goal we hope to reach. Much along these lines has been stated or implied in earlier parts of the book, but a brief recapitulation here may still be useful. Here then is a summary statement by Thomas McCall, one to which I in large measure subscribe. His statement of "theological desiderata" comes after his survey of current trinitarian options and his account of the biblical foundations for the doctrine of the Trinity.

> First, any acceptable doctrine of the Trinity must be a version of monotheism. Second, it will be wary of claims either that monotheism (or "real" monotheism) excludes real distinctions between the divine persons or that the divine "persons" must not be at all like "persons" in the more normal use of the term. To the contrary, a doctrine of the Trinity that arises from, and is consistent with, the biblical witness will maintain that the divine persons are persons in a robust sense of the term, and the proponents of such a view will insist that this is consistent with the account of monotheism that should matter most to Christians—it is consistent with the (Second Temple) monotheism of Paul, John, and the other authors of the New Testament. Third, such a doctrine will likewise insist that the Father, Son, and Holy Spirit are *homoousios*. Thus it will avoid all views that entail ontological subordination, and it will hold to the full divinity of the Son and Spirit as well as the Father. Finally, it will look for the strongest possible account of divine oneness or unity, and it will understand the "possible" in this instance to be constrained by the foregoing commitments (e.g., to the full divinity and real distinction of the Son and Spirit). And depending on the degree of commitment to the authority of the Latin tradition (and especially such statements as that of the Fourth Lateran Council), it will be wary of accounts of divine oneness that rely strictly on generic, functional, or collective unity.[10]

I will qualify this account with two reservations: First, McCall makes no mention here of the "relations of origin," the eternal generation of the Son and procession of the Holy Spirit; however I do not believe this should be taken to imply a rejection of the doctrine.[11] Secondly, I believe that one need not grant great authority to "the Latin tradition" (and certainly not to the Fourth Lateran Council) to be "wary of accounts of divine oneness that rely *strictly* on generic, functional, or collective unity." As I claim to have shown in Part I, we find, not merely in Augustine but in Gregory of Nyssa and the Cappadocians as well, the insistence on the numerical unity of the concrete divine nature. (Accounting for this will become a major task in subsequent chapters.) But with these qualifications, the statement presents an excellent summary of the goal we are hoping to attain.

---

[10] Thomas McCall, *Which Trinity? Whose Monotheism?* (Grand Rapids, MI: Eerdmans, 2010), 86.
[11] See the comments at *Which Trinity?*, 211–13.

22

Monotheism and Christology

The root from which the doctrine of the Trinity grew was the intersection of monotheism and christology. There is no doubt that Christianity arose on the soil of Jewish monotheism, and Christianity claims to be a monotheistic faith. It makes a difference, though, how monotheism is defined: for one thing, the definition will have a lot to do with what kind of doctrine of the Trinity (if any) is found acceptable. Thomas McCall has things exactly right with his title question: *Which Trinity? Whose Monotheism?* As an example of the relevance of this question, one scholar has proposed that Jewish monotheism, properly so-called, arose only in the late Middle Ages.[1] Even if such extreme views are rejected, the question, "Whose monotheism?" retains a great deal of force. According to Brian Leftow, "the Christian version of monotheism should complete, perfect, or fulfill its Jewish version. It should be a monotheism a Jew could accept as monotheistic, and a completion of Jewish monotheism."[2] Daniel Howard-Snyder adds Muslims to the list of those whose views determine what monotheism amounts to.[3] I think the line taken here by Leftow and Howard-Snyder is precisely wrong. Later Jewish monotheism and Muslim monotheism were both to a significant degree *defined by their opposition to the Christian doctrines of Trinity and incarnation.* To make those views the standard by which Christian monotheism is to be judged is a serious mistake. Nor is the situation greatly improved when Leftow adds, "Failing that, it should come as close to this as trinitarian orthodoxy permits."[4] To say this still leaves the anti-trinitarian God-concepts of Jews and Muslims as the standard—a standard to which, regrettably, the Christian doctrine of the Trinity cannot measure up.

---

[1] Peter Hayman, "Monotheism—a Misused Word in Jewish Studies?," *JJS* 42 (1991), 1–15; cited in Larry Hurtado, *Lord Jesus Christ: Devotion to Jesus in Earliest Christianity* (Grand Rapids, MI: Eerdmans, 2003), 32. Readers will quickly become aware of my indebtedness to Hurtado's massive, and highly respected, study.

[2] "Anti Social Trinitarianism," in McCall and Rea, *Philosophical and Theological Essays*, 72. (Leftow must have in mind Jews in the Christian era; earlier Jews were in no position to adopt a view concerning the Trinity.)

[3] "Trinity Monotheism," *Philosophia Christi*, 5/2 (2003), 402.

[4] Leftow, "Anti Social Trinitarianism," 72.

In contrast with this, McCall seems to be on solid ground when he proposes that we take as a standard "the monotheism of Second Temple Judaism as it was received and drawn upon by John, Paul, and the other authors of the New Testament."[5] By the time of Roman rule over Palestine, the hard lesson had finally been learned that "hedging their bets" by appealing to the gods of the nations along with the God of Israel was a path that led to no future for the Jewish faith or the Jewish people. The searing experience of exile, and the horrific persecutions under Antiochus Epiphanes, had driven this lesson home in a way that the preaching of the prophets by itself had never been able to do. And it was this faith in the God of Israel that formed the foundation for the faith of the earliest Christians. If a Christian understanding of monotheism is desired, surely this is the direction we must turn. Accordingly, the rest of this chapter will be devoted to two related topics. First, what was the character of the first-century Jewish monotheism that formed the context and foundation for the Christian proclamation? And second, how was this monotheism modified and enriched by the new-found faith in Jesus the Messiah?

SECOND TEMPLE JEWISH MONOTHEISM

The Judaism of the Second Temple era was monotheistic in this sense: Yahweh, the God of Israel, was the one and only God, Creator, and Lord of everything else in existence. Of particular importance was the *exclusivity of worship* that could be offered only to Israel's God.[6] Jews who accommodated to their gentile surroundings in many other ways—language, dress, dining habits, sports, and so on—nevertheless remained firm in their refusal to offer worship to any other person or deity. To transgress this restriction was perhaps the ultimate sin that any Jew could commit, a sin which automatically entailed separation from the Jewish people.

This exclusivity of worship was not, however, seen as inconsistent with what might seem to be rather extreme veneration of various figures, especially persons who play the role of God's "principal agent" as viewed in some particular context. These might include angels, historical figures such as Moses, or "hypostatized" divine attributes such as Wisdom. A striking example is found in the biblical figure of Enoch, concerning whom one tradition held

---

[5] *Which Trinity?*, 57.

[6] Hurtado clarifies: "Because the word 'worship' and its Greek and Hebrew equivalents can connote a variety of degrees and forms of reverence, I wish to make it clear that by 'worship' here I mean the sort of reverence that was reserved by ancient devout Jews for God alone, and was intended by them to indicate God's uniqueness. I use the term to designate 'cultic' worship, especially devotion offered in a specifically worship (liturgical) setting and expressive of the thanksgiving, praise, communion, and petition that directly represent, manifest, and reinforce the relationship of the worshipers with the deity." Hurtado, *Lord Jesus Christ*, 31n.

that at his ascent he was transformed into an angelic being and made head over all the heavenly court. This was unambiguously attested only in *3 Enoch* (about the fifth century C.E.), which identifies Enoch as "Metatron" (4: 2–3), a powerful heavenly being referred to in other ancient Jewish texts as well. In 4: 8–9, God tells the heavenly host that he has chosen Enoch to be "a prince and a ruler over you in the heavenly heights" (cf. also 10: 3–6). In *3 Enoch 9*, we are told of Enoch's transformation into a gigantic being from whom "no sort of splendor, brilliance, brightness or beauty" was missing, and in *3 Enoch* 10–12 we read of Metatron/Enoch's throne "like the throne of glory" (10: 1), his majestic robe (2: 1–2) and crown (12: 3–4), and we are told that God orders Metatron/Enoch to be called "the lesser YHWH," with a clear allusion made to Exod. 23: 20–21 ("my name is in him," 12: 5).[7]

Some scholars, seizing on evidence of this sort, have claimed that the "monolatry" of Israelites in this period was not as strict as might otherwise seem to be the case. Hurtado, however, argues convincingly that we must not obscure the difference between the veneration of such "principal agent" figures and the cultic practice of worship, which was directed solely to the one true God. He proposes, nevertheless, that the presence of these figures is important for our understanding of the origins of Christianity. "Along with the other two categories of divine agency thought (personified divine attributes and chief angels), the patriarchs reflect the ability of ancient Judaism to accommodate exalted figures alongside God. This may have enabled the first Christians to come to grips with their conviction about the exaltation of Jesus."[8] An important insight which emerges from this material is that the Jewish monotheism of this period was not primarily a metaphysical doctrine, though inevitably it had metaphysical implications. Rather, the focus was on *practice,* in particular the practice of worship, which by the insistence on exclusivity made sole allegiance to God central in Jewish religious life.

MONOTHEISM AND THE EARLIEST CHRISTIANS

When we turn to consider the earliest Christians, we find continuity with the Jewish monotheism of the age—and also some striking differences. Our earliest Christian writings are the letters of Paul, probably written in the 50s but taking us back to the time of his conversion, within a year or two of the

[7] Larry Hurtado, *One God, One Lord: Early Christian Devotion and Ancient Jewish Monotheism* (Philadelphia: Fortress Press, 1988), 55. This volume contains numerous examples of principal agent figures as they appear in various ancient Jewish texts. For further discussion of this and related topics, see Carey C. Newman, James R. Davila, and Gladys S. Lewis (eds), *The Jewish Roots of Christological Monotheism: Papers from the St. Andrews Conference on the Historical Origins of the Worship of Jesus* (Leiden: Brill, 1999).

[8] Hurtado, *One God, One Lord*, 51.

crucifixion. Paul is emphatic in his scornful rejection of the pagan deities and the worship practices directed at them, and insists that his converts take no part in such practices. ("You cannot drink the cup of the Lord and the cup of demons." 1 Cor. 10: 21.) Clearly, he thought of himself as continuing the Jewish insistence on the exclusive worship of the one God. At the same time, however, the place occupied by Jesus in his thought, and in the worship practices of the communities he established, was unprecedented in earlier Jewish experience. Jesus was "Christ," the Jewish messiah. He was also "the Son of God." Perhaps most significantly, he was *ho Kyrios,* "the Lord." To be sure, *kyrios* was used in Greek as a respectful term of address, equivalent to "sir" or "master." But it was also a reverential term addressed to deities. More than this, however, it was the Greek word commonly used as the translation for the tetragrammaton, YHWH, which by that time was no longer pronounced by Jewish worshipers. Paul himself uses *Kyrios* to designate God, and it functions for him as a Greek substitute for God's name. Hurtado points out that "it is remarkable that, in other citations of Old Testament passages which originally have to do with God, Paul applies the passages to Jesus, making him the *Kyrios:* Romans 10: 13 (Joel 2: 32), 1 Corinthians 1: 31 (Jer. 9: 23–24) 1 Corinthians 10: 26 (Ps. 24: 1), 2 Corinthians 10: 17 (Jer. 9: 23–24)."[9] An especially striking instance is found in 1 Corinthians 8: 5–6, where,

> in explicit contrast to the worship practices of the polytheistic environment, Paul affirms a two-part confession of "one God *[heis Theos]* the Father" and "one Lord *[heis Kyrios]* Jesus Christ" . . . In this astonishingly bold association of Jesus and God, Paul adapts wording from the traditional Jewish confession of God's uniqueness, known as the Shema, from Deuteronomy 6: 4, "Hear, O Israel: The Lord our God is *one Lord*" (*Kyrios heis estin* [LXX] translating Heb. *Yahweh 'echad*).[10]

Here the central Jewish affirmation of the one God is interpreted as *including Jesus Christ.*

There is also the amazing christological passage Philippians 2: 5–11, which I quote in full:

> Let the same mind be in you that was in Christ Jesus
> who, though he was in the form of God,
> did not regard equality with God
> as something to be exploited,
> but emptied himself,
> taking the form of a slave,
> being born in human likeness.
> And being found in human form,
> he humbled himself

---

[9] Hurtado, *Lord Jesus Christ,* 112.   [10] Hurtado, *Lord Jesus Christ,* 114.

and became obedient to the point of death—
even death on a cross.
Therefore God also highly exalted him
and gave him the name
that is above every name,
so that at the name of Jesus
every knee should bend,
in heaven and on earth and under the earth,
and every tongue should confess
that Jesus Christ is Lord,
to the glory of God the Father. (NRSV)

Here we have Jesus' pre-existence in an exalted state, describable as "in the form of God" (*en morphē theou*), and as "equality with God" (*to einai isa theō*), his voluntary self-humbling, and the exaltation subsequently bestowed on him. The depiction of that exaltation makes reference to Isaiah 45: 23, where God avows that "To me every knee shall bow, every tongue shall swear" (NRSV). The universal acknowledgment and obeisance that in Isaiah is directed to God, *is now to be given to Jesus*. Two additional points can be made concerning this passage. First, 2: 6–11 is widely recognized as having been an early Christian hymn, one that "likely originated much earlier than the epistle in which it is preserved."[11] But secondly, it is noteworthy that Paul *feels no need to explain or justify* these christological affirmations, or the application of the Isaiah passage to Christ. Rather, they are taken for granted as matters that will be readily understood and accepted by his readers, and can thus be made the basis for an appeal to them to exhibit similar humility and self-sacrifice. The constellation of beliefs, about God and about Jesus,

> that are in evidence here (and in other early Christian writings) has been termed by several scholars "Christological monotheism"—it is a monotheism in which Jesus is *honored and reverenced along with God* in a way that is unprecedented in pre-Christian Judaism.[12]

Hurtado goes on to point out features of the worship practices of the early Pauline Christians which show the remarkable place given to Jesus. There is prayer that is offered *through Jesus*—and at times, directly *to* Jesus. There are hymns about Jesus and to Jesus. There is the *invocation* of Jesus, memorably shown in 1 Corinthians 16: 22, in the prayer *marana tha*, Aramaic for "Our

---

[11] Hurtado, *Lord Jesus Christ*, 112.

[12] Richard Bauckham states, "The concern of early Christology was not to conform Jesus to some pre-existing model of an intermediary figure subordinate to God. The concern of early Christology, from its root in the exegesis of Psalm 110:1 and related texts, was to understand the identification of Jesus with God. Early Jewish monotheism provided little precedent for such a step, but it was so defined and so structured as to be open for such a development." "The Throne of God and the Worship of Jesus," in Newman *et al.*, *Jewish Roots*, 64.

Lord, come!" Apparently this Aramaic expression was so well known to Paul's gentile converts in Corinth that there was no need for translation or explanation; it must already have become a familiar part of their worship practice. Christians were to confess that "Jesus is Lord." They were baptized "in Jesus' name." There is the Lord's supper, the "Christian cult meal where the Lord Jesus plays a role that is explicitly likened to that of the deities of the pagan cults and, even more astonishingly to the role of God!"[13] Hurtado concludes that "when this constellation of devotional actions is set in the general first-century religious context, it is properly understood as constituting the cultic worship of Jesus."[14] What we have here, in fact, is a pattern of "binitarian worship"—and one that originated surprisingly early in the newborn Christian movement. A striking portrayal of such binitarian worship can be found in the slightly later book of Revelation. The author is intent on discouraging his readers from any compromise with idolatry, in the form of the emperor cult; he pleads with them to "be faithful unto death" (2: 10) if need be. He condemns the worship of "false and invalid objects of devotion" (e.g. 9: 2–21; 13: 4; 14: 9–11).[15] And the exalted angels who are instructing the seer specifically forbid his offering worship to them (19: 10; 22: 8–9). Yet in 5: 11–13 we find the heavenly host *worshiping the Lamb along with God*: "Worthy is the Lamb that was slaughtered to receive power and wealth and wisdom and might and honor and glory and blessing!...To the one seated on the throne *and to the Lamb* be blessing and honor and glory and might forever and ever!" Without doubt, this description of the heavenly worship provided a template for the worship that was to be offered, and that was in fact offered, in the churches for whom the book was written.

Paul's gentile churches were not, of course, the very first Christian groups, and many scholars have thought to find a divergence between them and the early Jewish circles of Christianity. Often, furthermore, the high christology evident in Paul's letters has been seen as the result of a gradual development that was heavily dependent on the general religious environment, especially the mystery cults. The evidence, however, provides little support for these speculations. The sharp opposition to pagan religious practices among first-century Jews, including Paul, argues against any major borrowing from pagan sources. What we can learn about the early Jewish Christian groups, both from Paul's letters and from the accounts in Acts, shows a devotion to Christ that is very much in line with what we find in the Pauline churches. There is actually a rather powerful argument from silence here, based on what Paul does *not* say on this subject. Paul was hardly timid or reticent in expressing his views when the faith he was promulgating was challenged! Indeed, his rhetoric became almost violent at times, as seen especially in Galatians. His

---

[13] Hurtado, *Lord Jesus Christ*, 146.   [14] Hurtado, *Lord Jesus Christ*, 138.
[15] Hurtado, *Lord Jesus Christ*, 593.

polemics were directed especially at the "Judaizers"—those who insisted that, in order to be fully accepted into the Christian movement, gentile converts must be circumcised and obey the Mosaic law. But there is in Paul almost a complete absence of controversy over his views concerning Jesus Christ. These matters are treated as well known and able to be taken for granted: "there is hardly any indication in Paul's letters that he knew of any controversy or serious variance about this exalted place of Jesus among the various other Christian circles with which he was acquainted."[16] Rather than showing evidence of a division between his own churches and the Jewish Christians of Judea, Paul's letters reveal that he was anxious to maintain fellowship between them, as shown especially in the collection for the Jerusalem Christians to which he devoted so much effort.

The early date at which these developments appear is also remarkable. Many scholars are eager to find an early group of "Jesus people" who reverenced Jesus as a wise teacher and leader, but did not subscribe to, and may have been unaware of, the high christology that appeared later on. Such groups, however, seem not to have left any historical traces, if indeed they ever existed. Hurtado states, "In historical terms we may refer to a veritable 'big bang', an explosively rapid and impressively substantial christological development in the earliest stage of the Christian movement."[17] According to Martin Hengel, "The time between the death of Jesus and the fully developed christology which we find in the earliest Christian documents, the letters of Paul, is so short that the development which takes place within it can only be called amazing."[18]

SOME ADDITIONAL MATTERS

Something needs to be said about the Holy Spirit. The Spirit was certainly not absent from the thoughts or the lives of the earliest Christians. For the most part, however, the Spirit was not made the center of attention, reflection, and worship as was Jesus Christ. Rather, the Spirit was the energizing power that made faith in Christ, and the new life in Christ, possible. The Spirit was seen at times in distinctly personal terms (Rom. 8:26–7; Eph. 4: 30; John 14: 26), but did not become the focus of thought, life, and worship in the way that this happened with Jesus. It was natural, then, that the subsequent development and struggles in the Church revolved around the respective places of Father and Son, with the Spirit often more of an afterthought. The Spirit is merely mentioned by name both in the Apostles' Creed and in the creed of the council of Nicaea. The council of Constantinople, in framing our "Nicene" Creed,

---

[16] Hurtado, *Lord Jesus Christ*, 135.   [17] Hurtado, *Lord Jesus Christ*, 135.
[18] In his *Jesus and Paul* (London: SCM, 1983), 31; cited by Hurtado, *Lord Jesus Christ*, 135.

had more to say about the Spirit. But to the chagrin of Gregory Nazianzen, that Creed does not directly affirm (though it clearly enough implies) that the Spirit is *homoousios* with the Father and the Son. So the recognition of the Spirit as a fully co-equal member of the Trinity took some considerable time—yet there is not at present any significant support for the idea that the Spirit should be understood in fundamentally different terms than those that are applied to the Father and the Son. For the remainder of this book it will be assumed, then, that we are dealing with a Trinity of Father, Son, and Holy Spirit, and not with Father and Son alone.

Finally, it is appropriate to acknowledge at this point that the conclusions of biblical scholarship drawn upon in this chapter are not by any means universally accepted. Regrettably, true consensus is very rarely achieved about important matters of New Testament scholarship. The views cited seem to be well-supported by the available evidence, but anything approaching a full defense of them here is out of the question; interested readers are urged to investigate the voluminous literature for themselves.[19] In the present context, this discussion serves to point out the conclusions that were in fact reached by the early Christians concerning Jesus Christ—conclusions which, in turn, provided the motivation that energized the development of the doctrine of the Trinity. This is so even if the chronology and the detailed process by which those conclusions emerged among the early believers remain controversial. Since I have drawn so heavily on Hurtado in this chapter, it seems appropriate to close by quoting the words with which he concludes his book: "In our time, as in the famous Galilean scene from the Gospels, for Christians and others as well, Jesus' question remains under lively debate: 'Who do you say that I am?' The history of earliest devotion to Jesus shows how answering that question can have profound ramifications."[20]

---

[19] Both Hurtado and McCall provide references to the literature; Hurtado, especially, refers to numerous sources containing views that dissent from his own.

[20] Hurtado, *Lord Jesus Christ*, 653.

23

Each of the Persons is God

The Father is God. The Son is God. The Holy Spirit is God. No one doubts that each of these sentences has an essential place in the doctrine of the Trinity. How the sentences are to be understood, however, is extremely controversial, even among those who affirm that doctrine. In this chapter, I begin by reviewing a way of understanding the sentences that, while historically momentous, has no significant support today. I then go on to consider various interpretations that have been proposed by contemporary trinitarians.

THE ARIAN SOLUTION: THREE GRADES OF DEITY

Arius, and those later anti-Nicenes whom we tend to call "Arians," had no difficulty in agreeing that each of Father, Son, and Holy Spirit "is God." Arius, according to Khaled Anatolios,

> combined Origen's emphasis on the real distinctions within the Trinity with an unflagging insistence on the utter singularity of the one unoriginated and Unbegotten God. Thus, while we can speak of a divine Trinity, only the first entity (*hypostasis*) is truly and fully God.... This doctrine does not deny the Son's divinity but presumes the framework of a graded hierarchy of transcendence in which it is possible to speak of variation in degree within the divine realm.[1]

For many of us today, this is likely to provoke a response of incredulity: "Either the Son is *God,* or he is not: there is no middle ground." If we do so respond, this very response is itself in large measure the result of the fourth-century trinitarian controversy, for one of the most important issues at stake in that controversy was precisely the absolute, all-or-nothing distinction between God the Creator and "everything else." For most of us the expression "true God from true God" in the Nicene Creed comes across merely as a verbal embellishment; we see no significant difference between "God" and "true

[1] *Retrieving Nicaea* (Grand Rapids, MI: Baker Academic, 2011), 17.

God." In the early Christian centuries this was not so. Lewis Ayres points out that "At issue until the last decades of the controversy was the very flexibility with which the term 'God' could be deployed. Many fourth-century theologians easily distinguished between 'God' and 'true God'."[2]

In view of the lack of contemporary advocates for Arian-like positions, it is not necessary at this point to rehearse the multiple arguments by which the pro-Nicenes resisted, and ultimately defeated, the Arian stance. It is worth our while, nevertheless, to review briefly the damage to Christian theology that results if the Arian position is accepted. First of all, of course, there is the simple fact that, on this view, Jesus Christ is *not God*—that is, not "true God." He can be called "God," to be sure, but that is merely a courtesy title, which does nothing to bridge the gulf between the Son/Logos and the Unbegotten, who alone is God in the full and proper sense. But it also follows that Christ is *not truly human*. Rather than being joined to a complete human nature, the Logos *takes the place* in Jesus of a human soul; Christ is a "mediator" not by being both divine and human, but by occupying an intermediate position which is neither one nor the other.

The conception of God is also altered in the process. Christ becomes a mediator in an ontological sense, an intermediate being between the true God and the realm of mundane existence. The need for such an ontological mediation implies, however, an extreme divine transcendence which denies to God, the Unbegotten, any direct involvement in the affairs of the creation. After the production of the Son/Logos, the work of creation is delegated to him, leaving uncompromised the stark separation between the transcendent "true God" and the created world. Furthermore, the focus of attention in the doctrine of redemption also shifts. The central moment is not the passion and resurrection, or even the incarnation itself. Rather, the key moment is the *production of the Logos,* who by mediating between the high God and everything else makes possible a kind of connection, albeit indirect, between God and us his creatures. It is precisely because the Son is *inferior in nature* to the Father that our redemption is possible. Anatolios sums up Gregory of Nyssa's response to this: "According to Eunomius, if the Son were as great as the Father, we would not be saved! But if the Son saves us because he is not as great as the Father, then we should really honor him more than the Father, and not less."[3]

IS EACH PERSON IDENTICAL WITH GOD?

One natural way to interpret "The Father is God" is by taking it to assert that the Father is *identical with* God. When the same interpretation is applied in

---

[2] *Nicaea and its Legacy* (Oxford: OUP, 2004), 14.
[3] *Nicaea*, 189. Anatolios cites *Contra Eunomius* 3.10.44.

the case of the Son and the Holy Spirit, this immediately rules out the possibility that "God" as said of the Son and the Spirit is merely a courtesy title, as it is for Arianism. Unfortunately, however, if each of the Persons "is God" in this sense, it follows that each Person is identical with each of the other two Persons, which is the heresy of modalism or Sabellianism. So a trinitarian who is attracted to the identity interpretation of "is God" must attempt to qualify it in some way so as to avoid the heretical conclusion. Several of the thinkers considered in Part II have taken this route.

For Barth and Rahner, each Person is identical, not with God *simpliciter* but with one of God's three "modes of being" (or "modes of subsistence"). However, it is difficult to know what a "mode of being" is supposed to be, given that it cannot be a *person* as we understand the latter notion.[4] There is also, of course, the difficulty in squaring the denial that the Persons *are persons* with the biblical depiction of Father, Son, and Holy Spirit—a difficulty which, in the end, leads both Barth and Rahner into outright inconsistency on this point.

Brian Leftow, as we have seen, begins by accepting both "the Father = God" and "the Son = God," which seems to commit him to accepting the conclusion that the Father is identical with the Son. So far as I can see, he has not yet managed to explain why that conclusion does not follow from his position as he has stated it. But he undoubtedly does not accept this conclusion and does not think it follows from his view. That view, I believe, is best interpreted as holding, not that the Father is identical with God, but that the Father is identical with "God-living-the-Father-life-stream." The Son, then, will be identical with "God-living-the-Son-life-stream," and so also with the Spirit. Given this, the three Persons will all be distinct from one another.

It remains true, however, that there is only *one* person, namely *God,* who performs all the actions and has all of the experiences attributed to all three trinitarian Persons, though to be sure each Person's experiences and actions occur in a different life-stream. And this means that in the Gospels we have the strange picture of a single person praying to himself, talking to himself, and answering himself—indeed, crying out to himself in anguished protest for having forsaken himself! And that, I submit, is too high a price to pay for whatever benefits Leftow's view affords us.

The attractions of Peter van Inwagen's relative-identity approach are readily appreciated. It allows us to say that each Person is "the same God as" God, and indeed that each Person is the same God as each other Person. But it blocks the inference from that to saying that each Person is *the same person as* each other Person, so we have three Persons but only one God. Over against that, there is the fact that the theory of relative identity has been rejected by a strong majority of logicians—and indeed, by van Inwagen himself, except as it is applied to

---

[4] We recall that for the Cappadocians, from whom the expression "mode of being" (*tropos huparxeos*) is derived, the expression is *not* employed to tell us what a divine Person *is*.

the Christian doctrines of Trinity and incarnation. I will not rehearse here the arguments given earlier against relative-identity trinitarianism; suffice it to say that support for it among defenders of an orthodox doctrine of the Trinity seems to be dwindling.

Jeffrey Brower and Michael Rea offer a modified relative-identity approach, in which relative identity is affirmed without denying the existence of the classical relation of identity. On their view, as we have seen, the term "God" becomes systematically ambiguous: it can refer to any one of the Father, or the Son, or the Holy Spirit. It seems clear, however, that this cannot be accepted. If what guarantees monotheism is that there is *only one* God, it cannot be the case that the expression "the one God" is ambiguous, referring to any of three distinct items.

On the whole, then, the option of interpreting "is God" in the doctrine of the Trinity in terms of identity does not seem promising. Taken without qualification, this option leads immediately to the modalistic heresy. So some qualification needs to be devised, to avoid the heretical conclusion—but all the ways of qualifying it so far proposed suffer from serious difficulties. It is hard to rule out in advance the possibility that someone might come up with a better solution, but to date nothing really hopeful has made its appearance.

DOES "IS GOD" EXPRESS A PROPERTY?

If "the Son is God" does not assert that the Son is identical with God, the most natural alternative is to say that "is God" attributes a *property* to the Persons.[5] But what property is that? And can such a view satisfy the other requirements for an orthodox doctrine of the Trinity? In order to explore this possibility, we shall consider some ideas of Edward Wierenga. (An essentially similar view is adopted by both Swinburne and Yandell, but Wierenga's version is preferred here, both because he develops it more fully and because the most significant critique of this approach, by Jeffrey Brower, is directed at Wierenga.)

Wierenga begins this part of his exposition by noting that the doctrine of the Trinity affirms all of the following:

---

[5] Marianne Meye Thompson points out that "'god' (*theos*) *is not a proper name, but a term that makes a predication about the person or reality so named.* The same holds true for the use of *elohim* in the OT, whatever its origin. Because in Hebrew, Greek, and English the respective terms *elohim, elim, theos,* and God are used both as names or designations of a specific figure and as labels for a class of beings, the point is often lost that 'God' comes to be a name by the way it is used, much the way 'Dad' or 'Mom' functions for children as the name of their parent, even though these are not their given names and are used for many other persons." *The God of the Gospel of John* (Grand Rapids: Eerdmans, 2001), 22–3; emphasis in original. Almost certainly, our modern tendency to think of 'God' primarily as the name of an individual strongly influences the tendency to interpret 'is God' as said of the Persons as an identity statement.

(A1)   The Father is God.

(A2)   The Son is God.

(A3)   The Holy Spirit is God.[6]

He notes that if the "is" here expresses *identity* this implies that Father, Son, and Spirit are all identical with each other, which contradicts the claim of the doctrine of the Trinity that they are distinct. He then goes on to propose an alternative:

> Philosophers commonly distinguish between the "is" of identity and the "is" of predication. Why not apply that distinction to these Divinity claims? In particular, since interpreting the copula in (A1)-(A3) as expressing *identity* leads directly to trouble, why not interpret it instead as making a *predication?* That is, instead of thinking of "is God" as meaning "= God", why not think of it as "is divine"? In that case, we can interpret (A1)-(A3) as
>   (A1''') The Father is divine,
>   (A2) The Son is divine,
>   and
>   (A3) The Holy Spirit is divine.
> Of course, whether this suggestion will help depends on what property the predicate "is divine" expresses.... [T]he concept of divine attributes can be employed to explain the content of "is divine". We noted above that such divine attributes as omnipotence, omniscience, being uncreated, and perhaps being eternal, are plausibly thought to be necessary for being a divine person. Let us make this explicit and hold that a person is divine just in case that person has the divine attributes.[7]

This interpretation, then, allows us to assert that each Person "is God"—i.e. *is divine*—without either affirming a plurality of Gods or collapsing the Trinity in modalistic fashion as the identity reading threatens to do.

Jeffrey Brower finds this proposal unsatisfactory. He writes,

> Even if we grant that the term *"deus"* or "God" in such contexts [as the Athanasian Creed] expresses a property possessed by each of the Persons of the Trinity, it is extremely implausible to say that the property it expresses is *divinity*, where this is to be understood as a property distinct from *deity*. If there really were a distinction to be drawn between *divinity* and *deity*, and if the Creed writers really intended to be predicating *divinity* rather than *deity* of the Persons, wouldn't we have expected them to use the Latin term *"divinus"* rather than *"deus"*?[8]

Furthermore,

> It is significant, I think, that even if the Creed writers *had* employed *"divinus"*, where they actually have *"deus"*, we would still have grounds for rejecting

---

[6] Edward Wierenga, "Trinity and Polytheism," *Faith and Philosophy,* 21/3 (July 2004), 287.
[7] Wierenga, "Trinity and Polytheism," 288–9.
[8] Jeffrey E. Brower, "The Problem with Social Trinitarianism: A Reply to Wierenga," *Faith and Philosophy,* 21/3 (July 2004), 297.

Wierenga's interpretation. Judging by the way these terms are used in Latin, there is no sharp distinction to be drawn between the properties of being divine *(divinus)* and that of being a God *(deus)*. Indeed, the terms *"divinus"* and *"deus"* seem to me to function in Latin in much the way that "human" and "man" function in English (at least when the term "man" is being used gender neutrally, for example, to translate the Latin term *"homo"*).[9]

There are two points to be made about this critique. First of all, contrary to what Brower has said, Wierenga does *not* contrast the two properties *divinity* and *deity*.[10] What he does is propose "is divine" as an *interpretation* of "is God," in contrast with reading the latter expression as an assertion of identity between each Person and God. Furthermore, the second part of the critique seems to undermine the first: if there is no significant difference between *divinus* and *deus,* why make an issue of the fact that the latter term is used rather than the former? Brower's real point, however, is rather different. What he (surprisingly) wants us to do is to read (e.g.) "deus pater" as "the Father *is a God*"—and so also for the Son and the Holy Spirit. The reason I say this is surprising is that for the main trinitarian tradition it is *entirely unacceptable* to describe each—or indeed any—of the trinitarian Persons as "a God."[11] We have noted Sarah Coakley's acerbic response to Richard Swinburne's use of such language in his own early statement of trinitarian doctrine, language which he wisely avoided in his more mature statement of the doctrine. But now Brower wants us to accept that very same language as an interpretation of the Athanasian Creed—and, presumably, of numerous other texts in the classical trinitarian tradition. Something, I cannot help but feel, has gone badly wrong here. If each Person is "a God," and each is distinct from each other Person, then we have at least three Gods, and that is not a direction we want to go.

Brower's own solution, stated briefly in the closing pages of his paper, is an early version of the "oneness in number without identity" solution, the solution which was further developed by him and Michael Rea. We have already seen reason to reject this solution, but Brower's presentation of it here is especially problematic. By appealing to this as an interpretation of the Athanasian Creed, he is in effect attributing to its author(s) this very difficult and controversial logical doctrine—and doing this without, so far as I can see, *any*

---

⁹ Brower, "Problem with Social Trinitarianism," 297–8.

¹⁰ In an earlier discussion of this exchange ("Objections to Social Trinitarianism," *Religious Studies,* 46 (2010),421–39, see 432–3), I mistakenly accepted Brower's criticism of Wierenga on this point. This present discussion replaces what was said there.

¹¹ One might object to this that ancient Greek and Latin lack the indefinite article, and so do not distinguish between "being God" and "being a God." This is unconvincing. Translators into modern languages that have an indefinite article will freely supply such articles when called for by the sense of an ancient text. The objection considered here implies that the translators of ancient trinitarian texts were uniformly in error in their translations in this respect, but this is (to say the least) implausible.

evidence whatever that he (or they) ever entertained such a notion. (I have argued that even attributing the notion to Aristotle, in the form in which Brower and Rea employ it, is unwarranted.[12]) But how much does the notion help, anyway? There is the Father, who is a God, and the Son, who is a God, and the Holy Spirit, who is also a God. Furthermore, each of these is distinct from each of the others. And each of them is distinct from *God,* who is, quite naturally, a God as well. By any normal method of counting, this gives us a total of four Gods! Brower's response to this has to be that we are counting incorrectly—that even though each of Father, Son, Holy Spirit, and God is "a God," and even though each of them is distinct from each of the others, they are nevertheless to be "counted as" one and only one God![13] Whether this response is satisfactory is left for the reader to judge.

Brower has several other criticisms of Wierenga, but most of them are criticisms of Social trinitarianism as such; these criticisms will be addressed in the next chapter. In the present context, the main question to be answered is this: Is it legitimate to interpret the locution "is God," in the Athanasian Creed and other trinitarian documents, as attributing to each trinitarian Person the property of "being divine"? In response, I turn to what is perhaps the most seminal of all "proto-trinitarian" texts, the opening verses of the Fourth Gospel:

> In the beginning was the Word, and the Word was with God, and the Word was God. He was in the beginning with God. All things came into being through him, and without him not one thing came into being. (John 1: 1–3a, NRSV)

"The Word was God" (*theos ēn ho logos*). By common consent, *theos* occupies the predicate position in this clause. Shall we then read it as "The Word was a God"? I know of no generally accepted translation that does so—and that can't be for lack of attention to this crucial text. That is a translation only an Arian could be happy with![14] The writer has already distinguished the Word from God, *ho theos*: "the Word was *with* God." (So the identity interpretation is ruled out here.) If he were then to tell us that the Word is *a God,* we would have a clear and direct affirmation of *another God* alongside of *ho theos*—but surely, this cannot be, and cannot possibly be what the writer intended. In the final clause *theos* is indeed a predicate, but it functions in effect as a predicate

---

[12] I remind the reader of Alexander Pruss's essay, "Brower and Rea's Constitution Account of the Trinity," in McCall and Rea, *Philosophical and Theological Essays,* 314–25.

[13] Once again, I remind the reader of the bigamist who argues that, in virtue of a novel method of counting he has devised, the two women to whom he is married "count as" one and only one wife.

[14] I am informed by Alan Padgett that the New World Translation, used by the Jehovah's witnesses, translates, "the Word was a god." And *The New Testament in an Improved Version,* published by a Unitarian committee in 1809, has "and the word was a god."

adjective, stating that the Logos has the property of *Godhood* or *deity*.[15] But if this is so, we have as good a precedent as could be imagined for Wierenga's proposal to interpret "is God" in the Creed along those same lines. And given the difficulties of other possible interpretations, I believe that is just what we should do.

---

[15] C. K. Barrett states, "*theos*, being without the article, is predicative and describes the nature of the Word. The absence of the article indicates that the Word is God, but is not the only being of whom this is true; if *ho theos* had been written it would have been implied that no divine being existed outside the second person of the Trinity." *The Gospel According to St John* (London: SPCK, 1960), 130. According to F. F. Bruce, "What is meant is that the Word shared the nature and being of God." *The Gospel of John* (Grand Rapids: Eerdmans, 1983), 31. See also Raymond E. Brown, *The Gospel According to John (i–xii)*, The Anchor Bible (Garden City, NY: Doubleday, 1966), 5. Brown asserts that the adjective form *theios* ("divine") was not used because it was too weak; in the Greco-Roman world, it was all too easy for something to be "divine." If so, this may provide an answer also to Brower's puzzlement as to why *divinus* was not employed in the Athanasian Creed.

24

The Trinitarian Persons are Persons

The trinitarian Persons are persons. That is to say, they are "distinct centers of knowledge, will, love, and action." This is a claim that has been argued for, indirectly but also at times directly, throughout the book to this point. I will not repeat all those arguments here, but will provide a brief summary designed to recall the points that have already been made. Most of this chapter, however, will be devoted to addressing the multiple objections to Social trinitarianism that have been raised by opponents of this view.

Since we postulated that our construction of trinitarian doctrine should take as foundational the pro-Nicene theologians of the fourth century, we examined the way the doctrine was understood by Gregory of Nyssa. The pro-Social character of his doctrine is apparent in his use of the "three men" analogy for the Trinity: As Anatolios states, "Gregory assumes the validity of the comparison and indeed validates trinitarian language by reference to it."[1] This conclusion is underscored by the conviction, common to Athanasius, Apollinarius, and all the Cappadocians, that the subject of all of the human experiences of Jesus is the divine Logos, God the Son. If this is so, then the Son has experiences the Father does not have, and there are within the Trinity (at least) two distinct subjects of experience—two "distinct centers of knowledge, will, love, and action." We also examined Augustine's trinitarian doctrine, noting that, in view of his "psychological analogies" for the Trinity, he has often been seen as an opponent of Social trinitarianism. This view, however, cannot be sustained in the face of his confession that those analogies fail at precisely the point at issue: "In the one person which a man is, I did indeed find an image of that supreme trinity . . . And yet the three things of one person were quite unable to match those three persons in the way our human plan requires, as we have been demonstrating in this fifteenth book."[2] It is *precisely because* there is in a single person just one instance each of memory, understanding, and will, that the image of the Trinity found in one such person is inadequate. These conclusions are strongly underscored when we examine the Fathers' use of scripture in their accounts of trinitarian doctrine. For all of the

[1] Anatolios, *Retrieving Nicaea*, 228.   [2] Augustine, *The Trinity*, bk 15, p. 435.

pro-Nicene Fathers, the sufferings of Jesus on the Cross are the sufferings of God the Son and not in the same way of God the Father. More generally, all of the words and actions of Jesus were understood to be words and actions of God the Son, the second Person of the Trinity. This is simply a fact about the Fathers' scriptural basis for the doctrine of the Trinity, and I submit that if we decide they were mistaken on this crucial point we have departed in a fundamental way from the theological enterprise that consumed their interest and attention.

Perhaps, however, a bit more needs to be said about this, in view of the distinction between the "economic Trinity" and the "immanent Trinity." Carl Mosser in effect charges Social trinitarians with exegetical naivety for collapsing this distinction, and he cites Fred Sanders to the effect that "Everyone is bound to be a social trinitarian at the economic level."[3] However, neither Mosser nor Sanders bothers to explain how the immanent–economic distinction bears on the point at issue here. For the pro-Nicene Fathers, to be sure, this distinction was of considerable importance. Texts reflecting limitations, weakness, and suffering in the Son were not to be taken, as the Arians supposed, as indicating a difference in nature between the Son and the Father. Rather, such texts pertain to the status of the Son with respect to the economy of salvation, and the weakness and limitations are those of the assumed human nature, rather than of the divine nature which the Son fully shares with the Father. But the economic–immanent distinction is *not* a distinction with regard to the *personal agent* who is the subject of both sets of attributes. On the contrary, what Christopher A. Beeley states concerning Gregory Nazianzen is true of all the pro-Nicenes: "By referring the lesser sayings to the Son in his incarnate form, Gregory is able to counter the claim that such texts prove that the Son is merely a creature and therefore not fully divine. Yet at the same time, when he distinguishes between unqualified and qualified reference to Christ, Gregory is saying that both kinds of statements refer to *the same Son of God*."[4]

Indirect support for a Social doctrine of the Trinity also emerges from the material in Part II in which we considered some trinitarian views that strive to avoid Social trinitarianism. Barth and Rahner develop similar views that share two important difficulties. First, it is exceedingly difficult to understand what a divine "mode of being/subsistence" can be, given that it is not a *person* as we now understand that notion. Secondly, even Rahner is forced into inconsistency because he cannot, in the end, persist in his denial of the mutual love of Father and Son within the Trinity. And Barth, with his greater overall engagement with the biblical text, is all the more forced to go a very long

³ Fred Sanders, "The Trinity," in J. R. Webster, K. Tanner, and I. Torrance (eds), *The Oxford Handbook of Systematic Theology* (New York: OUP, 2007), 45; cited in Mosser, "Fully Social Trinitarianism," in McCall and Rea, *Philosophical and Theological Essays*, 147.

⁴ *Gregory of Nazianzus on the Trinity and the Knowledge of God* (Oxford: OUP, 2008), 133; emphasis in original.

distance towards the Social doctrine he has officially repudiated. Leftow has constructed a version of the doctrine that combines a desire to be loyal to the tradition with a remarkable metaphysical inventiveness. Nevertheless, he is left with the view that the Gospels portray for us a single person praying to himself, talking to himself, answering himself, and crying out to himself in protest for having forsaken himself. Brower and Rea profess themselves opposed to Social trinitarianism (although their formal theory is compatible with a Social view), but say concerning the Persons only that they are "concrete particular non-properties."[5] I submit that the lack of a viable available alternative to a Social doctrine of the Trinity gives us additional positive reason to investigate the prospects for a doctrine of that kind. But at this point we need to examine further some of the objections to such an approach.

OBJECTIONS TO SOCIAL TRINITARIANISM

The objections that have been raised in the literature are numerous, so it is necessary to be selective. Many of those objections, however, are relevant only to a particular version of Social trinitarianism, or to some particular strategy employed by this or that adherent of the view. Here we will limit ourselves to some objections that apply (or are intended to apply) broadly to any Social trinitarian view as that perspective has been defined in this book. The most thorough critic of Social trinitarianism is Brian Leftow, and we can introduce the arguments in this chapter by citing the two "hard tasks" which, he alleges, Social trinitarians need to perform:

> [O]ne hard task for ST is to explain why its three Persons are "not three Gods, but one God", and do so without transparently misreading the Creed....
>
> A second hard task for ST is providing an account of what monotheism is which both is intuitively acceptable and lets ST count as monotheist.[6]

Clearly these tasks are closely related: If it can't be maintained that there is only one God, then the claim to be monotheistic will have to be given up. I believe, furthermore, that most of the criticisms that apply generally to Social trinitarianism (as opposed to some particular version or strategy) will be of the sort suggested by Leftow's two tasks. Perhaps I should say at this point that

---

[5] Rea, "The Trinity," in T. P. Flint and M. C. Rea (eds), *The Oxford Handbook of Philosophical Theology* (Oxford: OUP, 2009), 420. Note, however, what is said in Brower and Rea, "Material Constitution and the Trinity," *Faith and Philosophy*, 22/1 (Jan. 2005), 75 n. 7.

[6] Leftow, "Anti Social Trinitarianism," 54, 55. The majority of Leftow's criticisms (many of them quite acute) concern particular assertions or strategies that are not mandatory for Social trinitarianism as such. For additional discussion see my "Objections to Social Trinitarianism," *Religious Studies*, 46 (2010), 421–39; and Leftow's "Two Trinities: Reply to Hasker," *Religious Studies*, 46 (2010), 441–7.

the mere assertion that Social trinitarianism is "tritheistic" does not, by itself, count as an objection to the view—at least, not an objection that needs to be taken seriously. This often-made claim is, so far, merely a statement of disagreement. (And Social trinitarians, like other trinitarians, are used to disagreement and don't let it bother them!) But arguments have been offered to back up the disagreement, and those arguments do need to be taken seriously. Here, then, are some of those arguments.

Is God not a person?

According to trinitarians, the Christian God is the Trinity. Now if, as Social trinitarians assert, each of the trinitarian Persons is a person, and if the three together do not in some way literally constitute a "super-person," then God, the Trinity, is not literally a person but rather a community of persons. Some opponents of the Social view have seen in this a decisive objection to that view. Commenting on the "Trinity Monotheism" of J. P. Moreland and William Craig,[7] Daniel Howard-Snyder observes that, on their view,

> God has three persons as proper parts, but God, the Trinity "as a whole," is not a person. Strictly speaking, using personal pronouns to refer to God presupposes, on their view, the *false* proposition that God is a person. And here I do not mean by "person" anything distinctively modern or Cartesian or anything else (allegedly) objectionable. I have in mind the concept of whatever is, strictly and literally, the referent of a personal pronoun. Even in that minimalist sense of "person," the suggestion that the Christian God is not a person is most unusual, to say the least.[8]

To be sure, the fact that an assertion is "unusual" is not, taken by itself, a terribly strong argument against it. But Howard-Snyder reinforces his objection with an additional argument:

> First, recall the opening words of Genesis: "In the beginning, God created the heavens and the earth." Creation is an intentional act. An intentional act cannot be performed by anything but a person. God is not a person, say Moreland and Craig. Thus, if they are right, God did not create the heavens and the earth; indeed, He could not have done so. The first sentence of the Bible expresses a necessary falsehood. Not a good start![9]

Howard-Snyder considers the possible response that "a composite can 'borrow' properties from its proper parts"; he replies that "there can be no 'lending' of a property unless the borrower is antecedently the sort of thing that can

---

[7] See Ch. 17 above.
[8] Daniel Howard-Snyder, "Trinity Monotheism," *Philosophia Christi*, 5/2 (2003); also in McCall and Rea, *Philosophical and Theological Essays*, 107.
[9] "Trinity Monotheism," 121.

have it." Thus, if we are in fact immaterial souls (as many dualists insist), "it is strictly and literally *false* that if my arm is bleeding, I am bleeding."[10]

It seems to me that Howard-Snyder has discovered an extremely powerful method of argumentation—one that, if accepted, will have implications reaching far beyond the use he has made of it here. For example: if God is timeless, as the majority of the theological tradition has held, it will in any case be strictly and literally false to say that God *created* (past tense). Following Howard-Snyder's lead, then, we have a quick and easy refutation of divine timelessness. It is too bad this did not occur to Augustine, Boethius, and Anselm; we could have been saved so much heavy intellectual labor! Indeed, the reference to the bleeding dualist is itself rather curious. One hopes that, if a dualist friend were to cry out that she was bleeding, Howard-Snyder would first assist in getting the wound bandaged, before he pointed out to her that she had just refuted her own metaphysical view concerning the nature of human persons!

Clearly, something has gone wrong here. I believe, in fact, that Howard-Snyder's essay is a rather clear example of the tendency warned against in Chapter 21: the tendency to treat classic theological texts and expressions as if they were formulas in symbolic logic. Howard-Snyder summarily rules out of court, in this instance, the extremely widespread usage according to which groups of agents (including groups vastly less unified than the Holy Trinity) are said to perform intentional acts in virtue of such acts being performed by their members. No, the assertion that God—on a Christian view, the Holy Trinity—created the heavens and the earth is *false* unless the Trinity is, simply and literally, a single person. This insistence on univocal language flies in the face of virtually the entire theological tradition, which has insisted that *analogical* language is very much to be expected in our assertions concerning the divine; indeed, that it is indispensable. But not only that: it is widely recognized that in the doctrine of the Trinity, *more than* in many other areas of theology, our verbal and conceptual resources are stretched to the limit. On account of this it is here, even more than elsewhere, that analogical uses of language—such as, for example, the attribution of personal actions to the Trinity as a whole—are very much to be expected. Howard-Snyder's disregard of this virtually unanimous tradition is problematic, to say the least.

The insistence that the Christian God must be *a person* is probably reinforced by the history of polemics against views that have denied the personal nature of the divine—Spinozism, for instance, or absolute idealism; more recently Tillich, or John Hick in his pluralist phase. But those considerations are not relevant here. There is nothing "impersonal" about the Trinity, which is a closely coordinated unity of *three* persons. The divine nature is not in itself personal, but (like other natures) it *does not exist* "in itself," but only as

---

[10] "Trinity Monotheism," 121.

the common nature of Father, Son, and Holy Spirit. Nevertheless, it may be that Howard-Snyder will still want to insist that God must be a single person, period. Craig comments, "Unfortunately, Howard-Snyder evinces a disturbing proclivity toward unitarianism,"[11] and it is difficult not to agree. It is, of course, possible to define monotheism, and even theism, in ways that are incompatible with the doctrine of the Trinity, but Christians can and should reject those definitions. Historically, Judaism, Christianity, and Islam are regarded as the three great monotheistic religions, and Christianity has been trinitarian at least since the third century—and "binitarian" a good deal earlier than that.

How many divine beings are there?

Here we address a group of criticisms raised by Jeffrey Brower in his critique of Edward Wierenga, but which also occur in other writers as well. First he observes, "If Wierenga is right, and only the Persons can literally be said to have the divine attributes, then there is a perfectly good sense in which God [i.e. the Trinity] is *not* divine on his account."[12] He goes on to admit, "Of course, he could respond by pointing out that there is a derivative sense in which God is divine (since God is composed of three divine individuals who are literally divine)."[13] Now, a Social trinitarian will hold that each Person is God, and also that the Trinity as a whole is God; clearly this will require two different senses of "being God," or "being divine," though it is not clear that either sense need be regarded as "derivative" from the other. But as regards the divine attributes, what Brower says here is essentially correct: the Trinity is omnipotent, omniscient, and so on, *in virtue of the possession of these attributes by the Persons of whom it is composed.* It is open to Brower to worry about the adequacy of this, but the Social trinitarian will not find that Brower's worries as such constitute a forceful objection.

However, he goes on to argue that "if God is divine, where God is understood as [a][14] complex distinct from but composed of the divine Persons, then it would follow that there are four divine beings. But such a view certainly *seems* polytheistic—indeed, tetra-theistic as opposed to just tri-theistic."[15] Now, it is a little difficult to wrap one's mind around the idea that the Trinity is a "fourth God" in addition to Father, Son, and Holy Spirit! For one thing, this presupposes that each of Father, Son, and Spirit is "a God." But as we have

---

[11] William Lane Craig, "Trinity Monotheism Once More: A Response to Daniel Howard-Snyder," *Philosophia Christi*, 8/1 (2006), 105. Howard-Snyder has not stated his own view concerning the doctrine of the Trinity, though I do not think he means to reject the doctrine.

[12] Brower, "Problem with Social Trinitarianism," 298.

[13] Brower, "Problem with Social Trinitarianism," 298–9.

[14] I make this insertion as required by the sense of the sentence; its omission appears to be a typographical error.

[15] Brower, "Problem with Social Trinitarianism," 299.

already seen, Social trinitarians (and indeed *all* trinitarians) can and should reject this. The Trinity is nothing more nor less than Father, Son, and Spirit *together in their unity;* it is not a fourth Person, and certainly not a fourth "God," as if there were three Gods already!

But of course, Brower is not done yet. Even if we don't count the Trinity as a fourth divine being, we still have three such beings, and that, he will say, is two beings too many for orthodoxy. But is this really a problem that is unique to Social trinitarianism? Let Father, Son, and Holy Spirit be whatever the anti-Social trinitarian supposes them to be, and then let us ask her, "Is the Holy Spirit a divine being, or not?" If the answer is No, it appears that she has abandoned entirely any idea of an objective, ontologically real Trinity. Supposing she doesn't want to do that, it seems that the Spirit must *in some sense* be a divine being, though she may want to qualify this by saying that the Spirit isn't a *separate* divine being from the Father and the Son. But now it looks as though the Social trinitarian can say that as well. Brower, with his modified relative-identity theory, will say that the Spirit is *the same being as,* and *the same God as,* each of the Father and the Son, but is not *the same Person as* either the Father or the Son. (Perhaps better, the Spirit "counts as" the same being and the same God as the other two.) Now if this "impure" relative-identity theory is acceptable, it can equally well be employed by a Social trinitarian.[16] Unfortunately, we have seen reason to reject both "pure" and "impure" versions of relative-identity theory, so the task of explaining how the Persons are "one in being" remains. (It will be addressed in subsequent chapters of this part.) Up to this point, then, Brower has not identified a problem for Social trinitarianism as such, as opposed to any other version of the doctrine that retains a real, objectively existing divine Trinity.

Brower raises yet another issue, however, that is not easily disposed of. The Athanasian Creed requires us to believe, for example, that "the Father is almighty, the Son almighty, the Spirit almighty, yet there are not three almighties, but one almighty." Brower notes that "According to Wierenga, each of the persons *literally* has each of the divine attributes (this is precisely what makes them divine). But this already commits him to the existence of three almighties and three eternals, as well as three exemplifications of every other such divine attribute."[17] This certainly does seem to be a problem for Wierenga. But in the same way as was argued above, it seems also to be a problem for *any* trinitarian view that is committed to the real, objective existence of Father, Son, and Holy Spirit. We might ask Brower himself, "Is the Holy Spirit almighty and eternal?" The answer, of course, must be Yes—and so also for the Father and the Son. We

[16] Brower apparently considers relative-identity theory as an alternative to Social trinitarianism (see 301–2). But this relies on an unduly restrictive idea of what Social trinitarianism amounts to; as we saw in Ch. 15, van Inwagen is both a relative-identity theorist and a Social trinitarian as defined here.

[17] Brower, "Problem with Social Trinitarianism," 298.

go on to ask, "Are Father, Son, and Holy Spirit each distinct from one another?" Here also, the answer must be Yes—and the Creed agrees: "There is one Father, not three Fathers; one Son, not three Sons; one Holy Spirit, not three Holy Spirits." So according to the Creed itself, there are three distinct individuals, each of which is both almighty and eternal—yet there is only one almighty and eternal individual. Or so it seems. Once again, the difficulty does not seem to depend on anything distinctive of Social trinitarianism as such.

In view of this, I submit that we have a genuine problem in interpreting the Athanasian Creed. On the face of it, what the Creed asserts appears self-contradictory. Swinburne has asserted that "no person and no Council affirming something which they intend to be taken with utter seriousness can be read as affirming an *evident* contradiction."[18] It may be, nevertheless, that we should take seriously the possibility that some person, or some Council, might produce a statement that is *deliberately paradoxical,* and might state an evident contradiction to that end. I believe, however, that we should consider this possibility only as a last resort, if there is really no possibility of an interpretation that is logically consistent. What other options are there in this case? Brower, as we have seen, would interpret trinitarian doctrine in terms of "impure relative identity." But over and above the inherent objections to such a theory, it is monumentally implausible to attribute relative-identity theory to the author(s) of the Creed sometime in the fifth century, with no supporting evidence to suggest that they entertained such a doctrine. On the face of it, however, the Creed does seem to entail a contradiction: there are three almighty individuals, but there is only one such individual. Now, if the Creed were deliberately asserting a contradiction in order to make a paradoxical point, we would know already that what the Creed says cannot possibly be true. In that case, we would have the task of discerning, if possible, the truth that lies behind the paradox. As I have said, however, I believe we should take that line only as a last resort. For the time being, I will postpone this question about the interpretation of the Athanasian Creed until a later chapter—noting, in the meantime, that this is not a problem for Social trinitarianism as such, as contrasted with any other view that maintains an objectively existing Trinity.

CONCLUDING AFFIRMATIONS

Having spent a good deal of effort addressing some of the objections to Social trinitarianism, it seems appropriate to conclude this chapter with some additional affirmations. First, I cite a passage in which Anatolios reflects on Athanasius' conception of divine personhood:

[18] Richard Swinburne, *The Christian God* (Oxford: Clarendon Press, 1994), 180.

It has become fashionable to deny that early Christian theology conceived of divine "personhood" in terms anywhere resembling our contemporary understanding of this notion. Be that as it may, we should not overlook the ways in which a theology like Athansius's, in its careful adherence to the narrative biblical patterns of identifying Father, Son, and Spirit, finds itself depicting the relation between Father and Son in terms that intersect with some aspects of our modern notion of personhood. Certainly, to be a subject of conscious intentionality is integral to our modern notion of personhood, and the interactions of subjects so that they become mutually subjects and objects of each other's intentionality and affirmation is integral to our modern conception of intersubjectivity. But the attribution of conscious intentionality to the divine relations is precisely the point at issue in this passage,[19] not because Athanasius has a presciently modern conception of divine or human personhood but simply because he is beholden to the patterns of biblical narrative and symbol.[20]

The other point I wish to make is indebted to the understanding of "christological monotheism" that emerged in Chapter 22. Given the discussion there, I propose the following argument:

(1) The beliefs and worship practices of the early Christian communities, as depicted in the writings of the New Testament, constitute a valid and acceptable form of monotheism.

(2) The early Christians perceived God the Father and Jesus Christ as distinct persons—as "distinct centers of knowledge, will, love, and action."

(3) The early Christians exhibit a pattern of "binitarian" belief and worship, in which Jesus is honored, praised, and worshiped along with God the Father. *Therefore,*

(4) There is a valid and acceptable version of monotheism in which there is more than one divine person.

If this argument is accepted, we have a definitive answer to Leftow's challenge to provide "an account of what monotheism is which both is intuitively acceptable and lets ST count as monotheist." The argument does not, to be sure, provide an analytic definition of monotheism in terms of necessary and sufficient conditions; this is often difficult when we are dealing with broad-ranging and complex historical phenomena such as monotheism. (Compare "revolution.") Rather, it points to a concrete historical exemplar, a "paradigm case" against which other claims concerning the phenomenon can be measured.

I don't assume, of course, that the premises of this argument are beyond challenge, but I expect that Christian anti-Social trinitarians will have some difficulty in dealing with it. The second premise is merely a statement of fact concerning the depiction of God and Jesus in the New Testament; a challenge

---

[19] Anatolios has just given an extended quotation from Athanasius, *C. Ar.* 3.66.
[20] Anatolios, *Retrieving Nicaea,* 153.

at this point looks quite unpromising. The first premise can certainly be challenged, but Christians may well find it awkward to do so: this would position them in agreement with the Jewish leaders who, by the end of the first century, had expelled Jewish Christians from the synagogue because of their excessive exaltation of Jesus. So it seems that the most promising approach, for those who object to the argument's conclusion, is to contest the historical case that Hurtado and others have made for the third premise. It will be interesting to see what emerges along those lines!

25

The Communion of the Persons

If the results of the last two chapters are accepted, we have a Trinity of persons,[1] distinct centers of knowledge, will, love, and action, each of whom is fully divine, in possession of all the divine attributes. But in virtue of what do the three persons constitute *one God?* This question has yet to be addressed in any adequate way, and it will be the subject of the next four chapters. This chapter is devoted to the communion of the persons—their "oneness" in what might be termed a psychological sense.

It seems likely that one of the motivations for those who object to understanding the trinitarian Persons as persons "in our modern sense" is a concern about the modern propensity to glorify the "autonomous individual." We would not welcome a portrayal of a trinitarian Person as an existentialist hero! Such a concern, however, has been anticipated and forestalled by the Social trinitarians themselves. Cornelius Plantinga, for instance, states that

> Each member [of the Trinity] is a person, a distinct person, but scarcely an *individual* or *separate* or *independent* person. For in the divine life there is no isolation, no insulation, no secretiveness, no fear of being transparent to another. Hence there may be penetrating, inside knowledge of the other as other, but as co-other, loved other, fellow. Father, Son, and Spirit are "members of one another" to a superlative and exemplary degree.[2]

That is well said, and yet it is not unreasonable to ask for something more specific than Plantinga offers us here. Upon reflection, it becomes clear that there are two opposing dangers that need to be guarded against. On the one hand, there is the concern that, in spite of Plantinga's words of caution, a Social doctrine of the Trinity may attribute to the divine persons an excessive individuality and independence that compromises the divine unity. On the other hand, the emphasis on unity may end by obliterating the distinction of the persons, in spite of the Social theorist's desire to maintain such distinction. It

---

[1] In view of the arguments of the previous chapter, I will often hereafter refer to the trinitarian three simply as "persons," without the capital letter.

[2] "Social Trinity and Tritheism," in R. J. Feenstra and C. Plantinga (eds), *Trinity, Incarnation, and Atonement* (Notre Dame, IN: University of Notre Dame Press, 1989), 28.

appears, then, that we have a sort of continuum, marked at one end by excessive differences between the divine persons, and at the other end by a kind of unity that effaces their distinctness. Finding the right spot on this continuum for a viable Social trinitarianism promises to be a challenging task.

Complicating this task still further is the fact that here, perhaps even more than in other aspects of trinitarian doctrine, we are confronted by mystery that enormously exceeds our capacity for understanding. Thomas Nagel famously pointed out our inability to grasp "what it is like to be a bat," because a bat, though a fellow mammal, differs from us in having a sensory capacity, echolocation, which is alien to human experience. What then can we say about "what it is like to be God"? The mere thought of giving any account of this should cause us to recoil in awed silence. To say that this situation calls for epistemic humility seems a huge understatement. The very best we can do, I submit, is to send up a few hesitant and tentative probes in what we hope is the general direction of the truth, seeking to say something that is neither wholly unintelligible nor outrageously false. With this caution in mind, let us proceed.

We begin with a proposal that lies decidedly at the "unity" end of the spectrum. C. F. J. Williams, citing a poem by Browning in which a lover achieves perfect spiritual union with his beloved, but only for a "good minute," writes:

> The life of God is for all eternity, I suggest, what Browning's lover achieved only for a minute. Each of the Persons of the Trinity has knowledge and will of his own, but is entirely open to those of the other, so that each adopts those of the other, sees with his eyes, as it were.[3]

Williams's remarks can well be seen as a commentary on the traditional doctrine of the trinitarian *perichoresis*, or "mutual interpenetration" of the divine persons. It is, furthermore, crucial that the persons should be united in their dealings with the world, as expressed in the traditional formula, *opera trinitatis ad extra sunt indivisa*—"the external works of the Trinity are undivided." This should not be understood to mean that there are not individual acts of the persons in relation to the created world: if that were the case, we could not say that the Son, but not the Father or the Holy Spirit, was incarnate in Jesus of Nazareth. However, the three persons are *united* in their actions in a superlative way. With this much understood, we seem to be on the right track. Some other remarks of Williams, however, seem to suggest that the Three may function in such complete unity that there is literally but one set of mental states between them. He asserts that Father, Son, and Spirit "will the same thing with the same will (and) act in one in the same act...the wills of the divine Persons are...a unanimity which is actually a unity...the will of the lover and

[3] C. F. J. Williams, "Neither Confounding the Persons Nor Dividing the Substance," in Alan G. Padgett (ed.), *Reason and the Christian Religion: Essays in Honour of Richard Swinburne* (Oxford: Clarendon Press, 1994), 240.

the beloved coincide so completely that *there is a single act of willing.*⁴ This is puzzling, to say the least. If there is, literally, only one set of mental states between the three persons, one wonders what the point is of their being three rather than one to begin with. There is also a puzzle, noted by Brian Leftow, about *first-person* mental states:

> If three minds shared one such state—say, a tokening of "I am"—to whom or what does its "I" refer?...For Williams, the Persons, not the Trinity, do the tokening. The Trinity is not identical with any one Person. So no Person's "I" can refer to the Trinity...But if the Persons have just one mental state among them it is unclear how any one Person could refer just to himself.... [D]id the whole Trinity will, "the Son shall become incarnate"? The Son could not learn from that that *he* would become incarnate unless he could also think to himself, in effect, "I am the Son, so *I* shall become incarnate". But on Williams's account it is hard to see how the Son could do so.⁵

My conclusion here is that, in the last-cited quotation, Williams has overstated his case in a way that is inconsistent with other things he has said. Consider again his example of the lovers. "[T]he will of the lover and the beloved coincide so completely that there is a single act of willing." We can understand this to mean that both lover and beloved will, with undivided unanimity, that each shall love the other. But despite the talk about a "single act of willing," the lovers do not thereby lose the use of the personal pronouns! She wills both that "*he* shall love *me*" and that "*I* shall love *him*," and she may be entirely clear about the reference of each of the pronouns in question. That this reading is the one that actually coincides with Williams's intention is even more clear in the light of something he says just two pages earlier: "[T]he love of the Father is distinct from the love of the Son, and both from that of the Holy Ghost. If there were no distinction, the joy of sharing would be absent. Where there is no *meum* and *tuum*, there is no giving. We must not admit any confusion of the divine Persons."⁶ In view of this, I submit that the talk of a "single act of willing" is misleading and should be dropped.⁷ With this correction in mind, I believe Williams's suggestions are genuinely helpful. At the same time, however, he reminds us of a danger to be avoided, that of emphasizing the unity so strongly that the distinction of persons is lost.

Now we need to consider the possibilities at the other end of the spectrum, where the distinction of the persons is emphasized. It is absolutely clear, to

---

⁴ Williams, "Neither Confounding," 242; emphasis added.

⁵ Leftow, "Anti Social Trinitarianism," 69–70.

⁶ Williams, "Neither Confounding," 240.

⁷ One reader suggests, "It isn't clear to me that one couldn't affirm both (a) there is one thing willed (one state of affairs) and (b) there are three things willing along with (c) there is 'a single act of willing' (that is done by all three persons *together*)." I have to say that I find the notion of a single act of willing that is performed by three distinct agents difficult to comprehend. This may, however, be what Williams had in mind.

begin with, that there can be no possibility of the divine persons engaging, or attempting to engage, in conflicting activities, so that (for instance) the Son is attempting to bring about a certain state of affairs and the Father is seeking to frustrate him. Other objections aside, if such a situation is possible then the three persons cannot all be omnipotent, and perhaps none of them will be so. On the contrary, the trinitarian persons will, in Swinburne's words, "give their backing" to each other's projects—and necessarily so. In this sense, the persons must have "one will" between them. Carl Mosser seeks to make of this a general objection to Social trinitarianism:

> If the divine persons cannot differ because they necessarily act in concert with one another, then attributing distinct wills is superfluous. Attributing distinct wills to two or more persons *simply is* an admission of the possibility of differ-ence. If there can be no difference, then the individuals share a single will.[8]

The clear implication of this is that the persons cannot be "distinct centers of will," as Social trinitarians insist that they are. But Mosser is glossing over some important distinctions. The word "will" is ambiguous as between three distinct applications: it can refer to the *content* of one's will (the state of affairs that is willed), or to the *act* of willing, or to the *faculty or capacity* of willing. Mosser is asserting, in effect, that if it is impossible for there to be a difference in the content, then there cannot be more than one faculty of willing. But this is scarcely self-evident; it is a point that needs to be argued for.

Consider again Williams's pair of lovers. They have the same *content* of will—that each shall love the other. Does that cast any doubt whatever on the fact that each has his or her own distinct *capacity* of willing? To be sure, given the reality of human weakness, there is the possibility of inconstancy. But now suppose that, beginning at the moment when love first awakens, each is for all eternity so appealing to the other that no deviation from perfect mutual devo-tion is possible. Furthermore, this same mutual devotion guarantees that, for all eternity to come, neither will oppose or impede anything desired by the other. Do these suppositions cast any doubt whatever on the assumption that there is a distinct faculty of will for each of the lovers? At this point, to be sure, we are closer to what we take to be the situation with the Trinity than to any-thing realistically possible in human relationships. I believe, however, that this example suffices to show that Mosser's conclusion is too hastily arrived at.

Here is another point to notice: Even if the content of willing is the same between two individuals—even if it is *necessarily* the same—there can still be a difference in the *acts* of will performed by the persons. This can be seen in Leftow's example, cited above, of the incarnation. Father, Son, and Holy Spirit all will *that the Son shall become incarnate*. So far, there is "one will"

---

[8] Mosser, "Fully Social Trinitarianism," in McCall and Rea, *Philosophical and Theological Essays*, 145.

between them. The Son, however, wills *to become incarnate* (or, *that I shall become incarnate*)—something that is *not* willed by either the Father or the Holy Spirit. If the Son's faculty of will were not distinct from those of the Father and the Spirit, the Son could not in this way will something not willed by the Father or the Spirit—namely, *to become incarnate*. Once we have seen this, we can also see that Mosser's objection to Social trinitarianism on this basis is unsuccessful.

Similar difficulties arise for some ideas put forward by Michel René Barnes. In a perceptive study of the relation between Gregory of Nyssa's psychology and his trinitarian doctrine, Barnes points out that, for Gregory, each of Father, Son, and Spirit is a real individual, possessing will (*boulē*) and a faculty of moral choice (*proairetikēn*). However,

> There is nothing in Gregory's writings which requires that the wills of each of the Three be conceived of as separate wills....Gregory may link cognitive volition to real individuality, but the two kinds of existences have different origins, and there is nothing to require that the two kinds of existences necessarily overlap ontologically....In short, Three Individuals, but One Will throughout the Three, or, as Gregory puts it, "the motion of the divine will from the Father, through the Son, to the Spirit."[9]

It is clear that Barnes thinks contemporary trinitarian theology should follow Gregory's lead in this respect. But Barnes, like Mosser, fails to attend to the distinction between the content of will, the act of will, and the faculty of willing. Once we notice this distinction, we can see immediately that even if the content of will is the same for Father, Son, and Spirit, we simply cannot make sense of the biblical data if we refuse to attribute to them distinct acts of will and faculties of willing. An example was given in the previous paragraph: the Son, and only the Son, willed *to become incarnate*. This refusal would also negate the mutual love between Father and Son, for the act of will involved in loving another simply cannot be the same act as that involved in the other's love for oneself. (I assume that Barnes, unlike Rahner in some of his pronouncements, would not be willing to renounce the mutual love of the Persons within the Trinity.[10])

At this point, however, a further question can arise—one concerning which I am less sure of the correct answer. Consider the situation posited by

---

[9] Michel René Barnes, "Divine Unity and the Divided Self: Gregory of Nyssa's Trinitarian Theology in its Psychological Context," *Modern Theology*, 18/4 (Oct. 2002), 489. (The embedded quotation is from *On "Not Three Gods,"* NPNF 5/335.)

[10] Barnes seems to be committed to the view that, in considering the views of the Fathers, we ought to restrict ourselves to the conceptual resources available to them in their own times, rather than interrogating them in the light of conceptions that are salient for us today. However admirable this may be from the standpoint of historical accuracy, I submit that we can and must go beyond this if we are to make their views accessible and relevant to contemporary theological theorizing.

Swinburne, in which two of the divine persons initially "prefer" two different outcomes of a certain situation. His example was the direction of the revolution of the earth around the sun, and that may be as good an example as any other. (Who after all are we to speculate about the preferences of divine persons?) As I noted previously, it would have to be the case that both outcomes are good, but that neither is obligatory or such that there is overriding reason to prefer it to the other. (If there were such a reason, there could not be even an initial difference between perfectly wise and good divine persons.) Is such a situation possible, or not?

Upon consideration the possibility we are considering breaks down into two further possibilities. First, it must be possible that one of trinitarian persons in effect "proposes" some action for consideration. That is to say, one person can initiate such a "proposal" by himself; this does not need to be done by the entire Trinity acting together. And secondly, once this is done, the other two persons *may or may not* concur with the proposal; if they do not, this would result in a disagreement such as the one considered by Swinburne.[11]

Clearly, this can be allowed as possible without giving up our earlier claim that it is impossible for the divine persons to oppose each other's actions. One option would be the one proposed by Swinburne: the Father, in virtue of his status as "source of being" for the Trinity, has laid down in advance rules concerning the respective spheres in which each of the persons has priority, so that in a person's own sphere of influence his preferences take precedence over the preferences of the other two persons. If this solution is not appealing—Leftow thinks it creates a rather severe inequality between the persons[12]—there are other possibilities. I suggested in my comments on Yandell that there might be no need for such rules. Each of the persons, being perfectly wise and good, would recognize that it would be a bad thing for him to insist on his own preferences in disregard of those of another divine person. Because of this, each would refrain from acting on his own preferences until some mutually satisfactory solution could be agreed upon. This does not seem too much to ask from perfect wisdom and goodness!

So to repeat: *Is such a situation possible?* One might arrive at a negative answer in the following way: Always, in every such "choice situation," there will be one of the alternatives that is objectively better than the others, and a perfectly wise and good person will of necessity select that alternative. I believe, however, that the assumption that there will always be some "objectively best" alternative is one we should reject. For one thing, the assumption tends to negate the attribution to God of libertarian free will, understood in terms of alternative possibilities. There are other reasons for questioning

<hr>

[11] Here I employ temporal language in describing the deliberations of the divine persons; readers who find this language inappropriate are invited to replace it with their own, non-temporal paraphrase.

[12] Leftow, "Anti Social Trinitarianism," 86.

this assumption, but we won't go into them here. Even if that assumption is rejected, however, we might still find the envisioned situation problematic. Brian Leftow would object to it because "it seems a reasonable requirement that a genuinely omnipotent power be one whose use no other power is great enough to impede."[13] In the supposed situation, the power of one of the divine persons would be great enough to impede the exercise of another's power, and the latter (given Leftow's intuition) could not be omnipotent. This is so even if, due to the perfect wisdom and goodness of all three persons, no actual conflict could ever occur. If this intuition of Leftow's is found compelling, the solution would be to stipulate that it is metaphysically impossible for the persons' wills to differ in any respect whatever, including the sort of "initial preference" that is in question here. In that case, we could say that the "power" exercised by the persons is a *single* power, one that is absolutely incapable of being impeded, even under conditions which are themselves impossible. (Such a stipulation will seem more plausible if we assume—as I believe we should—that the three persons share a single concrete nature.[14])

After consideration, I find myself disinclined to make such a stipulation. We have already established that the Son (e.g.) is able to will things not willed by the Father or the Holy Spirit: the Son wills *to become incarnate,* but neither of the other persons wills to become incarnate. Why then, should it not be possible for the Son *initially to prefer* something that is not preferred by the Father or the Holy Spirit? Saying this allows us to attribute free will to each of the persons, and not merely to the Trinity as a whole, and it is more consistent with Social trinitarianism that personal functions such as willing should belong in the first instance to each person as such. I do not find Leftow's intuition, cited above, altogether compelling. One reason for this may lie in the somewhat different way we approach the various divine attributes. I am not concerned, as Leftow and some others are, to arrive at a general definition of, for example, "*x* is omnipotent," a definition which can then be tested to see if it fits the case of the Trinity, or of a divine person. Since there are no other candidates for omnipotence than God, I am content to define omnipotence *as a divine attribute*; I will say that "God is omnipotent" means that *God is capable of doing whatever it is logically possible for an absolutely perfect being to do.* This can be applied to the persons individually (each of whom is fully divine), but also to the Trinity as a whole, which is a (composite) divine being. Since a perfect being will never do anything that is morally wrong or substandard, actions of that sort are not included within the scope of omnipotence. It follows from this, then, that no actual conflict of will can occur as between Father, Son, and Holy Spirit; the exercise of their power in the world is single and undivided, just as the Fathers have said.

[13] Leftow, "Anti Social Trinitarianism," 65.

[14] A stipulation of this sort would be needed on Leftow's own view of the Trinity, though I am not sure whether he realizes this. There does not seem to be anything contradictory in the supposition that the one person, God, should have different preferences in his different life-streams.

Leftow, however, objects to my account of omnipotence: "if someone is omnipotent because he is 'able to do anything it is possible for a perfect being to do', then if a perfect being can't do moral evil, it seems that someone imperfect, who can do all a perfect being can and also do moral evil, could be able to do more—have a wider range of action—than someone omnipotent. But there cannot be a wider range of action than omnipotence gives one."[15] Two points in reply: First of all, it is metaphysically impossible that there be an imperfect being, able to do moral evil, who can do all a perfect being can do. (This may even be conceptually impossible: arguably, some of the things God does can as a matter of logic be done *only* by a being who is morally perfect.) But secondly, I don't find it absurd that there are some things an evil being can do that God, who is omnipotent and morally perfect, is unable to do. Even on the human level, there are some things that are possible for an unscrupulous person to do that a good person, regardless of her physical strength, is unable to do—for instance, the deliberate murder of a child.

This raises a more general question about the role played by intuitions—for example, about omnipotence or about monotheism—in a discussion such as this one. It is not feasible in general to disregard one's own clear intuitions. On the other hand, it is extremely plausible that one's intuitions on such matters are influenced by the way one is accustomed to think about the Trinity. (One could ask, not merely "Which Trinity?" and "Whose monotheism?," but "Whose intuitions?") Many of us, I believe, are accustomed to think about God in terms of what Rahner has termed "mere monotheism." (I don't say that this is true of Leftow.) If so, then some of the intuitions we have developed may need to be questioned and/or modified when confronted with the requirements of the doctrine of the Trinity. (We might also, to be sure, want to consider the "exegetical intuition" that the New Testament, in depicting the relationship between Jesus and the Father, is not portraying a single person talking to himself!) As I have said, however, I remain less than fully confident on the question as to whether the trinitarian persons might differ in their initial preferences. In the absence of further compelling arguments on either side, it seems to me that either answer to the question is consistent with the rest of what needs to be said concerning the Trinity. Once again, we should remember how slender our grasp is of these matters; some distant approximation of the truth is perhaps the best we can reasonably hope for.

APPLICATIONS AND THEIR LIMITS

In speaking about the communion of the divine persons we are close to the very heart of Social trinitarianism, so it seems that this ought to be the place

---

[15] "Two Trinities: Reply to Hasker," 443.

especially to look for applications of that doctrine. I believe that this is in fact the case. Perhaps the most central point is this: for those who find *personal relationships* to be central to what transpires between God and God's human creatures, a Social doctrine of the Trinity provides powerful reinforcement by finding such social relationships in the very being of God. On the other hand, for those who most naturally think of human God-connectedness in terms of union with (or absorption into) the unfathomably mysterious divine essence, the personalism inherent in Social trinitarianism may not be especially welcome. That is not to say that a "relational" understanding of union with God cannot be held in conjunction with an anti-Social view of the Trinity,[16] but such a connection seems somewhat less natural.

This point can be developed farther. It is not merely that Social trinitarianism, by exhibiting personal relationships within the very being of God, reinforces the understanding that God, the Holy Trinity, *wishes to enter into such relationships with us humans,* amazing though that may be. It seems to be biblical teaching that the disciples of Jesus are actually *drawn into* the personal relationships within the Trinity—enfolded in the love between Father and Son. This at least seems to be the implication of Jesus' words in John:

> "As you, Father, are in me and I in you, *may they also be in us,* so that the world may believe that you have sent me. The glory that you have given me I have given them, so that they may be one, as we are one. *I in them and you in me, that they may become completely one,* so that the world may know that you have sent me *and have loved them even as you have loved me.*" (John 17: 21b–23; emphasis added)

The applications of the doctrine of the communion of the divine persons are not yet finished. If the Trinity is in very truth a sort of divine community, are we not bound to ask what lessons we can derive from it for the life of our human communities? This opportunity was exploited early on by Gregory Nazianzen: "In the *Second Oration on Peace,* he encourages the discordant Christians in the capital to find harmony with one another by recognizing the internal harmony of the Trinity. All forms of peace and concord derive from the peace of the Trinity, he says, 'whose unity of nature and internal peace are its most salient characteristic'."[17] More recently, appeals to trinitarian doctrine to support various conceptions of human society have become more numerous and also more diverse. On the socio-political left, "Leonardo Boff is convinced that 'social' doctrines of the Trinity support (if not necessitate) a socialist economy, and the ST of Moltmann has been received as an inspiration and support for liberationist theological and sociopolitical agendas of all sorts."[18] On the other hand other theologians, aligned with a version

---

[16] For an example of this combination, see Eleonore Stump's *Wandering in Darkness: Narrative and the Problem of Suffering* (Oxford: OUP, 2010).

[17] Beeley, *Gregory of Nazianzus,* 230.

[18] McCall, *Which Trinity?,* 225.

of trinitarianism that emphasizes the "functional subordination" of Son to Father, use the doctrine to argue for a similar subordination of women to men.[19] By this time, surely, the alarm bells begin to ring. A note of caution (though not of outright rejection) is sounded by Miroslav Volf. He cites the slogan of Russian intellectual Nicholas Federov, "The dogma of the Trinity is our social program," but quickly states, "No arguments need to be wasted on showing that Federov's proposal is specious and his vision chimerical."[20] Nevertheless, he states, "the question is not whether the Trinity should serve as a model for human community; the question is rather in which respects and to what extent it should do so."[21] He notes that "the doctrine of the Trinity is employed to pursue primarily the project of re-arranging (world-wide) socio-economic structures." But "While such projects are by no means misplaced, the road from the doctrine of the Trinity to proposals about global or national social arrangements is long, torturous, and fraught with danger."[22] His own proposals, in contrast, consist of some sensitive, insightful reflections on the topics of "identity" and "self-donation."[23]

While I have little interest in criticizing Volf's proposals on these topics, I feel the need to underscore even more strongly than he has done the difficulty inherent in deriving general prescriptions for human society from the doctrine of the Trinity. Earlier (Chapter 3) we saw Carl Mosser's reminder to us of the many ways in which human societies are *unlike* the Trinity; it may be helpful briefly to recall that reminder:

> Human beings simultaneously experience interconnected political relationships, economic relationships, workplace relationships, sexual relationships, and extended family relationships. We also experience many social relationships that require inequality of position, e.g. parent–child, teacher–student, doctor–patient, commander–soldier, patron–client.[24]

Of particular importance is the presence in human societies and human relationships of precisely what is *not* present in the Trinity: disagreement and conflict. The management and (where possible) the overcoming of disagreement and conflict are central to the constructive ordering of human societies. In

---

[19] See McCall, *Which Trinity?*, 175–88; also Yandell, "How Many Times does Three Go into One?," in McCall and Rea, *Philosophical and Theological Essays*, 157–61.

[20] Miroslav Volf, "'The Trinity is our Social Program': The Doctrine of the Trinity and the Shape of Social Engagement," *Modern Theology*, 14/3 (July 1998), 403.

[21] Volf, "'The Trinity is our Social Program,'" 405.

[22] Volf, "'The Trinity is our Social Program,'" 406.

[23] Limitations of space do not permit me to comment on Volf's book, *After Our Likeness: The Church as the Image of the Trinity* (Grand Rapids: Eerdmans, 1998), in which he compares the ecclesiological doctrines of selected Roman Catholic, Orthodox, and Free Church theologians and relates those doctrines to their respective views of the Trinity. I will say, however, that his comments on the views of Cardinal Ratzinger make interesting reading, in the light of the latter's subsequent elevation to the papacy!

[24] Mosser, "Fully Social Trinitarianism," 146.

this respect, the Trinity may in some degree model for us the ideal to which we aspire, but certainly cannot show us the process by which it is to be reached.[25] If in spite of this we persist in finding social, political, and economic prescriptions in the Trinity, we are likely to be indulging in a process of circular reasoning.[26] We take our own social-political convictions, derived from whatever source, read them back, in a suitably disguised form, into the doctrine of the Trinity, and then "discover" in that doctrine the blueprint for a just society. There is, furthermore the very real danger that in the process we will distort the trinitarian doctrine by molding it in the direction of our preferred social program. We may indeed see in the Trinity a model of mutual love, openness, and (as in Gregory) of peace. And our aims for human society should include all these things, but detailed prescriptions must come from other sources.

[25] Volf's account of "self-donation" makes heavy appeal to the "*linear* movement of [divine] love—downward towards godless humanity" ("'The Trinity is our Social Program'," 41). In other words, precisely *not* (or not primarily) to the intra-trinitarian relationship of love between the divine persons.

[26] The danger of circular reasoning is highlighted in Karen Kilby, "Perichoresis and Projection: Problems with Social Doctrines of the Trinity," *New Blackfriars*, 81 (2000), 432–45.

26

Processions in God

The Son is eternally begotten of the Father; the Holy Spirit proceeds from the Father (and the Son). So say the creeds, but this key element in the doctrine of the Trinity has so far received only minimal attention in the present work. In the ancient Church, that the Son and the Spirit somehow owe their existence to the Father was universally accepted. The arguments about this concerned whether this origin came about through a temporal act of creation, as the Arians asserted, or whether it was, as the creeds insist, a matter of eternal "happenings" in the very being of God.[1] This was of course crucial for the pro-Nicenes, but in view of the lack of significant present-day support for Arianism, not too much has been said about it here. That contest, it seems, was won once and for all; no need to refight the battle in this generation.

But it would be rash to assume that this issue (or any other central issue concerning the Trinity) has been settled for all time to come. More recently, a critique of the doctrine of processions has come, not from Arians, but from otherwise orthodox Protestant evangelicals. We have already seen evidence of this in Part II, in the versions of the doctrine of the Trinity put forward by Craig and Yandell. This, however, is merely the tip of a good-sized iceberg. In his recent defense of the doctrine of the processions, Kevin N. Giles has identified over a dozen well-known evangelical theologians and philosophers who reject the doctrine.[2] No doubt Craig speaks for many of them when he states that this doctrine is "a relic of Logos Christology which finds virtually no warrant in the biblical text and introduces a subordinationism into the Godhead which anyone who affirms the full deity of Christ ought to find very

---

[1] Following the later Latin practice, I sometimes refer to the generation of the Son and the procession of the Spirit together as "processions." This is merely a terminological convenience; nothing substantive hangs on it.

[2] Kevin N. Giles, *The Eternal Generation of the Son: Maintaining Orthodoxy in Trinitarian Theology* (Downers Grove, IL: InterVarsity, 2012), 30–33. Among the better known figures mentioned are J. Oliver Buswell, Wayne Grudem, Lorraine Boettner, Millard Ericson, and Paul Helm. At an earlier stage, the Princeton theologians Charles Hodge and B. B. Warfield were at best ambivalent about the doctrine of the processions. Another extensive discussion of the movement to reject the processions will be found in Keith E. Johnson, "Augustine, Eternal Generation, and Evangelical Trinitarianism," *Trinity Journal*, 32 (2011), 141–63.

troubling."[3] Some would add to this that the doctrine is incoherent or unintelligible. In view of this challenge, it is necessary to develop at some length the rationale for this element of trinitarian doctrine. I begin by pointing out some of the metaphysical consequences if the doctrine of processions is abandoned. This is followed by a discussion of the biblical warrant for the doctrine, together with consideration of the charges that the doctrine is subordinationist or that it is unintelligible. The chapter concludes with a brief discussion of the ever-vexed question of the *filioque*.

What difference does the doctrine of processions make to the metaphysics of the Trinity? The answer to this question depends in part on another question concerning divine unity: are we to affirm, along with the pro-Nicenes, that the three persons share the numerically identical concrete divine nature? If not, and if the processions are also denied, we may have difficulty in arriving at even a minimally adequate affirmation of the unity of God. We have seen in our discussion of Yandell that he rejects both the processions and the unitary concrete divine nature. Because of this, he apparently has no way to exclude the possibility that each of the persons is an independent, ultimate source of being, a view that arguably crosses the line into outright tritheism. He does not, of course, affirm that this is actually the case, but that it is so may well be entailed by his position. In order to avoid that consequence, it would seem to be essential either that two of the persons derive their existence from that of the third (rather, the First!), or that all three depend for their existence on some fourth reality, presumably the divine nature or essence. If both of these are excluded, no other solution appears to be possible.[4]

It appears mandatory, then, that if the processions are denied we must affirm the unitary concrete divine nature. Craig's own view provides an example of this, in his single divine "soul" with its three sets of rational faculties. This alleviates the threat of tritheism, but there are difficulties all the same. If we take this line there seems to be considerable pressure to accept that the ultimate source of reality, and of deity, is not the persons as such but rather the non-personal divine nature which supports and enables their existence. Perhaps, however, this can be avoided if we specify that what is ultimate is simply the entire complex—the nature *together with* the three persons. Then we do not have the nature, in itself impersonal, as the source of the persons. But neither do we have any explanation for the existence of more than one person, or of the fact that there are three

---

[3] J. P. Moreland and William Lane Craig, *Philosophical Foundations for a Christian Worldview* (Downers Grove, IL: InterVarsity, 2003), 594.

[4] Stephen T. Davis suggests a possible alternative in the doctrine of *perichoresis*. According to Davis, "this Greek word, first formally used in this context by John of Damascus, means co-inherence, mutual indwelling, interpenetrating, merging. It reaches towards the truth that the core of God's inner being is the highest degree of self-giving love." *Christian Philosophical Theology* (Oxford: OUP, 2006), 72. This is certainly impressive, but still does not seem to exclude that the *being* of each of the persons is independent of the other two.

of them, as opposed to two, four, or some other number. The existence of the Trinity will be simply a *brute necessity*—a state of affairs which could not be otherwise, but for which no explanation is available. Brute necessities are perhaps not always fatal to metaphysical systems that include them, but neither are they especially welcome. If a certain state of affairs is said to be necessary—to be such that it *could not possibly be otherwise*—we naturally expect there to be some reason why this is so. If no reason is forthcoming, we may be inclined to think that the "necessity" in question amounts to an arbitrary postulation, something that is affirmed for no better reason than that it fills what would otherwise be an embarrassing gap in the system being expounded. One might of course ask whether the inclusion of the doctrine of processions makes things any better in this regard. The answer, I believe, is yes; later on something more will be said about this. The present point, however, is that the view now under consideration seems to be precluded from even looking for a further explanation on this point. I don't want to claim that the considerations advanced here constitute a proof that the doctrine of processions is essential. They do, I believe, suffice to make the point that abandoning the doctrine is not an especially attractive option.

NO BIBLICAL WARRANT?

It seems that the objection to the doctrine of processions based on lack of biblical warrant stems from a "hyper-Protestant" notion of theological method, according to which good theology consists simply of setting out, in a systematic arrangement, what is explicitly taught in particular passages of scripture.[5] This method, if carried out consistently, leaves little room for recognition of the theological tradition, except as a record of earlier attempts to properly arrange the biblical proof-texts. But leaving this to one side, a key impetus for the objection lies in the widespread view of contemporary scholarship that the Greek word *monogenēs,* traditionally translated "only-begotten" (e.g. in John 3: 16), means simply "only" or "unique," with no reference to an act of generation.[6] But even without that word, there is ample biblical warrant for the claim that the Son derives his being from the Father. Indeed, such a derivation is strongly implied by the very words "Father" and "Son," as the Church Fathers repeatedly emphasized.[7] The connection between the Father–Son relation and "begetting"

---

[5] On this see Giles, *Eternal Generation*, ch. 2, where he also offers numerous citations in which major Protestant theologians argue for a broader conception of theological method.

[6] This however is not certain. The best-attested reading for John 1: 18 is *monogenēs theos,* though many prefer instead the variant reading *monogenēs huios* (Son). If *theos* is accepted, this puts pressure on the interpretation of *monogenēs.* The adjective *monogenēs* must then distinguish *theos* who is the revealer from the unseen *theos* in the first part of the verse—and neither "only" nor "unique" serves that purpose well. F. F. Bruce, who accepts the reading *theos,* translates *monogenēs* here as "only-begotten": *Gospel of John,* 44.

[7] See Giles, *Eternal Generation,* 71–8.

is emphasized in Hebrews 1: 5 (quoting Psalm 2: 7), where God says, "You are my Son: today I have begotten you." If the eternal generation of the Son is denied, the Father–Son relationship must be viewed as having its inception with the incarnation. This, however, is implausible as a reading of some biblical texts, for instance, John 17, where Jesus, self-identified as the Son, refers to "the glory that I had in your presence before the world was made." Consider also Hebrews 1: 2, which speaks of "a Son...through whom also he created the worlds." Especially pertinent here is John 5: 26, a text heavily emphasized by Augustine: "For just as the Father has life in himself, so he has granted the Son also to have life in himself." To *have life in oneself* is most certainly a divine attribute; it is inconceivable that this could be said of a mere creature. But it is impossible that the one who eternally coexists with the Father (and this, I take it, is clear in the Gospel as a whole) should first receive this divine attribute at the time of his appearance in human form. Here the relationship between Father and Son is pushed far back, indeed to the very beginning.[8]

Alongside the Father–Son texts, there are other passages that strongly imply a relation of ontological dependence between Father and Son. The notion of Word or Reason (however *logos* is best understood) clearly implies such dependence. "Word" and "Reason" are not free-standing entities; a *logos* is the Word or Reason *of someone*. The text from Hebrews cited above continues by saying that the Son is "the radiance of God's glory and the exact representation of his being" (NIV); both "radiance" and "representation" imply a relation of dependence.[9] In Colossians 1: 15 Christ is "the image of the invisible God." And there are other texts besides. I would not wish to claim that these passages constitute a proof of the doctrine of the processions. They do, I believe, provide significant support, and should give us pause if we are inclined to see the Church Fathers as systematically mistaken on this important point.

SUBORDINATION AND THE PROCESSIONS

But what of the charge of subordinationism?[10] Here we do well to remind ourselves that the intellectual climate in which we exist tends to make notions of hierarchy and subordination extremely unpalatable. Such biases exist in every time, of course; in an earlier age theologians readily accepted hierarchical ideas in contexts where it would have been better if they had been challenged

[8] For an excellent discussion of this passage, with extensive reference to Augustine, see Keith Johnson, "Augustine, Eternal Generation, and Evangelical Trinitarianism," *Trinity Journal*, 32 (2011), 147–53.

[9] RSV and NRSV have "reflects" or "reflection" rather than "radiance," thus understanding *apaugasma* in a passive rather than an active sense. But a reflection also has a decidedly derivative character.

[10] For an extensive discussion of contemporary evangelical views concerning the relation between the doctrine of processions and subordinationism see Giles, *Eternal Generation*, ch. 8.

(e.g. in the attitudes toward women and slaves). But there is no doubt that our own time has carried egalitarianism to some fairly extreme conclusions, and we may well question the influence of this bias on trinitarian doctrine.

Even more interesting, and less familiar, is the point that the early Christians may not have been especially interested in the "equality" of Father and Son! The point comes out clearly in Hurtado's discussion of Justin Martyr:

> What Justin did face in his own time was, on the one hand, Jewish accusations that Christians worshiped two gods, and on the other hand, the internal threat of Christian teachings (Marcion, Valentinus, and other demiurgical traditions) that posited a sharp distinction between the creator deity and the God from whom the Son had come forth. Hence, characteristic of proto-orthodox Christianity, he emphasizes one creator of all, and one source and center of all divinity, including the Son/Logos. Justin clearly sought to deny that the Son/Logos was a creature, or an emanation from God like the sun's rays, or represented a partition in God such that the being of the Father was diminished. Yet he also wanted to account for the Son/Logos as a monotheist, and the only way he could do so was by attributing the source of the Son/Logos to the Father.... In the first two centuries, all texts from, and affirmed in, the developing proto-orthodox tradition, from the New Testament writings onward, reflect subordination Christology, the Son understood as the unique agent of the Father, serving the will of the Father, and leading the redeemed to the Father.[11] ...If, in the light of Arius, fourth-century Christians became jittery with anything that smacked of subordinationism, that is irrelevant for understanding Christian thought of the first two centuries.[12]

Note especially here the need to "account for the Son/Logos as a monotheist." One might perhaps say (using admittedly anachronistic language) that the motto of those early Christians was, "Binitarian worship, Yes; ditheism, No!" And in view of our discussion of Yandell, it may be that "attributing the source of the Son/Logos to the Father" in the interest of maintaining monotheism has not altogether lost its point with the passage of time.

Later on, the Fathers did become concerned with the issue of subordinationism—and rightly so, as Hurtado would agree. But we need to see how they

---

[11] Compare in this connection the following from Marianne Meye Thompson: "John's argument for the dependence of the Son on the Father constitutes an argument for their unity. Father and Son are not two independent deities and not 'two powers in heaven'. Rather there is—to quote the Gospel itself—one 'true God', the living Father, whose life is given to and whose divine power is exercised in and through Jesus, the Son, and through the agency of the life-giving Spirit." *God of the Gospel of John*, 232.

[12] Hurtado, *Lord Jesus Christ*, 647–8. In the light of Craig's disparaging reference to "Logos Christology," I cannot resist quoting Hurtado's further comments about this: "I want to reiterate that for Justin the Logos is first and foremost *Jesus*, whom Christians worship (*1 Apol.* 66–67), through whose death and resurrection believers are purified of their sins (*Dial.* 13: 41), and through whom now all nations can come to the light of the true God (*Dial.* 26).... Justin did not merely think about the Logos; Justin worshiped and loved him (*2 Apol.* 13: 4)." *Lord Jesus Christ*, 648.

addressed that issue; in particular, how they saw it in relation to the doctrine of the processions. Consider, in this regard, Christopher A. Beeley's account of Gregory Nazianzen's view:

> [F]or Gregory, the monarchy of the Father and the coequality and consubstantiality of the three persons not only belong together, but necessarily do so and in fact amount to the same thing. The priority of the Father within the Trinity does not conflict with the divine unity and equality, but is rather what causes and enables them. The Father, Son, and Holy Spirit are one God, sharing the exact same divine nature, only because the Father conveys that nature to the Son and the Spirit, while the consubstantiality of the Son and the Spirit with the Father is the corollary and the eternal result of the monarchy of the Father.
>
> To put it more sharply, Gregory is firmly rejecting the notion that the monarchy of the Father in any way conflicts with the equality of the three persons—on the grounds that it is precisely what brings about that equality....In the Trinity, then, dependence and equality are mutually involved in each other, however much the idea may run counter to certain ancient or modern sensibilities.[13]

For Gregory, we see that the origin of Son and Spirit from the Father is precisely what guarantees their equality: a son shares his parents' nature, and is not inherently inferior to the parents even though his very being is derived from theirs.

One might object, to be sure, that human parents have in turn parents of their own, whereas the divine Parent has nothing of the sort. This is certainly true, and the point was not lost on the ancient theologians. For Eunomius, "unbegottenness" (*agennēsia*) was *the* fundamental defining property of the divine nature; since Son and Spirit lack this property, their natures differ from that of the Father, and they cannot qualify as "God" in the full sense. The Cappadocians replied that unbegottenness is the *personal characteristic* of the Father, as is begottenness of the Son and "spiration" of the Holy Spirit; these properties are not, however, part of the common divine essence, which is fully possessed by each of the persons. One would think that contemporary trinitarians would find it uncomfortable to be thus in agreement with the most formidable ancient opponent of trinitarian orthodoxy! But if it is inconsistent with full deity for a divine person's existence to be dependent upon any other entity, we will have *three fully independent sources of being and godhood,* and tritheism lies close at hand. Note, furthermore, that the Father's own existence is not independent of that of the Son and the Spirit. Just as the Son and the Spirit proceed of necessity from the Father, so the Father of necessity generates the Son and is the source of being for the Spirit. No one of the three can exist apart from the other two; all three exist together of metaphysical necessity.

[13] Beeley, *Gregory of Nazianzus,* 209–10.

ARE THE PROCESSIONS INTELLIGIBLE?

Is the doctrine of processions in God intelligible? The best way to test the intelligibility of some view is to produce as clear a statement as possible of that view, and see whether it is capable of being coherently understood. Here, then, is my candidate for such a statement: *God the Father eternally communicates the totality of the one undivided divine nature to the Son and to the Holy Spirit, and in so doing brings about the existence of the Son and the Holy Spirit.*[14] This anticipates the results of the next chapter in presupposing the single concrete divine nature, common to the three persons. It takes no sides, however, on the question of the Son's involvement in the production of the Spirit. Is the statement intelligible? It seems to me that it is; I seem to myself to understand what is being said, nor do I see in it any contradiction or evident impossibility. One might ask, to be sure, *how* God the Father does this. Probably the best reply is that no further explanation can be given; at least, no one has ever succeeded in providing an illuminating explanation. But that no further explanation can be given (if that is indeed the case) is no proof of impossibility, much less of unintelligibility. The Fathers all recognized this as a topic of deep mystery; their primary concern was to exclude any notion of material generation, an idea that was all too familiar from the paganism of that age. Those who suspect the doctrine to be either unintelligible or impossible are invited to produce arguments to that effect; lacking such arguments, there does not seem to be much more that can be done by way of defense.[15]

But what of the claim, made earlier, that the doctrine of processions adds to our comprehension of the doctrine of the Trinity, as compared with a version that rejects the processions? Consider the familiar idea, going back to Richard of St Victor but represented in this volume by Swinburne, that the Trinity is

[14] To avoid misunderstanding, this "communication" does not presuppose the prior existence of the Son and the Spirit. For comparison: in ordinary reproduction, the parents communicate (some part of) their own being to their offspring, and thereby bring about the existence of the offspring. "Bring about," as used here, expresses a very general notion in which a state of affairs is the result of the activity of an agent; causation is one species of bringing about. (Note that the pro-Nicenes did not hesitate to identify the Father as the "cause" of the existence of the Son and the Holy Spirit.) For some additional statements of the doctrine of eternal generation, see Keith Johnson, "Augustine, Eternal Generation," 141 and 141n. For instance, the following from the Reformed theologian Louis Berkhof: "It is that eternal and necessary act of the first person in the Trinity, whereby He, within the divine Being is the ground of a second personal subsistence like His own, and puts this second person in possession of the whole divine essence, without any division, alienation, or change." *Systematic Theology* (Grand Rapids: Eerdmans, 1949), 94.

[15] Stephen T. Davis offers a different interpretation, one that is interesting but puzzling. He states that "No one divine Person caused any other divine Person to exist in any important sense." *Christian Philosophical Theology*, 76. (One wonders what "unimportant sense" is being allowed for here!) He takes the doctrine of processions to affirm that "The priority held by the Father as the 'fount of divinity' is entirely logical in nature. In my view, the Father's priority has to do only with the proper place to begin an explanation." *Christian Philosophical Theology*, 71. But he does not, so far as I can see, tell us *what is it that is to be explained* in such an explanation—given that the explanandum is *not* to be the existence of the Son or the Holy Spirit.

necessary because only in this way can divine love reach its perfection. Perfect love requires for its fulfillment a perfect object, which can only be another divine person. But the love of two for each other is perfected in their mutual love of a third; furthermore, each of the three persons is in turn loved by the other two. There does not, however, appear to be any correspondingly great gain by expanding the circle of perfect divine love even farther; thus, a community of exactly three divine persons.[16] Brian Leftow has criticized this final move, pointing out the reasons a married couple may have for wanting several children rather than only one.[17] Leftow's point is well taken, if the argument given above is taken as a proof of the Trinity of persons. (And Swinburne does rather seem to be taking it that way.[18]) But if taken as a plausibility argument rather than a proof, the idea seems to have considerable merit. It does begin to give us a grip, however slender, on a possible reason why there are three divine persons, no more and no less.

This line of thought cannot, however, be appropriated by a trinitarian conception that rejects the processions. The reasons given for why there is a Trinity of persons are based entirely on the surpassing value of its being so. But value can only be appreciated—can only be valued—*by a person,* that is by a rational agent. (A non-personal nature cannot value anything; humans in a comatose state make no valuations.) But on the no-processions view, at the point at which there is a person to do the valuing, the Trinity of persons is already in place. And so it is as was stated previously: for such a view, the Trinity of persons must be seen as a brute necessity.

This may, however, raise yet another question: If the Trinity is grounded in the Father's valuation of the great good of there being such, does this mean that the existence of the Trinity is a matter of *choice* on the Father's part? And would this not make the existence of Son and Spirit contingent, thus introducing inequality into the Trinity in an unacceptable fashion? This question, it turns out, was anticipated long ago by the Arians. They taxed the pro-Nicenes with the question whether the production of the Son was by will or by necessity, relying on the Nicene party to reject the notion that God was subject to necessity. But if not, then the Son must come to be through an act of the divine will, which would imply that he was created and is not of the same nature as the Unoriginate God. The pro-Nicenes, however, answered the question with another: Does God *exist* by will, or by necessity? The same dichotomy would seem to apply here as well, so the Arians were in effect trapped by their own

---

[16] For another interesting discussion of this argument, see Davis, *Christian Philosophical Theology,* 65–8.

[17] "Anti Social Trinitarianism," 81.

[18] There are additional reasons for rejecting the argument as a proof. For one thing, divine perfection must be a *possible* perfection, and the Trinity certainly has not been proved to be metaphysically possible. Furthermore, it is hard to refute decisively the idea that a single divine person might have in the universe an adequate object of its love.

question. The correct answer, in either case, seems to be *both*. God does not exist *unwillingly*; he is not "thrown" into the world, as Heidegger famously claimed to be the case with human beings. Rather, he joyously *affirms* his own existence—and yet, *it could not be otherwise* than that God exists. Similarly, the Father is not compelled to generate the Son and the Holy Spirit, but *it could not be otherwise* than that the Father does this. In Athanasius' words:

> So if the Son's existence is by nature (*physei*) and not from intention (*ek boulēseōs*), is he with the Father apart from willing and without the intention of the Father? Of course not! The Son is from the Father by will also, as he himself says, "The Father loves the Son and shows him all things" (John 5: 20). For just as [the Father] did not begin to be good consequent upon [a prior] intention (*ek boulēseōs*), and yet is good not apart from intention and willing—for what he is, he is willingly—so also the Son's existence, while not having its beginning consequent upon an intention, is nevertheless not apart from willing or the Father's purpose. Just as [the Father's] own subsistence is willful (*thelētēs*), so also the Son, who is proper to his essence, is not without his willing.[19]

At this point I wish to raise a different sort of question about intelligibility—the intelligibility, namely, of the process of the development of trinitarian doctrine.[20] In one sense, to be sure, there is no problem here about intelligibility. Empirically, the developmental process was what it was, and the facts about that process do not depend on whether we agree with much, little, or none of the result. I submit, however, that if we approach the process as trinitarians who reject the doctrine of processions, we will be confronted with puzzlement. As has already been noted, the derivation of the Son and the Holy Spirit from the Father *was not in question* in the ancient Church. It was a common assumption about which many disagreements revolved, but was not itself a matter of disagreement. In fact, it is reasonable to assert that the developmental process *could not have occurred* in anything resembling its actual shape, without that assumption. We have seen Hurtado's explanation of its importance in second-century christology, as a necessary means to refute the Jewish claim that Christians made of Christ a "second power in heaven," another god alongside the Father. (Note that the doctrine of a unitary concrete divine nature, common to the three persons, *was not available* at that early period; it emerged during the fourth-century controversies.) We really have no way to reconstruct the path along which Christian theology might have developed without this assumption.

Now, if we accept the main results of the trinitarian controversy, including the doctrine of processions, all this is as it should be. Alternatively, those who reject the doctrine of the Trinity altogether have here no particular cause for

---

[19] Athanasius, *C. Ar.* 3.66; quoted in Anatolios, *Retrieving Nicaea*, 152.
[20] Giles, *Eternal Generation*, chs 4–7, gives a detailed history of the doctrine of the eternal generation of the Son, emphasizing its centrality to the entire trinitarian development.

concern. But if one views that history as an (otherwise) orthodox trinitarian, yet rejects the doctrine of processions, there is a rather large problem. One is then endorsing the main results of a developmental process *that had at its very heart a fundamentally wrong assumption*—the assumption that the being of Son and Spirit is derived from the Father. Somehow—by luck, or by divine providence—this distorted and misguided process managed to reach an essentially correct conclusion! But luck is surely unacceptable as an explanation here, and it would be very strange to suppose that divine providence had guided the Church through a process which essentially involved such a fundamental mistake. If we view the other results of the process as correct, and as arrived at with divine assistance, I believe it would take an extraordinarily powerful objection to justify rejecting the doctrine of processions.

"... AND THE SON"?

The issues discussed in this chapter were originally worked out in the context of the eternal generation of the Son. But once the Holy Spirit had come to be acknowledged as the third person of the Godhead it was natural, indeed unavoidable, to extend to the Spirit the main conclusions of the discussion concerning the Son, and so the Nicene Creed asserted that the Spirit "proceeds from the Father." The Western Church, however, under the influence of Augustine, added the words, "and the Son" (*filioque*), and this became a topic of controversy between the Eastern and Western branches of the Church. It seems fair to say that this might have remained a relatively minor theological issue, had it not become embroiled in the political controversies between the Churches. At the present time, when there is less enthusiasm for anathematizing fellow Christians over small differences of doctrine, the *filioque* does not seem to arouse a great deal of passion. Yet the issue remains, and it is necessary to say something about it here.

The Eastern view on the topic is represented in the words of John of Damascus: "The mode of generation and the mode of procession are incomprehensible." Also, "We have learned that there is a difference between generation and procession, but the nature of the difference we in no wise understand."[21] This might seem unsatisfactory, in that the distinction between Son and Spirit depends on a difference of which we have no conception whatever. Furthermore, there seems little possibility of our grasping the difference. *What is communicated* to the Son and the Spirit cannot be different; in each case, it is simply the divine essence. Perhaps there is a difference in the

---

[21] John of Damascus, *The Orthodox Faith*, 820 A, 824 A; cited by Vladimir Lossky, *The Mystical Theology of the Eastern Church* (London: James Clark & Co., 1957), 55.

manner in which it is communicated to the two persons, but there seems to be nothing in this that one's mind could get a grip on. Still, that there is such an incomprehensible-to-us distinction in the being of God is hardly something we can rule out a priori.

Augustine's view, the foundation of later Western thought on this topic, is summarized by Gerald O'Collins as follows:

> the Spirit proceeds from the Father through the Son, the Son being considered the agent of the Father in this procession by equally producing the divine Spirit. (The Son's being equal in the production of the Spirit was and is important when facing Arian challenges to the Son's true and equal divinity.) What the Son does here, according to Augustine, happens "through the gift of the Father" and not independently, just as his divinity is derived from the Father. Being and acting in such a "derivative" way does not exclude being equal in divinity and in the production of the Spirit.[22]

This involvement of the Son in the production of the Holy Spirit is what was signified by the later addition to the creed of the *filioque*. Lossky states the opposition of the Eastern Church to this addition as follows:

> The Greeks saw in the formula of the procession of the Holy Spirit from the Father and the Son a tendency to stress the unity of nature at the expense of the real distinction between the persons. The relationships of origin which do not bring the Son and the Spirit back directly to the unique source, to the Father—the one as begotten, the other as proceeding—become a system of relationships within the one essence: something logically posterior to the essence.... The hypostatic characteristics (paternity, generation, procession), find themselves more or less swallowed up in the nature or essence which, differentiated by relationships—to the Son as Father, to the Holy Spirit as Father and Son—becomes the principle of unity within the Trinity.... The Greek Fathers always maintained that the principle of unity in the Trinity is the person of the Father.[23]

We will not attempt to decide here the merits of these objections on either side. Whether the failure to attribute to the Son a role in the production of the Spirit weakens the case against Arianism, or whether the dual procession from Father and Son threatens the real distinction between persons—these are questions we leave to be debated in another forum. It is important to note, however, that an alternative formulation exists that apparently has the potential to satisfy both sides. A number of early theologians, in both East and West, spoke of the origin of the Spirit as coming "from the Father through the Son" (*ek tou patros dia tou huiou*). This recognizes the Father as the "principal" source of the Spirit, the point which is most important to the Eastern Church

---

[22] O'Collins, *Tripersonal God*, 139.

[23] Lossky, *Mystical Theology*, 57, 58. It should be noted that, from the standpoint of the Greek Fathers, the denial of the processions would represent an even more extreme form of the tendency to find the unity of the Trinity primarily in the divine essence.

and was, indeed, recognized by Augustine. At the same time, it also involves the Son in the production of the Spirit, though the mode of this involvement is (wisely) left undefined. As a bonus, it offers us at least a glimmer of understanding of the way in which the Spirit is distinguished from the Son, a point which (as we have seen) remains obscure if the Spirit's origin is said to be from the Father alone.

An important point that can be gleaned from all this, I suggest, is that it reminds us once again how tenuous our intellectual grip on such matters is and must be. Divine wisdom simply has not seen fit to reveal to us everything we might like to know about these subjects, and our resources for investigating these matters for ourselves are limited, to say the least. Agnosticism and intellectual despair are not called for, but excessive confidence in the rightness of our own conclusions is unwise.

27

The One Divine Nature

What is meant, or what should be meant, by saying that the three persons of the Trinity share a single divine nature? It has been argued throughout this book, directly and indirectly, that this does not mean merely that they share a common generic essence, though admittedly some Social trinitarians have understood it that way. Rather, the three persons share a single concrete nature, a single instance or trope of deity. But is this consistent with the claim, argued for in an earlier chapter, that the Persons of the Trinity *are persons,* in a sense of the term closely analogous to our ordinary use of "person"? This is probably the most important philosophical question facing the view of the Trinity developed in this book, and it is the question addressed in the present chapter.

What exactly are we trying to accomplish? We cannot aspire to prove that the unity of the divine persons in a single concrete nature is really, i.e. metaphysically, possible—and no one should expect this of us. The divine Trinity is integral to the ultimate structure of reality, so the truths concerning its nature are metaphysically necessary, in the sense spelled out in Chapter 21 above. Conversely, any incorrect assertion about the nature of the Trinity is metaphysically impossible: in virtue of whatever is the actual truth, the incorrect assertion is something that could not be true; it is excluded by the fundamental structure of reality. But this means that we could prove the Trinity as we conceive it to be metaphysically possible only by proving to be actual—and to repeat, no one should expect that.

We may, however, attempt to show that the Trinity as we conceive it is *epistemically* possible—i.e. that the doctrine is not inconsistent with anything we know to be the case. This will include rebutting non-question-begging arguments that have been advanced against the doctrine. (Arguments that take as premises opposing views concerning God and the Trinity are in this context question-begging and need not be considered.) We may also attempt to show, so far as possible, that the doctrine is plausible, and that it not merely does not contradict known truths but is consonant with relevant things that we know. What success can attend these efforts can only be learned by making the attempt. Our present concern is to argue for the consistency of affirming both that the divine Persons are persons, in some full sense of the term, and that the three Persons share a single concrete nature, a single trope of deity. In pursuing this project, I will put forward several different ways of thinking about the Trinity; some from our previous reflections and some that are new.

It may be useful to review briefly the reasons why it is important to affirm a singular concrete divine nature. Scripture offers comparatively little on this topic. Jesus said "I and the Father are one," but not too much is said about how this oneness should be understood metaphysically. On the other hand, it is clear in the pro-Nicene Fathers—in Athanasius and the Cappadocians, as well as Augustine and the later Western tradition—that they affirmed a single concrete divine nature. We should take a moment to consider the metaphysical implications if this is denied. If this denial is combined with a rejection of the relations of origin, it will be hard to arrive at even a minimally adequate affirmation of divine unity; this became clear in our consideration of Yandell. So if we reject the unitary concrete divine nature, we will need more than ever to affirm the eternal generation of the Son and procession of the Holy Spirit. But how are we to understand this generation and procession? The result of these events/processes is to be the group of three divine persons, each with his own individual divine nature, his own trope of deity. How is this to be arrived at? One way of understanding this is found in Swinburne's earlier proposal, that

> if it is an overall best act that a solitary God share his essential almightiness, the only way in which this can be done is if he creates as a separate God what is God anyway, i.e., if he divides himself. The creation being everlasting, this is to be read as: he creates as a separate God what, but for his creative action, would be himself.[1]

Later, however, Swinburne dropped this idea, stating:

> I doubt that it makes any sense to talk of a non-physical being dividing itself—division only applies to extended and so physical substances.[2]

There is a further difficulty, alluded to at the end of the first quotation above: Since the processions are everlasting, there can never have been a time at which what was to be the nature of the Son and the nature of the Spirit was actually a part of the Father. We have, then, the strange idea that the divine essence exists eternally partitioned into three parts, due to the Father's eternal will that this should be so, rather than the divine nature's belonging in its entirety to the Father alone. I suspect we will be easily persuaded to agree with Swinburne's later thought that such a scheme is unworkable.

But if this is rejected, what is left? The only apparent candidate is Swinburne's later conclusion that the Son and the Spirit are created *ex nihilo*[3] by the

---

[1] "Could there Be More than One God?," 232.   [2] Private email.

[3] I am not forgetting that Swinburne chooses not to use this language. But the thought is there, even if the specific terminology is avoided.

Father—and created as (supposedly) co-equal divine persons. But surely, this cannot be accepted. We see, then, that the stakes are high, when we ask whether the three persons can share a single concrete divine nature. Indeed, the most reasonable conclusion would seem to be that an adequate conception of divine unity requires us to affirm *both* the eternal relations of origin within the Trinity, and the singular concrete divine nature.

TWO TRINITARIAN MODELS

We begin by recalling two models of the Trinity that are familiar from our examination of them in Part II, those of Brian Leftow and William Craig. The latter, it will be recalled, proposes a view of God as a "soul with three sets of faculties," these faculties enabling the lives of the three persons, Father, Son, and Holy Spirit. Leftow, in contrast, views God as a single person, who nevertheless has a three-fold life—three lives, in fact—as Father, Son, and Spirit. What I want to call attention to here, however, is a claim that the two models have in common. This claim is what I will term the "trinitarian possibility postulate," as follows:

> (TPP) It is possible for a single concrete divine nature—a single trope of deity—to support simultaneously three distinct lives, the lives belonging to the Father, to the Son, and to the Holy Spirit.

"Support" here does not represent any obscure or technical notion; the term is used in the ordinary sense in which we can say that the human body/mind/soul (no particular view on the metaphysics of human persons is assumed) "supports" the continuing conscious life of a human being. This, I submit, is an extremely important claim, a claim which, if accepted, represents a successful conclusion with regard to the question posed at the beginning of this chapter. It is important to note, furthermore, that if the claim is acceptable as applied to Leftow's anti-Social version of trinitarian doctrine, then it is also acceptable as applied to Craig's Social version.

Do Craig and Leftow offer anything more in support of their possibility postulate? Not much, I think. Leftow may think he has offered such support by means of his story about Jane, the time-traveling Rockette. If he does think this, I must disagree. Jane in the story differs from the rest of us by her ability to time-travel, but other than that she does nothing extraordinary or even particularly unusual. The "multiple Rockette" phenomenon that is observed results entirely from the time-travel device, which enables multiple, sequential segments of Jane's life to appear simultaneously in our common timeline. These features, however, do not carry over into the trinitarian application of the story. So far as the Trinity is concerned, we are left with the mere assertion that it is possible for the one person who is God to experience simultaneously three discrete, non-overlapping life-streams as Father, Son, and Holy Spirit. Leftow may feel that, even if there is nothing that closely corresponds to this in our ordinary experience, there is nothing about the story which shows that it is incoherent or impossible. And Craig undoubtedly would say the same about his own model of the Trinity. For what this may be worth, I am inclined to agree with both of them. Still, I would welcome some further support for this all-important claim of possibility, if such support were to become available.

Another question that arises is, supposing that the possibility postulate can be sustained, is there any way of deciding between the two models? Here I believe that a decisive argument is available—and that it favors Craig's theory over Leftow's. The argument concerns a simple but profoundly important grammatical device, namely the use of personal pronouns. We begin by asking: *When the pronoun "I" is used by a divine Person, to whom does the pronoun refer?* For Craig's theory, the answer is straightforward: When "I" is used by a divine Person, the reference is to that Person. When the Fourth Gospel portrays Jesus as saying, "I and the Father are one," the "I" refers to Jesus himself—the Son of God, the Second Person of the Trinity. Conversely, when the Father, speaking from heaven, says "This is my beloved son, in whom I am well pleased," the "my" and "I" refer to the Father, the First Person of the Trinity. Sometimes, to be sure, God is represented as speaking in the first person in contexts where no distinction of Persons is expressed. One way of interpreting this is to say that in such cases the entire Trinity is referred to, by an analogical usage in which the divine Community is viewed *as if* it were a single person. Another possibility is that "I" should be taken, in such cases, as referring to the Father. More will need to be said about this in a later chapter. In general, however, the situation for Craig's view (and for Social trinitarians generally) is reasonably clear.

In contrast to this, Leftow's view is in trouble on this issue, or so I will argue. The question, once again, is: *When the pronoun "I" is used by a divine Person, to whom does the pronoun refer?* Note first of all that, for Leftow as for Craig, the "I" can *only* be tokened by a divine Person—i.e. the tokening must occur in one of the three divine life-strands.[4] Now, so far as I can see, there are three, and only three, logically possible answers to our question. "I" as tokened by a Person can refer to that Person, or it can refer to God, the one divine person, or it might refer to either one, depending on context.[5] Since God is the only *person*, properly speaking, in the neighborhood, it might seem reasonable to assume that the pronoun refers to him. Unfortunately, if we make this assumption the results are not satisfactory. Suppose we address this question to God: "Did

---

[4] "[E]very event in God's life is part of the Father-Son-Spirit chorus line; God does not live save as Father, Son and Spirit." Leftow, "A Latin Trinity," *Faith and Philosophy*, 21/3 (July 2004), 312.

[5] It does not seem to be logically possible that "I" refers *both* to a Person and to God; "I" is a singular pronoun which cannot refer to both of two distinct items.

you suffer and die upon the Cross?" On the present assumption, the correct
answer to this question must be—can only be—Yes. (There is no one else—no
other divine person—who could have done this.) Now, suppose we were to
address to God the question, "Did you send your Son, a person distinct from
yourself, to suffer and die on the Cross?" Here the answer must be No, for two
distinct reasons: First, the divine Son is not the Son *of God,* but rather the Son
of the Father, which is a different matter. But second, the Son is *not* another
person than God, although he is another trinitarian Person than the Father.
Rather, the Son is the *same person* as God; he is, in Leftow's words, "God doing
something,"[6] namely God experiencing the Son-life-stream. We have, then,
the view that it was the one person who is God, and not any other person, who
suffered and died on the Cross. But this is a view that in the ancient Church
was regarded as a heresy, the heresy of "patripassianism"—or, to use the even
more apropos Greek term, "theopaschitism."[7] This, then, cannot possibly be
the right way to answer the question about the reference of the pronouns.

What about the answer that says that, when a divine Person tokens "I," this
can refer *either* to that Person or to God? This would, of course, require some
appropriate criteria that would enable us to decide, in a given case, which was
the correct referent for the pronoun. Perhaps this problem could be solved, but
there is another, more fundamental difficulty. I will introduce this difficulty
by citing a philosopher who is by no means a fan of Social trinitarianism, especially not of Craig's version. Daniel Howard-Snyder, in pointing out that God,
on Craig's view, is not a person, says:

> Strictly speaking, using personal pronouns to refer to God presupposes, on
> [Craig's] view, the *false* proposition that God is a person. And here I do not mean
> by "person" anything distinctively modern or Cartesian or anything else (alleg-
> edly) objectionable. I have in mind the concept of whatever is, strictly and liter-
> ally, the referent of a personal pronoun.[8]

Social trinitarians will not share in Howard-Snyder's shocked rejection of the
view that God, the Trinity, is not literally a single person. But it is hard to fault
the principle on which he operates here—that a person is "whatever is, strictly
and literally, the referent of a personal pronoun." A person is someone who
can say "I" of herself, and "you" to another person, and who can herself be
addressed in the same way. If we apply this principle to the present answer to
our question (the answer according to which the personal pronouns can refer
either to God or to a trinitarian Person), we get the result that God is, indeed,
a person, but that the three Persons are also persons; they also can correctly

---

[6] "God begetting is God, doing something…and so too Son and Spirit." Brian Leftow,
"Time-Travel and the Trinity," *Faith and Philosophy,* 29/3 (July 2012), 324.

[7] See Paul L. Gavrilyuk, *The Suffering of the Impassible God: The Dialectics of Patristic Thought*
(Oxford: OUP, 2004), 91–100.

[8] "Trinity Monotheism," in McCall and Rea, *Philosophical and Theological Essays,* 107.

refer to themselves as "I." This, however, gives us a total of four persons—the Holy Quaternity that is universally, and rightly, rejected. So this answer also gives no satisfactory result.

What is left, then, is the same answer that was given by Craig's view: when "I" is tokened by a divine Person, the referent is that Person. But this in turn implies that *God cannot refer to himself, or be referred to ("strictly and literally") by others, using personal pronouns.* But is this not to say that *God is not a person*? (Except, of course, in the analogical sense in which "God" (i.e. the Trinity) can be said to be a person also by Social trinitarians.) What sort of person is it that cannot say "I" of himself, and cannot be addressed as "you" by another person?[9] So if this third answer is the one we are forced to accept, it is clear that it is Craig's interpretation rather than Leftow's that we need to affirm.

EVIDENCE OF POSSIBILITY?

At this point I will introduce some empirical phenomena which provide at least indirect evidence in support of the possibility postulate discussed above. I am referring to the "split-brain" and "multiple-personality" phenomena documented in psychology. I believe these have often been avoided in discussions of the Trinity because of their abnormal, even pathological character. This reaction is entirely understandable and natural, yet I believe the phenomena have something important to tell us. But it is important to be clear about what is, and is not, being claimed here. I am *not* saying, in effect, "God is just like those crazy (or brain-damaged) people you read about in the psychology textbooks." To say that would be seriously objectionable, and the rejection of such a claim would be thoroughly justified. The phenomena are introduced for a single, specific reason: I believe they provide important indirect support for the trinitarian possibility postulate (TPP) discussed in the previous chapter. Readers who find no difficulty in accepting that postulate may feel free to disregard at this point the material on split brains and multiple personality. But for those (including myself) who do feel that some additional support would be welcome, I proceed to show how such support emerges from these two types of cases.[10]

Commissurotomy, or split brain, cases are familiar to many and have been widely discussed by philosophers. In certain hard-to-control cases of epilepsy

---

[9] Perhaps the Queen is such a person. (My thanks to Jane Robson for pointing this out.) But Her Majesty's inability to say "I" does not seem to result from a metaphysical obstacle.

[10] Some of the material concerning these two types of cases is taken from my article, "Persons and the Unity of Consciousness," in G. Bealer and R. Koons (eds), *The Waning of Materialism: New Essays* (Oxford: OUP, 2010), 176–81.

it has proved beneficial to sever the corpus callosum, the thick sheaf of nerve tissue which forms the main connecting link between the right and left cerebral hemispheres. In many instances this has lessened the severity of epileptic seizures. More surprisingly, this major surgical alteration of the brain has turned out to have relatively slight effects on the patient's normal, day-to-day functioning. However, under controlled experimental conditions some striking results have been obtained. In the interest of brevity I will describe here only two cases, both featuring manipulative skills. One of Roger Sperry's commissurotomy subjects, W. J., was asked to perform a task with his right hand that involved arranging blocks in a predetermined pattern. The right hand is primarily controlled by the left cerebral hemisphere, which is greatly inferior to the right hemisphere in its ability to perform tasks involving spatial orientation. As a result, the right hand was having difficulty with the assignment. And then,

> Slowly and steadily…the left hand creeps in, brushes aside the right hand, and starts building rather more efficiently. The experimenter is seen [on Sperry's film] pushing away the intrusive left hand. After a little while, along comes the left hand again. This time we see W. J. grasping the wrist of the left hand with the right, and pushing it away himself. But…after another pause, in creeps the irrepressible left hand once again. This time W. J. takes his left hand in his right, pushes it away—and sits on it, to stop it interfering further.[11]

Here is the other case:

> L. B., an intelligent eleven-year-old commissurotomy patient, was given a pipe to hold in his left hand; a screen prevented him seeing what he was holding. The pipe was removed, and he was then asked to write, with his left hand, the name of the object he had just held. The left hand is of course primarily controlled by the right hemisphere, which had received the "pipe" input from the left hand's tactual sensing of the pipe. Slowly and laboriously L. B., with his left hand, wrote "P" and "I". At this point the left hemisphere took over—using its ipsilateral control over the left hand—and, changing the "I" into an "E", swiftly wrote "PENCIL". The right hemisphere took over again, crossed out the letters "ENCIL", and *drew* a pipe.[12]

In each case, there is a conflict between the two cerebral hemispheres, each apparently operating on a different conception of how the assigned task is to be accomplished. Furthermore, a strong impression is created that we have here two *centers of consciousness*, each seeking to pursue its own agenda. This conclusion is not irresistible; it could be that in each case one of the hemispheres is not conscious but is instead proceeding "automatically," as one may perform many familiar actions without conscious attention. However, this

[11] Kathleen V. Wilkes, *Real People: Personal Identity without Thought Experiments* (Oxford: Clarendon Press, 1988), 139.
[12] Wilkes, *Real People*, 138–9.

does not seem at all a natural reading of the situation. The tasks involved are not familiar, routinized procedures like brushing one's teeth or walking along a familiar route. Rather, they involve novel, interesting tasks that receive their point precisely from the special instructions given by the experimenter. The most plausible reading of the situation, surely, is that both hemispheres are somehow conscious, and each is attempting to perform the assigned task in its own way. I submit that any theory about the mind that forces one to deny this incurs a significant empirical burden, by forcing one to reject the most plausible way of understanding the observed facts in cases such as these.[13]

Multiple personality has been somewhat less discussed by philosophers than commissurotomy,[14] and is more likely to elicit a response of skeptical disbelief.[15] Indeed, multiple personality remains a topic of controversy among psychiatrists, a fact which should lead us to be cautious in drawing conclusions from contested data. The position taken here will be that there is such a condition, defined as "two or more personalities occurring in one individual, each of which is sufficiently developed and integrated as to have a relatively rich, unified, and stable life of its own."[16] In cases of multiple personality the original personality seems to have become fragmented, leaving parts which are "separate mental aggregates, each with its own memories, which form the nucleus for new, independently functioning constellations."[17] Multiple personality may sometimes have its origin in childhood fantasy and role-playing, but the separate personalities gain a degree of autonomy that clearly distinguishes this syndrome from play-acting. The different personalities display different patterns of brain function, as seen by an EEG, and give different, but internally consistent, sets of responses to the Minnesota Multiphasic Personality Inventory.[18] The MMPI is an extremely sophisticated test, with lie-detection

[13] For me personally one of the strongest pieces of supporting evidence is indirect—essentially, an argument from authority. The neuroscientist John Eccles, whose philosophical leanings were strongly Cartesian, nevertheless admitted that in split-brain cases "there is remarkable evidence in favour of a limited self-consciousness of the right hemisphere." *Evolution of the Brain: Creation of the Self* (London: Routledge, 1989), 210. Such an admission, which contravened his own prior inclinations (as well as his published views stated in earlier writings) can only have been the result of strong pressure from the empirical evidence.

[14] The most outstanding exception is Ian Hacking's book, *Rewriting the Soul: Multiple Personalities and the Sciences of Memory* (Princeton: PUP, 1995). No one interested in multiple personality should miss Hacking's rich and provocative discussion. In ch. 16, "Mind and Body," Hacking discusses the ways in which several other philosophers have treated multiple personality.

[15] For readers who might be inclined to disbelief, I strongly recommend Richard Baer, *Switching Time* (New York: Crown Publishers, 2007). Baer, formerly a psychiatrist in private practice, later became Medical Director for Medicare for several Midwestern states. The book recounts the protracted, and ultimately successful, therapy of a patient with seventeen alters.

[16] William N. Confer and Billie S. Ables, *Multiple Personality: Etiology, Diagnosis and Treatment* (New York: Human Sciences Press, 1983), 16. The definition cited is taken from W. S. Taylor and M. F. Martin, "Multiple Personality," *Journal of Abnormal and Social Psychology*, 39 (1944), 281–300.

[17] Confer and Ables, *Multiple Personality*, 16.

[18] See Wilkes, *Real People*, 111.

scales built in; systematically faking responses without detection is considered virtually impossible. The syndrome may in some cases be exacerbated by unwise actions of the therapist (for instance, by showing excessive favorable attention to alternates that tends to reinforce their distinctness), but it exists outside the therapeutic setting and cannot plausibly be considered to be the result of therapeutic suggestion.

My present concern is not so much with multiple personalities as such, as with the apparent existence of *simultaneously conscious* multiple personalities in the same individual. Sally, the most prominent alternate of Morton Prince's patient Christine Beauchamp,[19] claimed to have been "intraconscious"[20] with Christine, aware of all of Christine's thoughts as well as actions, since her early childhood. Similarly Jeanne, the main alternate of William Confer's patient Rene, claimed to have been with Rene, and watching over her, virtually all of the time since they first "met" when Rene was 4 years old. Here again, as with commissurotomy, we have phenomena which seem to point to the simultaneous existence of two or more centers of consciousness in the same human individual.

Now, this evidence is not unimpeachable. Alternate personalities have delusions of their own; Jeanne, for example, was for a long time unwilling to recognize that she shared the same body with Rene! So it might be possible to develop a hypothesis according to which, in each multiple-personality patient, there is at any given time only one center of consciousness; the different personalities alternate, but never coexist in simultaneous conscious states. But developing such a hypothesis in detail would present a formidable challenge. Among the phenomena to be accounted for are the diverse memories of the different personalities. Sally remembered Christine's thoughts and actions, but emphatically as "hers" and not as "mine." (The name "Sally" was originally chosen because Sally disliked Christine and objected to being called by her name.) Sally was able to recall Christine's dreams in more detail than Christine herself could. On the other hand, Sally was uninterested in schoolwork and inattentive during lessons; she was quite unable to speak or understand French, a language in which Christine was fluent. (This came in handy when the therapist wanted to communicate with Christine while excluding Sally.)

Another range of data to be explained concerns the apparent interactions between the alternates and the principal personality, and between the alternates themselves. Both Jeanne and Stella, another alternate of Rene, considered that they had a need to protect Rene, which sometimes involved "taking over" when a situation arose which Rene was unable to handle. On one occasion

---

[19] This case was originally reported in Morton Prince, *The Dissociation of a Personality* (London: Longmans, Green, 1905); I am relying on the account given by Wilkes.

[20] "The technical term for a subordinate consciousness that is aware of the primary personalities' actions but not thoughts is 'co-conscious'; one aware of both actions and thoughts is 'intraconscious.'" Wilkes, *Real People*, 113n.

Stella phoned the therapist to say that Rene, after a traumatic experience, was determined to commit suicide by overdosing on her husband's Seconal and Valium. Stella was asked by the therapist to bring Rene to the emergency ward of the hospital, where he would meet her. Shortly thereafter, Rene did appear at the hospital, in a confused state with no recollection of how she had got there![21]

These few observations merely skim the surface of the phenomena that would have to be explained by a hypothesis that would deny the existence of simultaneous consciousness on the part of two or more personalities. It is my strong impression (subject, of course, to refutation) that any hypothesis that could do this would have to be both *ad hoc* and extremely complicated, and thus antecedently improbable. Once again, there is an empirical price to be paid, if one is determined to avoid taking the data at their face value.[22]

What conclusions should be drawn from these examples? There is, I think, no need to accept the conclusion that we have in these cases multiple distinct persons. In commissurotomy cases, the many-persons interpretation flies in the face of the overall unity and integration of the personality, outside the experimental situations that elicit the anomalous responses. In multiple-personality cases, on the other hand, there is an obvious, serious disruption of personal unity. But it is widely agreed that the objective of therapy for these cases (an objective which in many cases has been successfully achieved) is the reintegration of the original personality, with the fragments that have been "hived off" making their contribution to the resulting whole. But while there may not be multiple persons in these cases, it is hard to resist the conclusion that there are multiple centers of consciousness. And though this is less radical than the "many-persons" hypothesis, it has major implications of its own. For one thing, it undermines the formulas, "one person—one consciousness," and "one mind—one consciousness," which seem to be deeply entrenched in our thinking about these matters. Many would claim for these formulas the status of necessary truths, entailed by our concepts of *person, mind,* and *consciousness.* I am not certain whether this is correct or not, but if it is this may be a place where we are forced to revise our concepts under the pressure of experience. Such revisions, however, are far from trivial, nor are they easily accepted. I suspect that it is primarily resistance to this kind of revision that motivates

---

[21] Confer and Ables, *Multiple Personality,* 130.

[22] An alternative solution, of course, might be found in a radically skeptical approach to the multiple-personality data as a whole. Some readers might suppose that such skepticism is to be found in Hacking, but that would be a mistake. Hacking does not doubt that multiple-personality patients are mentally ill, nor does he consider that the illness is caused by the patient–therapist interaction. He does, however, lay heavy emphasis on the way in which not only the interpretation of the condition, but its actual manifestation and symptoms, are shaped by the climate of psychiatric and popular opinion about such cases.

the strong objection felt by many to attributing more than one center of consciousness to commissurotomy and multiple-personality subjects.[23]

I have gone into some detail about these cases because I believe they are relevant to the possibility postulate needed for Leftow's and Craig's versions of the doctrine of the Trinity. The cases, I maintain, provide strong empirical support for the following conclusion:

> (C1) In a number of actual cases, the human body/mind/soul supports simultaneously multiple centers of consciousness.

But if this is true, it is also true that

> (C2) It is possible for a single concrete human nature—a single trope of humanness—to support simultaneously two or more centers of consciousness.

What is actual is also possible; that much is clear enough. Furthermore, I believe it is highly plausible to equate a concrete instance of human nature with a human body/mind/soul. (Once again, I am avoiding a commitment to any one theory on the metaphysics of human persons.) But if so, we also have significant support for the "trinitarian possibility postulate" needed for the doctrine of the Trinity:

> (TPP) It is possible for a single concrete divine nature—a single trope of deity—to support simultaneously three distinct lives, the lives belonging to the Father, to the Son, and to the Holy Spirit.

This is not, to be sure, proved to be true by the data from psychology. Obviously enough, God is different from human beings, and (C2) could be true of humans without the possibility postulate for the Trinity being true as well. But anyone wishing to argue against the latter will be forced to locate the impossibility precisely in something true of the divine nature which is not true as applied to the human situation, and finding an objection of that sort may not be easy. What cannot now be said is that the very idea of a single "soul" with multiple centers of consciousness is incoherent—and that, I suspect, is where many would most readily have found an objection to the trinitarian possibility postulate. The phenomena from psychology go a long way towards demonstrating the conceptual coherence of such a view of the Trinity, and that is no small gain.[24]

---

[23] For an interpretation of the split-brain evidence that seeks to avoid recognizing multiple centers of consciousness, see Tim Bayne and David J. Chalmers, "What is the Unity of Consciousness?" in A. Cleermans (ed.), *The Unity of Consciousness: Binding, Integration, and Dissociation* (Oxford: OUP, 2003), 23–58; for a counterargument, see my "Persons and the Unity of Consciousness," 186–90.

[24] Trenton Merricks, "Split Brains and the Godhead," in T. M. Crisp, M. Davidson, and D. Vander Laan (eds), *Knowledge and Reality: Essays in Honor of Alvin Plantinga* (Dordrecht: Springer, 2006), 299–326, develops an extensive analogy for the Trinity by means of a story in which we are able to communicate with a split-brain individual only by corresponding separately

Before leaving this topic, we should take note of a criticism by Michael Rea directed at the attempt to understand the Trinity by analogy with the sorts of cases discussed above. He writes,

> My own inclination...is to think that neither of them compares the persons of the Trinity with *distinct* psychological subjects. Rather, each compares the Trinity as a whole with a *fragmented* psychological subject. The personalities of someone with multiple personalities are not substances; they are aspects of a substance. Plausibly, the same is true of the distinct 'centers of consciousness' that are elicited as a result of commissurotomy. Thus...modalism looms.[25]

With regard to the main point made by Rea—that in both sorts of cases we are dealing with "fragmented psychological subjects"—I am in agreement. However, this fact in no way undermines the use of such cases in support of the possibility postulate for the Trinity, as explained above. It is still the case that we have multiple centers of consciousness, supported by a single instance or trope of humanness, and so the argument I have made is unaffected by Rea's criticism.

---

with the person's two half-brains, Righty and Lefty. In his conclusion Merricks claims to "have defended the Doctrine from the charge of contradiction." He denies, however, "having a theory of the nature of the Trinity" (p. 323); thus he remains uncommitted concerning the application of his imaginary example to trinitarian doctrine.

[25] Rea, "The Trinity," 410.

28

Constitution and the Trinity

The material in the previous chapter makes, I believe, a strong case for the possibility postulate needed for Craig's and Leftow's accounts of the Trinity. However, we might reasonably wish for a more precise account of the relationship between the persons and the divine nature than is provided by the loosely defined "support" relation that has been employed up until now. Such an account, if one is available, could also serve to redeem a promissory note issued some time ago—the promise (or aspiration) to provide another account of the "unity relation" between the persons and the nature that for the ancients was provided by their doctrine of divine simplicity. The attempt will now be made to provide such an account, making use of the notion of *constitution* as it has been developed in contemporary metaphysics. I do not believe that the argument as developed to this point depends on the success of the present endeavor. However, if the effort is successful, it will round off and complete our metaphysical account of the Trinity in a way that might otherwise be difficult to achieve.

WHY CONSTITUTION?

The argument will develop in several stages. First, a general account and defense of the need for the constitution relation. Second, a more precise account of that relation, drawing on the work of Lynne Rudder Baker. Third, the application of that account to the multiple-personality situation. And finally, the application of the constitution relation to the Trinity. I begin by recalling some material from our earlier discussion of constitution in Chapter 16. Jeffrey Brower and Michael Rea explain the need for such a relation by pointing to intuitions which support

> (MC) In the region occupied by a bronze statue, there is a statue and there is a lump of bronze; the lump is not identical with the statue (the statue but not the lump would be destroyed if the lump were melted down and recast in the shape of a disc); but only one material object fills that region.[1]

[1] Brower and Rea, "Material Constitution and the Trinity," 62.

There is no doubt that common sense (one might say, the view of the ordinary person uncorrupted by philosophy!) would agree that there is only one material object in the region occupied by the statue. However, the man on the street (and some readers of this book) might tend to balk at the notion that the lump of bronze is a different item than the statue. Nevertheless, the reason they cannot be held to be identical is compelling. If an item *x* is identical with an item *y*, then *x* and *y* must have *all* of their properties in common. But that assuredly is not the case here, as is shown by the parenthesis in the principle (MC). The statue has the property of *being such that it would no longer exist were it to be melted down and the metal recast in another shape,* where as the lump of bronze lacks that property; it would still be the same lump of bronze after the recasting, only now in a different shape. So the relation between statue and lump cannot be identity, and we must look for another way to characterize the relation between them. What a number of philosophers have decided to say here is that the statue *is constituted by* the lump. We can still say that the statue *is* the lump, and the lump *is* the statue—but this is the "is" of constitution, which is distinct from the "is" of identity.[2] Once we recognize the existence of the constitution relation, it turns out to be extremely common, even ubiquitous. Flags, for instance, are constituted by, but are not identical with, the pieces of cloth of which they are made: if the cloth were bleached and redyed in another color the piece of cloth would still exist but the flag would be no more. Other examples, given by Baker, are "the relation that obtains between an octagonal piece of metal and a Stop sign, between strands of DNA molecules and genes, between pieces of paper and dollar bills, between stones and monuments."[3]

In spite of its apparent utility, the constitution relation has not been greeted with unanimous acclaim by philosophers. One way to avoid it is to hold that the "constituted objects"—statues, flags, dollar bills, and the like—are not, properly speaking, "real objects" in their own right. The statue, for instance, is nothing but a lump of bronze (or stone, or clay, etc.) which for the time being has the "accidental property" of being shaped like something or other, being placed on a pedestal in a museum, and so on. Art lovers, to be sure, may not welcome this way of describing their revered objects, but that may not be decisive. (In metaphysics, as in national finance, tough decisions sometimes need to be made in the interest of economy.) Baker argues forcefully and at length against such an approach, contending that metaphysics ought to take seriously the sorts of things that make a difference to people in their everyday lives.[4] The deficiencies of the approach become especially

---

[2] It has been evident to philosophers for a long time that "is" has multiple senses. In addition to these two varieties, there is the "is" of predication (discussed briefly in Ch. 23—"the Son *is God*"), and the "is" of existence ("*there is* a God").

[3] Lynne Rudder Baker, *Persons and Bodies: A Constitution View* (Cambridge: CUP, 2000), 27.

[4] See Lynne Rudder Baker, *The Metaphysics of Everyday Life: An Essay in Practical Realism* (Cambridge: CUP, 2007).

clear when we consider another example given by Brower and Rea: "cats and heaps of cat tissue."[5] Many of us, I believe, will be less than amused to be told that, when a cat is run over by a truck, nothing has been destroyed: rather, it is merely that a certain heap of cat tissue has been rearranged into a new configuration. Still, it is not practicable for us to examine all the objections to the constitution relation or all the alternatives that have been proposed to deal with the intuitions captured in Brower and Rea's (MC). The approach taken here is to assume that there is such a relation, and to see what can be learned from applying it to the Trinity. Trinitarian believers who are skeptics about constitution will have to find their own way forward in explicating the doctrine.

WHAT IS CONSTITUTION?

If we decide to countenance the constitution relation, there are various ways in which that relation can be explicated. The presentation here is based on Baker's version, with minor modifications. Her view of the relation makes essential use of two notions; the first is that of a *primary kind*. A thing's primary kind supplies the answer to the question, "What most fundamentally is x?"[6] Examples, from among the cases of constitution already given, would include statues, lumps of bronze or clay, cats, masses of cat tissue, pieces of metal or cloth, national flags, stop signs, and so on. Baker acknowledges that she does not have a general theory of primary kinds, but she suggests

> a consideration that would lead us to say whether a case is one of constitution [i.e. the appearance of an object with a new primary kind] or of mere property acquisition. If x constitutes y, then y has whole classes of causal properties that x would not have had if x had not constituted anything. The anvil acquires the property of being a doorstop by our enlisting a physical property of the anvil— its heaviness—for a special purpose: to hold open the barn door. The use of the anvil as a doorstop does not bring about instantiation of whole classes of properties that anvils per se do not have. On the other hand, *David* has many causal properties of different kinds that Piece [the chunk of marble that constitutes the sculpture *David*] would not have had if Piece had not constituted anything.[7]

And of course, a cat has innumerable causal properties that would not be possessed by the heap of cat tissue, were that heap not to constitute a cat.

The other notion required is that of *circumstances*, a general term which covers the answers, in different cases, to the question, "In virtue of what is y

---

[5] Brower and Rea, "Material Constitution and the Trinity," 61.
[6] Baker, *Persons and Bodies*, 40.   [7] Baker, *Persons and Bodies*, 41.

the kind of thing that it is?"[8] If *x* constitutes *y*, it does so in virtue of certain circumstances in which *x* finds itself; lacking those circumstances, *x* might exist without constituting anything. "[I]t is in virtue of certain legal conventions that a particular piece of paper constitutes a marriage license; it is in virtue of the arrangement of molecules that something constitutes a block of ice; it is in virtue of its evolutionary history that a particular conglomerate of cells constitutes a human heart."[9] Note that the circumstances may include features intrinsic to the item in question (the arrangement of molecules in the block of ice, the color patterns on the flag), but also features extrinsic to the item (the evolutionary history of the heart, the legal conventions for the marriage license, the existence of the nation that has adopted the flag as its symbol).

Assuming that these notions are now reasonably clear, it is possible to give a definition of the constitution relation. Suppose *x* has F as its primary kind, and *y* has G as its primary kind. Then *x* constitutes *y* at time *t* just in case

(i) *x* and *y* are spatially coincident at *t*;

(ii) *x* is in "G-favorable circumstances" at *t*;

(iii) necessarily, if an object of primary kind F is in G-favorable circumstances at *t*, there is an object of primary kind G that is spatially coincident with that object at *t*; and

(iv) it is possible for *x* to exist at *t* but for there to be no object of primary kind G that is spatially coincident with *x* at *t*.[10]

G-favorable circumstances, of course are precisely the circumstances in which an object of primary kind F must find itself at a given time in order to constitute an object of primary kind G at that time.

It is hoped that non-philosophical readers will not be put off by the unavoidably technical nature of this explanation. It may be, however, that the point can be more readily understood in terms of the examples. The piece of metal constitutes a Stop sign in virtue of its shape, color, and the words printed on it, but also in view of the traffic regulations which dictate that, upon reaching the sign, vehicles should come to a stop before proceeding. Lacking any of these things, the piece of metal could still exist (perhaps even shaped and colored just as it in fact is), but it would not be a Stop sign. If a piece of marble, as a result of some incredibly improbable series of collisions with other rocks in an avalanche, should come to have precisely the shape of Michelangelo's *David*, that piece of marble would not in virtue of this be a sculpture, because it has no connection with an artist or an artworld. And so on.

---

[8] Baker, *Persons and Bodies*, 41.   [9] Baker, *Persons and Bodies*, 41.
[10] Paraphrased from Baker, *Persons and Bodies*, 43.

CONSTITUTION AND MULTIPLE PERSONALITY

Now that the constitution relation has been clarified, we need to see how it might apply to the Trinity. However, I wish to approach this question by first applying it to the multiple-personality cases described in the previous chapter. Or rather, to a slightly modified and idealized version of those cases; making the changes at this point will facilitate the subsequent application to the Trinity. The changes to the ordinary multiple-personality cases will be three in number. First (and least momentous), we will assume that the individual in question has exactly three distinct personalities. Second, we will assume that these personalities have become extremely stable, in such a way that each functions continuously (possibly excepting periods of sleep), and will continue to do so for the remainder of the individual's life, though they must alternate in exercising motor control over their common body. Furthermore, the distinct personalities are incapable of being "recombined," as is the normal therapeutic objective for such cases. And thirdly, we will now abandon our neutrality concerning theories of human nature, and will assume that the metaphysical underpinning of the human personality is some kind of immaterial soul. (The objective here is not to take sides on the metaphysics of human nature, but rather to facilitate the move to the trinitarian case, where by common consent the divine nature must be understood as immaterial.)

How then might the notion of constitution apply to such a case? We can approach it like this: The *constituted kind* (the kind G of the schema presented above) will be the kind, *human personality*, the kind exemplified by each of the three personalities in question. The *constituting kind* (the kind F in the schema) can be understood as the kind, *human mind/soul*. And the "circumstances" in this case can be spelled out as follows: When the human mind/soul *sustains a conscious life-stream* (assumed to include appropriate elements of cognition, feeling, and volition), there necessarily exists a human personality. In the present case, the soul in question sustains *three distinct* life-streams, and so there are three distinct personalities. On the other hand, it is possible for a human soul to exist without sustaining any conscious life-stream at all; this would seem to be what occurs in cases of irreversible coma.

This so far leaves out, however, one element in the definition of constitution: the stipulation that the items *x* and *y* must be spatially coincident. If the human mind/soul is non-spatial, as many believe, this requirement cannot be satisfied (except vacuously).[11] And it clearly cannot apply to the case

---

[11] Baker states that her definition of constitution "does not rule out there being immaterial things or even immaterial things that are constituted." *Persons and Bodies*, 43. She does not, however, explain what should be done about the requirement of spatial coincidence, when applying the relation to objects that are non-spatial.

of the Trinity, assuming that God is non-spatial. In view of this, I propose to substitute for the first clause of the definition, "(i) x and y are spatially coincident at t," the following: "(i*) x and y *have all their parts in common* at t." (The same substitution should be made in the other clauses of the definition.) This should suffice to secure the needed "closeness" between x and y. And if, as is commonly thought, souls are metaphysically simple, then neither x nor y will have "proper parts"; what they share, then, will be only their single "improper part," which is the soul in its entirety.

CONSTITUTION AND THE TRINITY

How, finally, does the constitution relation, so understood,[12] apply to the Trinity?[13] On the face of it, the application is fairly straightforward. The constituted kind (G in the schema) is *divine trinitarian person;* the constituting kind (F in the schema) is *divine mind/soul* or *concrete divine nature.* The divine nature constitutes the divine trinitarian persons when it *sustains simultaneously three divine life-streams,* each life-stream including cognitive, affective, and volitional states. Since in fact the divine nature does sustain three life-streams simultaneously, there are exactly three divine persons. So far, then, all is as it should be.

There is, however, a remaining problem. This problem arises from clause (iv) of the schema: "it is possible for x to exist at t but for there to be no object of primary kind G that has all its parts in common with x at t." Making the required substitutions (and suppressing the time-index), we have (iv*) "it is possible for the divine nature to exist but for there to be no divine trinitarian person that has all its parts in common with that nature." But *is this* in fact possible? Note first of all that we are not speaking here of real, metaphysical possibility. To repeat this once more: The divine Trinity is inherent in the ultimate structure of reality, so whatever is true of its nature is true of metaphysical necessity;

---

[12] It will be apparent to the reader that by this time we have departed considerably from the Brower–Rea understanding of constitution, so the application to the Trinity will also need to be different. For them, the notion of "sameness in number without identity" is crucial, but that notion as they define it plays no role in the present discussion.

[13] One might wonder how Baker would view the application of her notion of constitution to the Trinity. A possible clue is given by the following quotation: "However, anyone who believes in the Christian Trinity is committed to there being a relation (besides proper parthood) between strict identity and separateness. So, an orthodox Christian believer is in no position to declare the claim that there is an intermediate relation between identity and separateness to be incoherent." *Persons and Bodies*, 27n. On the face of it, one might wonder about the relevance of this reference to the Trinity, which is mentioned nowhere else in the book. Almost certainly, however, the remark is aimed at Dean Zimmerman, who is indeed both an orthodox Christian and also an assiduous critic of Baker on the constitution relation. In any case, she does seem to agree that either constitution or a similar notion may be needed for the doctrine of the Trinity.

contrary states of affairs are excluded by the fundamental nature of being. What we are asking about, then, is conceptual possibility. We are asking, is it *consistent with the concept* of the divine nature that it should exist at some time or other without sustaining the existence of any divine trinitarian person? It seems to me that the answer is Yes. To be sure, it arguably is conceptually impossible for the divine nature to exist at some time without sustaining the existence of *any* divine person at that time. God is said to be the *living* God; God has life—*consciously experienced* life—essentially, and not contingently. There does not seem to be a coherently conceivable analogue in the divine case to the human situation in which a profound coma has the result that the human nature exists without sustaining any conscious life-stream. We can, however, conceive of the divine nature existing without sustaining *three distinct* life-streams; many people do in fact seem to conceive it thus. Trinitarians will hold that they are mistaken to conceive it in this way, but the mistake does not seem to be one of simple conceptual confusion. Yet if the divine nature sustained the life of only a single divine person, this would not be a *trinitarian* person; it would not be any one of Father, Son, or Holy Spirit. For the nature of a trinitarian person includes by definition an eternal, and necessary, relation to the other two persons; the Father, for instance, is of necessity the person who is eternally the source of being for the Son and the Holy Spirit. So it seems that the definition of constitution is satisfied in this case, always keeping in mind that we are speaking of conceptual possibility rather than of a real, metaphysical possibility for the divine nature to exist without sustaining the trinitarian persons. To be sure, some careful maneuvering has been required in order to reach this result, and some readers may find the resulting picture confusing or otherwise of doubtful merit. But the complexity of the application of constitution to the Trinity should not be surprising; as has already been noted, it is widely recognized that our previous conceptions are put under strain in our efforts to understand the Trinity, so conceptual modifications are not unexpected. I admit, nevertheless, that the application of the constitution relation to the Trinity would go more smoothly were no such modification required. Alas, reality—especially, *this* Reality!—apparently is not constrained to configure itself for our conceptual convenience.

We shall say, then, that the one concrete divine nature sustains eternally the three distinct life-streams of Father, Son, and Holy Spirit, and that in virtue of this the nature *constitutes* each of the persons although it *is not identical* with the persons. If we do say this, we are enabled to interpret in a coherent way some claims of the trinitarian tradition that may have seemed to amount to a contradiction. In Chapter 7 above, we noted that Augustine's doctrine of divine simplicity leads him to say that each of the Persons is identical with the divine essence. Now, since the relation of identity is both symmetrical and transitive, it follows directly from this that each Person is identical with each other Person—a consequence which Augustine steadfastly denies. It might seem, then, that Augustine—and with him, much of the subsequent tradition—is guilty of a logical fallacy at this point. However, I felt unwilling to attribute to a thinker of Augustine's stature and acuteness such a simple and obvious logical blunder. I conjectured, then, that the relation Augustine had in mind (perhaps, vaguely and inchoately in mind), was not identity as we understand it but rather some other "sameness" relation. I acknowledged, however, that I could not find, either in Augustine or in any other ancient theologian, any clear or helpful explanation of this "sameness" relation.

Recent trinitarian thought has not been unmindful of the need for such a relation. The notion of relative identity seeks to fill this need, and the Brower–Rea notion of "sameness in number without identity" serves the same purpose. Unfortunately, both of these approaches have been found wanting. I submit, however, that the constitution relation serves the purpose in an elegant fashion. Constitution is, as Baker emphasizes, very definitely a kind of sameness, even though it does not amount to identity. If the divine nature constitutes the Father, we can very well say that it is *the same as* the Father, and so also for the Son and the Spirit. Yet, the formal properties of the constitution relation prevent us from inferring from this that the three Persons are identical. The constitution relation is like identity in being transitive: if a constitutes b and b constitutes c, then a constitutes c. However constitution, unlike identity, *is not symmetrical:* if a constitutes b it follows that b does *not* constitute a. So if the divine nature constitutes the Father, the Father does not constitute the divine nature, and no identity of the Persons can be inferred. However, the "grammar" of constitution, the way we customarily talk about the constitution relation, readily explains why constitution is often mistaken for identity, even though the two relations are distinct. We say readily both that the lump of bronze *is* the statue and that the statue *is* the lump; the "is" here, rightly understood, is the "is" of constitution, and represents the fact that the lump constitutes the statue, but not vice versa. We might say, the "is-ness" is symmetrical, but the underlying constitution relation is not! And now we can say, the Father *is* the divine essence, and the essence *is* the Father, and so also for the Son and the Holy Spirit. Yet the Father is not the Son, the Son is not the Holy Spirit, nor is the Holy Spirit the Father. Augustine, I think (I hope!) would be pleased.

29

The Grammar of the Trinity

At this point we have all the pieces at hand for our final, metaphysical statement concerning the divine three-in-oneness. Before proceeding to that, however, it will be helpful to make some remarks about the grammar of the Trinity. Now, it is good advice in general that when philosophers speak about *grammar*—especially if the word is italicized—you should keep your hand on your wallet! More often than not, what philosophers do is take a few central theses of their own philosophical position and transmute those principles into grammatical rules. If allowed to succeed, this transmutation offers great advantages. It renders one's own view largely immune to attack: Who, after all, would want to argue with grammar? And it shows one's philosophical opponents to be not merely mistaken but linguistically incompetent, because they fail to recognize that the language in which they express their own views is grammatically defective.

The grammar on offer in this chapter is not of that sort. What I will present are a few grammatical observations concerning the doctrine of the Trinity. These reflections are needed because the doctrine is both subtle and complex, and offers traps for the unwary; apparently minor deviations from standard usage can have serious consequences. Furthermore, the long history of the doctrine has had the result that there are apparently conflicting ways of speaking about the Trinity that enjoy the sanction of usage and cannot simply be rejected in the interest of uniformity of expression. To guard against biased theorizing of the sort described above, I ask that these observations be tested against the actual trinitarian discourse of the Church and of Christian theology, as this discourse has developed over many centuries. I will not be smuggling in my own theoretical views under the rubric of "grammar"; rather, the arguments and results of the earlier chapters of the book are presupposed.

Without doubt, the central grammatical issues revolve around the uses of the word "God." There are, I will argue, at least three different and distinctive uses of this word that occur in the vicinity of trinitarian doctrine, and serious confusion can result if they are not properly understood and distinguished. We will consider them in order.

First, *"God" is used to designate Yahweh, the God of the Old Testament, who was known to Jesus as Father and whom he taught his followers to address as*

Father. This is the standard usage of "God" throughout the New Testament, as can be verified by a cursory reading of the texts. Unitarians consider this usage normative and definitive, and appeal to it in order to rule out as incorrect other uses of "God" that arise in trinitarian doctrine.[1] This would imply that the binitarian worship of the early Christians was idolatrous, because it involved *worshiping along with God* someone who was in fact a mere creature. As we shall see, however, this is by no means the only relevant use of the word in the New Testament texts. In trinitarian theology "God," understood in terms of this usage, is of course the First Person of the Trinity. It should be said, furthermore, that the use of "God" to refer to the Father remains by far the most common use of the word among later Christians. Prayer is offered *to* God, *through* Jesus (or, "in Jesus' name"); seldom to the entire Trinity. Jesus is the "Son of God," where "God" refers, and can only refer, to the trinitarian Father. The Spirit is the Holy Spirit *of God*—not of the Trinity. The usage of "God" to refer to the Father has been supplemented but by no means supplanted by later developments in trinitarian doctrine.

Second, *each of the three trinitarian Persons can be described as "God" and can be referred to, addressed, prayed to, and worshiped as God.* Here we need to recall that, as noted earlier, *"'god' (theos) is not a proper name, but a term that makes a predication about the person or reality so named."*[2] "God" as applied to the Persons states that each of the Persons *is God;* i.e. it ascribes to that Person the property of *divinity* or *deity.* It implies that the Person in question possesses all the attributes that qualify that Person as God in the full sense ("true God"), including omnipotence, omniscience, omnipresence, moral perfection, eternity, and whatever else needs to be included in the full package of divine attributes. In the New Testament it is said explicitly of Jesus Christ that he is "God" on several occasions; most notably in John 1: 1 and 20: 28, but also to be considered are Titus 2: 13, Hebrews 1: 8, Acts 20: 28, and Romans 9: 5. The use of this language is nevertheless restrained; no doubt in part to avoid confusion with the first usage stated above, which is, as we have noted, the common and predominant use of "God" in these writings. In particular, it is *not* allowable to reason thus: "God the Father is God, and Jesus Christ is God, therefore there are (at least) two Gods." Nevertheless, as we have already seen, the roles and functions attributed to Christ, and his status as the co-recipient of worship along with the Father, constrained the Church to recognize him as "true God," as fully and unambiguously divine. The Spirit, on the other hand,

---

[1] For a recent example of this, see Dale Tuggy, "Divine Deception, Identity, and Social Trinitarianism," *Religious Studies,* 40 (Sept. 2004), 269–87; for further discussion see William Hasker, "Has a Trinitarian God Deceived Us?" in McCall and Rea, *Philosophical and Theological Essays,* 38–51; Dale Tuggy, "Divine Deception and Monotheism: A Reply to Hasker," *Religious Studies,* 47 (2011), 109–15; and William Hasker, "Deception and the Trinity: A Rejoinder to Tuggy," *Religious Studies,* 47 (2011), 117–20.

[2] The quotation is from Thompson, *God of the Gospel of John,* 22–3; emphasis in original.

is not explicitly said to be God in the New Testament texts, a point that was exploited in the fourth century by those who balked at recognizing the Spirit as divine. But the roles and activities attributed to the Spirit, and not least the invocation of the Spirit in the baptismal formula, led to his recognition as a full, co-equal member of the divine Triad.

A further point that needs to be made here is that *sometimes one Person is spoken of as divine in what seems to be an exclusive manner; nevertheless, such expressions should not be taken as excluding the other two Persons.* A striking example of this is found in the Gloria, which says, speaking to Christ: "Thou only art holy; thou only art the Lord." Here lordship and holiness clearly are seen as specifically divine attributes. (Christ has already been addressed as "Lord God.") But if Christ *only* is the holy Lord, what of the Father and the Spirit? However, the prayer goes on to say:

> Thou only, O Christ, *with the Holy Ghost*
> art most high *in the glory of God the Father,*

and so the Father and the Spirit are included along with the Son, in spite of the apparently exclusive reference in the first line quoted. (Whatever the field of candidates from which Christ was singled out as the "only" holy Lord, it did not include the Father and the Holy Spirit.)

This sort of apparently exclusive reference to one Person only is far more common in the case of the Father, so it becomes important to insist that *when the Father is referred to as "God," this should not be taken as an identity statement in such a way as to exclude the Son and the Holy Spirit.*[3] This issue arises in as late, and mature, a statement of trinitarian doctrine as our Nicene Creed (from Constantinople 381), which states:

> We believe in one God the Father almighty, maker of heaven and earth, of all things visible and invisible;
>   And in one Lord Jesus Christ, the only-begotten son of God, begotten from the Father before all ages, light from light, true God from true God, begotten not made, of one substance with the Father, through Whom all things came into existence.[4]

Here in addition to the "one God" who is the Father, we have Jesus Christ who, while clearly distinct from the Father, is himself said to be "light from light, true God from true God..." In addition, then, to the "one God," we have another person, distinct from the first, who is also said to be God. So there is, on the face of it, an inconsistency, but one that does not seem to have troubled

---

[3] Augustine: "And when [a man] hears the Father called the only God, he must not exclude the Son or the Holy Spirit from that title, for he is of course the only God together with whomever he is the one God with; so too when we hear the Son called the only God, we must accept it without in any way excluding the Father or the Holy Spirit." *The Trinity,* bk 7, pp. 234–5.

[4] Text from J. N. D. Kelly, *Early Christian Creeds,* 2nd edn (London: Longmans, 1960), 297.

the Church. It is clear enough what has happened. The Creed now *includes the Son and the Holy Spirit within the Godhead;* notwithstanding the first clause of the Creed, the relationship of the Father to the "one God" is not simple identity. The Father *is* God, to be sure, but not in such a way that the Son and the Holy Spirit are excluded.

Yet a third usage is one in which *"God" is used to refer to the Trinity as a whole.* This usage, unlike the first two, finds no explicit sanction in the New Testament—and yet, for trinitarian Christianity, it is unavoidable. In answer to the questions, "What is God?" or "What do you mean by 'God'?," an answer framed in terms of just one trinitarian Person would be, though correct, nevertheless incomplete. A full answer needs to include *all three* of Father, Son, and Holy Spirit—which is to say, it needs to mention the Trinity. The full and complete answer to the question, "What do Christians understand God to be?," can only be, "God is the Holy Trinity of Father, Son, and Holy Spirit."

But while the use of "God" to designate the Trinity is in some sense the metaphysical "bottom line" for trinitarian theology, it is not correct to view this as the primary use of the word, even within the context of that theology. Clearly it is a less frequent usage, and it came along comparatively late, becoming prominent only after Augustine. And it seems infelicitous to try to make this the primary usage of "God," and to explain the Godhood of the Persons in terms of it; for instance, by saying that the Persons "are God" because they are *parts* of God, the Trinity. If we go that route we will face the difficulty (noted in our discussion of Craig in Part II) of finding some sense of "part" such that the Persons are "parts of God" in that sense, and such that their being such is necessary and sufficient for the Persons' being divine. It is much better, I believe, to explain the Godhood of the Persons as was done above, in terms of their possession of the divine attributes of omnipotence, omniscience, perfect goodness, and so on. ˙

As we have seen, however, this can lead to the question, "Is the Trinity divine?" For knowledge, power, and goodness are characteristics *of persons,* and the Trinity, on the view defended here, is not a person but rather a community of persons. To this the reply must be that the Trinity, while not literally *a person,* can nevertheless be regarded in some contexts, and spoken of, *as if* it were a single person, in the way this is often done with closely unified groups of human beings. Would it be more accurate to describe the Trinity as powerless? When in fact the three Persons together exercise a single, transcendent power that can never be in conflict with itself? Or that the Trinity is ignorant, when each of the three Persons knows everything that exists to be known? To be sure, it may be that the manner of speaking in which personal attributes such as knowledge are ascribed to the Trinity as a whole will be found unsatisfactory by unitarians and those who sympathize with them. But it is no part of the agenda for trinitarian Christians to develop a way of talking about God that will be acceptable to unitarians. Summing up, then, the relationship between the Persons and the Trinity can be stated as follows: *Each Person is wholly God, but each Person is not the whole of God.*

I believe that the considerations presented here should serve to resolve most of the "grammatical" issues that arise concerning trinitarian doctrine. However, there is one traditional, and highly regarded, creed of the Church that presents special problems, and requires separate treatment. I speak, of course, of the "Athanasian" Creed which, while it does not enjoy the sanction of an ecumenical council, is deeply entrenched in the theology and piety of the Western Church.

THE ATHANASIAN CREED

This Creed, of course, has nothing directly to do with Athanasius; it seems rather to have been crafted sometime in the fifth century by a follower of Augustine's version of trinitarian doctrine. Some Social trinitarians would be willing to dispense with it, considering it to be an overwrought expression of some of the questionable tendencies of Latin trinitarian thought. I believe, however, that this option should be considered only as a last resort, if no acceptable interpretation can be found. And I will argue that there is, in fact, a perfectly reasonable way to understand the Creed that does not conflict with the Social trinitarianism espoused in this book. I begin by setting out the text in full:

> We worship one God in the Trinity and the Trinity in unity, without either confusing the persons or dividing the substance, for the person of the Father is one, the Son's is another, the Holy Spirit's another, but the Godhead of Father, Son and Holy Spirit is one, their glory equal, their majesty equally eternal. Such as the Father is, such is the Son, such also the Holy Spirit: uncreated is the Father, uncreated the Son, uncreated the Holy Spirit; infinite is the Father, infinite the Son, infinite the Holy Spirit; eternal is the Father, eternal the Son, eternal the Holy Spirit; yet they are not three eternals but one eternal, just as they are not three uncreated beings or three infinite beings but one uncreated and one infinite. In the same way, almighty is the Father, almighty the Son, almighty the Holy Spirit, yet they are not three almighty beings but one almighty. Thus, the Father is God, the Son is God, the Holy Spirit is God; yet they are not three gods but one God. Thus the Father is Lord, the Son is Lord, the Holy Spirit is Lord; yet they are not three lords but one Lord. For, as the Christian truth compels us to acknowledge each person distinctly as God and Lord, so too the Catholic religion forbids us to speak of three gods or lords.
>
> The Father has neither been made by anyone, nor is he created or begotten; the Son is from the Father alone, not made nor created but begotten; the Holy Spirit is from the Father and the Son, not made nor created nor begotten, but proceeding.

So there is one Father, not three Fathers; one Son, not three Sons; one Holy Spirit, not three Holy Spirits. And in this Trinity there is no before or after, no greater or lesser, but all three persons are equally eternal with each other and fully equal. Thus in all things, as has already been stated above, both unity in the Trinity and Trinity in the unity must be worshiped. Let him therefore who wishes to be saved think this of the Trinity.[5]

Over and above its elegance of expression, this Creed displays some distinct advantages in comparison with the Nicene Creed. It treats the three Persons in a fully coordinate fashion, removing the awkwardness in which the Father is said to be the "one God" and yet both Son and Holy Spirit are also accorded divine status. It unequivocally asserts the full equality of all three persons, even as it recognizes the origin of Son and Holy Spirit from the Father. It emphatically affirms both the oneness and the threeness of God, and finds no conflict between them.

But—and this is a big "but"—can this Creed be consistently affirmed by a Social trinitarian? Indeed, can it be consistently affirmed by anyone at all? It is fairly clear, I think, that the Creed requires a unitary concrete divine nature, so Social trinitarian views that deny this will be unable to subscribe. This is not, of course, a problem for the Social trinitarian view defended in this book. But it has been alleged that the Creed is inconsistent with any Social trinitarian view whatever; this I take it is the upshot of Jeffrey Brower's critique of Wierenga's view, noted in Chapter 24 above.

The principal difficulty lies in those passages of the Creed that assert both the divine oneness and the divine threeness in what appears to be the same context, so that we seem to have instances of the arithmetical formula, "(1 + 1 + 1) = 1." Some of these passages, however, are less troubling than others. When it is said that "the Father is God, the Son is God, the Holy Spirit is God; yet they are not three gods but one God," this is exactly what we should expect. It is no surprise at all to find the Creed insisting that each Person is God, but that the three together are *one* God, and not three Gods.[6] And the rationale for this is given when the Creed asserts that "they are not three uncreated beings or three infinite beings but one uncreated and one infinite."

The three together are *one being, one substance,* and this again is no surprise, certainly not if we accept that they have between them a single trope of deity, a single concrete divine nature.

Our perplexity increases, however, when the Creed speaks of particular divine attributes. For example, "almighty is the Father, almighty the Son, almighty the Holy Spirit, yet they are not three almighty beings but one

---

[5] Text from J. Neuner and J. Dupuis (eds), *The Christian Faith,* 6th edn (New York: Alba House, 1996), 16.

[6] This is, of course, completely consistent with the different uses of "God," as explained earlier in this chapter.

almighty." Brower notes that "According to Wierenga, each of the persons *literally* has each of the divine attributes (this is precisely what makes them divine). But this already commits him to the existence of three almighties and three eternals, as well as three exemplifications of every other such divine attribute."[7] This does seem to be a problem. But it is not a problem only for Social trinitarian views such as Wierenga's. On the contrary, the problem exists for any trinitarian view that posits a real, objective distinction between the divine Persons. As was noted previously, we might ask Brower himself, "Is the Holy Spirit almighty and eternal?" The answer, of course, must be Yes—and so also for the Father and the Son. We go on to ask, "Are Father, Son, and Holy Spirit each distinct from one another?" Here also, the answer must be Yes—and the Creed agrees: "there is one Father, not three Fathers; one Son, not three Sons; one Holy Spirit, not three Holy Spirits." So according to the Creed itself, there are three distinct individuals, each of which is both almighty and eternal—yet there is only one almighty and eternal individual. Or so it seems. The problem does not depend on anything distinctive of Social trinitarianism as such.

At this point, then, we are confronted with a genuine difficulty in interpreting the Creed. It might be tempting to suppose that at this point the Creed is being deliberately paradoxical, openly flouting the requirements of logic in order to display the faith's superiority to all such mundane considerations. I believe, however, that this is an interpretation that we should consider only if there is no defensible way to construe the Creed that avoids such paradox. My proposal is that we should understand such expressions as "they are not three almighty beings but one almighty" as imposing what may be termed, in a strict sense, *grammatical* rules. That is, the Creed is laying down *rules for how we are to speak* about the Trinity. That such a construal is not alien to the Creed's intention is clear enough when the Creed states, "the Catholic religion *forbids us to speak* of three gods or lords."

To see how this might work, recall a statement made by Lewis Ayres in characterizing "pro-Nicene" theology. According to Ayres, a mark of such a theology is "a clear version of the person and nature distinction, entailing the principle that whatever is predicated of the divine nature is *predicated of the three persons equally and understood to be one*."[8] Is this not exactly what we have in the Creed? Omnipotence—almightiness—is predicated equally of Father, Son, and Holy Spirit, belonging to each of the Persons in virtue of his possession of the entire, undivided, divine nature. However, this attribute is "understood to be one"—i.e. we are not to speak about "three almighty beings," leading to questions such as "What happens when one almighty being opposes another?," and pointing in the direction that might lead us to speak of three Gods. We need not understand the Creed as denying that there are three

---

[7] Brower, "Problem with Social Trinitarianism," 298.
[8] Ayres, *Nicaea*, 236; emphasis added.

divine Persons, each of whom is almighty; indeed, the Creed itself says exactly that. What is at stake here is a *restriction on how we are to speak* about these three almighty Persons: we are *not* to speak of them as three different Powers, which might lead to the unfortunate lines of thought mentioned above.

This interpretation is reinforced, I believe, when we consider that the Creed is very much an expression of an *Augustinian* doctrine of the Trinity. Commentators on Augustine have noted that much of his exposition seems to be concerned with *how we are to speak* about the Trinity as much as with the Trinity itself.[9] And surely, this is what we ought to expect from Augustine. He is deeply conscious of the inadequacy of our grasp of trinitarian matters— which of course did not keep him from writing a lengthy book on the subject! He is convinced of the spiritual benefits that can come from a deeper under- standing, but also of the dangers if our thinking on this topic goes astray. What more natural, then, than for him to guard especially against ways of speaking about the Trinity that might lead those whose grasp of the topic is inadequate (and that really means, all of us) into harmful misunderstandings.[10] In a pas- sage that bears directly on our present subject, Augustine writes,

> And so the Father is wisdom, the Son is wisdom, the Holy Spirit is wisdom; and together they are not three wisdoms but one wisdom; and because in their case to be is the same as to be wise, Father and Son and Holy Spirit are one being.[11]

But why not say "three beings"? For scripture does not forbid this, as it does forbid us to say, "three Gods." Augustine replies,

> Human inadequacy was trying by speech to bring to the notice of men what it held about the Lord God its creator, according to its capacity,... It was afraid of saying three beings, in case it should be taken as meaning any diversity in that supreme and ultimate equality.[12]

In passages such as these we have clear precedent, and very possibly the actual source, for the Creed's refusal to say "three eternals" or "three almighty beings."

This, then, is my proposal for understanding the Creed. The Creed is not concerned to deny arithmetical truths such as "$(1 + 1 + 1) = 3$." Rather, it is laying down *rules for our speech* about the Trinity, rules that forbid us to say things that might imply "any diversity in that supreme and ultimate equality." There is no logical paradox here, though there remains the verbal appearance of paradox that is unavoidable and perhaps even welcome. And the Creed on this interpretation is fully consistent with the Social trinitarianism advocated

---

[9] So Hill: "In general it is well to bear in mind that in these books [5–7] he is not so much talk- ing about God the Trinity, as talking about how to talk about God the Trinity." Augustine, *The Trinity*, 186.

[10] For Augustine's exploration of these terminological issues, see esp. *The Trinity*, bk 7.

[11] *The Trinity*, bk 7, p. 226.

[12] *The Trinity*, bk 7, p. 229.

in this book.[13] But to repeat this just once more: the problem being addressed is in no way a problem for Social trinitarianism in particular, as opposed to other trinitarian views that embrace an intrinsic, ontological distinction between the Persons. If some other solution to the problem is considered to be preferable, in all likelihood that solution also will be one that a Social trinitarian can happily accept.

---

[13] But will we in fact be able consistently to observe the Creed's prohibitions? Perhaps not; appropriateness of speech is highly context-dependent, and in discussing philosophical theology we often find ourselves saying things that would be inappropriate in a creedal or liturgical context. Clearly, conflicts of this sort are of less moment than disagreements in fundamental doctrine.

30

The Metaphysics of the Trinity

In the first chapter of Part III, I undertook to "present the central issues of trinitarian doctrine in a series of clear-cut steps." At this point I will briefly rehearse those steps, and then I will proceed to show how by following them we are able to arrive at a coherent, meaningful, scripturally adequate, and theologically orthodox doctrine of the Trinity. In Chapter 22 the theme of "Christological monotheism" was developed, showing how the Jewish monotheism of the earliest Christians was modified and enriched as a result of the impulsion they felt to affirm Jesus of Nazareth as the Son of God, and to worship him as such. In Chapter 23 we considered the trinitarian assertion that each of the Persons "is God," and concluded that this is best understood as attributing to each of the Persons the attribute of deity or Godhood. In Chapter 24 the central claim of Social trinitarianism, that each of Father, Son, and Holy Spirit is a person, a "distinct center of knowledge, will, love, and action," was set forth and defended. Chapter 25 is devoted to the communion of the persons—to what is sometimes described as their "perichoretic unity." Chapter 26 expounds and defends the processions in God, the doctrine of the eternal generation of the Son and the procession of the Holy Spirit. In Chapter 27 we expounded the doctrine that the three persons share a single, concrete divine nature, a single trope of deity; the intelligibility, coherence, and importance of this doctrine have been defended. Chapter 28 advocates the view that we can helpfully understand the relationship between the persons and the divine nature in terms of the metaphysical notion of constitution; the persons are not identical with the divine nature but are constituted by that nature. Finally, Chapter 29 sorts out some grammatical considerations that enable us to navigate our way through the sometimes confusing varieties of linguistic usage concerning the Trinity. What remains is for the present chapter to show how all these points can come together in a concise and accurate statement of the doctrine of the Trinity.

The doctrine of the Trinity arose because devout Jewish monotheists became followers of a man, Jesus of Nazareth, in whom they found the presence, holiness, and authority of God visibly embodied. Very early on after his death and resurrection they were found to be according to Jesus an exalted status and to be engaging in what amounted to a pattern of binitarian worship—of worshiping Jesus along with God. This was not an abandonment of monotheism but rather the transformation of a monotheistic faith from within, as a consequence of new revelatory experiences. The process of working out the relationship between Jesus and God became a vitally important theological concern of Jesus' followers for the first four centuries and beyond; the results of this process took the form of what we know as the doctrine of the Trinity.

It was evident from the beginning that Jesus was a "distinct center of knowledge, will, love, and action" from the Father—a distinct *person* from the Father. There was, however, no inclination to make of the Christ an independent deity, a "second God" along with the Father. Rather, the Son was worshiped and praised *together with* the Father, and his dependence upon the Father was emphasized in multiple ways: by the Father–Son terminology, by calling him the *logos* (Word or Reason) of God, and by stressing his willing obedience to the Father in his earthly mission. In the final, developed form of trinitarian doctrine this dependence was recognized in the doctrine of the "eternal generation" of the Son—and also, of the "eternal procession" of the Holy Spirit, who was accorded equal divine status with the Father and the Son.

The existence of Son and Spirit as divine beings did nevertheless pose a challenge to the monotheism which the early Christians were determined to maintain. One possible line was to affirm that Son and Spirit were divine in some lesser, subordinate sense, which would leave the Father alone as the "one true God." This line of thought reached its climax in the Arian controversy, the main result of which was the realization that the Church confronted a forced choice: Either the Son is *God*, "true God," God in the same sense as the Father is God, or he is a mere creature, "God" only by courtesy. Faced with this option, the decision was unequivocal: the Son and the Holy Spirit are indeed true God, fully and completely divine. To say that each of the three persons "is God" means that each of them displays, in the fullest sense, those attributes which are essential to a person's being God: almightiness, omniscience, perfect goodness, eternity, uncreatedness, and whatever others there may be.

Even given the derivation of Son and Spirit from the Father, the idea that there are *three different beings*, each of whom is fully divine, seems seriously problematic. Because of this, the "pro-Nicene" theologians of the late fourth century came to embrace the view that there is a *single* divine being or substance which somehow is at once Father, Son, and Holy Spirit. Clarifying this notion presented them with a formidable challenge, and still presents us with such a challenge today. Also important for upholding monotheism is the affirmation of *unity of will and operation* between the three divine persons; not only do they never in fact act in disharmony or oppose one another's projects, but it is simply impossible that this should ever occur.

The task for contemporary trinitarian metaphysics is that of making intelligible these claims that are integral to the doctrine of the Trinity, and doing so in a way that will be recognizable as coherent even by those who do not accept the claims. All the key elements in the present proposal have been explained and defended in earlier chapters of this book; what remains is merely to bring them together in a single, concise statement.

It was evident from the beginning that Jesus was a person distinct from the Father. But his existence as a distinct divine person was not limited to his earthly life: the Son was with the Father and shared his glory "before the world existed" (John 17: 5). So the doctrine of the Trinity affirms that there is, from all eternity, a distinction within God of three persons, three subjects and centers of consciousness—Father, Son, and Holy Spirit—each of whom is fully and equally divine. But this community of persons cannot be liable to degenerate into individualism and conflict, as so often happens with human communities. The doctrine of *perichoresis*—of the mutual indwelling and interpenetration of the divine persons—shows why it is that this does not and cannot happen. The three persons, while distinct in their actions (only the Son became man as Jesus of Nazareth), are necessarily united in their purposes and in their actions towards the world.

This personal union and communion of the persons does not, however, say everything that needs to be said about the divine unity. The doctrine of the Trinity affirms that the three persons are together a *single concrete being*—that they share between them a single trope of deity, a single concrete instance of the divine nature. This claim can be modeled by the notion of a single mental substance, or soul, supporting simultaneously three distinct conscious lives, three distinct streams of experience. Certain phenomena of psychology seem to show that something like this actually occurs among human beings; these phenomena support the conceptual possibility of this occurring in the divine case, and contribute to the plausibility of its being actually, metaphysically possible. (The latter, however, cannot be demonstrated, any more than the doctrine of the Trinity as a whole can be demonstrated.) It can also be said that the divine nature or substance *constitutes* each of Father, Son, and Holy Spirit, using the notion of constitution in a way closely analogous to its use in contemporary metaphysics. It is conceptually possible for the divine nature to exist without constituting (for instance) the Holy Spirit, but under the circumstances in which that nature supports the Spirit-life-stream (circumstances which do in fact obtain, and do so of metaphysical necessity) there exists the person of the Holy Spirit, a member of the divine Trinity.

The explanation for this three-fold sharing of the divine nature is given in the doctrine of processions, which affirms that the Son is eternally begotten from the Father, and the Spirit eternally proceeds from the Father through the Son. The doctrine asserts that, even as a human parent gives part of his or her being to become the being of an offspring, so the Father eternally makes it the case that the divine nature, which is originally the being of the Father alone, becomes in its entirety also the being of the Son and of the Holy Spirit, without thereby being divided or separated from the being of the Father. That this occurs is not a contingent choice on the Father's part, but rather is a necessary consequence of the perfection of the Father, a perfection which could not be perfectly fulfilled apart from the Father's eternal communion with the Son and the Holy Spirit.

For Christians, the full and final answer to the question, "What is God?" is and can only be, "God is the Holy Trinity of Father, Son, and Holy Spirit." The Trinity is not a single person, but the closest possible union and communion of the three divine persons. Yet in virtue of the closeness of their union, the Trinity is at times referred to *as if* it were a single person. The Trinity is divine, exhibiting all the essential divine attributes—not by possessing knowledge, power, and so on distinct from those of the divine persons, but rather in view of the fact that the Trinity consists precisely of those three persons and of nothing else. It is this Trinity which we are to worship, and obey, and love as our Lord and God.

Selected Bibliography

Adams, Robert M., "Divine Necessity," in Robert M. Adams, *The Virtue of Faith and Other Essays in Philosophical Theology* (New York: Oxford University Press, 1987), 209–20.

Anatolios, Khaled, *Retrieving Nicaea: The Development and Meaning of Trinitarian Doctrine* (Grand Rapids, MI: Baker Academic, 2011).

Augustine, *The Trinity*, with introduction, translation, and notes by Edmund Hill OP (Hyde Park: New City Press, 1991).

_____ *On Christian Doctrine*, tr. G. W. Robertson (Indianapolis: Bobbs-Merrill, 1958).

Ayres, Lewis, *Nicaea and its Legacy: An Approach to Fourth-Century Trinitarian Theology* (Oxford: Oxford University Press, 2004).

_____ *Augustine and the Trinity* (Cambridge: Cambridge University Press, 2010).

Baer, Richard, *Switching Time* (New York: Crown Publishers, 2007).

Baillie, Donald W., *God was in Christ* (London: Faber & Faber, 1948).

Baker, Lynne Rudder, *Persons and Bodies: A Constitution View* (Cambridge: Cambridge University Press, 2000).

_____ *The Metaphysics of Everyday Life: An Essay in Practical Realism* (Cambridge: Cambridge University Press, 2007).

Barnes, Michel René, "Rereading Augustine's Theology of the Trinity," in S. Davis, D. Kendall, and G. O'Collins (eds), *The Trinity* (Oxford: Oxford University Press, 1999), 145–76.

_____ *The Power of God: Dynamis in Gregory of Nyssa's Trinitarian Theology* (Washington DC: Catholic University of America Press, 2000).

_____ "Divine Unity and the Divided Self: Gregory of Nyssa's Trinitarian Theology in its Psychological Context," *Modern Theology*, 18/4 (Oct. 2002), 475–96.

Barrett, C. K., *The Gospel According to St John* (London: SPCK, 1960).

Barth, Karl, *Church Dogmatics, i/1. The Doctrine of the Word of God*, tr. G. T. Thomson (Edinburgh: T. & T. Clark, 1936).

_____ *Church Dogmatics, ii/1. The Doctrine of God*, tr. T. H. L. Parker *et al.*, (Edinburgh: T. & T. Clark, 1957).

_____ *Church Dogmatics, iv/1. The Doctrine of Reconciliation*, tr. G. W. Bromiley (Edinburgh: T. & T. Clark, 1956).

Bauckham, Richard, "The Throne of God and the Worship of Jesus," in C.C. Newman, J. R. Davila, and G. S. Lewis (eds), *The Jewish Roots of Christological Monotheism* (Leiden: Brill, 1999), 43–69.

Bayne, Tim, and David J. Chalmers, "What is the Unity of Consciousness?" in Axel Cleermans (ed.), *The Unity of Consciousness: Binding, Integration, and Dissociation* (Oxford: Oxford University Press, 2003), 23–58.

Beeley, Christopher A., *Gregory of Nazianzus on the Trinity and the Knowledge of God* (Oxford: Oxford University Press, 2008).

Berkhof, Louis, *Systematic Theology* (Grand Rapids, MI: Eerdmans, 1949).

Berkouwer, G. C., *The Triumph of Grace in the Theology of Karl Barth* (London: Paternoster Press, 1956).

Brower, Jeffrey E., "The Problem with Social Trinitarianism: A Reply to Wierenga," *Faith and Philosophy,* 21/3 (July 2004), 295–303.

———— and Michael C. Rea, "Material Constitution and the Trinity," *Faith and Philosophy,* 22/1 (Jan. 2005), 57–76.

Brown, David, *The Divine Trinity* (La Salle, IL: Open Court, 1985).

Brown, Raymond E., *The Gospel According to John (i–xii),* The Anchor Bible (Garden City, NY: Doubleday, 1966).

Bruce, F. F., *The Gospel of John* (Grand Rapids, MI: Eerdmans, 1983).

Campbell, C. A., *On Selfhood and Godhood* (London: Allen & Unwin, 1957).

Champion, John B., *Personality and the Trinity* (New York: Revell, 1935).

Coakley, Sarah, "'Persons' in the 'Social' Doctrine of the Trinity: A Critique of the Current Analytic Discussion," in S. Davis, D. Kendall, and G. O'Collins, (eds), *The Trinity* (Oxford: Oxford University Press, 1999), 123–44.

———— (ed.), *Re-Thinking Gregory of Nyssa* (Oxford: Blackwell, 2003).

Confer, William N., and Billie S. Ables, *Multiple Personality: Etiology, Diagnosis and Treatment* (New York: Human Sciences Press, 1983).

Craig, William Lane, "Trinity Monotheism Once More: A Response to Daniel Howard-Snyder," *Philosophia Christi,* 8/1 (2006), 101–13.

———— "Another Glance at Trinity Monotheism," in T. McCall and M. C. Rea (eds), *Philosophical and Theological Essays on the Trinity* (Oxford: Oxford University Press, 2009), 126–30.

————"Toward a Tenable Social Trinitarianism," in T. McCall and M. C. Rea (eds), *Philosophical and Theological Essays on the Trinity* (Oxford: Oxford University Press, 2009), 89–99.

Crisp, Oliver D., and Michael C. Rea (eds), *Analytic Theology: New Essays in the Philosophy of Theology* (Oxford: Oxford University Press, 2009).

Cross, Richard, *The Metaphysics of the Incarnation: Thomas Aquinas to Duns Scotus* (Oxford: Oxford University Press, 2002).

———— "Latin Trinitarianism: Some Conceptual and Historical Considerations," in T. McCall and M. C. Rea (eds), *Philosophical and Theological Essays on the Trinity* (Oxford: Oxford University Press, 2009), 201–13.

———— "Two Models of the Trinity?," *Heythrop Journal,* 43 (2002), repr. in Michael Rea, (ed.), *Oxford Readings in Philosophical Theology,* i (Oxford: Oxford University Press, 2009), 107–26.

Davis, Stephen T., *Christian Philosophical Theology* (Oxford: Oxford University Press, 2006).

———— Daniel Kendall SJ, and Gerald O'Collins SJ (eds), *The Trinity: An Interdisciplinary Symposium on the Trinity* (Oxford: Oxford University Press, 1999).

Dummett, Michael, *Frege: Philosophy of Language* (London: Harper & Row, 1973).

Eccles, John, *Evolution of the Brain: Creation of the Self* (London: Routledge, 1989).

Emery, Gilles, OP, and Matthew Levering (eds), *The Oxford Handbook of the Trinity* (Oxford: Oxford University Press, 2011).

Feenstra, Ronald J., and Cornelius Plantinga, Jr. (eds), *Trinity, Incarnation, and Atonement: Philosophical and Theological Essays* (Notre Dame, IN: University of Notre Dame Press, 1989).

Franks, R. S., *The Doctrine of the Trinity* (London: Duckworth, 1953).

Garrigou-La Grange, Reginald P., *The Trinity and God the Creator*, tr. G. Eckhoff (London: Herder, 1952).

Gavrilyuk, Paul, *The Suffering of the Impassible God: The Dialectics of Patristic Thought* (Oxford: Oxford University Press, 2004).

Geach, Peter, *Logic Matters* (Oxford: Basil Blackwell, 1972).

_____ "Ontological Relativity and Relative Identity" in Milton K. Munitz (ed.), *Logic and Philosophy* (New York: NYU Press, 1973), 287–302.

Giles, Kevin, *The Eternal Generation of the Son: Maintaining Orthodoxy in Trinitarian Theology* (Downers Grove, IL: IVP Academic, 2012).

Gregg, Robert C., and Denis E. Groh, *Early Arianism: A View of Salvation* (Philadelphia: Fortress Press, 1981).

Gregory of Nazianzus, *Faith Gives Fullness to Reasoning: The Five Theological Orations of Gregory Nazianzen* (Leiden: E. J. Brill, 1991).

Gregory of Nyssa, *On "Not Three Gods," to Ablabius, Nicene and Post-Nicene Fathers*, 2nd ser. 5/331–6 (Grand Rapids: Eerdmans, 1976).

_____ *Against Eunomius, Nicene and Post-Nicene Fathers*, 2nd ser. 5/33–248 (Grand Rapids: Eerdmans, 1976).

_____ *The Great Catechism, Nicene and Post-Nicene Fathers*, 2nd ser. 5/471–509 (Grand Rapids: Eerdmans, 1976).

Gunton, Colin E., *The Triune Creator: A Historical and Systematic Study* (Edinburgh: Edinburgh University Press, 1998).

Hacking, Ian, *Rewriting the Soul: Multiple Personalities and the Sciences of Memory* (Princeton: Princeton University Press, 1995).

Hanson, R. P. C., *The Search for the Christian Doctrine of God: The Arian Controversy, 318–381* (London: T. & T. Clark, 1988; pbk edn Grand Rapids: Baker Books, 2005).

Hartill, Percy, *The Unity of God* (London: A. R. Mowbray, 1952).

Hasker, William, "Tri-Unity," *Journal of Religion* 56/1 (Jan. 1970), 1–32.

_____ "Analytic Philosophy of Religion," in William J. Wainwright (ed.), *The Oxford Handbook of Philosophy of Religion* (Oxford: Oxford University Press, 2005), 421–46.

_____ "A Leftovian Trinity?," *Faith and Philosophy*, 26/2 (2009), 154–66.

_____ "Has a Trinitarian God Deceived Us?" in T. McCall and M. C. Rea (eds), *Philosophical and Theological Essays on the Trinity* (Oxford: Oxford University Press, 2009), 38–51.

_____ "Constitution and the Trinity: The Brower–Rea Proposal," *Faith and Philosophy*, 27/3 (July 2010), 321–8.

_____ "Objections to Social Trinitarianism," *Religious Studies*, 45/4 (Dec. 2010), 421–39.

_____ "Persons and the Unity of Consciousness," in George Bealer and Rob Koons (eds), *The Waning of Materialism: New Essays* (Oxford: Oxford University Press, 2010), 175–90.

_____ "Deception and the Trinity: A Rejoinder to Tuggy," *Religious Studies*, 47 (2011), 117–20.

_____ "Dancers, Rugby Players, and Trinitarian Persons," *Faith and Philosophy*, 29/3 (July 2012), 325–33.

_____ "How to Think about the Trinity," in Colin P. Ruloff (ed.), *Christian Philosophy of Religion* (Notre Dame, IN: University of Notre Dame Press, forthcoming 2013).

Hayman, Peter, "Monotheism—a Misused Word in Jewish Studies?," *Journal of Jewish Studies,* 42 (1991), 1–15.

Hengel, Martin, *Jesus and Paul* (London: SCM, 1983).

Hodgson, Leonard, *The Doctrine of the Trinity* (New York: Charles Scribner's Sons, 1944).

Hoffman, Joshua, and Gary S. Rosenkrantz, "Platonistic Theories of Universals," in Michael J. Loux and Dean W. Zimmerman (eds), *The Oxford Handbook of Metaphysics* (Oxford: Oxford University Press, 2003), 46–74.

Holmes, Stephen R., *The Holy Trinity: Understanding God's Life* (Milton Keynes: Paternoster Press, 2012).

Howard-Snyder, Daniel, "Trinity Monotheism," *Philosophia Christi,* 5/2 (2003), 375–403; repr. in T. McCall and M. C. Rea (eds), *Philosophical and Theological Essays on the Trinity* (Oxford: Oxford University Press, 2009), 100–25.

Hunsinger, George, "Karl Barth's Doctrine of the Trinity, and Some Protestant Doctrines After Barth," in G. Emery OP and M. Levering (eds), *The Oxford Handbook of the Trinity* (Oxford: Oxford University Press, 2011), 294–313.

Hurtado, Larry, *One God, One Lord: Early Christian Devotion and Ancient Jewish Monotheism* (Philadelphia: Fortress Press, 1988).

_____ *Lord Jesus Christ: Devotion to Jesus in Earliest Christianity* (Grand Rapids, MI: Eerdmans, 2003).

Illingworth, J. R., *Personality Human and Divine* (London: Macmillan, 1894).

_____ *The Doctrine of the Trinity* (London: Macmillan, 1909).

Jacobs, Nathan, "On 'Not Three Gods'—Again: Can a Primary-Secondary Substance Reading of *Ousia* and *Hypostasis* Avoid Tritheism?" *Modern Theology,* 24/3 (2008); corrected version available at www.nathanajacobs.com.

John of Damascus, *Exposition of the Orthodox Faith, Nicene and Post-Nicene Fathers,* 2nd ser. 9/1–101 (Grand Rapids: Eerdmans, 1976).

Johnson, Keith E., "Augustine, Eternal Generation, and Evangelical Trinitarianism," *Trinity Journal,* 32 (2011), 141–63.

Kelly, J. N. D., *Early Christian Doctrines* (London: Adam & Charles Black, 1958).

_____ *Early Christian Creeds* (London: Longmans, Green & Co., 1960).

Kerr, Fergus, "Trinitarian Theology in the Light of Analytic Philosophy," in G. Emery OP and M. Levering (eds), *The Oxford Handbook of the Trinity* (Oxford: Oxford University Press, 2011), 339–45.

Kilby, Karen, "Perichoresis and Projection: Problems with Social Doctrines of the Trinity," *New Blackfriars,* 81 (2000), 432–45.

Kripke, Saul, "Naming and Necessity," in D. Davidson and G. Harman (eds), *Semantics of Natural Language* (Dordrecht: D. Riedel, 1972), 253–355.

Laird, John, *Problems of the Self* (London: Macmillan, 1917).

Leftow, Brian, "A Latin Trinity," *Faith and Philosophy,* 21/3 (July 2004), 304–33.

_____ "Modes without Modalism," in P. van Inwagen and D. Zimmerman (eds), *Persons: Human and Divine* (Oxford: Clarendon Press, 2007), 357–75.

_____ "Anti Social Trinitarianism," in T. McCall and M. C. Rea (eds), *Philosophical and Theological Essays on the Trinity* (Oxford: Oxford University Press, 2009), 52–88.

———— "Two Trinities: Reply to Hasker," *Religious Studies,* 49 (2010), 441–7.

———— "Time-Travel and the Trinity," *Faith and Philosophy,* 29/3 (July 2012), 313–234.

———— "On Hasker on Leftow on Hasker on Leftow," *Faith and Philosophy,* 29/3 (July 2012), 334–39.

Lossky, Vladimir, *The Mystical Theology of the Eastern Church* (London: James Clark & Co., 1957).

McCall, Thomas H., *Which Trinity? Whose Monotheism? Philosophical and Systematic Theologians on the Metaphysics of Trinitarian Theology* (Grand Rapids, MI: William B. Eerdmans, 2010).

———— and Michael C. Rea (eds), *Philosophical and Theological Essays on the Trinity* (Oxford: Oxford University Press, 2009).

MacMurray, John, *The Self as Agent* (London: Faber, 1957).

Merricks, Trenton, "Split Brains and the Godhead," in T. M. Crisp, M. Davidson, and D. Vander Laan (eds), *Knowledge and Reality: Essays in Honor of Alvin Plantinga* (Dordrecht: Springer, 2006), 299–326.

Moltmann, Jürgen, *The Crucified God,* tr. R. A. Wilson and John Bowden (New York: Harper & Row, 1974).

———— *The Trinity and the Kingdom,* tr. Margaret Kohl (Minneapolis: Fortress Press, 1993; originally published by Harper & Row, 1981).

Moreland, J. P., and William Lane Craig, *Philosophical Foundations for a Christian Worldview* (Downers Grove, IL: InterVarsity, 2003).

Mosser, Carl, "Fully Social Trinitarianism," in T. McCall and M. C. Rea (eds), *Philosophical and Theological Essays on the Trinity* (Oxford: Oxford University Press, 2009), 131–50.

Neuner, J., and J. Dupuis (eds), *The Christian Faith,* 6th edn (New York: Alba House, 1996).

Newman, Carey C., James R. Davila, and Gladys S. Lewis (eds), *The Jewish Roots of Christological Monotheism: Papers from the St. Andrews Conference on the Historical Origins of the Worship of Jesus* (Leiden: Brill, 1999).

O'Collins, Gerald, *The Tripersonal God: Understanding and Interpreting the Trinity* (New York: Paulist Press, 1999).

Plantinga, Alvin, *The Nature of Necessity* (Oxford: Clarendon Press, 1974).

Plantinga, Cornelius, Jr., "Social Trinity and Tritheism," in R. J. Feenstra and C. Plantinga (eds), *Trinity, Incarnation, and Atonement* (Notre Dame, IN: University of Notre Dame Press, 1989), 21–47.

Prestige, G. L., *God in Patristic Thought,* 2nd edn (London: SPCK, 1952).

Prince, Morton, *The Dissociation of a Personality* (London: Longmans, Green, 1905).

Pruss, Alexander, "Brower and Rea's Constitution Account of the Trinity," in T. McCall and M. C. Rea (eds), *Philosophical and Theological Essays on the Trinity* (Oxford: Oxford University Press, 2009), 314–25.

Radde-Gallwitz, Andrew, *Basil of Caesarea, Gregory of Nyssa, and the Transformation of Divine Simplicity* (Oxford: Oxford University Press, 2009).

Rahner, Karl, *Grundkurs des Glaubens* (Freiburg: Herder, 1976).

———— *The Trinity,* tr. Joseph Donceel, with introduction, index, and glossary by Catherine Mowry Lacugna (New York: Crossroad, 1997).

Rea, Michael C., "The Problem of Material Constitution," *Philosophical Review*, 104 (1995), 525–52.

_____ (ed.), *Oxford Readings in Philosophical Theology*, i. *Trinity, Incarnation, Atonement* (Oxford: Oxford University Press, 2009).

_____ "Relative Identity and the Doctrine of the Trinity," *Philosophia Christi*, 5 (2003), 431–46; repr. in T. McCall and M. C. Rea (eds), *Philosophical and Theological Essays on the Trinity* (Oxford: Oxford University Press, 2009), 249–62.

_____ "The Trinity," in Thomas P. Flint and Michael C. Rea (eds), *The Oxford Handbook of Philosophical Theology* (Oxford: Oxford University Press, 2009), 403–29.

Richardson, Cyril, *The Doctrine of the Trinity* (New York: Abingdon Press, 1958).

Sanders, Fred, "Entangled in the Trinity: Economic and Immanent Trinity in Recent Theology," *dialog*, 40/3 (Fall 2001), 175–82.

_____ "The Trinity," in John R. Webster, Kathryn Tanner, and Iain Torrance (eds), *The Oxford Handbook of Systematic Theology* (New York: Oxford University Press, 2007), 35–53.

Sidelle, Alan, *Necessity, Essence, and Individuation* (Ithaca, NY: Cornell University Press, 1989).

Stead, G. Christopher, *Divine Substance* (Oxford: Clarendon Press, 1977).

_____ *Philosophy in Christian Antiquity* (Cambridge: Cambridge University Press, 1994).

Stump, Eleonore, *Wandering in Darkness: Narrative and the Problem of Suffering* (Oxford: Oxford University Press, 2010).

Swinburne, Richard, "Could there be More than One God?" *Faith and Philosophy*, 5/3 (July 1988), 225–41.

_____ *The Christian God* (Oxford: Clarendon Press, 1994).

_____ *Was Jesus God?* (Oxford: Oxford University Press, 2008).

Taylor, W. S., and M. F. Martin, "Multiple Personality," *Journal of Abnormal and Social Psychology*, 39 (1944), 281–300.

Tertullian, *Treatise Against Praxeas*, tr. Ernest Evans (London: SPCK, 1948).

Thompson, John, *Modern Trinitarian Perspectives* (Oxford: Oxford University Press, 1994).

Thompson, Marianne Meye, *The God of the Gospel of John* (Grand Rapids, MI: Eerdmans, 2001).

Tuggy, Dale, "Divine Deception, Identity, and Social Trinitarianism," *Religious Studies*, 40 (Sept. 2004), 269–87.

_____ "Divine Deception and Monotheism: A Reply to Hasker," *Religious Studies*, 47 (2011), 109–15.

_____ "On the Possibility of a Single Perfect Person," in Colin P. Ruloff (ed.), *Christian Philosophy of Religion* (Notre Dame, IN: University of Notre Dame Press, forthcoming 2013).

Turcescu, Lucian, "'Person' versus 'Individual', and Other Modern Misreadings of Gregory of Nyssa," in S. Coakley (ed.), *Re-Thinking Gregory of Nyssa* (Oxford: Blackwell, 2003), 97–109.

_____ *Gregory of Nyssa and the Concept of Divine Persons* (Oxford: Oxford University Press, 2005).

van Inwagen, Peter, "And Yet They are Not Three Gods, But One God," in Thomas Morris (ed.), *Philosophy and the Christian Faith* (Notre Dame, IN: University of Notre

Dame Press, 1988), 241–78; repr. in T. McCall and M. C. Rea (eds), *Philosophical and Theological Essays on the Trinity* (Oxford: Oxford University Press, 2009), 217–48.

———— and Dean Zimmerman (eds), *Persons: Human and Divine* (Oxford: Clarendon Press, 2007).

Volf, Miroslav, "'The Trinity is our Social Program': The Doctrine of the Trinity and the Shape of Social Engagement," *Modern Theology,* 14/3 (July 1998), 403–23.

———— *After our Likeness: The Church as the Image of the Trinity* (Grand Rapids, MI: Eerdmans, 1998).

Webb, Clement C. J., *God and Personality* (London: Allen & Unwin, 1919).

Weinandy, Thomas, *Does God Suffer?* (Notre Dame, IN: University of Notre Dame Press, 2000).

Welch, Claude, *The Trinity in Contemporary Theology* (London: SCM Press, 1953).

Wierenga, Edward, "Trinity and Polytheism," *Faith and Philosophy,* 21/3 (July 2004), 281–94.

Wilkes, Kathleen V., *Real People: Personal Identity without Thought Experiments* (Oxford: Clarendon Press, 1988).

Williams, C. F. J., "Neither Confounding the Persons Nor Dividing the Substance," in Alan G. Padgett (ed.), *Reason and the Christian Religion: Essays in Honour of Richard Swinburne* (Oxford: Clarendon Press, 1994), 227–43.

Williams, Rowan, "Redeeming Sorrows," in D. Z. Phillips (ed.), *Religion and Morality* (Basingstoke: Macmillan, 1996).

Wolterstorff, Nicholas, "Between the Pincers of Increased Diversity and Supposed Irrationality," in William J. Wainwright (ed.), *God, Philosophy, and Academic Culture: A Discussion between Scholars in the AAR and the APA* (Atlanta, GA: Scholars Press, 1996), 13–20.

Yandell, Keith, "The Most Brutal and Inexcusable Error in Counting? Trinity and Consistency," *Religious Studies,* 30 (1994), 201–17.

———— "How Many Times does Three Go into One?" in T. McCall and M. C. Rea (eds), *Philosophical and Theological Essays on the Trinity* (Oxford: Oxford University Press, 2009), 151–68.

Young, Frances M., *From Nicaea to Chalcedon: A Guide to the Literature and its Background,* 2nd edn (Grand Rapids, MI: Baker Academic, 2010).

Zachhuber, Johannes, *Human Nature in Gregory of Nyssa: Philosophical Background and Theological Significance* (Leiden: Brill, 2000).

Zizioulas, John D., *Being as Communion: Studies in Personhood and the Church* (Crestwood, NY: St Vladimir's Seminary Press, 1985).

Index

Made in the USA
Coppell, TX
21 January 2022